Pete Brown used to advertise beer for a living before he realized that writing about it was even more fun, and came with even more free beer. He contributes to various newspapers, magazines and beer trade press titles, writes the annual report on Britain's cask ale market, sings beer's praises on TV and radio, and runs an influential blog.

In 2009, Pete was awarded the Michael Jackson Gold Tankard Award and named Beer Writer of the Year by the British Guild of Beer Writers.

(No, not that Michael Jackson, the other one).

PETE BROWN

HOPS AND GLORY

ONE MAN'S SEARCH FOR THE BEER THAT
BUILT THE BRITISH EMPIRE

PAN BOOKS

First published 2009 by Macmillan

First published in paperback 2010 by Pan Books
an imprint of Pan Macmillan, a division of Macmillan Publishers Limited
Pan Macmillan, 20 New Wharf Road, London N1 9RR
Basingstoke and Oxford
Associated companies throughout the world
www.panmacmillan.com

ISBN 978-0-330-51186-5

For Liz,

with profound and sincere apologies,

for reasons that will become acutely obvious

to the attentive reader

'We are not here to sell a parcel of boilers and vats, but the potentiality of growing rich, beyond the dreams of avarice.'

Samuel Johnson,
after arranging the sale of his late friend Henry Thrale's brewery
to Barclay Perkins for £135,000

'If I were asked under what sky the human mind has most fully developed some of its choicest gifts, has most deeply pondered on the greatest problems of life, and has found solutions, I should point to India.'

Max Müeller,
nineteenth-century orientalist

'I cannot tell you where you should look for me if you send out any pinnace to meete me. I live at the devotion of the wind and the seas.'

From a letter by James Lancaster,
Commander of the Company's first fleet, to the Directors of
the Honourable East India Company, 1601

CONTENTS

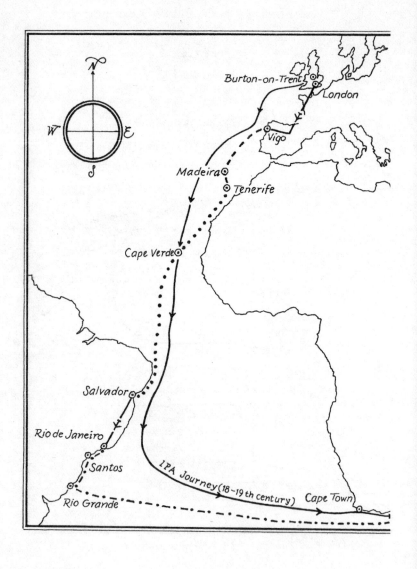

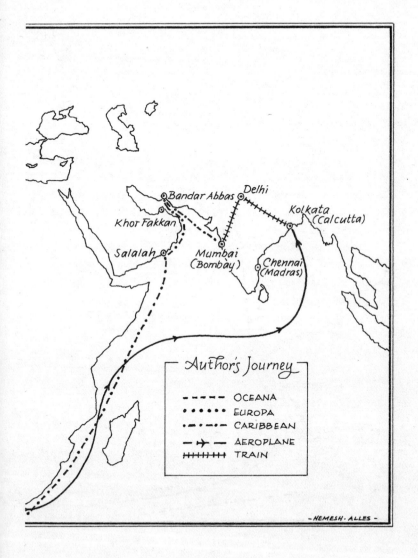

Author's Journey

- - - - - OCEANA
· · · · · EUROPA
- · - · - CARIBBEAN
- ✈ - AEROPLANE
++++++ TRAIN

- HEMESH · ALLES -

Author's Note

The names of three people have been changed in this text: one for legal reasons, one at the person's request and one because the guy was a bit of a knob and I felt it would be unfair to make this so clear and then use his real name, though it's unlikely he'll ever read this because, as I say, he was a bit of a knob.

Everyone else is here under their real names and everything written is true, recounted as it happened, albeit with a bit of judicious editing every now and then, which is only to stop the reader getting bored or confused.

Oh, and mum – sorry about all the swearing.

DOG WATCH

'Oh, you contrary old bitch, how do you keep *doing* this?'

I throw my weight against the wheel, spitting obscenities at the sails as they flap and harrumph against the dense stars. The sails shouldn't be flapping – or harrumphing, for that matter – and it's my fault they are.

Neither my bulk nor my foul mouth have any effect on the compass – it's still mocking me with a heading of two-oh-five degrees. I push harder at the wheel, turning it two spokes at a time. For some reason it'll spin and rattle without effort to port, but insists on making a sluggish and obstinate grind of any correction to starboard. My wrecked arm starts to complain yet again, wondering why shooting pains from wrist to bicep are not a strong-enough hint for me to give it a rest. Denis, the Slovenian 'police judge' with whom I'm sharing my 2 a.m. stint at the wheel of an ancient ship, languidly leans over and lends a hand, easing her round.

Soon the wheel has gone through a full rotation and the rudder meter indicates almost ten degrees to starboard. I can sense *Europa* pretending not to notice, trying to ignore me. And then slowly, grudgingly, she starts to move back to her correct course.

Every time you move the wheel, it takes about two hundred feet – twice the length of the ship – for it to work through and affect the course. So as the compass nears two-two-five degrees, which is the course I should be steering, I spin the wheel back rapidly, bringing the rudder to zero. The 'Grand Old Lady', as ever, has ideas of her own. Even though I've now put five degrees back to port on the rudder, she's gallivanting off up past two-thirty . . . two-forty . . .

The ship starts to flip-flop from side to side. Waves splat on planks of the main deck, and I wince as I imagine the clattering dishes in the galley below, the rest of the crew rolling in their bunks, cursing the *debiel* on the helm.

The ship's big brass compass, face the size of a dinner plate, illuminates mine like the torches we held under our chins when we read ghost stories as children. It glares at me accusingly as, gradually, I settle *Europa* back on to a reasonably steady course, and everything falls quiet again.

'Ten seconds,' I say to Denis as he lies back on the bench, arms behind his head, 'I take my eyes off her for ten seconds . . .'

He knows how it is. We all do. For fifteen minutes she'll behave, meandering by no more than two degrees from two-two-five, the steady south-westerly course the captain has instructed us to follow on our rotating shifts for two days now, steering our tall ship to Brazil half an hour at a time, through day and night. And then you steal a look at the stars, thickly packed because the half-moon is only just rising with the night two-thirds gone. And as you try to identify the few constellations you learned to recognize as a kid, which was the last time you saw stars like this, you'll see a shooting star. And this is a big one, sinking gracefully towards the dancing waves like a parachute flare, a thick felt-tip wake drawing slowly across the black velvet, chunkier and more satisfying than the usual (because shooting stars are routine now) blink-and-they're-gone, fibre-point traces that leave you struggling dumbly to think of a wish, wondering if it still counts if you only articulate it five seconds later. And as the star or meteorite or piece of space junk or whatever it was vanishes, you remember what you're supposed to be doing; you look back down at the compass and to your dismay the ship has jumped as surely as if she had lifted herself out of the waves and flopped down again, tossing like an insomniac, and she's sailing twenty degrees off course.

It's not your fault of course: it's the wind. The weather is coming from your port side, fairly strong, and you're averaging around seven knots. But the wind is capricious. When it gusts, the ship blows to starboard, and you have to balance this out by giving the rudder a few degrees to port. When it drops – and doesn't it always decide to do that just when you choose to look heavenward – the rudder does what it's been trying to do, and steers you into the wind. And then you're off on the mad tiller waltz, taking several minutes to correct something that happened in seconds, all the time fearful that one of the permanent crew is finally going to lose their rag and yell and ask you just what the fuck you think you're doing, but of course they're mostly Dutch, and wouldn't raise their voices even if you rammed a container ship.

We're nearing the equator now, about three hundred miles out from the Cape Verde islands. Over the past few days it's become too warm to wear a fleece on these night watches. That devious wind is still blowing from the northeast but it has warmth in it now, even in the dead of night. Soon it will be too hot down below to lie in our bunks at all, and the sloop deck will be crowded with people trying to doze under the stars, despite the noise and the stumbling feet in the dark, as Janet or Margriet trips over sleepers while trying to find and shake awake whoever is due to take over for day watch at 4 a.m.

When I first came aboard, I thought that being dragged from my bunk at a quarter to midnight would be an ordeal, but I'm enjoying dog watch more than any other part of the voyage so far. Being at the helm of a beautiful century-old ship, really sailing her, is one of the highlights of my half-consumed life. As *Europa* settles down, the splash and hiss of the waves on her hull is joined by the voice of the wind in the taut rigging, halfway between a ghostly moan and a Gregorian chant. Bombs of phosphorescence explode in the black water, transforming our wake into an under-lit seventies-style disco dance floor. A shoal of flying fish erupts from the portside bow. During the day they resemble buzzing insects. Now, the rising moon catches and highlights them, silver dots arcing over the waves, like the reflections from a glitterball on the walls of a wedding reception. I listen to the spooky music, soak in the moon and sea's light show, and stand grinning to myself, alone in an ambient disco in the middle of the Atlantic Ocean.

I'm drinking down this time, gorging on the space and peace, allowing my head to unwind. I cherish every second of it. In the last ten months I've had no time to reflect at all. I've not thought about what I'm doing, about the impact it's having on my life, my sanity, my health, my marriage. There wasn't time for anything apart from work and planning. Now, having been aboard *Europa* for ten days, having grown a semi-convincing beard and acquired a deep face-and-forearms tan, I'm finally starting to let myself think about what I've got myself into, what I've set out to do.

And the output of this thinking is that I'm worried. I'm scared that I'm failing, that perhaps now I can only fail in everything I embarked upon. By the strictest standards, I've already failed in my primary quest, my real reason for being here. And in terms of secondary objectives – personal goals, underlying motivations, sub-plots and diversions – I'm also moving very much in the wrong direction. I think of the upset I've caused, the sacrifices I've made. Why the hell am I doing this? Is it really worth it? Shouldn't I just admit that I've overreached myself? I can't just give up now. Or can I?

'Mike says it'll toughen you up a bit.'

My wife's words and the amused look on her face as she said them – the laugh with just a tiny hint of meanness, born only from her frustration with me and my idiot ideas and cack-handed attempt to execute them – play on a loop in my head every five minutes.

Anyone can become tougher. Even the weediest person can go to the gym every day for six months and, while they may never make that comic-book transition from sand-covered victim to Charles Atlas, they'll be stronger than they were before they started. Guaranteed. But there are some qualities that, if you don't have them to start with, no amount of work is going to develop. And then there are circumstances. Simple bad luck. Oversights and bad planning.

I can't do anything but stay on the ship until we reach Salvador, our first port in Brazil. But I could fly home from there – ten, maybe twelve hours back to Liz, and a couple of months of peace and relaxation instead of two more months on this fool's errand. Christ, what was I thinking? But of course, I wasn't thinking. We've already established that.

Failure. It would mean withdrawing in shame from the frustrating, joyous, agonizing, weird, addictive, unfashionable-but-you-know-what-sod-fashion-fuck-fashion world of beer writing.

I don't want to think about this any more.

Whatever happens when we reach Brazil, nothing changes the fact that I am sailing – not flying, not powering – sailing across the Atlantic, on a ship that takes your breath away. This ship, which I'd feel privileged even to see, is my home for three weeks. This journey, even this moment, makes everything worth while. I've consummated my relationship with the sea, and I'm head over heels. I suspect there will be higher peaks of stress and lower troughs of despair to come (and I'm so right), but here and now the waxing moon has risen, sewing a wide silver swathe across the sea, turning it into the carpet of a magical playground, a fairy-tale theatre and oh you devious, obstreperous cow, how the *fuck* did you sneak on to one-ninety?

PART ONE

BURTON

A POISONED TANKARD? · A BEER OF GREAT CHARACTER
A DIFFICULT CONVERSATION, FOLLOWED BY A FORTUITOUS ONE
SIX MONTHS ON GOOGLE · 'BEER TOWN' · BREWING DAY

CHAPTER ONE

A POISONED TANKARD?

It was the beer's fault. It usually is.

Though when you consider that beer is the most popular drink in the world, consumed by billions on a daily basis, and not a single soul among those billions had done what I was about to attempt to do in the cause of beer, I have to shoulder at least part of the blame myself.

I don't mean that I got drunk and did something I regretted. I did get very drunk. And I did something I would come to regret bitterly at frequent intervals. But one did not lead to the other: I caused most of the damage while perfectly sober.

What I mean is, this was one of the increasingly frequent occasions when I got carried away after spending too much time with the kind of people you meet when you let beer start to mean more to you than simply the best long drink in the world. When I simply forgot myself. Forgot reality. Not for the first time, the ideas and associations that surround beer, what beer *means*, intoxicated me more effectively and more devastatingly than mere alcohol ever could.

My voyage across the Atlantic on a century-old tall ship – and the larger quest of which it was merely part – began long before I turned up at a sun-blasted port to board *Europa* with too much luggage and a cask of beer that was both much more, and much less, than it seemed. You could say it began in the pub with Chris, ten months before I boarded the ship. That's where the idea was born. I soon recognized it had been gestating for much longer, waiting for its moment. But it was in the Duke of Argyll in Soho, just before Christmas, that the idea burst forth, silently screaming.

The timing might have been important. Two days before Christmas, the city is still just about present, but its thoughts are elsewhere. This is the time when 'Londoners' who weren't born here get ready to leave. The focus of the city is not on itself, where it normally rests 100 per cent of the time, but on the places it's draining away to for Christmas. Half the population is leaving town at the same time, and that makes Christmas unique: London shuts down. It's when Londoners briefly think across a slightly broader horizon.

Chris, Liz and I like to think of ourselves not only as Londoners, but also as interlopers. Chris and I are proudly Yorkshire, unapologetically Barnsley, and Liz is . . . Welsh. But among us we'd knocked up a lifespan of London life. We'd lived in the city longer than some people born here who we now worked with. We felt it was our right – if not a birthright, then a right purchased in beer money – to stake a little territory of our own. And tonight, after our annual Christmas ritual of Japanese food and present exchange, that territory was the Duke of Argyll.[1]

The Argyll is a Sam Smith's pub. Chris and I love the fact that Sam Smith pubs are cultish in both commonly used senses of the word. They look like they haven't been decorated since the 1970s, but not in a bad way. They only stock their own brands of everything. They don't advertise. They don't talk to writers or journalists, even those who love them. They don't even have a website. They're a bit funny about allowing brewery tours. If Willy Wonka had been into beer

---

1. Japanese food followed by seedy pubs had become our own unique Christmas tradition. None of us knew why it had to be Japanese food in the middle of Soho, but that's the point of Christmas traditions – creating them, and allowing them to become special without allowing cynicism's usual threatening interrogation.

instead of chocolate, he would have been called Samuel Smith.

The Argyll cashes in some of the otherwordliness all Sam Smith pubs share and buys a little normality with the proceeds, which allows it to integrate into normal society and pass itself off as a normal pub to the less observant Soho toper, and it was busy with people who looked entirely normal.[2]

Chris and I were discussing that day's *Evening Standard*, which had run a two-page feature proclaiming that pubs were cool again – on the grounds that Kate Moss said they were. Our grouchy conversation had sent Liz off to the toilet and then the bar, possibly throwing in a detour to make a phone call to someone who wasn't interested in talking about beer and pubs.

The conversation had been fairly beery all night. Two weeks previously, I'd won an award for my second book about beer, *Three Sheets to the Wind*. It was the third award I'd won for writing, but the first one for beer writing, and the first one that came with a fat cheque, stashed inside a Budweiser Budvar tankard.[3] It was a travel bursary, and seemed to bring with it not just congratulations for managing to ponce around the world drinking beer at someone else's expense, but also an expectation that, having pulled it off once, the winner could now do it again, only better.

---

2. Normal by Soho standards, that is.

3. The first time I won anything was for a story inspired by a poster in the school corridor when I was ten. My gripping yarn about giant mutant hornets ridden by evil goblins thrashed the living daylights out of the runner-up, and not just because he was eight years old and the only other entrant. The last time I'd won something was the *Time Out* short-story competition in 1994. My delight was lessened only slightly by the fact that in the wake of my victory, *Time Out* abandoned the competition. Sixteen years between my first two prizes. Twelve years between the last one and this one. My writing career was gaining momentum.

This 'better' bit wasn't (just) paranoia. Whereas most of the awards doled out at the British Guild of Beer Writers' Annual Dinner[4] allowed the winner simply to bask in glory, the Budvar Travel Bursary was awarded to the writer the judges felt 'could most benefit' from the cheque for a thousand quid. In other words, it wasn't saying I'd written the best beer-themed travel book – or travel-themed beer book – of the year. It was saying I was the writer who needed the most practice.

The award had come in the middle of a creative drought. I'd been trying for almost a year to come up with an idea for a new book. Now the award, while welcome, was making me feel an obligation to come up with a bigger, better idea than travelling 45,000 miles around the globe in search of the true meaning of beer.

'Maybe I'll write a piece of investigative journalism about Sam Smith's,' I said. 'Start work as a barman and infiltrate the organization. Find out why they're so secretive. What they've got to hide. How they came to own so many pubs in London, given that they're based in Yorkshire and these pubs must be worth a fortune.'

Chris looked at the door and said nothing. This wasn't going well.

'You know, I'm not saying you're a shit travel writer or anything like that,' he said.

'Thanks.'

'But if you want to call yourself a travel writer, haven't you got to write about an actual journey?'

---

4. Yeah, I know. The British Guild of Beer Writers sounds like one of those weird cultural cul-de-sacs that get featured in the guest-publication round on *Have I Got News For You*. But let me ask you this: who do you think knows best how to party – the British Guild of Beer Writers (www. beerwriters.co.uk) or the Pylon Appreciation Society (www.pylons.org)? Compared to those guys, we *rock*. I'll bet.

Chris accompanied me on key parts of my travels for *Three Sheets*, and feels more qualified than most to advise on my writing career.[5]

'The thing about travel writing is,' he continued, 'it suggests you actually write about travelling. Don't get me wrong, you went to some nice places for *Three Sheets*. But shouldn't you be writing about a journey rather than just the destination?'

He had a point.

'Maybe', I replied. 'The problem with beer is, traditionally, it's a localized product. It's never really gone on any big meaningful journeys because it never travelled that well. I suppose I could recreate Jacobsen's journey from Munich to Copenhagen when he brought back the yeast that created Carlsberg. Or I could maybe retrace the route of the German brewers who colonized the United States.'

These ideas weren't filling me with enthusiasm. Chris was now picking his teeth and staring vacantly at the bar.

I carried on thinking. Maybe there was something better. 'Hey, there's the journey made by beers from Burton-on-Trent to the Baltic in the eighteenth century. That might be interesting . . .'

I tailed off. My mouth fell open. I'd just spotted the elephant in the room. 'Oh. Oh, shit.'

'What?' asked Chris.

'You've just made me think of an idea.'

'Why "oh, shit" then? Isn't that good?'

'I'm not sure it is, no.'

---

5. At this point, I need to plead for leniency from the reader. The pub-based bet or challenge between mates has launched so many madcap travel books in recent years that, as a literary device, it's become the non-fiction equivalent of 'It was a dark and stormy night'. If this *were* fiction, I wouldn't start it here – I'd come up with a different way in. But this is how it really happened, word for word. Some of us really do say 'Yes' when everyone else would say, 'Don't be so fucking stupid.'

'I always give you your best ideas. What's this one then?'

It was a big journey all right. I only didn't spot it because it was *too* big. But now Chris had made me think of it, in an instant I had no choice. It had enslaved me as soon as it appeared.

'I'm just going to have to think about how I break it to Liz. She's coming back.'

The idea sat there fully formed, grinning at me, a fourth entity at our table. Nervously, I grinned back at it. I knew immediately that I was going to do it. This was a real adventure, something that would make people stop and ask, are you sure? Something that might even make them worry for my safety. Now that I thought about it, I realized this story, its place in history and beer folklore, had been bothering me, gathering around me like thunderclouds for several years. Now, the storm was about to break. And it was going to be a big one.

'Erm, Liz? You know when I went to the Great American Beer Festival last year? Remember what I told you about my favourite beers? Well . . .'

CHAPTER TWO

A BEER OF GREAT CHARACTER

Fifteen months and half a world away from the Duke of Argyll, the streets of the Mile High City were a tide of people flowing towards the Denver, Colorado Convention Center.

Inside the vast hangar of the Center, I was discovering that American beer festivals are nothing like their English cousins. On previous visits to the States I'd been blown away by the unslakable thirst for experimentation among American brewers, but this was the motherlode. Beyond the glitzy stands staffed by hot-pants-wearing hotties giving out samples of Bud, Coors and Miller Lite, the aisles were crowded with funky, farmyard-spicy Belgian-style ales, spritzy sweet-and-sour fruit beers, mellow red ales, sweet Scottish ales, dark German bocks, smoked porter from Alaska, even a recreated sahti, a Finnish speciality that's brewed with bread yeast inside a hollowed-out log and filtered through pine needles. There were more beers here than I could ever sup in the three days of the festival, even though they were served in four-ounce shot glasses. I felt a duty to sample as many different styles as I could.

Yeah, right.

I was kidding myself. I knew what I was looking for.

In 2004, when I was writing *Three Sheets to the Wind*, I instantly fell in love with Portland, Oregon, particularly with India Pale Ale from the city's Bridgeport brewery. It wraps you in deep hop aromas of pine and citrus, before dipping you in a bath of fruit and flowers and leaving you with a delicious bitter tingle at the end. When I first tasted it, no beer had ever tasted as good before.

A year later, I remembered it the same way I did my first mouthful of real curry. I was a twenty-year-old student, and I felt that I was tasting in colour for the first time. And while you can eat the same curry again (and again), you can never again taste it for the first time. No curry has ever tasted as good since. How could it? Now, I was in a similar situation with beer. My Great American Beer Festival (GABF) sample of Bridgeport IPA was, I knew, identical to that first sip in Portland, but it didn't taste the same. Bridgeport is not available in the UK,[6] but I'd discovered another IPA – Goose Island from Chicago – that was obtainable from Internet-based wholesalers. Goose Island regularly appears in most lists of best beers from around the world, and at this time I was buying it by the case. It not only converted my mates from lager to ale, it also converted their wives and girlfriends from wine to beer. Especially among those who preferred a Kiwi Sauvignon blanc, whose citrussy, grassy character it resembles, Goose Island never failed to produce a delighted comment along the lines of 'I still don't like beer, but I love this.'

Out of sixty-nine different categories at the festival,[7] six were variations on pale ale. And despite the fruit beers and the spontaneously fermenting beers and the smoked beers and wheat beers and whatever else, the most fiercely contested category was 'American-style India Pale Ale', with ninety-six beers entered for judging. The American craft-beer scene was as smitten by IPA as I was. If you wanted to be taken seriously as an American ale brewer, you had to have

---

6. In Portland I'd asked them if they exported their beer. They replied, 'Sure, we sell in six states now!'

7. There are *not* sixty-nine different styles of beer. But the only way you'd win this argument with an American craft-beer enthusiast is by pretending there are even more.

an India Pale Ale in your range. Amid such wild eclecticism, it was the standard by which brewers were judged, comparable from coast to coast.

There are many archaic terms and acronyms in the naming of beer: XXXs, XXXXs, even a 6X; there are 3Bs, ESBs and SBAs; 70/-, 80/- and 90/-; double drops and single hops. All have historic meanings as brewing terms, even if many have become disconnected signifiers today. But IPA is more than a brewer's term. It's a legend – a fable that anyone at GABF could have faithfully recited to me.

Many IPA labels are illustrated with line drawings of sailing ships that, along with the name, evoke a sea-salt whiff of high adventure. I knew the story well – I've recounted it, hazily, in both my previous books. Even back then in Colorado, it was a story that felt like it had been worn shiny, the edges rubbed off by endless repetition.

In one sentence: India Pale Ale was a beer style created specially for the British Raj in India.

The blurb on the back label of every IPA bottle and in every coffee-table beer book elaborates the story along similar lines. In the eighteenth century there were thousands of Britons living in India. They demanded their creature comforts, and one of the most difficult to provide was beer. Before refrigeration and modern brewing biochemistry, the Indian climate made it impossible to brew locally, so beer had to be imported. The trouble was, this involved a sea journey that took anywhere between three and six months, through rough seas and harsh climates, and the beer arrived flat, sour and undrinkable. Then, someone recognized that high alcoholic content and high levels of hops both helped preserve beer. They created a strong, hoppy beer, and laded it on to eastbound ships. When it arrived in Bombay and Calcutta, it had not only survived the journey, it had also gone through an amazing, unexpected conditioning process on board that left it light, bright and sparkling, perfect for the climate.

Thanks to the American craft-brewing boom, it's a story that's now more famous in the States than in Britain. Because America has gone hop-crazy.

Most people sort of know that beer is made out of hops, even if they don't know what hops are. The building blocks of beer are actually hewn from malted barley, but hops are used to season beer, like herbs in cooking, giving beer its characteristic bitterness as well as most of its aroma. When Americans started to create craft beers based on old European styles, they quickly realized that American hops, particularly the varieties that thrived around Portland and the rest of the Pacific North West, were far more aromatic than their European cousins. Now, hoppy aromas – and, more importantly, bitterness – are characteristics you either love or hate. Most people who 'don't like' beer are put off by the bitterness, and that's the fault of hops. But if you do like it, American hops offer flavour to make your toes curl. Craft brewers began searching the archives and history books for beers that were characterized by high levels of hoppiness. And they rediscovered India Pale Ale.

When every brewer started creating hoppy IPAs, hopheads started asking for more. America has the most vibrant craft-beer scene in the world because it combines a reverence for the past with a confident, sometimes arrogant belief that however good these great old beers were, they can be improved upon. Here, at GABF, were the results.

Over three days I used Bridgeport and Goose Island as base camp to explore new peaks of hoppiness. From California's Stone brewery came Arrogant Bastard, a beer that informed us we probably wouldn't appreciate it, as we didn't have refined-enough tastes. Over at the Falling Rock – the brewpub brewers go to when they want to drink rather than pour their own beers – a single pint of Maharajah IPA put me to sleep.[8] But the one that made the greatest impression was Dogfish Head. Sam Calagione, the founder of this Delaware brewery, is an enormously charismatic guy in his mid-thirties. His brewery's motto – 'Off-centered beers for off-centered people' – reflects both a very astute entrepreneurial sense and a desire to redefine what beer can be. Sitting proudly on Sam's stall at GABF was Randall the Enamel Animal, an 'organoleptic hop transducer module' that filters the extremely hoppy Dogfish Head 90 Minute IPA (9 per cent ABV or alcohol by volume) and 120 Minute IPA (21 per cent ABV – yes, 21) through a fat plastic tube crammed full of raw hops. To make the beer, y'know, a bit more hoppy.

That this centuries-old British beer style was driving innovation across an entire industry in the United States, an industry growing at 10 per cent annually while the likes of Budweiser, Miller and Coors were looking at flat sales year after year, begged a rather obvious question. In India Pale Ale, American style, I'd found the greatest beer I'd ever tasted, that I then believed I ever would taste. It was based on an historic English recipe. So why was it so much more popular and exciting in the supposed beer desert of the USA than in its homeland? Why couldn't I find beers like this in England?

If you have even the vaguest knowledge of beer, you're now sitting there thinking, hang on a minute, even I've heard of IPA. Greene King IPA, that's a famous one, isn't it? Well . . . no, it's not. It's a perfectly decent beer. It was the runner-up Championship Beer of the Great British Beer Festival a few

---

8. This was not entirely due to the combination of jet lag and absurdly high 10 per cent ABV: apart from their use in brewing, hops are a powerful soporific – hop pillows are a popular remedy for insomnia.

years ago.[9] But true IPAs were – and in America still are – around 6 to 8 per cent ABV. Greene King, like almost all British IPAs, is less than 4 per cent. You wouldn't describe it as a particularly hoppy beer, and it's not even that pale. Deuchars IPA from Edinburgh has also won the top prize at the Great British Beer Festival. It is at least pale, and is definitely hoppier than many British cask ales. I order it whenever I see it on the bar. But at 3.6 per cent, it simply doesn't have the intensity of flavour I'd come to love. The Yanks were beating us at our own game, quite embarrassingly.

By the time I was sitting in the Duke of Argyll fourteen months later, I'd found a few exceptions to the transatlantic IPA rule. Marston's Old Empire, St Austell Tribute, Thornbridge Jaipur and Meantime IPA all took cues from North American brewers and used North American hops. In particular Greenwich's Meantime brewery made a real effort to rediscover the true history of IPA, and, at 7 per cent, they maintained that their beer was as faithful to the original style as possible. But much as I loved these beers they were few and far between, and not always easy to get hold of.

India Pale Ale was the greatest beer that ever lived. In its modern incarnation it was my favourite style. But its story always felt a little incomplete to me. I was always waiting for a more detailed telling that never came. The journey that gave birth to IPA, the old sea route from England to India around the Cape of Good Hope, remains the greatest journey beer has ever made, and was made at a time when most brewers couldn't even deliver their beer to the next town in good condition. Didn't anyone else think this was extraordinary? This journey around the Cape used to kill people!

---

9. And even though some segments of the audience booed when the result was announced, and even though the building was struck by lightning shortly after, it was not a fix, because the judges come from a broad range of backgrounds and taste the beers blind.

And India, still one of the most exotic and mysterious places on Earth, was back then – for the English at least – a thrilling, glorious adventure. Didn't this story need fleshing out a little? Turning into a proper story?

And then I realized something else. Something that could reclaim this beer and bring it home. For all the experimentation that had happened in the States: the recreation of old recipes, the use of new ingredients, the super-high levels of hops, the alcohol levels on a par with wine – the one thing no twentieth- or twenty-first-century brewer had done was recreate the journey that gave birth to the style in the first place.

All this flashed through my mind in those first few seconds in the Duke of Argyll, and that's why I said 'Oh, shit.' Because as soon as the idea presented itself, I knew what I was doing next.

'I'm going to recreate the journey of India Pale Ale,' I announced to Liz and Chris. 'I'm going to get a brewer to brew me a cask of traditional IPA, and I'm going to take it by sea to India, around the Cape, for the first time in at least a hundred and forty years.'

CHAPTER THREE

A DIFFICULT CONVERSATION, FOLLOWED BY A FORTUITOUS ONE

'You fucking tosser.'

'Sorry.'

'I said you're a tosser!'

'I know. I was just saying sorry.'

I hate upsetting Liz. It's not that I'm scared by her anger (though I am), it's just that it seems like such a foolish thing to do. If you love someone, and if your best memories all have one thing in common, which is the two of you being happy together in the same place at the same time, then why would you ever hurt or annoy them? Whenever I upset Liz it's by accident, which makes me a very clumsy person, emotionally.

Oh, this had been such a stupid idea, I could see that now. Liz had been nothing but supportive when I wrote my last two books. While she hated the fact that I disappeared inside my head for long periods of time while writing, she had accompanied me on some of the trips for *Three Sheets* and they were experiences we would both remember for ever. But taken together, the whole thing had been an ordeal too, for both of us. I had failed to appreciate how much my schemes and ideas affected the person I shared my life with. There was a line between asking your partner to be supportive of your ideas and decisions, and displaying a flagrant disregard for their feelings. A line between suggesting the possibility of a few days in Belgium, and announcing a three- (or four-, or six-) month disappearing act. I'd just found that line, and not only crossed it, but pointed at it and laughed as I did so. Well, that was that.

'Look, it was just a thought,' I said. 'I was excited about it, but I should have thought it through before just announcing it like that. It's OK, just forget it. It probably wouldn't have come together anyway. I don't have to do it.'

Liz glared at me with exasperation. 'No, you do. You do. That's the problem. You've got to do it. It's a very good idea and in fact I insist that you *do* do it. But you're still a tosser for thinking of it. How could you?'

My declaration became like one of those awful sentences people say in the heat of an argument, and instantly regret but can never unsay. Liz was right of course. Having had the idea, I had to go through with it. That didn't mean she had to like it, but she knew me better than anyone, and understood how important it was for me to explore something that felt like new ground in writing about beer, and much more besides.

There had to be much more to the basic IPA story. But as well as proving or disproving the myth – that this sea journey alchemized the beer in some way – the voyage would have many more facets. I was planning to do it in 2007 – the year India was celebrating sixty years of independence from British rule, as well as marking the 150th anniversary of the Sepoy Rebellion, when the East India Company's own army rose against it, and the 250th anniversary of the Battle of Plassey, commonly regarded as the start of British rule in India.

I also liked the idea of travelling by sea. Fascination and wonder at the ocean rests somewhere deep inside millions of us, sometimes acted upon, more often simply dreamed about. Did I really like the sea, or just the idea of it? Should we be rediscovering it, at a time when awareness about global warming had reached a kind of tipping point and we were beginning to question our right to hop on a plane every five

minutes? A look on the website of a company specializing in
travel on container ships (the first of so, so many to come)
revealed that travelling from the UK to Cape Town on a
cargo ship – a huge, oil-guzzling container ship – gave you
a carbon footprint fifty-six times smaller than the same
journey by plane. What if you could get there under sail? Liz
was right. She often is. I had to do this journey.

I needed to go to work on three fronts: arranging a sea
journey that hadn't existed since the opening of the Suez
Canal 138 years ago; persuading a brewer to help me by
brewing a beer they didn't normally make and hopefully
giving me at least a barrel of it for free, and delving into
history, finding out the truth of the IPA story, what it was
really like, why it really went to India, who drank it when it
got there, and why it disappeared so quickly and completely
from our collective beery consciousness.

The best place to start, at least on the last two, would be
Burton-on-Trent, the spiritual home of IPA. I needed to think
about whom I would contact and how I would approach it.

And then, three days after New Year, I received an email
that, if I were superstitious, I would have hailed as proof that
this trip was more than a mad idea: it was destiny. It was an
email from Rudgie.

Rudgie and I worked together when he was marketing
manager for English Rugby, and I'd been employed by a
marketing consultancy. We worked on a marketing plan that
covered everything from grass roots to the English national
team, with the overall aim of improving the profile of English
Rugby to such an extent that England would win the Rugby
World Cup in 2007. I'd last spoken to him in 2002, when I
quit the brand consultancy. I guess that when England won
the Cup in 2003, four years ahead of schedule, Rudgie must
have decided there wasn't much left for him to do.

According to the email, he was no longer working for
English Rugby. He was working for Coors, one of the

country's biggest brewing concerns. He was based in their main office. Which was in Burton-on-Trent. He was looking after innovation and speciality beers, hoping to create interesting new projects. And after not having seen me for five years, he just wondered if there were anything beery I might be interested in talking to him about?

Paul Rudge was made for the beer business. He has the avuncular manner that has clients, suppliers and little old ladies in the street calling him Rudgie within seconds of meeting him. I bet even the Queen would call him Rudgie.[10] He began his career at what was then Bass before moving to English Rugby. Between that and joining Coors, he had a short spell as marketing manager for Durex. Having spent his entire professional life selling sport, sex and beer, you'd call him the ultimate lad's lad if only he displayed the slightest trace of the boorish insensitivity and inability to treat women as equals that label would imply.

American brewer Coors bought most of what used to be Bass plc just after the millennium, and as part of the deal acquired extensive brewing archives, which, once I explained my quest, Rudgie promised to get me into. But now they brewed Carling, the UK's biggest lager, Grolsch and Reef, and alcopop available in a variety of fruity flavours. So when I thanked Rudgie for the archives and said, 'Now I just need to figure out how to get the beer,' I was surprised when he replied, 'Well, I was just coming to that.'

'How do you mean?'

'We've also got White Shield.'

'Ah. Oh. I see.'

---

10. Rupert Ponsonby, a brilliant campaigner for the image of beer generally, does some PR for Coors. Rupert is almost as posh as the Queen (it's often been observed that the posher you get, the more you have in common with the poorer classes – Rupert is so posh he doesn't just wear hand-me-downs, he wears his grandfather's suits) and *he* calls Rudgie Rudgie.

When Coors ended up with almost everything Bass owned apart from Bass ale itself, they were left with a hole in their business. It was a small hole admittedly, but it was a legendary ale-shaped hole. They filled that hole with Worthington.

After merging with Bass in 1926, this one-time Burton rival took a back seat to Bass itself. Now it was being promoted again. Worthington White Shield, available only in chunky dark brown bottles with a stylish shield and dagger logo, had always been a beer that made aficionados raise their eyebrows reverentially and sigh, 'Ahhh, White *Shield*' at the mere mention of its name.

'And did you know', said Rudgie, 'that until people started calling it White Shield 'cos of the label design, and although these words aren't on the label any more, it used to be called Worthington India Pale Ale? Or that the recipe has hardly changed since it went to India in the mid-nineteenth century?'

'No. No, I did not.'

'Well then. We make it in the Museum Brewery. Tiny plant, about eighty years old. It's called the White Shield brewery now. So how do you fancy getting in there and brewing your own batch of it, maybe make a few tweaks to get it back to the original ballpark recipe, and taking a cask of it to India?'

See? I told you he was a nice bloke.

For the first and last time in relation to my quest, the words 'this could be easier than I thought' passed my lips.

CHAPTER FOUR

SIX MONTHS ON GOOGLE

It was only after I'd deeply upset my wife, got one of the country's biggest brewers involved and sold the idea of a book that I decided to find out whether it was actually possible to recreate the sea route taken by India Pale Ale in the mid-nineteenth century. It turned out that taking a 30-kilogram barrel of beer on an 18,000-mile sea journey that no longer exists was not going to be as easy as it sounds.

The main problem – and it's fairly crucial – is that no one goes anywhere on ships any more. You only have to leaf through even the self-consciously adventurous travel guides. There's always a section telling you how to get to a particular place. It starts by giving you details of flights and airports, and then, for those feeling brave, it might tell you about trains and buses. But there is never anything about getting there by sea, save for a few narrow straits criss-crossed by ferries.

This just didn't seem right. Admittedly I'd never considered going anywhere by sea before now. But even without having experienced it, I quickly grew defensive on behalf of sea travel, and lamented its passing. Didn't anyone else? Wasn't *Titanic* the biggest-grossing film of all time? OK, bad advertisement for ocean travel. But before the iceberg came the glamour, the elegance, the romance and stateliness. From yachts to ocean liners, when ships were the only way of seeing the world, travel meant so much more than it does now. There was no way you could take it for granted the way the bored business-class suit does a 747–400, where the wine list has become more interesting than the fact that he's tens of thousands of feet above the clouds on his way between London and Manhattan. From the eighteenth century, when death at sea shrank from being probable to merely possible, through to the 1960s, when jumbo jets redefined the world, both the destination and the journey would have been something to remember for-ever. Now, for most people, sea travel meant either the grim, greasy floating transport-cafe experience of the ferry, or the ocean-going old people's home of the cruise ship. It wasn't much of a choice. And I quickly discovered that neither offered a passage from England to India.

The historical research wasn't going too well either. The Burton archives were punctured by holes where past researchers had been. No one at the British High Commission in India had ever heard of India Pale Ale. William Dalrymple, who knows more about the British in India than anyone alive if his superb books on the subject are any indication, had heard of IPA, but only because his dad used to work in a brewery. 'To be honest, it's something I have only come across in this country,' he replied kindly to my unsolicited email. 'I never heard of it in India – all my East India Company heroes seemed to drink pipes of Madeira.' Was the whole IPA story merely an exaggeration? Wishful thinking on the part of the beer industry? No. It couldn't be.

India Pale Ale first embarked on its passage a century before the Suez Canal existed. The tall ships set off south-south-west out of the Channel, past Cape Finisterre on the northern coast of Spain, and headed for the rocky, volcanic islands of Madeira, the Canaries or the archipelago of Cape Verde off the North African coast. Here they would pick up fresh water, fruit and vegetables, and maybe a few delicacies such as Madeira wine to trade.

That was the easy part. Sometime after Cape Verde, they would lose the north-east trade winds and enter the hot, still, muggy Doldrums. This was the point where death sometimes became a realistic possibility, as ships that depended upon wind could be robbed of motion and left to sit on a flat, salty mirror for weeks on end.

Sometimes they'd be carried slowly westward by the equatorial current, and would call at the Portuguese trading settlement of Rio de Janeiro to take on fresh supplies once more. Alternatively, if they got lucky – and later, when steam replaced sail – they would make it to St Helena, a tiny island in the South Atlantic that the English East India Company had made their own in 1659.

Finally, they would reach Africa's southern tip. Unless the wind looked particularly promising, there would be a brief respite in Cape Town to sample the beautiful grapes. And then the notorious Cape itself: once known as the Cape of Storms, an early example of rebranding to the Cape of Good Hope didn't prevent old sea dogs from telling frightened passengers that, if they listened carefully, they might still be able to hear the ghostly screams of the doomed *Flying Dutchman*'s crew.

Yeah, that sounded good. As someone with so little experience on water, I didn't even know if I got seasick or not. That was definitely the route for me.

Those who survived the Cape entered the Mozambique Channel, and followed the East African coast, where Somali pirates are still attacking shipping, and finally traversed the Indian Ocean, back up through the tropical latitudes to Bombay, Calcutta or Madras.

This was the route I had to follow. The question was, who the hell would take me on it?

Cargo ships have always taken passengers. If you're terrified of flying, how else are you going to get to your cousin's wedding in Sydney or South Africa? Ninety-eight per cent of the world's cargo still travels by sea, which means they must go everywhere. Of course, no ship has followed the route I wanted to take since Suez opened in 1869. When your business is shipping cargo as cheaply and quickly as possible, why would you? No problem, I thought. I'd get a ship to South Africa, wait around for a bit, then pick up another ship from there to India, maybe with a few nice stops along the way, perhaps in Mauritius, Zanzibar, Madagascar and the Seychelles: truly exotic place names full of colourful smells and dockside adventure.

Strand Travel, who book passengers on cargo ships, offered plenty of options for getting to South Africa, but none from there to India. I wrote explaining what I was trying to do, and that I hadn't found a straightforward answer on their website. They replied that there were no ships from South Africa to the Indian Ocean, and suggested I look at their website for more details. The Sail Training Association said they would see what they could do, and then studiously ignored every follow-up contact I ever made. By April these responses, plus a very alluring brochure from The Tall Ships People, full of fantastic-looking voyages, none of them anywhere close to India, were all I had in my inbox.

'You drive me mad!' said Liz one day. 'You need to phone!'

I phoned the woman at The Cruise People, who assured me, 'What you are trying to do is completely impossible. There is no shipping that goes from South Africa to India.'

'You mean, no shipping that you handle.'

'No, I mean no shipping at all.'

Later, her boss emailed me and told me there had been a container ship that went from Durban to Mumbai (modern-day rebranded Bombay), but it had just stopped doing that route. He assured me the woman I had been speaking to was looking into it for me. I never heard from them again.

It was hopeless combing the outer reaches of the Internet like this. What I needed was a specialist travel agent, someone who organized Travel with a capital 'T' and pointed and laughed at squares like me who queued at Heathrow to board flights with businessmen and families with screaming children. But where would I find someone like that? Did such a place even exist? It must do. But where?

Salvation turned up bearing one of the most unlikely names I'd ever heard.

It was June. Nothing had happened apart from, having first pissed off Liz by having the idea six months earlier, I was now pissing her off even more with my perfect inability to drag it into reality, and the stress and moping this drove me to.

I thought of going by Suez. Of cheating and doing the last bit by plane. Of chartering a ship. I couldn't accept that this journey might be impossible. I knew that somebody else, somebody who wasn't me, would have been able to make it work. There were so many ships in the world! People knew people who owned those ships or worked on them. There were ships on the seas, and there were ports in India. This, at least, I knew. But after six months, I had been unable to put them together, and it felt like a black snake thrashing in my guts.

I wrote to the 'secretariat' of the British Guild of Travel Writers, who canvassed as many members as she could think of. I took some comfort from the inevitable reply, when it came from the Guild's chairman: 'I did a bit of asking but drew a bit of a blank (which is great from one point of view; nobody else is doing anything like this!).'

At least I was failing in an original and interesting manner.

When another email arrived later that afternoon from somebody called Station Weggis, I read it fleetingly, seeing another 'no', when in fact, that's not what it was saying at all.

I only went back to the email because I thought 'Station Weggis' was the best name I'd ever heard. It was so unlikely. In fact it turned out that Station Weggis was not the person's name at all, which disappointed me. I'd been looking forward to typing the words 'Dear Station' in response. Station Weggis was in fact where Urs Steiner worked, and it was he who had written to me. Now Urs Steiner is still a pretty cool name. No flies on Urs. Sounds like a character from a Sven Hassel novel. But it's no Station Weggis.

Weggis (I never found out why 'Station Weggis' comes up in the 'name' field on emails) is a company that specializes in booking container-ship travel. I hadn't come across them before because they don't really have a web presence. But I immediately warmed to them for two reasons. Firstly, because 'Station Weggis' is not a remote outpost in the Arctic, as words like 'station' or 'base' imply, but sits in Switzerland, tiny and landlocked, and I loved the idea of someone being in a country hundreds of miles from the sea and thinking, 'You know what this place needs? A company that deals exclusively with shipping.'

The second reason I fell in love with Station Weggis is that it's where Urs Steiner goes to work every day. And Urs Steiner was my saviour.

Urs hadn't in fact said no. He'd said the dates might be a problem, and he'd said I would have to go to Brazil on one ship, and then take another ship back across the Atlantic. The dates were all wrong, that was true enough. Urs said I would have to board my first ship on 5 September. I couldn't do that. I couldn't leave the UK until 17 September. But there were two things that kept me coming back and prod-ding this ghost of a possibility. The first was that Urs used the word 'Batavia'. I hadn't mentioned Batavia in my email, but here he was saying:

> If you emphasize the trade route to the former
> Batavia, you could choose the following sailing:
>
> Voyage 2301: Commodore
> Santos/Brazil – Itajai/Brazil – Paranagua/Brazil –
> Itaquai/Brazil – Durban/South Africa – Singapore

'The former Batavia' is the current Indonesia, and was once the heart of the Dutch spice trade. And the only person who would know something like this is someone who, like me, had at least a fleeting interest in the history of sea voyages. Someone who might actually be interested in what I was trying to do. And this revealed that I could get from Brazil – even Durban – to Singapore. From there, Urs explained, I could wait for about two weeks, then get another container ship from Singapore back to India, probably Chennai (formerly Madras). It wasn't strictly historically accurate, and it would probably cripple me financially, but it was possible.

The second reason I persisted was the photograph that Urs had attached to the email; the photograph of the first ship, the ship that would get me to Brazil. I clicked it open, and when it appeared on my screen I turned into a watery minor female character in a BBC costume drama. I gasped. I put one hand over my heart. My eyes filled with tears. And, no, I'm not exaggerating. No dramatic effect here. You ask the people who were sitting next to me, who looked at me strangely and asked if I were all right.

So this is what love at first sight felt like. Urs had sent me a picture of *Europa*:

> Part one you follow the trade winds which were used
> by the old East India vessel with an old bark (see
> picture). She is sailing on September 5 from
> Amsterdam via Lisbon – Tenerife to Salvador/Brazil
> (arriving October 28). The vessel will proceed down
> to Argentina. Embarkation would also be possible in
> Lisbon or Tenerife. This is the only sailing this year.

She was the most beautiful thing I had ever seen in my entire life.[11] You can tell how beautiful she was (we're talking about *Europa* now) because look – I was calling her 'she', not 'it'.

---

11. Apart from my gorgeous wife, of course.

Until that point I'd believed the only people who could get away with calling ships 'she' were those who really lived at sea, or who appeared in black and white movies starring Jack Hawkins and, preferably, Denholm Elliott. If anyone else did, they were being pretentious. Well, you could call me whatever you liked, but I wanted this ship. A low, slender white hull curved up and tapered to an elegant bow. Three wooden masts reached up into a cloudless sky, brilliant white sails furled, looking like they were crying to be let down so she could leap off through the sapphire sea. Oh, and look at that – Urs knew about the trade winds too. He knew more about my quest than I did.

But I couldn't do it. I just couldn't leave the UK on 5 September. This is the only sailing this year. It hit me like a punch in the stomach every time I read it. And then, I finally read the preceding sentence properly: embarkation would also be possible in Lisbon and Tenerife. I wrote back – when was she due to leave Tenerife? Urs replied: 29 September. That gave me two weeks to get from the UK to Tenerife, by sea; sod it, I'd cheat, by plane if necessary, just to get on that ship. She was due to reach Salvador, Brazil, at the end of October. And a few days later I would board the *Caribbean*, the other container option, the one that didn't follow the old Batavia route. She didn't stop in South Africa either, but did sail round the Cape, up the East Coast of Africa and across the Indian Ocean, called at a few ports in the Middle East and then Nhava Sheva, India.

Where was Nhava Sheva? I looked on a map of India and couldn't find it anywhere. It wasn't in the index of the Lonely Planet guide. It was probably some flyblown place in the middle of nowhere and it would take me about a month to get from there to Mumbai. After a few days I remembered Google. Nhava Sheva: India's biggest port. Located in Mumbai.

'This one would – if it stays like that, work out very well!'

wrote Urs, lovely Urs, the first person with access to passenger berths on the world's ships who gave a toss about my quest. There were still gaps to fill, but there was the basic route. I knew I could get from the UK to Tenerife somehow. After six months of fruitless effort, I was leaving for India in another three.

Things started to move quickly. There were two options for getting to Tenerife by the 29th. I could take a ferry to northern Spain, then a train to Madrid, another train from Madrid to Cadiz, and a ferry from Cadiz to the Canaries. That would be fine. It would cost few hundred quid, and take about a week. Or.

Or.

Or I could narrowly miss *Oceana*, a P&O cruise ship (it left Southampton thirty-six hours before I was able to board it), fly to Vigo in northern Spain, which was cheating but only a few hundred miles of cheating, catch up with *Oceana* there and not only get to Tenerife in style, with a week to spare before *Europa* sailed, but also visit some of the other islands the old East India Company ships called at along the way. It was highly unorthodox to spend only four nights on board a cruise – the 'Canaries Carousel' as it happens – that lasted for a total of fourteen nights. And I would of course have to pay for the whole fourteen nights. And it would cost me the same astronomical amount of money whether I went alone, or shared my cabin with someone else. What kind of fool would do that?

The kind of fool who would phone his wife and say, 'Love, I've got a great idea. I'm going to make it up to you for buggering off, by giving you a really special time the week before I leave you. What do you say to a luxury ocean cruise, followed by a few days in Tenerife?'

'A cruise?'

'Yeah!'

'A *cruise*?'

'. . . What?'

'How old do you think I am?'

'It'll be fantastic!'

'It'll be my worst nightmare! My dad thought he was a bit too young when he went on a cruise for his seventy-fifth birthday!'

'Yeah, but he enjoyed it, didn't he? I was going to suggest asking him if you didn't want to go.'

'You are not going on this with anyone apart from me. A cruise though!'

I convinced myself she was secretly pleased at the prospect.

I started to make preparations. I still had the brochure, 'Sailing Adventures 2007', from The Tall Ships People in Devon, which was full of handy hints and a kit list. Seasick? 'Nelson was (frequently!) It usually only lasts a few days.' Most ships had ship-to-shore phones. All training would be given and you didn't have to do anything you didn't want to. This all sounded good. Travel insurance, sun cream, warm clothing – balaclava, scarf, fleece and gloves were all essential: 'it can be very cold at sea even in July and August!' Lots of socks, especially thick ones, and a slight ripple of concern at the advice on underwear, 'it is always a good idea to bring more than you think you will need.' I was going to have to pack for both winter and summer. 'Travel light!' they then had the gall to recommend. How? And as I needed to write my account of the trip as I went, that meant laptop, books and sheaves of notes too.

My favourite part was the advice about money. It wasn't strictly essential, as the cost of the cruise was inclusive of everything apart from bar bill and souvenir T-shirts, sweatshirts and 'smocks etc.', which was good as I probably wouldn't have room to pack a smock. But we may want to take some cash with us just in case, as 'there will be opportunities to go ashore for chips etc.'.

I had a whole list of elements still to sort out: visas for

India and Iran, a canal boat from Burton to either London or Liverpool, accommodation in Tenerife and Brazil, getting to Vigo, and figuring out what I was going to do when I finally arrived in India lugging a barrel of beer. I assumed that, having taken six months to get the main elements in place, these final bits would be relatively straightforward. I was utterly mistaken of course.

I was going to be away from home for about four months. That meant I would be earning no money for at least five And as the weeks before the start of the voyage fell away faster than the items on my To Do list, I felt myself sinking, drowning. I was losing control, each day beginning with a new set of deadlines, and ending with 'Phew, I managed to survive another one.'

And while all this was happening, I had a beer to brew.

CHAPTER FIVE

'BEER TOWN'

Whenever I go to Burton I get an irresistible urge to eat curry.

It's part of a weird feeling I get that predates any association between Burton and India. The first time I came here, pitching for an advertising account years ago, I was struck by a seemingly random urge to experience the typical British Friday night out. Not just my idea of a good night out, but the Friday night most representative of the typical night across the country. When botanists classify species they select a sample that they declare as the type specimen, the Platonic archetype that defines the essence of the species, and to which all other examples are compared to determine if they are the same species. I was struck by the sense that Burton would offer the Platonic archetype of the British Friday night. That first time, I believed it was just a random thought. But every time I came back I felt it again, far more than I have in notorious drinking towns like Portsmouth, Newcastle or Nottingham. Now, back in town with a mission, I discovered that it wasn't just me: Burton had recently won a poll to be named the most average town in the UK.

Burton-on-Trent has a red-brick, low-rise high street called High Street. It has all the big chain names, shopping malls and multiplexes that are bleaching Britain of any regional variation. So fine, it's average, but why is it more average? I began looking at it more closely, and realized what it was. The average British town is circled by superstores, malls and multiplexes, which are there to be driven to. In

Burton, you can pull into a vast car park, go for a meal at
Frankie & Benny's, then see a Hollywood movie at the
Cineworld multiplex, before popping into the twenty-four-
hour Sainsbury's or the drive-thru KFC on your way home,
all right in the centre of town. This big-box version of
commerce only hit Britain in the last twenty or thirty years,
which is why any other town has these delights on its formerly
leafy outskirts. Burton is more average than the rest –
uniquely average – because these bland names and formats
have colonized its heart, and there's nothing else in its flat
streets, no iconic architecture or quirky layout, to break them
up. It's as if there were no town in the town centre at all
before the malls and multiplexes came, no individual identity
there to be eroded by these cathedrals of commerce.

What kind of town could have found itself with so much
empty space in its heart twenty or thirty years ago?

There are clues in the street names and street furniture.
The massive multiplex car park is just off Worthington Way.
Outside Cineworld stands a sculpture in which film reels
dance with what appear to be wooden barrels. Across the
street, the main shopping mall is called Cooper's Square. A
common-enough name, but as the bronze statue just outside
Boots confirms here we're talking specifically about the craft
of cooperage, the making of barrels.

These vast urban spaces, now colonized by identikit commerce, were once breweries. All of them.

The shopping mall used to be John Bell's brewery. The
multiplex and its car park used to be Bass. The public library
was Worthington. Behind the storm fencing and DANGER
KEEP OUT signs outside the derelict Riverside shopping
centre and the abandoned Club Extreme, the Salt's brewery
well still runs beneath the litter-strewn concourse, workers'
Portaloo and graffiti informing us in emotive and disapprov-
ing terms that Fat Jodie of Derby is liberal with her sexual
favours, complete with her mobile phone number.

In the middle of the nineteenth century the name of Burton-on-Trent was world famous. Burton was the greatest brewing town the world has ever seen, a wonder of the industrial age and a celebrated jewel of Queen Victoria's British Empire. It was as far from average as it's possible to imagine: time and again, it left visitors gasping for words to describe the immensity of its industry. In 1872, the *Burton Daily News* painted a vivid picture:

> One no sooner enters the town of Burton than he begins to be oppressed by a sense of brewery on the brain . . . There are breweries to the right, to left, in front, and in rear. Huge piles of casks, arranged as we see shot and shell in an arsenal, rise high above the walls flanking the streets. You meet a locomotive coming serenely down the street drawing a long tail of trucks loaded with barrels full of beer, or with grains on their way to the dairies.[12] A scent of brewing ever floats upon the air . . . Walk whither you will, the breweries are interminable. Bass, left behind half a mile on the left, springs into sudden being again on the right front; and when you are looking for the Town-hall you find a few more acres of Bass right in the centre of the town. Not less ubiquitous is Allsopp; and when haply, for a brief space, you manage to escape from under the shadow of these two giants the skirmishing work is taken up at all points by Ind Coope, Worthington, Salt, Nunneley, Evershed, Robinson, and others *quos narrare longum est*. It is impossible to realize that Burton is a town with breweries in it; the inevitable impression is that Burton consists of a congeries of breweries, in the interstices between which and around their edges a town has diffidently grown up, and exists on sufferance, while the

---

12. There's little waste in brewing. Spent brewing grains are a very popular meal among the bovine sorority.

ground on which it stands is not required for brewery purposes.

And yet, you rarely see beer even mentioned in accounts of the Industrial Revolution or the Victorian golden age of industry and prosperity that followed it. Even in Burton itself, there's little reverence now, no real sense of being in a historic brewing town.

Walking down Burton High Street, I passed Wetherspoons and Yates's and wondered why they were not speciality beer bars recreating some of the countless brews that were born here, festooned with displays rejoicing in the proud history of names that were once celebrated around the world, the lifeblood of an empire. I wanted to tear the bricks up and dig my fingers into the soil to find the past, pick the town up and shake it until greatness fell from its pockets.

But I knew enough about the curious character of this place to understand that no amount of coercion would get it to sing unless it felt good and ready. I had to try though: the history of Burton was the history of India Pale Ale. Without knowing one, I'd never find the other.

Burton has always been a fiercely belligerent, independent town. Burtonians have a history of being a stubborn people who go their own way, doing things differently, and protesting against anything they see as wrong. During the English Civil War, Burton was fought over bitterly and almost destroyed because it refused to declare allegiance for either side. Edward Wightman, the last man to be burned at the stake in Britain for the crime of heresy, was a Burton man (and a publican[13]).

---

13. Wightman was burnt in 1611 at Lichfield 'for calling himself the Holy Ghost and holding very dangerous heretical and blasphemous opinions'. It takes a story like this to make you realize that, even taking into account the Thatcherite abomination of 'care in the community', there has been modest progress over the last 400 years in our treatment of the mentally ill. On the other hand, if things had stayed the same we'd get to burn David Icke . . .

And although Lady Godiva rode naked through the streets of Coventry in her famous protest against tax, she actually lived in Branston Manor, a possession of Burton Abbey.

Perhaps this spirit is the product of an extraordinary run of bad luck that, if you weren't one of the many it killed, could only make you tougher. Over the last eight hundred years, Burton has been destroyed by fire, flooded, devastated by midsummer hailstorms, torched by anti-Royal nobles, flooded again – and again and again – hit by hurricanes, earthquakes, Zeppelins, and in 1944 was the site of the largest man-made explosion ever to hit Britain. When disaster is seemingly an everyday occurrence, you need to have a bit of steel in you if you're not going to drop everything and run for the hills, and Burtonians certainly seemed to possess it. Maybe it's something in the water. After all, water is why there's a town here in the first place.

Sometime between the sixth and ninth centuries – sorry if that's a bit vague, but we're talking about the Dark Ages, when writing was often discouraged with the aid of fire and pointy sticks, so accounts vary – an Irish nun by the name of Modwen arrived in England and stayed at a monastery in Whitby for a while before setting off on a pilgrimage to Rome.

She got as far as the River Trent.

The Trent has always been broad and powerful, and crossing it had to be undertaken carefully. Modwen spotted an island in the middle of the river, and wisely figured that this would be a safe crossing. When she reached the island, she found a spring or well in the centre of it. Perhaps she took a drink straight away. Perhaps something else extraordinary happened. But once she was on the island, Modwen forgot all about Rome, and stayed there, building churches and using the water from the well to treat the sick. Her fame as a healer spread, and one day a young boy was sent to her with a seemingly terminal illness. Using the waters from the well on the island now known as Andressey, Modwen cured him, and 'while under Modwen's care he resided on Andressey . . . [he] there received no inconsiderable share of his education at her hand'. Eventually the boy left, grew up – and became King Alfred the Great.

Modwen eventually did get to Rome, but always stopped off in Burton while passing to build another church. She obviously partook of the mystical Burton spring waters herself whenever she was popping by to carry a few bricks or do a bit of roofing, because she lived to see her 130th birthday. Modwen was duly canonized after her death, and buried on Andressey.

A century later, the splendidly named Wulfric Spot, a wealthy landowner with huge holdings across the country, and confidant of King Ethelred 'the Unready', decided to pay tribute to Modwen. Wulfric was the son of Lady Wulfruna, the founder of Wolverhampton, and great-great-grandson of Alfred the Great. Perhaps Wulfric realized that without Modwen's ministrations, his bloodline (not to mention Wolverhampton) would never have existed.[14] In 1004, he founded an Abbey at 'Byrtune',[15] just across the river from Andressey, and had Modwen's remains moved to a shrine there.

Burton Abbey was built to honour Modwen, so it was opposite Andressey. But the Trent was a major river, and the important crossing at Burton Bridge was built in a more convenient place, about half a mile downriver. The track between the abbey and the bridge soon became a busy street

---

14. I refuse to make a joke here about the world perhaps being a better place if Wolverhampton had never existed. Some of my best friends are from Wolverhampton. OK, they're not.

15. It's almost certainly a total coincidence that when you say it aloud, this sounds a lot like 'Beer Town'.

catering to the needs of travellers and pilgrims, and is now Burton High Street.

Like any abbey, Burton brewed its own beer. Hard evidence dates back to the early twelfth century, when records show that one of the abbey's tenants at Wetmore was Frawin the brewer. By 1295, people were writing ditties about how 'The Abbot of Burton brewed good ale'.

Beer was an essential part of any monk's diet. Burton Abbey's records show that the daily allowance for each monk was 'one gallon of strong ale often supplemented by one gallon of weak ale'. But the monks had to think about more than their own needs. Abbeys and monasteries had a duty to provide shelter and sustenance to travellers and pilgrims. Given that the bridge down the road was such an important crossing of such a difficult river, Burton Abbey would have had more than its fair share of thirsty guests. Although there is no documentary evidence, it's likely that this is how the town first started to acquire its reputation for brewing.

It was a reputation that survived the Dissolution of the Monasteries in 1540. When we did this period in history at school, I was left with the impression that 'dissolution' meant Henry VIII personally turning up at each monastery in the land at the controls of a rudimentary wrecking ball, cackling and yelling, 'That's it, run, you tonsured bastards!' while tossing half-eaten deep-fried chicken legs over his shoulder.

But it turns out that it didn't happen that way. Britain had already invented the civil service by then, and the mockingly orderly auditing and division of monastic assets was a bureaucratic process that took five years to complete. As we all know, when you're on official business you have to keep meticulous records so you can file your expense claims later. That's how we know that in November 1545, two receivers from the Court of Augmentation – Richard Goodricke and John Scudamore – travelled up from London to sort out Burton Abbey. They stayed in town for four days, and duly submitted their bar tab on their return home. The solitary bottle of wine probably didn't raise any eyebrows. But they must have had a bastard of a job explaining how they got through 'forty-seven gallons of ale'.

By 1604 there were forty-six brewers in Burton (forty-five once Edward Wightman had been burned at the stake), serving a population of 1,500. These would in fact have been publicans brewing their own beer, the equivalent of modern brewpubs, but even by the standards of the time that was a high number. Transport links consisted of muddy, rutted roads along which beer would have been heavy and costly to move. And such a journey meant that even if you persevered, it was likely that the beer would have been rendered undrinkable when it arrived at its destination. If you were near the coast, of course, transport was a little easier. But Burton was isolated and landlocked. The Trent may have flowed to the coast at Hull, but its weirs and falls made navigation by boat impossible. Nevertheless, some beer made it. Burton ale was being sold in London, at the Dagger in Holborn and the Peacock Inn in Gray's Inn Lane, as early as 1630. And when Samuel Pepys proclaimed his fondness for Hull ale, it's likely that what he was drinking may have come by ship from Hull, but had actually been brewed in Burton.

Today, beers from distant lands are inevitably seen as premium to whatever is brewed locally, and are usually sold in bottles rather than on draught. The same was true back in the very earliest days of beer being transported further than the next valley. Burton ale was strong, reassuringly expensive, and targeted at the 'fashionable market'. In 1707 Farquhar's *The Beaux Stratagem*, a play performed in London, begins with Boniface, a Lichfield innkeeper, welcoming a guest who requests some 'much famed' ale. Boniface boasts, 'I have in my cellar 10 tuns of the best ale in Staffordshire; 'tis smooth as oil, sweet as milk, clear as amber, and strong as brandy.'

In 1709, a collection of songs was published, one featuring the following praise of Burton ale:

> Give us noble Ale
> Of the right Burton pale
> And let it be sparkling and clear.

And writing in his magazine the *Spectator*, in May 1712, essayist Joseph Addison found that it was doing a good trade at Vauxhall Gardens: 'We were now arrived at Spring Gardens, which is exquisitely pleasant at this time of the year. We concluded our walk with a glass of Burton ale and a slice of hung beef.'

That same year, an advertisement in the London *Post Boy* for an auction of the household goods and furniture of His Grace, James, the Late Duke of Hamilton, includes 'Four Hogsheads of fine Burton-Ale'. From then on, Burton ale crops up regularly in auctions of household effects of people either recently dead or moving on.

But what made beer from Burton so special? Robert Plot was the first to stumble towards the answer back in 1680. While visiting Burton during the research for his *Natural History of Staffordshire*, he observed that 'they have an art in this county of making good ale . . . as clear and palatable as one would desire any drinke of this kind to be.'

Having got so close to the right answer, he then concluded that Burton brewers did this by 'putting alum or vinegar into it whilst it is working'. He wouldn't be the last person to accuse Burton's brewers of adulterating their water. But as Molyneux commented in 1869: 'The "potable" condition of the ale assumed by [Plot] to be rapidly acquired by a low form of adulteration, is, in reality, one of the peculiar characteristics of the Burton ale, and attributable exclusively to the chemical or natural properties possessed by the water of which the ale was then, as now, made.'

At the time of Plot's visit, 'Modwen's Well' on Andressey

was still being used for the treatment of 'scorbutic diseases', or ailments of the skin and eyes, and a century later that same well was the source of the 'boyled water' for the most celebrated 'clear and potable beere' on the planet. There are many such wells throughout Burton, and it has always been those wells, not the Trent, from which the brewers have drawn their liquor. As Plot demonstrates, at that time they had no idea what made this well water so special, and wouldn't find out until the nineteenth century.

It may just be coincidence that water with legendary healing properties also turned out to be the best ale-brewing water anywhere on the planet. But it would be one heck of a coincidence.

Water is not just the basis of beer, it's the key to everything, the most important player in this story. Because a single generation after Plot drank up his beer and left Burton along roads 'proverbial for deep ruts and miry obstructions', water in a very different guise would transform the fortunes of this landlocked town, making the name of Burton-on-Trent synonymous with strong, quality ale throughout the country and – unprecedentedly – far beyond.

CHAPTER SIX

BREWING DAY

On a chilly August morning (it was that kind of summer), the day India woke with a massive hangover after the official celebrations of sixty years of independence from British rule, I arrived at Burton train station for the sixth time in as many months, looking forward to the prospect of something a little more alive than dusty archive searches.

Walking down Station Street into the town centre on a cold, clear day like this, you inhale the rainy flagstones smell of freshly brewing lager as columns of white steam rise into a cobalt sky. Yards further on, you're challenged by the other brewing smell: the wet, sugary, loamy fug of mashing. Most of the old breweries may have gone, but Burton still brews 15 per cent of all the beer drunk in the UK, storing it in *Apollo* rocket-sized lagering tanks that stand in ranks on both sides of Station Street.

I mentioned this walk into town later to Rudgie, and he nodded before adding, 'Of course, what people don't realize is that one of the first buildings you pass – the one with all the white steam coming up from it? It's not a brewery. It's the country's largest kebab meat factory.' He squinted philosophically into the morning air. 'I think that's quite fitting, really. Middle of Burton.'

The White Shield brewery must cause at least a moment's confusion for the more fundamentalist beer aficionado. Its continued existence means you have to give due credit to the vast, American-owned multinational lager brewer that rode into town a few years ago and bought the place. A tall, square red-brick tower, the brewery sits apart from the looming old buildings housing the Coors Visitor Centre and Museum of Brewing. Nestling in the middle of a large courtyard among the stables for the dray horses and the collection of old drays, it's a simple, striking building, partially hidden by its neighbours' corrugated-iron walls and sloping roofs. A tall arched doorway and a neat, high round window are separated by gold letters spelling WHITE SHIELD BREWERY, with the red and white shield and dagger logo.

Most of the brewery inside dates back to the 1920s, but it was reassembled here in 1977 when the then Bass Museum was built to commemorate Bass's bicentenary. Until a few years ago it was called the Museum Brewery, and recreated tiny runs of old beers from Burton's past, mainly for special occasions, or for sale in the museum gift shop.

Steve Wellington took over as head brewer at the Museum Brewery in 1993. He claims to have been brewing in Burton since 1965, and the only grounds for disbelieving him are that he doesn't look anywhere near old enough. He would have to be in his mid-sixties, and I simply don't believe he is. He's stocky and ruddy cheeked, but mid-fifties would be a much more reasonable guess. 'I must have brewed two or three hundred different beers since then,' he smiled, looking fondly up at the brickwork. 'Got through most of 'em too.' I remembered Modwen and her reputed 130-year lifespan. Steve would have drunk an awful lot of Burton water over the decades. Maybe he wasn't lying after all.

In 2001, Steve heard that production of Worthington White Shield was being discontinued. After Bass and Worthington merged in 1926, White Shield wasn't a priority. 'Worthington's' became an indifferent mass-market bitter competing with John Smith's and Tetley's. Production of White Shield was contracted out to other brewers in the early seventies, and the once-famous bottled beer seemingly received a little less attention each time it was shunted from one regional brewer to the next, an unwanted, neglected child. By the late 1990s it was being brewed at the King & Barnes brewery in Horsham, Sussex. When it was announced that that brewery was about to close, amid the outcry and rush to save beers such as Brakspear, few people noticed the footnote to the story: Worthington White Shield was about to follow former competitors such as Samuel Allsopp and Thomas Salt into obscurity.

'So I just phoned up and asked if we could have it, and we brought it back home,' said Steve casually, neglecting to mention that the beer was ceremonially welcomed home by an honour guard from the Staffordshire Regiment, and celebrated with the construction of a new £80,000 bottling line.

Steve still enjoys playing with those other historic beers when he can, but brewing a resurgent White Shield had become a full-time job for him and his fellow brewer Jo White. In 2006 it was named best bottled beer at the Great British Beer Festival, and a year later Steve was named Brewer of the Year by the All-Party Parliamentary Beer Group. White Shield is a stunning beer, in both sense of the word. It balances generous IPA hoppiness with dollops of malt, combining with that famous Burton water and a treasured, ancient yeast strain to create a muscular 5.6 per cent ABV ale with all sorts going on: bags of fruit, loads of spices, a hint of freshly baked bread, some treacle, caramel and toffee, all suspended in a fine balance, with no one flavour overpowering the others. I've seen grown men almost weep at how well this beer goes with mature cheddar.

And Steve and Jo were going to let me mess around with it.

Over the last seven or eight years, I must have read fifty different descriptions of the brewing process, and visited just as many breweries where I've had it explained to me on the ground. But I'd never watched it happen before, let alone taken part.

I'd told Steve that I wanted a beer that was around 7 per
cent ABV, packed full of hops, with dry hops in the barrel,
brewed with traditional Burton well water.[16] 'There was an
old IPA called Bass Continental that was last brewed about
sixty years ago,' he explained. 'It was brewed for Belgium
and based on recipes that went back to Bass pale ales in the
1850s, so it's pretty authentic. It was six and a half, so we're
upping it to seven. We're using Northdown hops, which are
very aromatic, pale English and crystal malts. We're using
two different Worthington yeasts, and water from Salt's well,
rich in gypsum. It's still running, a thousand feet down under
the middle of Burton.'

I was delighted. Steve had created a meta-Burton IPA,
with contributions from three of the four biggest names in
Burton's history. He was calling it Calcutta IPA, because
that's where I was hoping to take a four and a half gallon
cask of it.

Inside the building, the brewery itself is a 45-foot-high
tower of scaffolding, girders and pipes, with ancient tubs
made of metal and rich, shiny wood squatting at various
levels. It doesn't look like it should work, but it's been brewing
great beer for over eighty years.

The idea behind the traditional tower brewery is that once
you've got the raw material up to the top, gravity does the rest
of the work. We climbed the stairs carefully, avoiding various
beams, pipes and levers that stuck out at odd angles, threatening a bump on the head here, a torn shirt there. As we
peered from the top platform an ancient electric winch rattled

---

16. White Shield is brewed with Burton well water. But for all its mass-
market beers, Coors, like most big breweries, strips the water of all its
mineral content before adding back in what each beer needs. You can
understand why they do it, but in an historic context it does seem sadly
perverse to remove from Burton beer the reason there are breweries here
in the first place.

into life and hoisted up a heavy, bulging sack. The winch was the newest piece of kit in the place, and Steve had attempted to rig up a pulley system using his car instead before reluctantly admitting that it needed to be fitted. I helped him position the sack over a large hopper. He secured it with a rope, donned a facemask and handed me one, along with a wicked-looking, hook-shaped metal cutter. 'Well, Pete, this is it,' he said. I hooked and slit the bottom of the sack, and 100 kilos of pale malt fell hissing into the hopper, instantly filling the air with a heady aroma of caramel and breakfast cereal. Steve threw a few handfuls of crystal malt on top. 'It's not much,' he said, 'two and a half kilos compared to a hundred of the pale, but it adds a really biscuity note to the flavour.' A whiff of toffee joined the party as the crystal malt fell in a shaded stripe on our huge pile of pale.[17]

I slid on the mask as a crunchy grinding noise drowned out speech and the malt disappeared through the bottom of the hopper, like sand in an hourglass, to be roughly cracked and broken, then mixed with hot water. It reappeared from the end of a fat copper pipe with a temperature gauge sitting on top, a thick, lumpy gloop now, slopping and sputtering on to the shiny slotted plates at the bottom of a wide copper tub lined with chocolaty wood with the words 'Mash tun no.1' stencilled on the side. With the temperature held steady at 66 degrees Celsius (the wooden lining is for insulation), a malty, porridgy steam twisted around us, making my hair curl and my stomach rumble.

'Right!' said Steve, 'that's it for ninety minutes. It sits there

---

17. Malting is one of the great arts of brewing. There are many different types of malt, graded by colour. The colour comes from roasting, much the same way coffee beans are roasted. The greater the roast, the deeper and richer the flavours. Lager malt is very lightly roasted, hence its pale colour, whereas Guinness malt is charred. The same barley grain can be made to yield quite a different array of flavours depending on how it is malted.

mashing now. This is when the enzymes in the malt get to
work and the complex sugars are converted into simpler,
fermentable sugars. Fancy a walk through the museum?'

The Museum of Brewing is Britain's premier tourist attraction dedicated to beer.[18] From my previous visits to the
archives I was already familiar with the waxworks of early
brewers and biochemists, the reconstruction of a Victorian
pub parlour, the reel of retrospectively hilarious early TV
ads, and the pride and joy, which I'll never tire of looking at
– a working train layout depicting Burton as it was in the
1920s, still Beer Town even though the decline had set in.
After many hours of research, the stuff on transporting beer
was as familiar to me as my own name. But one thing I
hadn't noticed before was a smattering of framed photographs of brewery workers through the years. Steve pointed
to a snap of a Bass football team taken in the late fifties.
'Look, there I am,' he said. He was at least eighteen in the
picture, meaning the most conservative estimate possible
would make him sixty-five now. I started to suspect that,
among all his other talents, he was also a Time Lord. 'That
label must be wrong, it wasn't really the late fifties,' he said,
blushing, as if reading my thoughts, 'that must have been
more like the mid-sixties.'

Whatever you say, Steve. Or should I call you . . . Doctor?

After ninety minutes, we headed back to Mash tun no.1.
A turn of a lever and the infused, malty mash drained through
the slotted copper plates in the bottom of the tun, leaving the
spent grains in a coagulated mush inside. But we weren't

---

18. Or, rather, it was. As I was completing this book, Coors announced
the closure of The Visitor Centre, the Brewery Tap, the museum and the
archives as a cost-cutting measure. As the book goes to press, the beer
community and the people of Burton are united in the attempt to try to
save this unique, irreplaceable resource. This book would have been much
weaker without it.

finished with them yet. Now we got to do the sparging, one of many satisfying brewing terms that always summon up red wavy lines from Microsoft™ Word™. We blasted the malt with fresh hot water to rinse out any residual sugary extract from the husks. It's vital to stop the sparge at just the right point – when there's enough sugar for the strength of brew you're after, but before lipids, fats and other undesirables start to wash through. And, yes, I am just pretending I know what lipids are. At this stage we'd stopped referring to our brew as mash: it was now wort, another wonderful wavy red line word. The wort ran glistening into a trough, from which we took a glass to taste. It was the colour of weak tea, and tasted like very sweet hot tea with a digestive biscuit dunked in, the grain's maltiness now infused with its converted sugars.

While I was enjoying my malty cuppa, Steve squinted into a little gadget called a refractometer, which measures the sugar content. 'Apart from this thing and the electric winch, we're brewing pretty much exactly as they would have brewed India Pale Ale in the 1830s,' he said. When the reading was where he wanted it to be, our wort had the right level of sugar, or 'specific gravity', to fuel a fermentation that would give us our 7 per cent beer. It had taken, funnily enough, around another ninety minutes.

The only problem with our tea analogy is that the wort hadn't yet been boiled – that came next. From the network of copper pipes and troughs, the wort ran into a big kettle known as the copper. Traditionally all brewing vessels were made out of copper. 'It reduces the level of sulphide in the water,' explained Steve. 'You get less of the Burton snatch' (the sulphurous whiff from the minerals in Burton well water). Burton brewer Marston's are proud of it and champion it in their beers – it's part of the unique character of Pedigree, their flagship brand. But it's not a flavour Steve wants in his beer.

While vessels are made from copper, *the* copper is the

vessel that celebrates the fact. If you've ever seen the inside of a brewery, the copper is the vessel with a broad, squat bottom tapering to a long, thin chimney. It's the icon of the whole process, appearing on medals in beer competitions and all kinds of beery logos. After decades of boiling and constant scrubbing (cleanliness *is* godliness in brewing) the walls eventually become paper-thin membranes and have to be replaced. 'She's done over two thousand brews in the last ten years,' said Steve, stroking the White Shield copper. 'Not bad for eighty, but she's starting to look it, I suppose.' When this overhaul comes around in big breweries, copper is almost always replaced by stainless steel, but they still refer to the vessel as the copper. Home brewers might do this step of the process in a plastic tub, but even to them, it's the copper.

Part of the fondness for it is because it's home to the process that converts a crude wort into something special. If we let the wort ferment as it is, it would be beer, but not very appetizing beer. The copper is where the hops are added. It's closer to seasoning a dish in cookery than anything else, but as Steve opened a porthole held in place by fat rivets that made it look like part of the *Nautilus*, and a cloud of steam enveloped me and plastered my hair to my forehead, it felt more like alchemy.

Many brewers today use compressed hop pellets or even concentrated hop extract. It disappoints the purist, though I'm not sure many drinkers could taste the difference in the finished product. But we were doing things properly, and that meant using whole hops. They came tightly packed in a sack, dry and olive-coloured, individual leaves like delicate insect wings.

It's a well-known scientific fact that it's impossible to be in the same room as a brewer when there are hops present without him demanding that you take a handful and crush them in your palm to release their essential oils. Ever since I first did this, it's become a highlight of any brewery tour for me, the piney, resinous perfume staying on the skin for hours afterwards. It's the clean essence of the beers I love, and I hanker after it when I try hoppier and hoppier brews. But our palates are all different. There were a couple of photographers doing a project in the museum and brewery, and they were following our work. After crushing hops in their palms for the first time, one verdict was, 'It smells like vomit.'

As I poured in 2 kilos of Northdown hops, the steamy aroma changed immediately. A delicate floral waft filled the air, clean and fresh. Five minutes later as the brew was starting to bubble, it had disappeared again as the hop aroma compounds broke down, and the malt reasserted itself. These hops would give us our essential bitter bite. Towards the end we'd add more; they would remain chemically intact, and give the beer that wonderful aroma.

And then it was coming to the boil. From nowhere, a thick, creamy foam started to break through the soggy blanket of hops sitting on top of the wort. 'It's a vigorous boil, this one,' said Steve, as a blizzard of foam covered everything. A second later we could see nothing but a cloud of sweet, herb-tea-smelling steam, the signal to slam shut and seal the porthole. Here and there, steam seeped out of creaking old joints, and the brewery started to feel like a sauna.

'More waiting now. That needs to boil away for forty-five minutes,' said Steve. He nudged me. 'Time for a beer I think.'

It was also time for lunch. With Steve and Jo, Ian Ward (Rudgie's colleague in marketing), Kevin, a visiting American brewer who likes to pop in on Steve whenever he can, Rupert Ponsonby and his colleague Eleanor, who were in town for a meeting, plus the photographers, it became a bit of a party.

Steve revealed that this wasn't the first time he had resurrected Bass Continental. He'd brewed some in 2002 for the Queen's Golden Jubilee, bottled some and forgotten about the rest. He rediscovered it five years later, reseeded it with yeast, and put it into new bottles, two of which he now produced from his pockets. It was 6.5 per cent, and at these levels beer doesn't go off, it improves with age just like vintage wine. It tasted winey, almost fortified, vinous and fruity and spritzy.

'So this is, like, the same chassis as our beer?' I asked.

'Yes, but we've put in a more powerful engine.'

Calcutta IPA was going to be a great beer.

Rupert brought out some cheese from under the table. Not just any cheese, this had been coated in a skin of hop leaves. When we sampled beer and cheese together, the flavours combined and leapt into the stratosphere. This ale was the best of wine and the best of beer, together in the same glass! Scaling heights neither could have achieved on their own! Like Spiderman and Batman teaming up, Marvel and DC combined, but with no enemy to defeat, unless that enemy was crap beer. It was quite strong to be drinking at lunchtime, and I'm not ruling out the possibility that it went to my head a little quickly.

Jo, the other brewer, is an earthy, relaxed Rhea Perlman-like figure with the filthiest laugh any female has ever had, a laugh that would make Sid James sit up in his grave, a laugh that, as Rudgie commented later, 'could pickle cabbage'. Only beer as good as this could have distracted me enough from noticing when this laugh disappeared with Jo back into the brewery for the next stage.

By the time we realized our forty-five minutes were up, finished our drinks and ambled back, Jo had added the late hops that would give the beer its aroma. The whole building was laced with fat drops of condensation dripping from the rafters as the wort was pumped out of the copper and over the heat exchanger. It ran glistening in rivulets over coils of pipes with cold water running inside, and then into the tall, cylindrical fermenting vessels in the next room. Now, the final step: the pitching of the yeast. I opened a vent and poured in gloopy yeast from a plastic bucket. It seemed a little anti-climactic and disrespectful given that I was kicking off the part of the process that is nothing short of miraculous, but that's simply how it's done. The yeast would get to work as soon as it left the bucket, and would be left to munch away for three or four days, eating sugar, pissing alcohol.

'Now, I don't see why you should just get the easy jobs,' said Steve, handing me something that looked like a hoe. The soggy grain husks from the mash were still packed tightly in the bottom of tun no.1, compacted by water pressure into a cake about eighteen inches thick. My job was to scrape them out through a narrow opening, down a chute to the ground where they fell into sacks to be taken away for cattle feed. It was hard work because it all happened above head height, and the grain cake took some breaking up. But after months of reading, writing, thinking and talking, this methodical, physical work was as therapeutic as a candle-lit massage, and I carried on long after Steve said, 'All right, Pete, you can stop now,' after we'd made the symbolic point and taken the humorous photos, until the job was just about finished.

After fermentation, the beer would be transferred into a conditioning tank, where it would mature and mellow for four weeks, until four and a half gallons of it would be drawn off into a cask for me to take to India.

We'd brewed the beer. I'd involved all these people and taken up their time, and cost this brewery money. Along the way, Steve, Rudgie and Jo had become friends. I couldn't let them down. There was no turning back now.

I already knew that, when I picked up my cask, I was going to anthropomorphize it. As we returned to the Brewery Tap and the afternoon took on that pleasantly hazy quality you get when you drink without getting too drunk and the day's work is already done, I announced that he would be called Barry. It seemed like a writer's cute trick to give a name to the barrel of beer I was about to share so many adventures with, allowing it to acquire a personality, and we made joking references to Wilson, Tom Hanks's basketball friend in the film *Castaway*. What could be the harm in imbuing a harmless, inanimate object with 'pretend' personality traits?

What harm indeed.

PART TWO

REMUS

A LETTER OF INTRODUCTION TO MR HICKEY

A CURRY AND A PINT AT THE COOPER'S

JOHN COMPANY GOES HUNTING PEPPER

A VERY IMPORTANT PASSENGER · PIVO BURTONSKI

BARRY THE BRUISER

CHAPTER SEVEN

A LETTER OF INTRODUCTION TO MR HICKEY

William Hickey was a rake.

Like fops and dandies and bounders and rum coves, rakes don't really exist any more. There are people who behave in a similar fashion, but the delicacy and subtlety has drained from our sober perception of their behaviour. Today, we'd probably call a rake a pisshead, and that would be doing a disservice to Hickey and his kind.

One of my favourite quotes about drinking is from Samuel Johnson, Hickey's near-contemporary, who among many other memorable epithets once said, 'A man who exposes himself when he is intoxicated, has not the art of getting drunk.' The rake understands that there *is* an art to getting drunk, that altering your mental state and joyously loosening your inhibitions doesn't have to mean conversing in ever-decreasing circles, putting your pants on your head and thinking with your groin, or emptying your stomach into the gutter. Hickey did occasionally disgrace himself – and in style[19] – but after

---

19. Like the time he returned home, already very, very drunk, to find his sisters just about to leave for a masquerade (fancy-dress party) at the nearby opera house. They insist he should accompany them, and as he has no costume, they dress him up as a nun: 'The novelty of it attracted universal admiration. I was the cause of much wit and fun.' And then . . . 'I reeled about, singing, talking sad nonsense, and jostling every person that came in my way, every now and then tumbling and unable to rise until assisted by the bystanders. These falls, the heat of the place, and a few glasses of champagne at last produced sickness; and I relieved my overcharged stomach by a very copious vomiting of claret and all the mixture I had that

an unsteady adolescence he managed to embrace the positives of good cheer and raucous merry-making while avoiding embarrassing himself or offending others. 'I certainly have at different periods drank freely, sometimes to excess', he confessed, 'but it never arose from sheer love of wine; society – cheerful companions and lovely, seducing women – always delighted and frequently proved my bane; but intoxication for itself I detested.'

Hickey felt it was his 'particular good fortune to meet with uncommonly generous and disinterested whores and rogues', people whom, according to Peter Quennell, the editor of a mid-twentieth-century edition of his memoirs, were 'sophisticated, rich, extravagant, devoted to the social life and the pleasures of the table, yet distinguished by [their] love of elegance and by a deep regard for art and learning'. What better aspiration could there be in life! In Hickey's day even rogues would greet you with formal courtesy and a witty bon mot before throwing up on your shoes or challenging you to a duel for looking at their bird.

'Pray, sir, did you perchance spill my bumper of claret?'

'My fine fellow! I believe I may be found guilty if tried of such an affront against Dionysus! Perchance you would like to make something of it?'

'Oh, you naughty rogue! Permit me to escort you outside, where, together, we shall admire the constellation of Cassiopeia.'

'But, sir, tonight the bounteous heavens are denied us by London's grey shroud of fog. How is such star-gazing possible?'

---

day poured down my throat. My white dress was soon in a very filthy condition; nor was the effluvia I emitted of the pleasantest nature; so far otherwise that my till then close followers were glad to retire to more respectful distance, leaving me upon the floor like a hog, rolling and wallowing in my own nastiness.'

'My good man, I promise you'll be seeing stars by the
time you have tasted the exquisitely tooled leather of my
boot. You fucker.'

By which time, both parties had forgotten all about the
spilled claret, and hooked up with two of Covent Garden's
finest ladies of the night.

Hickey was born in 1749 and wrote his memoirs in 1810.
Though heavily edited and censored at various points in
history, they've rarely been out of print since. After reading
the first thirty pages, I realized it was pointless underlining
the quotable parts – I was highlighting the entire text. As
Hickey warns early on, 'there are many low and indelicate
anecdotes related, and many gross and filthy expressions
used'. It's irresistible. He recounts tales of a life almost lived,
a life that fell short of its potential, with a rueful tone. But
even when attempting to shock the reader with tales of his
overindulgence, he never quite succeeds in sounding completely repentant. He could have been the inspiration for
Rowley Birkin QC, the *The Fast Show* old soak who, week
after week, ended an unintelligible yarn with the catchphrase
'I'm afraid I was very, very drunk' and a roguish glint in his
eye.

Like Birkin, Hickey was a lawyer, though to read him
you'd imagine law was something you could simply fall into
and make up as you went along. In Bengal in the 1780s, it
was just that. Perhaps the reason his name is referenced
fondly in almost every account of British Calcutta is that he
was the perfect man to prosper there.

The British are famous for their questing, adventurous
spirit. James Cook discovered Hawaii and became the first
man to chart the eastern coast of Australia when most Europeans rarely left the town they were born in. Robert Falcon
Scott died during his expedition to the South Pole on foot
because doing it with dogs, like the Norwegian Amundsen
(who both beat him there and, more importantly, survived),

was cheating. Even today, if you hear of someone trying to get across the Atlantic in a balloon, hitch-hike round Ireland with a fridge or circumnavigate the globe in a bathtub, chances are they'll be British, giving a plucky thumbs-up to the cameras as they sink beneath the waves.

This is the spirit that enabled a relatively small island nation to create the biggest empire the world has yet seen. Whatever you think of the mixed legacy of that empire, you can only admire the intrepid bravery that drove it.

So it's curious that in many smaller ways, this nation of adventurers is conservative, terrified of the new. While the British may be first out of the gate when it comes to travelling to the ends of the earth, when they get there they expect to have their home comforts to hand. Mediterranean holiday resorts are full of restaurants that eschew ripe local produce and freshly caught seafood in favour of full English breakfasts, pies, eggs, gammon and deep-fried fish all served with compulsory chips. The key legacy of the British abroad is the spread of our native tongue. Our sole concession to breaking down the global language barrier is to speak ever more slowly and loudly to those who don't understand us, meaning the rest of the world speaks far better English than we speak anything else.

This paradoxical attitude – we'll go absolutely anywhere, but we insist on taking a bit of home with us – is nothing new. As Peter Quennell said of Hickey and his pals: '. . . they made no concessions to the Indian climate – they wore heavy laced uniforms, curled and powdered wigs, skin-tight breeches and tight polished boots. Nor did they often trouble to acquire the usage of a native tongue . . . Hickey seems to have learned no more than was sufficient to give his host of menials their appropriate orders.'

After two relatively short visits, Hickey returned to India a third time and settled there in the 1780s, around the time pale ale was first being exported in serious quantities. The

British started as they meant to go on, as soon as the voyage
from England began. Hickey writes that on his second voyage, 'As we drank freely, we were frequently half-seas-over
by supper, were consequently frolicsome and noisy, which
offended our commander.'

Hickey wasn't all that wealthy by Calcutta standards, but
still had sixty-three servants, including two who were
employed just to cool his drinks. The typical Company clerk
had even more. He would be woken in the morning by a
posse of respectful servants. A barber shaved him, cut his
fingernails and cleaned his ears. He was served tea and toast
for breakfast, while a hairdresser prepared his wig. After a
contemplative smoke of the hookah, he'd be taken to the
office in a procession, carried in a palankeen with standard
bearers clearing his way. He arrived at work around nine in
the morning and worked until midday in hot weather. When
it was cooler he might put in an extra half hour, arriving at
ten, leaving at one thirty.

A hearty lunch followed. Hickey tells on his first arrival in
India how he sat down to lunch at one, and two hours later
the Governor gave a toast, 'A Good Afternoon', which was
the signal to break up. The custom was then to have an
afternoon nap, but instead Hickey went for a walk to drink
tea with some acquaintances. He returned home, dressed,
and was picked up for dinner at 7.30 p.m.

The dinners and balls were endless. People would drink in
groups at each other's houses first, arriving late in loud,
dishevelled groups, battered and bruised by their short journeys, blaming potholes and bad lighting. Hickey once turned
up at a ball with the skin scraped away from one side of his
face, but still proceeded to be the life and soul of the party.

There was a half-hearted attempt at pacing, with wine
being diluted with water during dinner. When dessert had
been served and a few loyal healths drunk the ladies with-
drew and the gentlemen sat down to the serious business of

disposing of three bottles of claret each. It would have seemed oddly unsocial for a gentleman to drink less when, as a Mrs Fay wrote, 'every lady (even your humble servant) drinks at least a bottle'. The men would demonstrate their drinking prowess by piling up empty bottles on the table in front of them.

William Hickey had found his version of paradise. 'I had many invitations to large dinner parties, which often led me into excess, it being the custom in those days to drink freely,' he writes. He made himself at home instantly:

> Having partaken of several entertainments given at the Tavern by Captain Sutton and other gentlemen, I thought it incumbent upon me to return the compliment and accordingly bespoke the handsomest dinner that could be provided, for forty, at the Harmonic Tavern. On the day appointed, thirty-nine sat down to table, all of whom did ample justice to the feast, drank freely, some of my guests remaining until three in the morning, when they staggered home well pleased with their fare, and declaring I was an admirable host ... I, who had always been disposed to conviviality, soon rendered myself conspicuous, and by the splendour of my entertainments gained the reputation of being the best host in Calcutta.

It was a bold claim to make in a town where drink allegedly accounted for a third of the high mortality rate, but it's a claim none has disputed.

Hickey survived and returned home in 1808, a departure which, according to Kincaid, 'must have made people realize that an age was ending, for he had been so constant a figure at every party, always on the racecourse of an evening in his chariot, the noisiest at every supper, trotting down the law-court corridors every morning, wracked with headache but still bubbling with gossip'.

One age ended, but another was beginning. The excesses

of Anglo-Indian society would never again hit the heights (or depths, if that's how you choose to look at it) of Hickey's day. Madeira and claret suffered steep declines in fashionability and sales. But another drink was about to take their place, a drink that was a little easier on the liver, if not the pocket, and was to become a powerful symbol of English supremacy in the Raj. Hickey would have adored it. And on the eve of my journey to reintroduce it to India, I felt it was only appropriate to organize a send-off of which he would have been proud.

CHAPTER EIGHT

A CURRY AND A PINT AT THE COOPER'S

The Brewery Tap at the Coors Visitor Centre and Museum of Brewing had been recently and expensively refurbished. The old fellas who had spent their lives working for Bass looked slightly uncomfortable on the minimalist leather benches, as incongruous on their own turf as the cask ales from Steve Wellington's White Shield brewery sitting next to megabrands like Coors and Carling on the bar, their traditional wooden handpumps forsaken for sleek, shiny aluminium cylinders.

A glass wall flanked the bar, through which you could see a beer cellar that could easily have been a laboratory. With one notable regular recently named Brewer of the Year, and others possessing the ruthless demands for consistency that only former brewery employees can, you knew the beers in that cellar must be kept in immaculate condition.

Tonight, there was a new one in there.

'Do you want to see him?' Rudgie asked as he, Chris and I sat down with pints of Worthington White Shield.

I felt nervous about meeting Barry for the first time. With the enormity of the journey we were about to undertake together finally sinking in, it seemed inappropriate, like seeing the bride the night before a wedding. 'No, I think I'll wait till tomorrow.'

'But you'll have a drink from his brother surely? We've got Bernard open.'

OK, so the barrel anthropomorphism thing was getting out of hand. But I was about to get a preview of my beer. Rudgie returned from the cellar with tasting glasses of a deep amber brew. A sniff of the glass revealed a massive nose of tropical fruit-salad aromas. In the mouth there was a bitter, resinous spike, so intense it conjured a sensation of bubble-gum just above my tongue, and after that a surprisingly short finish. It just sort of tailed off.

'It's young,' we all agreed. The right elements were all in there, but hadn't quite settled down and got to know each other. No one thought it was the best beer they had ever tasted. But I could tell everyone was excited about what it might become.

Here was my first practical lesson in the history of India Pale Ale. In the eighteenth century most private households brewed their own beer. In the houses of the landed gentry brewing was a fine art, using only the best ingredients. Beers would be brewed strong and cellar-aged for at least a year before drinking, with the best ones cracked open for family celebrations. These 'October ales' (that was considered the best month to brew them) were prized for their keeping qualities, and drunk from small, liqueur-sized glasses – a luxury in those days – etched with barley and hop motifs.

In 1773 a young William Hickey dined with the Marquis of Rockingham at his home in Grosvenor Square, and sampled such a beer:

> I was much pleased with some delicious ale which his lordship said had been brewed at Wentworth (his seat in Yorkshire) upwards of twenty-five years before. It was so soft and grateful to my palate that I was induced to take a second glass; upon which Mr William Burke, who sat next to me, cautioned me to mind what I was about, the liquor I was so approving of being infinitely stronger than brandy and more likely to intoxicate. Undoubtedly, after drinking the second glass, I felt my head light and rather giddy.

Our Calcutta ale echoed these old beers, because their keeping qualities meant that they stood the best chance of getting to India intact. IPA evolved from October beer. Perhaps its miraculous transformation on the voyage was simply an accelerated version of what happened to these strong ales as they sat in cool country-house cellars.

Nine months before, when the idea for this expedition had first reared up in the Duke of Argyll, one of the first things I envisioned was a curry in Burton the night before I set off to India. We would invite all the brewers remaining in the town to attend, and taste a bunch of different IPAs. When I first mentioned this to Rudgie we agreed that it would have to be Balti Towers, a bring-your-own-booze restaurant on Station Street – how could it not be? But Lisa, Rudgie's colleague, disagreed. She was in charge of persuading our guests – who as a rule have refined palates – to attend. She booked us in to Jee-Ja-Jee instead, one of those Indian restaurants that has replaced flock wallpaper with bare brick, has square black plates and lots of chrome, and recognizes that spicy doesn't always have to mean fiery. Even though they were fully licensed, they allowed us to take a few bottles of our own.

I hadn't realized how many brewers there are still in Burton. Small-scale craft brewing is undergoing a renaissance across the UK, with more breweries now than at any time in the last fifty years. And in Burton, as well as Coors and Marston's, there are at least four other small breweries. Under the radar, it was becoming a beer town once again.

It didn't quite work out as I'd hoped.

Thanks to my organizational chaos, I'd scheduled my departure for the week Steve Wellington was on holiday. In the days leading up to the event, brewer after brewer sent their excuses and apologies. When Rudgie, Chris and I sat down in Jee-Ja-Jee, we were joined by Ian Ward, Rudgie's marketing colleague who was just about to defect to Marston's, and two craft brewers, neither of whom had the slightest clue as to why they were there.

Ian explained my quest to Geoff Mumford, founder of the

highly respected Burton Bridge brewery, and John Saville from the Burton Old Cottage Beer Company. Neither had any idea who I was. As Ian spoke, they responded with puzzled nods and guarded expressions, as if this were perhaps some kind of wind-up, or they'd just realized they were trapped in a room with a lunatic. But they both looked like men who wouldn't pass up the offer of a free curry.

Conversation was stilted over dinner, but things started to ease a little when the plates were cleared away and we set about the various Burton IPAs we'd brought with us. Burton Bridge's Empire Pale Ale is an award winner, brewed to a full 7.5 per cent with an earthier, spicier flavour than other beers I'd tasted. Marston's Old Empire was less demanding, but still hoppy and full-bodied. Finally there was Worthington White Shield, its live yeast creating a mini cumulonimbus of dense foam at the mouth of each freshly opened bottle.

I felt then that I'd been unfair to English beers. While I still loved my big American IPAs, they were one-dimensional compared with these. If all you want is a big hoppy smack to the head that rattles your teeth – and sometimes I do – the American ales are wonderful. But here were British beers – authentic IPAs – that balanced this high hop content with a richer, heavier dose of malt. Both hops and malt are capable of imparting fruity flavours to beer, but they evoke different kinds of fruit. Hoppiness is citrussy, like a New World Sauvignon blanc. When it gets to higher levels and intensifies, the lemons, limes and kiwi fruit are joined by mango and papaya. Malt on the other hand tends to impart ripe berry flavours, more like a Shiraz or Cabernet Sauvignon. While the American beers are dramatic and assertive, their English counterparts were complex and subtle, displaying the benefit of centuries of tradition.

The beers made Geoff and John a little more comfortable, and they started to trade bad puns and bitchy asides about their bigger rivals. But I still felt that this wasn't turning into the celebration of beer that I'd hoped for.

Then, Ian produced the beer that changed everything.

For much of its history, Bass was run by not one, but three different families, and was known as Bass, Ratcliff and Gretton. In 1869 Richard Henry Ratcliff ordered the brewing of a special strong ale to celebrate the birth of his son, Richard Henry Junior. As we've seen, these celebration beers were brewed strong and meant for keeping. Perhaps Richard Henry Junior – Harry to his mates – enjoyed a bottle or two on his twenty-first birthday, or on the day in 1894 when he replaced his father on the brewery's board. He died prematurely in 1902. Over the years, bottles of Ratcliff Ale surfaced at auctions. Most buyers kept them as collector's items, eventually selling them on again, but occasionally someone would drink one and it would become that bit rarer. In 2006, Steve Wellington decided to have a clear-out of the cellars at the brewery, sifting through boxes and crates no one had disturbed for years, and discovered a stash of beers that included a sizeable number of bottles of Ratcliff Ale. Having started the evening with a strong ale that was too young, that would mature, it was fitting that we finished with one that had aged longer than its brewers could ever have imagined.

Ian used a bottle opener to chip away carefully at the wax that had sealed in the cork for 138 years. Black flakes snowed on the white tablecloth, and Ian eased out the cork.

The beer poured almost black under the soft halogen lights. It faded to the sides of the glass, where it clung grainily. Everyone around the table was silent.

Even with the glass a foot away from me, I was getting a whiff of something like vintage port. Drawing it close I inhaled deeply – and then did so again, and again. You always have to beware when looking for words to pin down complex aromas like this for fear of sounding pretentious or,

worse, like a TV wine critic.[20] But it was irresistible. My nose
was filled with aromas of dried summer fruit, rich raisins,
plums and brandy, so vivid I could almost see them. Behind
the vintage port and brandy lay vanilla, fresh red fruit,
cinnamon, buttered leather, a tiny hint of smelly cheese. And
– sorry about this – Caramac bars.

'Like the inside of a Bombay taxi driver's jock strap,' said
Rudgie, prompting a predictable volley of enquiries as to
how he's obtained his olfactory knowledge of soiled Indian
underwear.

We could easily have carried on like this and forgotten
actually to taste the stuff. I swirled a mouthful, and the leather
came to the fore, bringing cedar wood with it. As I swallowed
there was just a hint – a ghost – of old oak closets.[21] It made
me think about the man this ale had been brewed for. It had
been created to celebrate his birth. He had been dead for
over a century, and here we were drinking his beer. 'This
beer is proof that ghosts exist,' I announced, or maybe just
wrote in my notebook, having no idea what I meant. The
alcohol had disappeared decades ago, but I was drunk on
sheer sensory stimulation.

Taking a second sip there was a faint impression of
incense, like in an empty church after a service, a maltiness
that made me appreciate the link between 'malt' and 'malt
vinegar' (particularly when it's evaporating off hot chips), and
a pleasant, warming taste of cough sweets with a miraculous
drying finish on the tongue, rounding up all that complexity
and leaving no loose ends. Of course, beer wasn't supposed
to taste like this. A brewing purist would have spat the stuff
out. But it rewarded an open mind and a curious palate with
an unforgettable experience.

---

20. One prominent wine celebrity said Ratcliff Ale tasted like his grand-
mother's staircase.

21. OK, the wine critic was right after all. Sorry.

'The insole of a footballer's boot,' said Rudgie, trying a bit too hard now.

Finally, the brewers were captivated. We became poetic. Passionate. Maybe it hadn't happened quite the way I'd hoped, but finally I had Burton's brewers talking excitedly to each other about the story of Beer Town. 'We're drinking Burton's heritage,' said Geoff solemnly, 'and, boy, it stands up to it.'

We probably didn't need any more to drink by the time we left Jee-Ja-Jee, but I insisted that my last drink before leaving Burton for India had to be at the Cooper's Tavern.

The Cooper's doesn't even look like a pub, more an unassuming, double-fronted red-brick house. It's down a back street forty yards or so off a main road, and you'd never find it unless you were looking for it specifically – but I've already said too much. If you visit Burton, and your heart is pure, maybe the Cooper's will reveal itself to you.[22]

We walked into a utilitarian drinking room with a red-tiled floor, wooden benches and tables along the walls, a Victorian fireplace and a piano shoved into one corner. A shelf ran along two walls, lined with a dusty, random collection of ale bottles. Streetlights shone through the etched glass windows, casting shadowy Bass & Co. logos on to the wall opposite. It seems laughably obvious to mention this, but there was no jukebox or plasma-screen telly.

At the far end of the main room, through a sparse hallway with doors leading to the toilets (outside, naturally) and into the private quarters of the house, we came into a second, smaller room. On one side was a narrow corridor, down which the bar ran. It was just like the bar in any other pub, except where there should have been stools with punters and

---

22. Also, if I'm honest, they do run a fair bit of local advertising, they're listed in the *Good Beer Guide*, and they have these little business cards with maps on. But let's not spoil the romance by thinking about that.

a view of the room, there was a whitewashed brick wall. To get a drink you had to stand self-consciously at the corner of the bar, peering around a bookshelf of tatty paperbacks and down the corridor to ascertain which beer taps faced the wall. Real-ale casks lined the rear of the bar. The walls opposite – the ones we could see without craning our necks and squinting – were crowded with tiny individual chalkboards telling us what beers were on, and what was coming next.

All this was charming enough, but what made me fall profoundly in love with the Cooper's was the seating arrangement here in the parlour. The room was made entirely out of corners, with no middle. Down one nook there were narrow benches with two or three hogsheads serving as tables. Cosy, it was clearly a place for regulars. But there are regulars, and there are local legends. From the end of the bar to the back corner of the room, beneath the chalkboards, ran a high seat raised slightly from the floor. It reminded me of the special, more comfortable booths in old churches that were reserved for rich families, enabling congregations to miss the whole point of Christianity even as they gathered to worship. These were seats where elders gathered to look down on the rest of us. Because even if you'd never been in the Cooper's before, if you knew anything about pubs – shit, if you knew anything about human nature – you just KNEW that you did not sit in these seats. You didn't sit in them if the pub was very busy, and every other seat was taken but these seats were still free. You didn't sit in them if the pub were empty and you were the only drinker. It was obvious that you did not sit in these seats unless you had been a Burton brewer for several decades, and could remember drinking in here when the person now pulling your pint was still a twinkle in a Bass imbiber's eye.

The Cooper's, as well as being a beer temple, was a true pub, a place where any member of society with the exception of Alistair Darling could imagine himself welcome. George

Orwell once described his perfect pub, the Moon Under Water, before admitting that it didn't actually exist. I wish with all my heart that I could have bought him a pint at the Cooper's.

When we took our seats, the people at the next table whipped out accordions and fiddles from under their table and began playing folk music, which is not something I normally like, but in a pub like this, on a night like this, everything is different. When they finished jamming their first number we clapped enthusiastically. Their leader blushed and mumbled, 'Gosh, that's never happened before.'

We only stayed for one. It didn't seem the evening could get much better after that.

CHAPTER NINE

JOHN COMPANY GOES HUNTING PEPPER

When the Honourable East India Company was incorporated in 1600, there was no such place as India. Or, rather, there was, but 'India' was completely interchangeable with 'The Indies', a catch-all term for anywhere east of the Cape of Good Hope and west of the Azores – in other words, most of the as-yet-unexplored planet, including the entire American continent.[23]

What we now know as India was a shaky Islamic empire to the north, squatting atop a scattered array of independent kingdoms, each with its own language and customs. The Company, eventually, would pull most of these together into one country.

It's easy to fall into the trap of thinking about empire builders as simple megalomaniacs, and, at the time, the English sported the twirly moustaches and pointy beards to pull off this kind of schtick convincingly. But the Company was formed with no grand designs of empire building. In the beginning, all it was trying to do was buy some pepper from a group of tiny islands to the south-east of the Indian subcontinent.

While the common man would try to humanize 'John Company', it went around referring to itself as 'the Grandest Society of Merchants in the Universe'. It invented the model of the modern corporation. At its height it controlled half the

---

23. While Europe may have realized its mistake centuries ago, we still haven't got around to renaming the West Indies.

world's trade, and was responsible for a tenth of Britain's income. It financed the Industrial Revolution, created the City of London as a financial centre, laid the foundations of the British Empire, and is largely responsible for the existence of Hong Kong, New York, Singapore and South Africa as we know them today. More importantly though, its adventures would ultimately lead to Britain's love affair with chicken tikka masala, and the evolution of the beer that pairs with it better than anything else.

And yet, thinkers as far apart on the political spectrum as Adam Smith and Karl Marx thought the Company was evil and wished to see it destroyed. It was condemned by white racists as a traitor to its nation, which is ironic given that the Company actually invented modern racism. Those of a more liberal disposition might see the needless deaths of millions upon millions of Indians, or the fact that, over its history, most Company profits derived from being the biggest and most aggressive trafficker of hard drugs the world is ever likely to see, as bigger stains on the corporate copybook. Writing when the growing excesses of corporate power are warping the planet, Nick Robins claims the East India Company outstripped 'Walmart in terms of market power, Enron for corruption and Union Carbide for human devastation.'

Allegedly there are ten miles of shelves of Company archives in the British Library. But there is no blue plaque marking the spot where the Company's sprawling headquarters once stood, no trace of its acres of warehouses. Britain doesn't know how to deal with the legacy of a corporation that shaped the country more than any other, and yet has such an abhorrent record as a corporate citizen. So we just ignore it. The only memorial to the Company in the City of London, a district once built around it, is a tiny pub. But perhaps this is appropriate: from the very start, the Company's antics were drenched in booze.

When the charter to found the Honourable East India Company was granted by an elderly Queen Elizabeth I in 1600, the merchants wanted something a little more powerful than a normal merchant ship for their first expedition. They bought a 600-ton warship, renamed her the *Red Dragon* and had her refitted as their flagship. The supervising committee provided a barrel of beer every day for the shipwrights, so that 'they leave not their work to run to the alehouse'. Encouraging drinking on the job may have seemed questionable, especially when you were counting on the product of that labour to stay afloat and keep you alive. But it was a necessary measure: Britain was being shut out of the Spice Race, and there was no time to lose.

Pepper, nutmeg, cinnamon, cloves, caraway and cumin had been vital to the European diet for centuries, preserving food longer, masking the taste of foul meat, and harbouring alleged healing properties. They had been traded overland since Roman times, making the whole of Western Europe dependent on Italian and Turkish traders, via the Venetian republic. Europe lived in Asia's shadow.

This changed in the late fifteenth century, when Spain and Portugal pulled together to become the most powerful naval force in the world. Columbus sailed west to find a new route to the Spice Islands and cut out the Venetians, while Vasco da Gama rounded the Cape of Good Hope and turned up off the Indian coast. Da Gama was a murderous lunatic who delighted in killing Indians in the most gruesome ways he could think of.[24] He ended centuries of peaceful trading across the Indian Ocean and rerouted the spice trade 'to the

---

24. Such as the time he captured twenty trading vessels off Calicut, taking 800 prisoners. In God's name, he cut the hands, feet and noses off every one of them. Then, displaying the kind of subtle wit that Bernard Manning would have admired, he sent this pile of carrion to the local ruler, with an accompanying note suggesting that he make a curry with it.

greater advantage of Christendom', which makes it all OK then.

This in turn prompted the Dutch to form their own trading company and get in on the action, and it was the sight of heavily laden Dutch ships sailing up the Channel that prompted English nobles and merchants to petition the ailing Queen for permission to form a company with a simple mission, 'Let us be sole masters of the pepper trade.' The beer-fuelled shipwrights did their job, and in February 1601 four ships set sail under James Lancaster.

Lancaster made it to Sumatra and the local rulers threw a fabulous party to welcome him. Here, he became the first Briton to sample a beverage that would become notorious in British India. Arak is described somewhat kindly by William Dalrymple as 'Indian Absinthe' and by another writer as 'Indian schnapps'. But a more appropriate analogy would be 'Indian meths'. It's still made by a method unchanged in centuries. Take one palm tree, cut off a thick, flowering stalk and bind the stump tightly with rope. Hang a pot underneath to catch the sap. Drink it straight away for a pleasant sweet, aromatic taste reminiscent of coconut milk. Alternatively, leave it out in the hot sun all day while a violent fermentation takes place. That's it. Serving suggestion: drink until you fall over.

Lancaster's arak was so potent that 'a little will serve to bring one asleepe'. He diluted it, and managed to stay awake for the gamelan orchestra and dancers. Days later, he and his crew got to sample an Acehnese underwater cocktail party. Guests sat in a river up to their armpits in water while servants paddled among them with delicacies and arak. In 1613, one such party attended by the British lasted four hours. Two of them died the next day from 'a surfeit taken by immeasurable drunkenness'. They were among the first of thousands of Europeans who would lose their lives to this insanely potent drink.

The Company was slowly forced from the Spice Islands, outgunned, outclassed and out-brutalized by the Dutch. The encounter produced some outstanding tales of heroism, the way British defeats always do, and the Dutch finally agreed to give England a little island on the other side of the world called Manhattan as compensation. But England was effectively out of the Spice Race.

There were other compensations. Between 1607 and 1611 ships were ordered to explore the Indian Ocean on their way to the Spice Islands, to see if they could find anything en route that might be more valuable to trade with the islanders than English tweed. Which is why, in 1608, William Hawkins became the first Englishman to set foot on Indian soil, at a boggy, swampy, mosquito-infested backwater called Surat.

Surat was the main port of the largely landlocked Mughal Empire. The Portuguese, French and Dutch were also hovering around, but all the Western powers existed completely at the sufferance of the emperor and his local representative. The 'Portingalls' had already been in the Imperial court for a century when Hawkins set off on the ten-week-long trek to the court at Agra to make his case and beg for trading rights.

Despite the best efforts of the 'Portingalls', Hawkins made himself popular with the Emperor Jahangir, largely by becoming his main drinking buddy. He pointed out to those who doubted his methods that by the end of each day, Jahangir was so wasted on booze and opium his supper had to be 'thrust into his mouth by others'. Maybe so, but in his sottish state, Hawkins was no match for the politicking of the Portuguese. He left the Imperial court in 1611, emptyhanded.

The Company's twelfth fleet arrived in 1612, and were told they had won temporary trading rights. As they awaited confirmation, the commander, Thomas Best, insisted that his men should be on their best behaviour, not creating any embarrassment or giving the emperor any reason to think they were being disrespectful. It was no use. He recorded that he had to have two men ducked from the yardarm for jumping ship on the Sabbath and getting 'drinking drunke with whores ashore'.

The battle for trading rights would carry on for a century. In the meantime, the Europeans were permitted to build trading establishments known as factories in Surat, with their traders referred to as factors. The chief factor was known as the President, and so Surat became the first English Presidency in India.

Factories were permanent establishments where the English could buy goods when the price was favourable and store them until the arrival of the fleet from home. By 1620 there were two hundred factors across a dozen trading centres around Surat and in the soon-to-be-abandoned Spice Islands. They were hard places to live in. Over the course of the Company's history, half its servants died while stationed in India. Drink was often blamed: when there was nothing to trade there was nothing else to do.

Captain Symson claimed arak was 'good for the gripes . . . in the morning laxative and in the evening astringent', but he did admit that a binge on the stuff made drinkers 'so restless that no place is cool enough; and therefore they lie down on the ground all night which occasions their being snatched away in a very short time'. The consensus seemed to be that arak fell 'upon the nerves . . . causeth shaking of the hands in those that drink a little too much of it, and . . . casts them into incurable maladies'. But despite all this, it was 'drunk in drams by Europeans'.

While drink obviously played its part in high mortality rates, not a single servant of the East India Company ever had the benefit of the six vaccinations deemed necessary for my welfare before I set off on my own voyage to India. The water was polluted, and carried cholera and dysentery. Drinks such as beer were safer than water because the liquid had been boiled and sterilized, but people got the wrong end of the stick. Even as late as 1840, it was believed that there was something in booze that counteracted the effects of polluted water, rather than that brewed or distilled liquor was simply free from those pollutants. Many who were dying of disease drank heavily in an attempt to cure themselves, and so hastened their demise.

When Thomas Roe, an ambassador from the court of King James, arrived in India to negotiate on the Company's behalf, he must have wondered if he ever stood the slightest chance of currying favour with Jahangir. He found the Surat factors were prone to frequent bouts of drunkenness and to 'other exorbitancies proceeding from it'. The Company was continually embarrassed by the behaviour of its employees, 'prostituting the worthiness of our Nation and Religion to the calumnious Censure of the Heathen'.

But the heathen didn't really seem to mind that much. Jahangir's father, Akbar, had already witnessed the excesses of Europeans before the arrival of the English, and had been quite understanding about it. He published a special decree permitting the sale of intoxicating spirits to them. 'They are born in the element of wine, as fish are produced in that of water,' he reasoned, 'and to prohibit them the use of it is to deprive them of life.'

On the other side of the subcontinent from Surat, the meanderings of one particular English drunkard were to have a profound effect on the Company's fortunes. Sailing along the Coromandel Coast, Francis Day negotiated with the nawab, the local ruler, to buy one square mile of land near the village of Madraspatnam, where he built a fortified trading post and named it Fort St George. Captain Trumball, who served with him, recorded in his journal: ' 'Tis no strange thing for Mr Day to be drunke. Drinking with Moores and Persians at Ballisara he so disguised himself in their presence that they sent him away in a Pallankeene out of which he fell by the way . . . And another time he made himself so drunk he Ran into the Sea.'

Roe had insisted that 'it is an error to affect garrisons and land wars in India . . . if you will profit, seek it at sea and in quiet trade.' Nevertheless, with its strong walls and garrison of soldiers, thriving Madras pointed the way forward.

And if factors had it tough, the troops had it even worse. It was claimed that those troops who survived the voyage to India died of drink soon after they arrived. They would turn up in Bombay, probably long after they were needed, scurvy-ridden and dressed in rags, wandering the streets, 'seeing all provisions being still very scarce and deare and none of the publicke houses will be persuaded to entertain or dyet them'. Of the 360 men patrolling the walls of Madras, most had chosen the posting over the only other alternative offered: rotting in an English jail.

There was nothing to do other than drink. And if you were going to misbehave when drunk – and many did – it was far better to be an officer than a private. One drunken soldier was a bit rude to a Mr Bradyll. Unfortunately Bradyll sat on the tribunal that tried such crimes, and the private was given thirty-nine lashes. Whereas when Captain Wyatt, returning to the barracks at dawn after a night's drinking, decided a sentry had looked at him a bit funny and responded by flying into a rage, thrashing him, running him through with his sword, then jumping up and down on the dead man's face, this was dismissed as high spirits. The Company felt that it would be punishment enough for Wyatt to be stripped of his commission, because being a gentleman, he 'would naturally feel this disgrace keenly'.

Despite the fact that they were probably seeing double, and therefore thinking their rivals had twice as many troops as they really did, the Company's ships and soldiers grad-ually rolled back Portuguese dominance. In 1661, Charles II was gifted Bombay as part of the dowry when he married

Catherine of Braganza, daughter of the Portuguese king. Charles had no use whatsoever for a few islands and a lot of water,[25] and in 1668 he happily leased it to the Company for '£10 per annum . . . yearly, forever'. With Madras and now Bombay, the Company was a sovereign power in Asia, trading on its own land rather than being the guest of a local ruler.

In 1682, the Company was finally driven from its last outpost in Bantam in the Spice Islands. The Presidency at Surat was relocated to the more militarily defensible position of Bombay, and within twenty years the settlement had become a thriving colony of 60,000 people.

Given that the average life expectancy of a European stationed there was three years, the major Bombay landmark was the English cemetery. Amid the disease-carrying insects and dirty water, Dr Fryer, a Company surgeon, blamed Portuguese arak (which the dirty bastards made from jellyfish, apparently) and loose women. In Surat he had been entertained with 'good scoops of brandy and Delf's beer till it was late enough', but on arriving in Bombay he declared that the English lived: 'in Charnel-houses, the Climate being extremely Unhealthy . . . whence follows Fluxes, Dropsy, Scurvy, Barbiers [elephantiasis] . . . Gout, Stone, Malignant and Putrid fevers, which are Endemial Diseases: Among the worst of these, Fool Rack [arak] . . . and Foul Women may be reckoned.'

It was all very well being able to produce a potentially highly toxic spirit from a palm tree (and perhaps some jellyfish) in less than a day, but the Company's servants were Englishmen, dammit. And what do Englishmen drink? That's right. John Ovington, a ship's chaplain, wrote an account of his visit to Surat in 1689: 'Europe Wines and English Beer, because of their former Acquaintance with our Palates, are

---

25. The archipelago was later filled in to become Greater Bombay.

most coveted and most desirable Liquors and tho' sold at high Rates, are yet purchased and drunk with pleasure.'

This hadn't always been the case. In the early days of Surat, supplies of everything from home were infrequent and uncertain. In 1621, one visitor remarked, 'And further concerning their Drinke, is it not a very great part water? Some Wine and Sider and but little Beere.' With supplies of decent booze limited, the factors were caught between arak and a hard place.

Some small amounts of beer did make it in good condition. Indian guests at factory dinners were amazed by the bubbles and froth when bottled beer was opened. 'It is not the sight of the drink flying out of the bottle', described one observer, 'but how such liquor could ever be put in.'

At a party to 'commemorate the day they left England and their wives', Johan-Albrecht de Mandelslo, a German nobleman who visited Surat in 1638, remarked that the place was 'well provided with . . . excellent good sack, English Beer, French Wines, Arak and other refreshments'. When the drinking got out of hand, the ration was capped to a measly 'half a pint of brandy together with one quart of wine at any meal'.

Every day at noon, the factors in each of the presidencies of Surat, Bombay and Madras would file into the main hall and sit at the public table in order of seniority. Disease-ridden and wretched, they would endure the stifling heat in wigs and flowered coats, toasting each other with wine drunk from rhino horns, which they believed to be an antidote to poison. European wines were imported from France, Germany and Italy. 'English' was good claret to which brandy was added to enable it to withstand the harsh climate. The factors were paid very little, and the table provided eight or nine courses with a variety of drinks all at John Company's expense. Well, it did until a certain president started to become a little too liberal with the drinks tab.

Joseph Collett went to the Indies in 1712 to take up the

governorship of Benkulen, a ramshackle outpost on the coast of Sumatra that was supposed to be sending home ships full of pepper, but was in fact draining rather than filling Company coffers. It was a place where only 'the disgraced and the truly desperate' ended up. Convicts often hung themselves in their cells rather than accept a posting there.

On his arrival in Benkulen, Collett was shocked at the dissolute state of the men, commenting that one Mr Ballard 'drank himself dead a few weeks after his arrival', while another much-anticipated recruit turned out to be no more than 'a notorious drunkard, a profane swearer and a scandalous defamer'. Collett wrote to London promising to sort things out, claiming he was effecting a 'reformation of manners' and the pepper cargoes would soon flow.

The Company may have found this easier to believe if it weren't for the public table's drinks bill for the 'monstrous month' of July 1716. At one time it had been compulsory for factors to dine there. By now it was optional, but the factors pretended not to notice. 'You tell us that all now are diligent, no drunkenness and revelling permitted, all candles are out and all gone to bed before ten at night . . . which is owing to the regular living and good table you keep,' thundered the Company. So how, they would like to know, did Collett wish to explain that the nineteen people under his command had, in one month, made their way through: '74 dozen and a half of wine [mostly very expensive claret], 24 dozen and a half of Burton Ale and pale Beer, 2 pipes and 42 gallon of Madeira wine, 6 Flasks of Shiraz [Persian wine], 274 bottles of toddy, 3 Leaguers and 3 Quarters of Batavia arrack, and 164 gallons of Goa [toddy].'

This bar tab surely makes Joseph Collett one of the greatest drinkers of all time. But he wasn't finished yet. Somehow, only a year later he'd wangled promotion to President of Madras. In October 1718, the Company wrote a thick letter, casually mentioning two enclosed declarations of war with Spain, before coming on to what was really bothering them – the drinks bill for the public table at Fort St George: 'This is an extravagancy that every one of you ought to blush at the thought of. To give 9 Pagodas [30 rupees] a dozen for Burton ale. If you must have liquors at such prices, pray Gratify your Pallats at your own, not our Expence.'

This was an ignominious debut in India for 'Burton Ale and pale Beer', but an important one. Before now students of IPA have believed the first Burton beers went to India in the 1820s; the first pale ales from anywhere in the 1780s. But while they cannot have been exported in great quantities, the outrage of the Company at Collett's antics proves that Burton ale and pale ale – if they are not the same thing – were already so famous they were being referred to by name, and were luxury items in India over a century before the name 'India Pale Ale' was coined.

Soon after Collett's disgrace, the public table was replaced by a more parsimonious food allowance. Rather than living monastically, the factors began roaming the streets and bazaars of their new homeland. Taverns and punch-houses sprang up in the now bustling towns, serving both neat arak and a punch that used it as a base. Merchants and army officers would call on each other in the mornings, greeting each other with draughts of punch made with arak and water, 'which, however cool and pleasant at the moment was succeeded by the most deleterious effects'.

Imports of Indian cotton and silk textiles eventually eclipsed pepper, the original cargo the Company was formed to seek. Raw silk, indigo, and later coffee and tea, helped the Company become a great power at home, and it was reconstituted as a permanent joint-stock corporation, the first of its kind.[26] People began to question the wisdom of allowing

---

26. Previous corporations were granted the right to exist by royal, then parliamentary assent. This was given on a temporary basis and usually

such a powerful corporation to have monopoly power, and interlopers and pirates began roaming the Indian Ocean. Parliament began a power struggle with the Company that would last for centuries, but in the meantime, thanks to commercial might and no small measure of corruption, the Company held the upper hand. It won the right to keep a standing army and navy, and was permitted to gain land by military conquest, and rule thereafter.

In 1707 the last great Mughal emperor, Aurangzeb, died, causing a vacuum at the heart of the Empire. Power gradually transferred to the local nawabs, and, after over a century of trying, in 1716 the Company finally won its treasured farman (trading permit) from the weak, disinterested new Emperor Farrukhsiyar. The right to carry on trade free of duty in large parts of the Mughal Empire represented the most extensive commercial and territorial privileges ever granted to a foreign power, and the Honourable East India Company was now free to pursue profit pretty much as it pleased.

Next in the Company's sights lay Bengal, a place where John Company's worst excesses would reach new heights, where its insatiable thirst for profit – followed closely by its insatiable thirst for colossal amounts of booze – would lead to the rape of an economy, the unnecessary decimation of a people, some fabulous parties and the birth of an incredible beer. From this perspective, I suppose we can't really complain that – given none of this is all that widely known today – this last development is the least well documented of the Company's legacies.

---

related to a specific project, such as the building of a canal, and had to include an element of public good. The BBC is one of the few remaining examples of this kind of corporation.

CHAPTER TEN

A VERY IMPORTANT PASSENGER

Peter Kay does a routine about uncomfortable silences while travelling by taxi, and the need to fill them with excruciating conversation. He can never resist asking the driver, 'Been busy?' and 'What time y'on till?'

Imagine this, except instead of a taxi you're on the back of a wooden cart painted bright red and covered in beer logos. And instead of sitting next to a cab driver, you're standing next to a tall man in a long, chocolate-brown overcoat with red piping and matching bowler hat, who is strapped to a tiny, sloping seat by a fat brown leather harness, occasionally giving a light flick of his riding crop to a muscular and gaily braided shire horse called Carling who is pulling you – just the two of you – through a more-average-than-average English town.

If you were doing this as part of a procession, you might feel merely self-conscious. But if you were jangling along early on a Tuesday morning, hungover, your fillings rattling as the metal-rimmed wheels argued with the tarmac, in the middle of a stream of traffic that was otherwise perfectly – what's the word? – average, the pressure to break the silence would collide with the acute embarrassment nurtured by permed and bespectacled middle-aged women staring at you from pelican crossings, and you would start to sound as awkward as an IT student on a blind date who has just been joined by the local vicar.

'So do you do this often?'
'Nice horse, isn't it?'

'Do you like horses, then?'

As each question left my lips, I died a little inside.

Coors were sending me off in style. The dray was taking me through town to the White Shield brewery, where we were to meet Barry, Janet Dean – Burton's MP – and a horde of curious journalists waiting to speed me upon my way. Everything went to plan except the bit about the journalists. Despite the skills and tireless devotion of Lisa in the Coors press office, Carling, his driver and I were greeted by Rudgie, Ian, Chris, the Coors photographer and Lisa herself.[27]

When he appeared, squat and silver, he already had 'Barry' written across his top in something that was possibly lipstick. I was touched: I'd only just invented him as an anthropomorphic beer cask and already he was making friends. Steve and Jo had written a good luck message on the label, and I was overwhelmed by the kindness everyone had shown; the time and money they'd devoted. Sure, this was a great PR opportunity for Coors (although clearly not as great as I'd believed) but there was no cynicism about this, no sense that what I wanted to do was being twisted for ulterior motives. After so much panic and dismay and self-doubt, to know that this curious combination of large corporate brewery and well-respected micro-brewery was rooting for me, that they were my friends, was humbling. I had to succeed not just for myself, but for them too.

Janet Dean arrived and nodded politely as I explained what I was doing and how I hoped it would help make Burton famous again. We posed for photos together in front of the White Shield brewery and in front of the dray. I sat on Barry, attempted to carry him, was given a substitute barrel that was empty, and carried that instead. Finally, fortified by more samples of young Calcutta IPA from Bernard, we

---

27. Lisa didn't give up though. Apparently we still made the front pages of the local papers the following day.

hoisted Barry on to the dray. Thirty minutes later we were at Horninglow Basin, ready to board the first of four boats that were to take Barry and me to India.

After securing passage halfway around the world on a variety of different vessels, I'd assumed booking a canal boat from Burton to London would be easy, so I left it quite late. You have to return canal boats to the same yard from which they're hired, so that meant a round trip. At the recommended cruising speed of four miles an hour, London and back would have taken three weeks, and cost more than a holiday of the same length in a villa on a Greek island complete with flights and transfers. Canal-boat hire is eye-wateringly, inexplicably expensive. In Burton's heyday, when the canals were lined with robbers, it cost as much to get the beer from the town to the sea as it did to get from the English coast to India. Little had changed: even though the nice people at Viking Afloat gave me a 25 per cent discount for a compromised round trip from Rugby to Burton and back,[28] the cheque I wrote for a week on a barge in the West Midlands was bigger than the one that paid for a month on a tall ship crossing the Atlantic.

As Chris, Graham, another mate, and me picked up the boat in Rugby everyone we spoke to asked if we were waiting for anyone else to join us.

'No. Why does everyone keeping asking that?' I replied to Gary, who was finally showing us aboard the boat.

'Well, it's just . . .' Gary gestured to the canal. After hopping over two other moored boats, we'd arrived at *Remus*.

We needed a four- or five-berth boat, which would have been maybe 40 feet long. *Remus* was a nine-berth boat, the

---

28. That way I would recreate the first part of the original journey by canal, then the journey after 1840 by train. OK, the IPA trains from Burton went into St Pancras and today's train from Rugby went to Euston, but I didn't have to tell anyone that.

only one they had left when they confirmed my booking. And it was 68 feet long. The maximum length of boats allowed on the canals was 72 feet.

The immense size wasn't the only striking thing about *Remus*'s appearance. We all know what canal narrowboats look like. They're hand-painted in dun green or royal blue, beautifully decorated with flowing vines of roses, ornate detailing and illuminated names. They speak of a slow, simple life where people can take pride and as much time as they like to get their compact little boat exactly as it should be. And as they glide noiselessly along the water between fields of ripe corn, they sing silently to us of a rural, Arcadian England that we can still attain if we wish hard enough.

Not *Remus*.

Remus was fluorescent mustard-yellow with ketchup-burgundy trim, a lurid hot-dog condiment boat, a warning to cruisers who knew what they were doing: danger, twats on the water.

And then there was that name. It confused me. Having spent months looking at boats and ships of all kinds, I'd acquired full working use of the term 'she'. Boats are always 'she'. But this one had a bloke's name.

We'd hired a big, bold transsexual monster of a barge.

It was an eventful three days battling with *Remus* to get to Burton. Four miles an hour may be the maximum speed on the canals, but the average is two, and we had fifty-five miles to do. I was William Bligh and Ahab rolled into one, urging us on, yelling with frustration each time a stupid bend grounded our stupid long boat on the stupid bank once more.

At a time when we can get to India in eleven hours by plane, slowness was partly the point of the adventure. And this was the slowest stage of all, slower than walking speed, as Graham repeatedly demonstrated when he got off for a stroll and then had to wait for us to catch up. Slowness was the appeal of the canals, an escape from the modern day. It was meant to be relaxing, soothing.

Instead, I'd invented extreme canal boating by mistake.

Graham had left us the previous lunchtime, and Chris and I managed to get to Burton about an hour before we were due to meet Rudgie in the Brewery Tap. Now, eighteen hours later, after more photos of us getting the barrel on to the barge, we were joined on board by Rudgie and Ian.

My departure felt muted. As we unlocked *Remus*, turned on the engine and nudged our way out into the canal, there was no fanfare, no crowd waving goodbye and wishing us Godspeed, just Lisa and the photographer deciding they'd got enough, before trudging back up the bank with a casual wave.

As Chris took his place at the tiller, I was twittering with excitement, showing Ian and Rudgie around, working out our timing.

I took Barry's picture and emailed it to Liz.

'Barry looks cute,' she texted.

'Cute, but heavy,' I replied.

'I'm saying nothing about your compatibility on that score,' she fired back.

With the engine running and Burton sliding past, I could content myself that my journey had finally begun, and there was little I could do but surrender myself to it. And through this chink in my tunnel vision of getting everything organized, and finishing everything off, after nine months of determined planning, the enormity of what I'd done surged in at me. Here we were on day one. I'd already spent about £7,000 on booking the main stages of the voyage. I'd created the first real strain on my marriage, and caused serious disruption to the rest of my life. All to take a barrel of beer to India.

'What am I doing? What the fuck am I doing?' I couldn't make my limbs work. This was serious. Except it wasn't serious, it was a child-like whim, but I'd allowed it to become serious, when it had no right to be. I'd involved too many people, pushed it too far. 'I'm a fully grown adult. I'm mature! Is this a mid-life crisis? What's going on? Why am I doing this?'

'But everyone seems to think it's such a great idea,' said Ian.

'That's because they're not the ones doing it! They think it's a good idea that I'm doing it, sure. But they think I'm insane!'

'Maybe you should have thought about this a little earlier, Pete,' said Chris, swinging the tiller.

From the canal Burton looked newly built and middle class, all lines of pleasant houses with gardens backing on to the water. After half an hour we slid under a bridge welcoming us to 'The home of Marston's Pedigree' in a cheery mid-twentieth-century modernist typeface, and gazed at the Albion brewery, its surrounding army of articulated lorries reminding us how unfashionable our own mode of transport had become over the last couple of centuries. After that we left the town behind, and ran with the A38 in a straight line, south-west towards Birmingham. The rolling thunder of commercial traffic robbed us of any pretence of being in a rural idyll. But this was primarily a story about industry. The canals may now be populated almost exclusively by leisure craft, but they were built for the forerunners of Eddie Stobart and my own particular favourite, Norbert Dentressangle.

We said goodbye to Chris after a pleasant pub lunch a few miles and two hours later, and the remaining three of us got back on the water. I'd picked up maps of the canals when we boarded *Remus* back in Rugby. You expect these kinds of maps to be painstakingly, obsessively hand-drawn, to look like they could perhaps date back to the 1940s, and they didn't disappoint. Each came with an evocative subheading. 'Trent Waters' offered to guide us through '90 miles of inland waterways through the Trent and Soar valleys', and 'East Midlands Canals' boasted '150 miles by water through the English shires'. They took in places with delicious names like Braunston Turn, Smeeton Westerby and Hampton Magna, and thoughtfully warned us that towns such as Daventry, Hinckley and Nuneaton closed early on Thursdays. I doubted that twenty-first-century consumers would allow early closing anywhere (the maps were last updated in 1996) but I was sure that even fully open, they would feel only half awake.

Canal-side shops were neatly noted, as were pubs that still had names like the George and Dragon, the Three Horse-shoes and the Blacksmith's Arms. When you're sitting in a bar in Shoreditch nursing a four-quid bottle of imported beer while a DJ fiddles with his iPod in the corner, it's easy to sneer and build up a mocking image of the kind of person who takes canal boating seriously. I know this because I have done so. But now we were on the water, I was starting to think of it as an excellent idea. Canals linked Britain before the arrival of the railways and motorcar. And as we twisted away from the road, we were seeing the country in a parallel dimension, one where people still used words like 'motorcar'. It felt great, if you could block out the real world long enough.

There was one feature on the maps that I was less happy about: carefully hatched-in chevrons, which indicated where the locks were. So far we had negotiated four, which meant we had twenty-two to go. On the way up, Chris, Graham and I had gelled into a super-efficient lock-negotiating team. But Chris and Graham had now left. A couple of hours later Rudgie disembarked, leaving just Ian, Barry and me. Ian could only stay with me until around lunchtime the following day, and Barry wasn't helping with anything. According to the maps, I reckoned Ian would be jumping ship smack in the middle of a dense flight of eleven locks at Atherstone on the Coventry Canal.

I'd read that seasoned boaters, those who can sense the mood of their vessel through the gentle touch of their fingers on the tiller, can do locks single-handed, but even they would rather not. As a first-time cruiser on a 68-foot-long monster barge, it was out of the question.

Liz had been making vague noises about joining me for the last few days, without ever actually saying yes, and a sudden flurry of work meant she was now emphatically saying no. I called a few other friends and asked if they'd like to come up and help, but while they all liked the sound of it (or at least pretended to) I was giving them less than a day's notice.

As we entered the Birmingham and Fazeley Canal a gentle flurry of falling leaves started to fill the air and then, when the fresh breeze turned blustery, the flurry turned to a blizzard, and *Remus* became drunk, the wind shoving the bow from one bank to the other in a grand, arcing stagger. As the sun sank, Ian tried his hand on the tiller and immediately hit a moored boat, thanks to *Remus* completely ignoring him as he swung around to change direction. He didn't want to touch it after that, which meant I was in sole charge of a boat that had been difficult to start with and was becoming increasingly erratic, a boat on which I would be alone the following day. I started to panic.

There was no one left to call. And then, with time running out, mounting despair pushed me to a solution that was either inspired or terrible, depending on how you looked at it. I could do this. It just meant swallowing a little pride. Well, maybe more than a little. In fact, thinking about it, I was going to have to force down pretty much the full stock of pride I'd managed to build up throughout my adult life.

I'd organized an 18,000-mile journey that experts on sea travel said was impossible. I was sailing across the Atlantic. I was going on a real adventure, something most of my friends admired, but said that they themselves dare not do. And on the very first day of the voyage, on the easiest part of the whole thing, the bit that elderly couples do with ease, I picked up the phone, punched in a number I usually only dial religiously every Sunday (before *Heartbeat* comes on) and said, 'Hello, Mum? I need your help.'

*

If I ever exhaust my repertoire of common procrastination techniques, I may idly compile a top-ten list of sentences you never, ever want to hear trail off into an ominous silence following the word 'but . . .'

'Normally this would be a minor disciplinary matter.'

'I really, really like you as a friend.'

'We'll probably be able to save your right leg.'

All lurch from good to nightmare with the addition of that three-letter word. But I'm sure that at the top of my list would be the sentence Liz said to me over the phone on a sunny Wednesday afternoon as I stood with my BlackBerry in one hand, phone in the other, attempting to steer a rebellious *Remus* with my arse:

'You're my husband, and I love you.

'But . . .'

Minutes after I'd driven my wife into such unchartered waters of exasperation, something happened that I believed would signal not only the end of my voyage, but also my marriage. There was no way, I thought, that Liz's patience would withstand this.

Day two had started well enough. The alarm woke me at seven o'clock, and we were under way by ten past. There was no rush on the return leg to Rugby, but a quick start just felt right. The silver water was glazed with mist that slunk in hollows until hours later, when the sun rose high enough to burn it away. Rabbits and sheep were the only other creatures up and about, and soon all we could hear was birdsong underscored by *Remus*'s clanking rattle. We fitted in washing and teeth cleaning and bacon rolls and mugs of tea around the navigation of the canal and between locks.

Life is so slow on the canals, you start to feel it's actually going backwards. I was surrounded by things I hadn't seen since I was ten years old. Swallows gathered on the telephone wires spanning the canal, contemplating their own flight to warmer parts. In among the blackberries were other bushes with bright red fruit I now remembered were called rosehips – at least, that was their common name. The technical term, as we learned at school, was 'itchybacks', thanks to the furry seeds you found if you broke open the thick red flesh, designed by nature for mushing up, dropping down your friends' collars and grinding into their skin through their clothes, guaranteeing a hot rash and an amusing afternoon of writhing in a small, plastic grey chair.

Everything about this trip felt like a return to the junior-school classroom, apart from the beer obviously. It wasn't just the itchybacks and the swallows and the blackberries, but unbidden memories of harvest festival, Ratty and Moley and Badger, and knowing the names of things.[29] I was getting reacquainted with the rhythms of nature, having forgotten about them for thirty years. They seemed quite important again now.

The nature of the canal changed constantly, from the seedy bit in the middle of a grim town where teenagers

29. In fact, there's more of a link between our story and *The Wind in the Willows* than I originally realized. After Christmas carolling, back at Mole's house: 'The Rat, meanwhile, was busy examining the label on one of the beer-bottles. "I perceive this to be Old Burton," he remarked approvingly. "SENSIBLE Mole! The very thing!"' The book's original illustrations by Arthur Rackham show Ratty uncorking what is clearly a bottle of Bass, with its distinctive triangle. Beer being drunk freely in a children's book! It's a wonder British society survived, amazing that a whole generation didn't grow up to become alcoholics. Thank goodness today's children's literature is so much more wholesome.

discarded WKD bottles and used condoms under bridges and the water teemed with supermarket plastic bags and budget-brand soft-drink cans, through wide, open scenery you thought had disappeared from England for good, and past brief tableaux of stone-built pub, painted riverboat and lush rushes that were so picture perfect you'd want to wrap a bow around them and give them as presents to the people you love.

Ian and I made great progress and got lucky with Atherstone locks. I used the minutes when the boat was slowly rising to nip inside for loo breaks and, as the day wore on, for the application of sunscreen. These were the only times I was away from the tiller for the entire day. At the time I thought I didn't have much choice, and I didn't really mind because it was absorbing, good fun, and Chris had done most of the steering on the way up so I wanted to get a good go. But it was a devotion to the cause that I was about to spend weeks regretting.

The locks took us up a long staircase from open fields into the middle of busy Atherstone town, and we'd just emerged, triumphant, from the final one at the tail end of lunchtime when my phone rang. The reinforcements were almost here.

In most ways this was a very happy occasion, but I hadn't planned for it to be quite like this. My mum had been on her own since Dad died in 1996. Now, at the age of sixty-one, she'd been dating the nice man who lived across the road and had, a few weeks ago, made it official: they were an item. I was thrilled for her, very keen to meet Dave, and not just because he happened to be a Barnsley FC season-ticket holder. I hoped they hadn't heard the desperation in my voice when I phoned, and that they'd see the opportunity to spend an unseasonably warm day or so on a canal boat as just the kind of impulsive, romantic thing a new couple would enjoy. I seemed to have pulled it off.

As we pulled away from Atherstone back into rolling,

open country, I directed Dave by mobile to a pub where he parked the car. We pulled over to the bank when I saw them standing on a bridge, and swapped Ian the soon-to-be marketing manager of Marston's Beer Company for my mum, a twinkly-eyed, cheerful-looking sixty-five-year-old bloke in a Barnsley FC baseball cap, and Missy the Attention Deficit Disorder Dog, who started gurning like a raver and straining at her harness the moment she saw me, and didn't stop until we said goodbye twenty-four hours later.

Just as we were finishing our first cup of tea, Ian phoned to say that he was back in the office in Burton. It had taken us over a day to get here, and the distance back was a mere twenty-three miles by road. I suddenly felt like a child playing Let's Pretend, like I was doing something silly. But I reminded myself again that slowness was the point, and that I was taking the precise route taken by Burton India Pale Ale to the docks in London, taking just as long as the beer once did. We only had two locks left to face, and I figured I had the hang of steering. We were sorted, happy, and relaxed.

Well, we were for about twenty minutes.

Remus was getting worse. Several times, I would swing the rudder around sharply to line him/her up, and s/he would just keep going along her previous course, ignoring the tiller, until I had to switch swiftly into full-throttle reverse to avoid hitting a boat or the bank. Inevitably, as soon as we started reversing *Remus* would respond to the tiller and swing sideways, bows blocking the canal to oncoming boats, stern lodging itself in the mud and thick brambles of an earth bank. To the untrained eye of someone who had, say, just met me for the first time in the last half hour or so, I looked like I didn't have a clue what I was doing.

After eight hours on the tiller without a break, a tiller that was significantly more juddery than it had been four days ago, my right arm was starting to feel all wrong. Shooting pains went from my elbow to my shoulder with increasing frequency, and my muscles had turned to jelly. I switched to steering with my left, and found that I couldn't pick up a cup of tea with my right. When my phone rang, I fumbled as I took it out of my pocket, almost dropping it.

It was Souheila, from the visa agency. I'd left the visas I needed to enter Iran and India until the last minute. I didn't want to go to Iran, but my container ship, the *Caribbean*, stopped there three days before it was due to reach Mumbai. I had no plans to leave the ship, but I still needed to have a visa to be in Iranian waters. It was a bit of a thrill, telling people I was going to Iran at a time when the rhetoric between the lunatic-bastard Holocaust denier who ran that country and the lunatic-bastard warmonger in the White House, who genuinely believed God spoke to him personally on a regular basis, was reaching new heights. But the visa process was straightforward and routine.

'I've heard back from Tehran, and they have refused your visa,' said Souheila.

'What? Why?'

'I don't know. This is the first time they have ever refused a tourist visa that I know of.'

A man on a boat passing us glared at me and yelled, 'No phone calls while you're in charge of a boat! That's a fifty-quid fine!'

The front of the boat started nudging out towards him as he passed. I was losing control again. 'Is there an appeal process? Can I find out why? It's just ... I don't need the visa until late November, but I actually leave the country on Sunday and it's now Wednesday evening.'

Amazingly, she didn't say, 'Well, maybe you should have applied for your visa earlier than last week then, fool.' She actually said, 'I'll phone them and see what I can do. But tomorrow is a holiday in Iran. The office will be closed until Monday.'

There was no way I was getting an Iranian visa before I

had to leave. And without an Iranian visa, there was a real danger that I might not be allowed on the *Carribbean* for the longest leg of my voyage, from Brazil to India.

I hung up, staring at my phone as if it had bitten me. Immediately, it rang again. It was Liz.

'I just phoned Souheila to check about your visa and it's—'

'I know. She just phoned me. What am I going to do?'

'Well, maybe you should have applied for your visa earlier than last week, fool.'

'Can you do anything? Can you think of anyone to phone? I need to try to email Urs at Station Weggis. See what his take is. He won't be at the office now.'

'I already Googled them to try and get their phone number. Did you know, the first link that comes up talks about voyaging to Iran and says the most important thing is to leave five weeks for the visa process? I'll try them on the phone for you. I don't know why. Joan's here in the office and she says she wouldn't do anything for you. I mean, that's Joan, but she has a point. Have you any idea how busy I am this afternoon?'

And that's when she said it – or rather, didn't.

'You're my husband and I love you, but . . .'

Possibly the nicest thing that could ever come after that 'but' was 'you've really let me down' or 'sometimes you're an idiot'. I didn't want to think about what the other alternatives might be.

I apologized across a whole array of subjects, and hung up. I needed to email Urs, sure that Liz wouldn't be able to raise him on the phone. And then we came to a corner, and I swung the rudder around as far as it could go, and the boat carried on going in a dead straight line, heading for the centre of a small barge with a man sitting in the back, staring at us with growing alarm.

I hit reverse, but we weren't slowing fast enough, and then we were going backwards, and the front was spinning round, and the stern crunched into the bank and muddy water splashed the deck, and we were stuck, completely blocking the Coventry Canal.

I looked up. The man on the boat in front wasn't screaming with rage, but he still looked unsettled. I stuffed my phone and BlackBerry into my pockets and went forward to talk to him, walking up the narrow strip along the side of the boat, holding on to the rails along the roof, as we had been shown. We hadn't hit the man's boat. I apologized profusely, again, and he was understanding about it. The only thing that had suffered catastrophic damage was any sense of credibility in the eyes of a man who could conceivably be my future step-father.

So now I just had to get the boat back facing the right way, and with the business day running out, see if I could do anything to save the back half of my voyage to India. I needed to work fast. I walked back down the side of the boat to the deck. And that's when – with my brand-new mobile phone in one pocket and my freshly upgraded BlackBerry in the other – I fell in the canal.

CHAPTER ELEVEN

PIVO BURTONSKI

Poor old John Evelyn.

The English diarist and keen gardener must have thought it was a gilt-edged invitation to social advancement when he agreed to loan his beautiful London home to a mysterious seven-foot-tall man whom everyone had to pretend not to know was Pyotr 'Peter' Alexeyevich Romanov, Tsar of Russia.[30] In 1698, Peter was in the middle of an eighteen-month-long 'incognito' tour of Europe, during which he tried everything from shipbuilding[31] and town planning to catching butterflies and pulling teeth (presumably not at the same time). Evelyn could only watch in dismay as Peter blew his cover in the most spectacular fashion, ordering his hangers-on to dump him in a wheelbarrow and push him through the hedgerows and precious flowerbeds whose contents would later become the first Crabtree & Evelyn products before storming inside and demonstrating his virility by smashing the furniture to matchwood.

I choose to believe that Peter the Great's discovery of and subsequent love affair with English beer on this trip was entirely unrelated to his violent behaviour. The fact that he

---

30. It was a giveaway that he went around with a delegation referred to as 'The Grand Embassy', saying, 'Yeah, my official title is Peter I, but everyone calls me Peter the Great! Yeah, they do. Huh, don't know where they get it from. Yes, that's Peter . . . the . . . Great. Shall I spell it for you?'

31. Specifically he helped build a Dutch East Indiaman, the *Peter and Paul*, which had been specially laid out for him.

spent most of the time with a bottle of Burton ale in one hand while demolishing Evelyn's cottage with the other has nothing to do with anything. But it was the start of a relationship that would transform the fortunes of Beer Town, and provide the unlikely basis from which a landlocked Midlands town would ultimately become the principal supplier of drinks to a global empire.

While the Tsar was busy partying in London like a seventeenth-century proto-Keith Richards, Burton's merchants and landowners were just across town, lobbying for an Act of Parliament that would permit the works needed to make the River Trent navigable by boat. The Trent Navigation Act was passed that year, and a decade later Burton had access to Hull and the sea. Shipping to London was now straightforward and Burton ale gathered nationwide fame. Daniel Defoe toured the whole of Great Britain between 1724 and 1726, and when he passed through Lichfield, he commented: '. . . the ale is incomparable, as it is all over this county of Stafford. Burton is the most famous town for it . . . the best character you can give to ale, in London, is calling it Burton ale.'

And across the North Sea and into the Baltic, new markets beckoned. The Staffordshire brewers first looked across the waves to buy rather than sell. Suddenly able to meet a much bigger demand for Burton ale, ambitious publicans went into business as fully fledged professional brewers. Such was the reputation of Burton's water, these entrepreneurs often moved into town from elsewhere. Burton's first recorded brewer, Benjamin Printon, set the trend when he relocated in 1708, and was ready to ship his beer as soon as the navigation was complete. Demand was obviously brisk, and soon Printon and other fledgling brewers like him faced a new high-quality problem: there wasn't enough wood to make all the barrels they needed. Brewers depended on 'good English oak', which had to be cut from thick trunks with no low branches, because

knots would render a stave unusable. At one time England
had been covered in such trees, but since the defeat of the
Spanish Armada and the emerging English maritime supremacy that plays such a central role in our story, the hills
had been denuded. The wood the brewers sought for barrel
staves had been turned into the hulls and masts of East
Indiamen.

With new access to sea routes, the brewers soon heard
that perfect timber was to be had in abundance in Peter
the Great's Russia. Peter had staggered home in love with
Western Europe, and wanted to be closer to it. In 1703 he
built himself a new city on the banks of the River Neva, and
named it with his characteristic modesty. St Petersburg was a
grand project that required innumerable craftsmen of every
stripe, each obviously the best in their field. Allegedly among
this army of imported labour were a number of Staffordshire
glassblowers. Perhaps it was they who saw the quality of the
local timber being used, and reported it back home. And
maybe it was they who, homesick and thirsty after a hard
day's palace building, suggested that the ships coming to buy
timber could bring beer to trade.

Hull became a thriving port through which sizeable quantities of Burton ale were shipped to St Petersburg and Riga.
Molyneux described 'Pivo Burtonski' as 'high coloured and
sweet, and of remarkable strength', qualities that he claimed
– and make of this what you will – 'appeared specially suited
to the Russian temperament'. He insisted that Peter was
'immoderately fond' of Burton ale, claiming his 'devotion
to it is rumoured to have been excessive'. This would seem
true enough given one guest's less-than-enthusiastic description of a banquet thrown by Peter at the Imperial Court in
St Petersburg: 'As soon as you sit down you are expected to
drink a cup of brandy, after which they ply you with glasses
of adulterated Tokay and other vitiated wines, and between
whiles with a bumper of English beer.'

Peter the Great died in 1725, after an impressive and fun-packed forty-three-year rule. Half a century later, Catherine, the next 'Great' ruler of Russia, shared many of her predecessor's appetites. Once describing herself as 'frank and original as any Englishman',[32] she kept alive the Imperial tradition of drinking copious quantities of strong English ale, and Burton's fame spread.

In the town itself, most of this growth was driven by one man. In 1742 Benjamin Wilson bought the Blue Stoops, a pub on the High Street that, like all pubs then, brewed its own beer. With his son – imaginatively also named Benjamin – he turned it into Burton's biggest commercial brewery, and was soon doing most of his business through the Baltic ports. By 1774 father and son were struggling to keep up with demand.

In 1777 the Trent and Mersey Canal opened, linking the busiest ports on either side of the country and intersecting with nine other newly built canals. Burton found itself in the middle of a highly integrated transport system that linked it to the biggest markets in the UK, and ports that gave it access to the rest of the world.

One man who understood the importance of good transport links better than most, whose name would travel further and live longer than any other, was William Bass. Born just

---

32. On other occasions she described herself as 'Catherine the second, Empress and Autocrat of all the Russians at Moscow, Kiev, Vladimir, Novgorod, Czarina of Kasan, Czarina of Astrachan, Czarina of Siberia, Lady of Pleskow and Grand Duchess of Smolensko, Duchess of Esthonia and Livland, Carelial, Twer, Yugoria, Permia, Viatka and Bulgaria and others; Lady and Grand Duchess of Novgorod in the Netherland of Chernigov, Resan, Rostov, Yaroslav, Beloosrial, Udoria, Obdoria, Condinia, and Ruler of the entire North region and Lady of the Yurish, of the Cartalinian and Grusinian czars and the Cabardinian land, of the Cherkessian and Gorsian princes and the lady of the manor and sovereign of many others.' I guess it depended on what mood you caught her in, or perhaps how much Burton ale she'd had.

over the county border in Hinckley, Leicestershire, Bass had
already led a very successful professional life by the time he
decided to open a brewery in Burton. He ran a carrying
service between Manchester and London, and would often
stop off in Burton-on-Trent.[33] Beer may have been cumber-
some to carry by road, but Burton was also renowned for the
manufacture of hats – a far more portable commodity. Over
the years, casks of ale crept on to Bass wagons to London,
and empty casks were brought back. Between September
1762 and May 1763, Bass delivered 113 casks of Burton ale
to London publicans. Wagons would leave pubs and arrive at
pubs, and pubs provided the pick-up and drop-off points
along the way,[34] so Bass had a detailed knowledge of the
brewing industry.

When the Trent and Mersey opened, Bass perhaps saw a
less-than-certain future for his carrying business. At the age
of sixty, he bought a disused brewery on Burton High Street
and sought a piece of the Baltic trade. But through his wagon
business, he sold far more beer in Manchester and London.
His main customer in the capital, the Burton Coffee House
in Cheapside, shows how Burton's fame was spreading at
home as well as abroad. When William died in 1787 his son
Michael pushed forward relentlessly, cutting out the agents
and pioneering direct trade in the Baltic, and visiting Manchester and London to drum up business there.

By the 1790s there were nine 'common brewers' in
Burton, all supplying thirsty locals but brewing far greater
quantities for export. In his 1798 history of Staffordshire,

---

33. It's a common misconception that Bass worked for Pickfords, who are
still in the business of moving stuff about today. He didn't. His business
was his own, though it was eventually sold to Pickfords after the brewing
took off, and Pickfords were used to carry Bass beer around the country.

34. An arrangement that still has echoes in any suburban English bus
timetable today.

Stebbing Shaw boasted: 'So great is the celebrity of this place for its ale brewed here, that, besides a very considerable home consumption both in the country and in London . . . vast quantities have been exported to Sweden, Denmark, Russia and many other kingdoms.'

Such was the esteem of Benjamin Wilson's ale, those who couldn't get enough of it were prepared to pass off inferior Burton ale in its place. In 1803, Michael Bass received a request from a customer in Königsberg for thirty casks of ale and a branding iron bearing the name 'B. Wilson'. Asking the brewer to provide the branding iron to complete the forgery was perhaps rubbing their noses in it. Bass resolved to take Wilson's Baltic supremacy from him. It was the start of a rivalry between the two firms that would run for generations.

While Bass eventually succumbed to the temptation of forgery,[35] his true desire was for his own brand to be held in such esteem. But neither his fraud nor his daring ambition succeeded in the Baltic, and eventually, wounded, he retired to focus on building up the business to Manchester and London. This failure to displace Wilson, and search for business elsewhere, would ultimately save his brewery and give his son Michael Thomas Bass the supremacy he craved.

Burton's brewing boom was built on shaky foundations. Shipping heavy casks of beer on the canals was fraught with danger. The floods that often hit the town were particularly frequent around this time, and both river and canal would freeze during the winter, blocking traffic completely.

Even when the routes were open, pilfering by the boatmen was common. And then they were just so bloody slow. Michael Bass wrote repeatedly to Pickfords, his carrier, raging

---

35. Such skulduggery throws a different light on the future counterfeiting of the Bass brand, which would prove the biggest headache for Michael's son, Michael Thomas, through much of the nineteenth century.

at them to buck their ideas up, telling one agent: 'If people could depend upon the time you engage to deliver goods, you would have many more tons in a year from this place than you have.'

Getting the beer to sea was only the beginning. By the early 1790s relations with France were deteriorating and there was war in the Baltic. French privateers were roaming the North Sea, and the Hull ships began travelling in convoy for protection.[36] And pilferage didn't stop once the beer finally made it to the coast. Bass was always writing letters like the one where he thanked an agent in Hull 'to see this ale stowed in the ship in such a manner that the crew may not get at it'.

But these were high-quality problems, born of burgeoning success. Plaudits like Stebbing Shaw's tell us two vital facts about Burton ale. Sure, it was great-tasting beer. But lots of people were brewing great beer. At the height of the Baltic trade a single London brewer was turning out more than double the entire output of all Burton's breweries combined. Burton's importance was out of all proportion with its size. Because the second fact, hidden just below the surface, is that Burton ale had remarkable keeping properties. The only way a beer could be enjoyed so widely is if it were up to the rigours of the journey. More than anything else, it was this remarkable longevity that would make Burton world famous.

---

36. In September 1797 the *Culloden* was captured by the French on her way from Inverness to Hull, with six cases of champagne on board bound for Michael Bass's cellar. But she was recaptured by a boat of colliers also bound for Hull, and Bass got his champagne after paying £3 6s. 8d. to the Admiralty. Maybe it's because I'm a Yorkshireman, but I love this story. It's a state of war, and what must have been a reasonably heavily armed ship captures the *Culloden*. Then a bunch of miners sail past and go, 'Eyup, lads, looks like there's a spot o' bother 'ere', steam in and say, 'Nah then, Jean-Pierre, I don't think this belongs to you, does it, flower?' Not even pirates can fuck with miners.

But not yet. Within a few years, those brewers who survived in Burton would be dreaming of the days when they had the luxury of fretting about pilferage on the canals.

The fog of war was rolling in over Europe, and Michael Bass fretted that 'that Damned Bonaparte will throw everything on the continent into confusion'. His fears proved well founded. In 1806, Napoleon succeeded in blockading all of Europe to British shipping, including the Baltic ports. Burton's Baltic beer trade was dead with a few strokes of the quill.[37]

This was too much for Wilson. He sold up, leaving his business to his nephew, Samuel Allsopp. Even though Samuel's brother Thomas has been congratulated in Hamburg by none other than Marshal Blücher himself on the 'bonne bière' produced by Wilson and Allsopp, there was no way through to the continent. Some small exports were squeezed out through Liverpool to Belfast, Dublin and the West Indies, but the bulk of volume had to be offloaded domestically. Allsopp became desperate to sell his beer. He set up agencies in West Bromwich, Hull, Manchester and Liverpool, paid agents 5 per cent commission, threw out free samples to London publicans – but even when he got orders they were sporadic, and delivery was often more difficult than it had been up the canal to Hull. His ale was darker than people liked and eventually he was forced to write to his customers to ask 'whether Pale Ale or that of a darker Colour is most liked by you'.

The fact that Michael Bass had failed to challenge Allsopp's Baltic supremacy now worked in his favour. With the legacy of his father's carrying business, he had cultivated contacts in London, Manchester and increasingly Liverpool.

---

37. Well, that and the talents of the most fearsome military genius Europe had ever seen.

As Burton's breweries began to close, Bass showed steady growth.

Finally, Napoleon was defeated, the continental system collapsed, and Allsopp and the rest of Burton's brewers looked forward to a resumption of the good old days. But it wasn't to be. In 1820 Russia suddenly abolished all duties on Burton beer then, with the capriciousness that only an absolute ruler can pull off, reimposed them two years later. A Mr Stein, formerly the Member of Parliament for Bletchingley and described by his peers as 'entirely devoted to the service of his country wherever it did not interfere with his own interest', had seen a shrewd business opportunity, and opened a porter brewery in St Petersburg. The Russians still loved English-style beer, but they could now brew their own. Burton's Baltic lifeblood was still once more – this time for good.

By this point there were only five brewers left in business in Burton, from a peak of thirteen. Michael Bass stood triumphant at the top of the much-reduced pile. He was clearly a strong-willed man, and probably didn't allow himself to be distracted from his celebrations by the fact that the combined output of all Burton's brewers was lower than it had been forty years before.

In March 1822 Allsopp issued a notice to the domestic market that was nothing short of a fire sale:

> In consequence of the sudden prohibitory measures adopted by the Russian Government affecting various exports from Great Britain, Wilson & Allsopp of Burton-upon-Trent will directly offer to the public a quantity of rich pale ale and fine flavoured ale of uncommon strength, brewed expressly for that market, at a reduced price of 2s 6d per gallon at Burton . . . it is too well known to need comment that the ale from this brewery has stood pre-eminent and unrivalled in the Baltic market for the

last 40 years; and without affecting to presume on the
unvaried preferences shown to their ale, they do not
hesitate to express their full confidence that a trial will
secure general approbation.

These repeated allusions to pale ale suggest that the strong,
sweet beer that was so 'specially suited to the Russian temperament' wasn't going down well at home. Burton ale was
recognized as a unique style, respected, but much stronger
than the everyday beers people were accustomed to.[38] After a
spell of glory that died just as it was hitting its stride, it
seemed that Burton's destiny was as a producer of revered
but small-scale speciality beers.

The course of beer history changed one wet, cold winter's
night early in 1822. While he was in London trying to secure
new business, Allsopp received an invitation to dinner from a
Mr Campbell Marjoribanks. Mr Marjoribanks (pronounced
'Marchbanks') had made his fortune as captain of the *Arniston*,
an East Indiaman, sailing her to India and back on three
voyages between 1795 and 1803. In 1807, he was elected to
the Company's board of directors, and by 1819 he was serving his first term as chairman. When he issued his invitation
to Allsopp, he had either just begun or was about to begin his
third term.

As the two men dined at Mr Marjoribanks's elegant Upper
Wimpole Street mansion, Mr Allsopp recounted his tale of
Baltic woe: the sudden loss of his entire market, the govern-
ment's refusal to bail him out, and the bleak prospects ahead.
When he finished, Mr Marjoribanks said, 'But why not,
Allsopp, leave the cold climates, and try the warmer regions

---

38. *The Treatise On Adulterations of Food*, published in 1820, featured tests
that had been carried out on various liquors to determine their alcohol
content. Samples of Burton ale were between 6 and 9 per cent, while
'common London-brewed ale' was between 5 and 6, and porter between
4 and 5.

of the earth? Why do you not make an attempt on the Indian market?'

'I never heard of it,' replied Mr Allsopp.

'There are five thousand hogsheads of English beer sent to Madras and Bengal every year,' said Mr Marjoribanks, 'and, what is more to your purpose, it is a trade that can never be lost; for the climate is too hot for brewing, unless at a distance so great that the carriage must eat up all the profits; and no tariff can ever affect you.'

Marjoribanks had pitched this shrewdly – the circumstances that crippled the Baltic trade could not happen again, because India was a British property. But before we can continue eavesdropping on this conversation (which, if we choose to believe it, was recounted word-for-word decades later to a journalist who stood in awe of Samuel Allsopp and what he had by then achieved[39]), before we hear how it ultimately set the course for not just Allsopp, or Burton, but for the entire development of beer and the global brewing industry, we need to ask a few questions.

Why had Marjoribanks chosen to speak to Allsopp when London was home to huge, successful brewers who dwarfed him in scale and were much nearer the East India Company's dockyards?

And what did Allsopp mean when he said of the India trade, 'I never heard of it'? Was he being disingenuous? He must have been aware of the trade conducted by Marjoribanks's Honourable Company. There wasn't a citizen in England who didn't know about John Company, even one

---

39. J. Stevenson Bushnan's 1853 book *Burton and its Bitter Beer* offers the most definitive account ever written of the birth of Burton India Pale Ale, but is written entirely from Allsopp's point of view. The author describes the brewer as 'a man of high courage, and with a spirit as stanch as ever warmed the breast of a true English gentleman'. And that's him just warming up.

with his face turned perpetually to the Baltic. Maybe he meant he'd simply never heard of beer as a significant part of this trade. That would be more understandable. But even then, it would mean that he was completely unaware that, by the time of his dinner, Bengal had become an English fiefdom where the finest drinks known to humanity were swilled alongside fatal firewater; a tropical dominion where Burton ale had already been celebrated and squabbled over for a hundred years.

CHAPTER TWELVE

BARRY THE BRUISER

I sat on *Remus*'s foredeck on my own, shivering occasionally, gulping whisky frequently. Mum and Dave had gone to bed, happy and bashful like teenagers, after a canal-side beer-garden dinner and a rare England football victory on the big screen inside. Barry sat in the galley, saying nothing, but I could sense a certain quizzical air emanating from him. He was sizing me up, finding me wanting.

Having begun this voyage feeling that I'd put too many people to too much inconvenience, I was nearing the end of this first stage believing that I'd let everyone down, including myself. I'd created this grand adventure of going halfway around the world, and two days in, at thirty-nine years old, I'd had to call my mum to come and help me. And since she and her brand-new boyfriend had turned up, I'd behaved like someone who couldn't really be trusted even to cross the road to the shops without someone holding his hand.

'It'll toughen you up.'

I couldn't get Liz's words off a tape loop in my head. Like a druggy sequence in a bad spy film, she became more mocking each time I ran it. I knew it would toughen me up. I was prepared for hardship, looked forward to embracing it. *But on the canal trip?*

Each time I heard her words, I replayed the fall into the canal in crystal-clear, high-definition slow motion. I'd become confident, nonchalant about walking up and down the four-inch-wide walkway on the side of the boat. I was sure of my footing, trying to be like Gary at the boatyard rather than a clumsy, nervous novice. And, anyway, I had on my special deck shoes that I'd bought from a special shop that sold wet suits and those cool James Bond underwater thingies that are basically a propeller in a yellow fibreglass housing with a couple of handles, designed for sneaking up on villains' yachts undetected.[40] I didn't even notice the splashes on the deck from where I'd churned up the water trying to power out of the weeds. I put one foot down and had already lifted up the other to step confidently from the edge of the boat back on to the main deck, and the foot that was touching the edge slipped from the wet metal with a loud squeak.

I've no idea how long it takes to fall into a few feet of water. It's probably less than a second, but it felt like so much longer. I knew I was going to be able to save myself. As I was in mid-air, touching nothing, I knew my foot would find purchase once again on the deck. As my feet got wet, I thought, no problem, I can land kneeling on the edge. Up to my shins, I was thinking, this is fine, I can grab the railing and hold on, and it will be a near miss that we can all laugh about. Then my left knee clanged sharply on the metal hull, shooting pain, and I missed my grip. Up to my waist I still knew I would hold myself and fall no further. Up to my chest, I thought, OK, this is bad, but these canals are very shallow. I'll let myself go, then punch the bottom with my feet and bounce back on to the deck. I'll barely be in long enough to get wet. As my head went under I realized I'd been mistaken about how shallow the canal was. As I sank further and the gravy-like water went up my nose and still there was nothing beneath my feet, something broke inside my head. I yanked myself up with my arms, still clinging to the side of the hull.

---

40. Given that the shop was on the Embankment in the middle of London, judging from the range of these items they stocked there must be an awful lot of Bond villains working in the City.

My mum helped drag me back on the deck like a sopping bin bag.

Like Bill Murray in *Groundhog Day*, I could think of many, many other short passages of time I wished I'd been able to relive in such vivid detail instead of this one.

My phone was dead. The BlackBerry, a couple of days later, recovered. Mum is never better than when she is in a crisis. She took both and laid them out to dry, transferring my SIM card to her phone so I could carry on having my visa nightmare.

I'd gone into shock. Dave had already indicated that, understandably, he wasn't comfortable taking *Remus*'s tiller, particularly after s/he had started trying to travel down the canal sideways. I knew we had to get a few more miles under our belt before we moored for the night, although looking back, I have no idea why – we were in no great rush any more. The sun was sinking. And even though I dripped until I was standing in a splashy puddle, I wouldn't leave the tiller to change out of my filthy, wet clothes. I stood there shivering, accepting cups of tea, saying nothing, thinking I was behaving normally.

Inside my head, I was screaming.

That's it. That's the last straw. Liz will divorce me now.

I was sure of it, from the instant the water closed over my head. Her frustration with me had been growing exponentially as I became more stressed and inefficient in the run-up to the start of the voyage. Here was final proof that she'd accidentally married an idiot.

I texted her the news, and of course her only thought was to check that I was OK. When I came out on the foredeck clutching the bottle of whisky, I'd phoned her back to say goodnight, admitting I thought she would be furious.

'You're joking, aren't you? It's the only thing that's cheered me up all day.'

That was OK then.

'All the girls at my jewellery-making class thought it was very funny.'

Right.

'And my cab driver on the way home thought it was hysterical.'

I felt an enormous wave of relief. But I also felt ridiculous. 'I don't think I can do this. I don't think it's going to work. The thing with the visa, and then falling in . . . I think it might be an omen. This was such a bad idea, I think I should jack it in as a bad job.'

I suppose on some level I thought I was offering her an opportunity to say she didn't want me to go, to talk me down from the ledge and attempt to get our lives back to normal. I wanted her to say 'I'm so glad you said that. It's time to end this business.' Instead, she laughed. Only my wife can laugh scornfully and mockingly, yet in a loving, supporting way. 'What? So on day two of your journey, you fall in the canal and that's it? You spend months talking about how you're going to sail across the Atlantic on a tall ship and then at the first hurdle you say, right, that's it, I'm going home? Don't be ridiculous.'

Tough love. The slap across the hysteric's chops. For the first time since my dip in the soupy water, I felt warmth that wasn't entirely whisky-based. 'You're the loveliest wife in the world,' I said.

'And you're the funniest husband in the world. Now go to sleep.'

But I didn't. I couldn't. When Liz hung up I was back on my own in the dark, fretting about the problems and obstacles that were bobbing up and squelching around me. My tiller-arm screamed with agony whenever I moved it. The knee I banged on *Remus*'s metal hull throbbed sickly. My right nostril burned raw where canal water had shot up it. I worried about what might be in that water, and like the cholera-struck factors in Surat, I drank enough whisky to make sure anything living in my stomach wouldn't survive the night.

I scribbled in my notebook by the light of my head torch. There was no other light, no sound apart from the blood rushing in my ears like the throb of the barge's engine, and my breathing, which sounded like the *Tardis*. I wrote until my handwriting became illegible, saving me from the embarrassment of having to read the drivel I was submerging myself in towards the end.

Our final day on the canal dawned beautiful and quiet. It wasn't just an absence of noise; it was like the canal was doing its best to present itself, a naughty child who has been bathed and tidied up and dressed in her Sunday best, pretty and demure and charming. The silvery surface, burnished by just a breath of mist, was smooth as glass and empty of other boats. When we got under way, even *Remus*'s engine seemed quieter and more polite than it had been. We cleared our last couple of locks easily, and spent the morning inside an advertisement for canal-boat cruising.

The nature of the canal continued to change constantly. Round one corner we entered stage left on to a broad, flat plain, miles of Midlands farmland stretching away. From here, even Coventry in the hazy distance didn't look shit. We didn't hit the bank once.

As I executed a flawless ninety-degree turn into the arm where the boatyard lay, nudged in next to the other boats, handed back the keys and nodded sagely on learning that our steering problems were probably due to an early crash knocking the rudder out of its cup, I already felt changed from when we'd picked up *Remus* a week before. The concerns of office life seemed small and far away. I was windswept and sunburned, and knew what time the sun rose and set and what phase the moon was in. I'd worked out how to use my new nautical watch, which had a compass, barometer, information about the tides and the moon, and in case of emergencies was just about big enough for a helicopter to land on. For the first time since I finally grew too old to stay in the Scouting movement without appearing sinister, I felt like I belonged outdoors.

So after saying goodbye to the lovebirds, I felt a little guilty boarding one of the Virgin high-speed trains that had regularly thundered past us as we puttered along the canal. I was back in London in an hour. It had taken me three days to travel the first fifty-four miles of the old IPA route, and sixty-two minutes to do the next eighty-five. You can see why the idea of trains caught on.

I spent the brief journey home thinking about the canals, following them into the distance when the train ran parallel with them. I wasn't sad to abandon *Remus* early, but I would have loved it if we could have got to London on the water. The Regent's Canal, which ends at Limehouse Dock where the old East Indiamen were loaded, runs just a mile or so south of my house. I hoped that one day I would see London from the canal's perspective, a hidden side to the city that would change my perception of it, just as I now thought of the Midlands as a region that was fascinating, multilayered and often beautiful.

By India Pale Ale's heyday, most of it was coming down from Burton to London by train. When St Pancras Station was built, giant arched cellars were incorporated to hold thousands of hogsheads of Burton ale before it could be transferred for shipping.[41] Midland Road, around the station, was packed with bottling firms who would add their own branding

---

41. I hoped to be able to see those cellars, and one day I would: after the end of the events described in this book, I returned to London just as the station reopened as St Pancras International, the most beautiful, elegant shopping mall I have ever seen, with a record-breaking long champagne bar and – back then – no pub. There's no trace, evidence or record of Burton pale ale: one of the arches is M&S. Another is a WH Smith. One, of course, is a Starbucks.

to the beer before sending it to every corner of the English-speaking world, which, back then, meant most of the planet.

As I disembarked at Euston, a few hundred yards down the road from St Pancras, I had specific cause to mourn the passing of the beer-carrying industry that once dominated this corner of London. When I collected Barry, I gave no thought to what he might be like to carry. I certainly didn't want to put him inside a wheelie bag for this part of the journey, because I knew he was going to want his photograph taken. But now I was at the back of the train, on my own, at the end of a long platform, with my computer bag, wheeled duffel bag and a 30-kilogram beer barrel. I tried to cradle him and managed a waddling walk of ten yards or so, to the first point where the luggage trolleys should have been. I couldn't get very far like that, so I hoisted him on my shoulder for the next part. I had to stop and put him down every twenty yards or so. There was not a single trolley on the whole station, just empty corrals. I huffed and grunted and staggered and weaved as the platform cleared and the station staff gathered for a chat and watched me impassively.

It took me twenty minutes to get from the platform, across the eternally busy station concourse, and down two flights of steps to the taxi rank. By the time I was in a cab I was wild-eyed and spitting hatred for the city I was about to leave for several months. We needed a better solution for carrying Barry.

When I undressed that night, the whole of my left bicep was a livid, multicoloured bruise from where I'd carried him. My left arm was tenderized like a piece of steak, vying for sympathy with my banged leg and a useless right arm I was now pretty certain was displaying the symptoms of repetitive strain injury.

If I'd realized then that this was merely a taste of the anguish this barrel had in store for me, I'd have left the bastard on the platform at Euston.

PART THREE

OCEANA

CHAPTER THIRTEEN

BOOZING AND BRAWLING IN BENGAL

When John Keay wrote 'There are few highlights in the Calcutta saga and no heroes . . . it is not a pretty story', he was showing remarkable restraint. Bengal was the stage on which, unfettered by the constraints of Western civilization, the merchants, officers and soldiers of the East India Company could give full vent to their urges and desires. And at the heart of Bengal is Calcutta, a city variously described as both hell and paradise on Earth, capital of John Company's India, and final destination for the lion's share of the beer that came down the canals from Burton and out into the Atlantic on its long journey.

Europeans were already trading in Bengal when William Hawkins was still at Agra getting drunk with his new best mate, the Emperor Jahangir. But unlike Bombay and Madras, which stood on land the Company now owned, in Bengal they traded entirely at the local nawab's pleasure. This irked the appropriately named Governor John Child, who wanted more, always more. Famously regarded as a bit of a bastard even by his rapacious peers, Child believed the Company needed to transform itself from 'a parcel of mere trading merchants' into a 'formidable martial government in India' . . . to secure 'a large, well-grounded sure English dominion in India for all time to come'.

Sitting at home safely in London, Child declared war on the Mughal Empire. A ragged band of soldiers and merchants fought skirmishes against a bemused emperor and his hundreds of thousands of troops up and down Bengal's swampy

Hooghly River delta for several years, until being forced to pay humiliatingly large tributes and damages when peace was finally brokered. In return the commander of the Company forces, a weary merchant called Job Charnock who believed the conflict had 'only rendered our nation ridiculous', was granted land and tax-raising powers over four villages near the river. One of these, Kalighat (named in honour of the bloodthirsty goddess Khali) gave its name to the thriving trading community that sprung up there, and Calcutta was born.

The idea was for the city to be near the trading centres upriver, but close enough to the sea to allow access to ships. It paid off – by the middle of the eighteenth century Calcutta was a thriving city that attracted Bengali traders and crafts-men in their tens of thousands. It made the English the most powerful traders in the region, and John Company became the world's first global corporation.

Indian garments could be bought so cheaply they could be shipped back to Britain and sold at a healthy profit, and still cost less than domestically produced goods. The revenues were used to finance the slave trade, and Britain prospered. Joseph Addison, the Burton-ale-loving *Spectator* owner, remarked in 1711 that London was an 'emporium for the whole Earth . . . The single dress of a woman of quality is often a product of a hundred climates . . . the scarf is sent from the torrid zone . . . the brocade petticoat rises out of the mines of Peru and the diamond necklace out of the bowels of Indostan'. Words such as bandana, calico, chintz, dungaree, gingham, seer-sucker and taffeta entered the language, and England became fashion-obsessed. This world of extravagant clothes produced in Asian sweatshops controlled by multinational corporations, and sold at home to a fickle populace at prices that put domestic producers out of business, is almost unimaginable today.

To be fair, there was one big difference: back then India

was a rich country, accounting for a quarter of global manu-
facturing output compared with England's measly 2 per cent.
It had its poor and it suffered from famine, just as it does
today, but the wealth of the emperor and his local nawabs
was rumoured to be immense. As far as the Company was
concerned, there was just one problem: increasingly, they
would rather all that treasure was theirs.

After being granted full trading rights in 1716, the Company gleefully ignored the small print and did whatever they
liked, paying a tiny fraction of the tax and tributes they were
supposed to. This was clearly outrageous: it would be like a
major corporation today – a newspaper publisher for example
– dictating policy to the government without paying a single
penny in tax.

The nawabs, ever more dependent on English cash, were
starting to become fearful of their power in Bengal. One ruler
likened Europeans to a swarm of bees, 'of whose honey you
might reap the profit, but if you disturbed their hive they
would sting you to death'. Eventually Siraj ud-Duala, new
nawab of Bengal, declared war and drove the English from
Calcutta. Those who didn't escape were taken prisoner and
confined to a tiny, overcrowded cellar. From an alleged 146
captives, only 23 survived. The veracity of the account of the
'Black Hole of Calcutta' has since been disputed bitterly by
Indian historians, who point to some glaring inconsistencies.[42]
But exaggerated or not, this one act of atrocity was used by
the Company as moral justification to exact whatever revenge
it pleased.

Enter Robert Clive, a man who didn't exactly earn his

---

42. The man who wrote the definitive account describes how bodies were
packed in too tightly to move, then later tells how a friend made his way
across the room to sit next to him on a bench. The cellar had one tiny
barred window, through which hardly any air entered, and yet the Indian
gaolers allegedly gathered round this to watch and taunt the prisoners.

place in the pantheon of great military leaders, more sort of shoplifted it after tricking everyone into looking the other way. If Clive had been around today he would probably have been auditioning for *The X Factor* between running dodgy Internet scams out of Nigeria and doing odd jobs for Halliburton. The content of his letters home from India to his father can be summarized briefly as 'I wanna be a STAR!'

For a common merchant with no formal military training he certainly displayed an aptitude as a commander and strategist. He'd just saved Madras from the French when the Company ordered him to retake Calcutta, with the distinguished Admiral Watson leading the navy. The young upstart and the distinguished commander took an immediate dislike to each other.

They soon reached the fortress of Baj-Baj, which guarded the Hooghly River. According to Surgeon Ives, who chronicled the campaign, while Clive waited for dawn to assault the fort with his crack troops, 'one Strahan, a common sailor belonging to the *Kent*,' clearly drunk, staggered forwards, waded across the fort's moat and managed to 'imperceptibly get under the walls'. He then decided that he could take on all the *bashtards*, and scaled a breach in the walls that had been made by the ships' cannons. He reached the top, much to the bemusement of the nawab's men, 'at whom he flourished his cutlass, and fired his pistol . . . Then after having given three loud huzzas, he cried out "The place is mine."'

Several of his merry shipmates ran to his aid, and found him bloody but unbowed, still defending himself with only a broken cutlass and his 'incomparable resolution'. As chaos descended, English troops piled into a free-for-all and the fort's garrison fled. The only fatality, a Scots captain, was an early victim of friendly fire, 'unfortunately killed by a musket-bullet from one of our own pieces'. For all the glory given to Clive of India, it was in fact a gang of violent binge drinkers who won the first battle in the conquest of Bengal.

Watson was delighted that one of his own sailors had upstaged the prissy Clive. He made a show of disciplining the badly hungover Strahan, who confessed his crime but 'hoped there was no harm in it'. As he was led away to an imaginary flogging, he swore under his breath that he 'would never take another fort by himself as long as he lived, by God'.

Calcutta itself soon followed, the biggest altercation being a spat between Clive and Captain Eyre Coote, as to who had really retaken the city and who was the bestest hero.

Crying 'Nine-eleven!' – sorry – 'Black Hole!' Clive now swept through Bengal with ease. The only real battle, against the French at Chandernagore, was won by Watson's navy. Largely a spectator, Clive's biggest worry was arak. Of the dodgy, potent drink, Bengal produced the most lethal variety, and through necessity a daily ration was issued to enlisted men in the field. They were ordered to drink it on the spot, but the custom was to hoard it until they had enough for a really good session. When Chandernagore fell, Clive was so concerned about his men encountering the swarms of arak merchants that he marched them a mile north of the city before making camp.

The famous Battle of Plassey was the final conflict between Clive and Siraj ud-Duala. Taught in schools as a great military victory, it was actually, as Nick Robins points out, more like a corporate takeover. Clive simply bribed most of the nawab's allies with promises of a share of the loot if they stood and watched instead of joining in, then reneged on his promises and kept most of it for himself and his cronies.

Suddenly, the Indian nobles realized they had lost their supremacy. They rallied the emperor to meet the English in a decisive battle at Buxar in 1764, and when they lost, the Company ruled the whole of Bengal. From now on, the broken Mughal Empire, beset on all sides, increasingly became a puppet administration. In kingdoms they didn't own directly the Company planted 'residents' in the nawab courts, who bent India's rulers to the corporate will.

Within the space of a few frenetic years, the East India Company had transformed from a society of merchants to a sovereign body with a large standing army and tax-raising powers in one of India's richest provinces. They wasted no time in proving just what a bad idea it was to put taxation in the hands of an entity whose sole purpose was the maximizing of shareholder revenue. Local weavers and peasants were oppressed and brutalized, and the Company seemed almost not to recognize that it had any obligation to govern beyond raising tax revenue.

In the eyes of the average Company employee, India meant one thing: profit. They came out as poor merchants on rubbish salaries, with the aim of achieving a 'competence', making enough money to retire home and adopt the lifestyle of the landed gentry. Before Plassey, almost every one of them had huge loans outstanding with Indian moneylenders. A dozen years later, the phrase 'a lass and a lakh a day' was coined to describe their lifestyle, a lakh being a hundred thousand rupees, largely consisting of generous presents from state officials and Indian merchants, and a lass being one of the many mistresses, or 'bibis', they took in a land where unmarried Western women didn't exist.

These fabulously wealthy men had little entertainment and were fabulously bored, as bored as their predecessors in the factories in Surat so long before. And so, just like their ancestors, they drank. It was estimated that a third of all hospital cases arose from liver complaints. In 1760, measures were put in place to try to limit the distillation and sale of arak in Calcutta, but fifteen years later Alexander Mackrabie, puritanical secretary to the governor, found the city still teeming with arak sellers, 'to the ruin and ill-health of the lower class of people'. The upper classes, newly posh, used it as the basis for punch, mixed with sugar, citrus juice, water and spices.

In 1769 the monsoon failed. The Mughal rulers had been well prepared for famine. Strict measures preserved food stocks, and anyone found profiteering from the crisis was brutally punished. But the new English 'nabobs' decided to show the heathen a different way of doing things. At the first sign of shortages, English merchants bought up all the rice they could find and watched the price increase a hundred-fold. The Company itself was keen not to miss out. Where the nawabs had given tax relief during famine, the Company increased the rate. Driven off the land, peasants flocked into the streets of Calcutta, imagining there would be aid for them there.

The first full report into the famine took a while to reach the top of the To Do list – a hundred years, to be precise. The Company no longer existed by the time William Hunter compiled the first comprehensive account from its records in 1870:

> All through the stifling summer of 1770 the people went on dying. The husbandmen sold their cattle; they sold their implements of agriculture; they devoured their seed grain; they sold their sons and daughters, till at length no buyer of children could be found; they ate the leaves of the trees and the grass of the field; and in June 1770 the Resident . . . affirmed that the living were feeding off the dead. Day and night a torrent of famished and disease-ridden wretches poured into the great cities . . . The streets were blocked up with promiscuous heaps of the dying and dead.

Warren Hastings, the future governor of Bengal, estimated around 10 million dead – between a third and a half of the population of lower Bengal. The Company didn't allow this minor inconvenience to trouble their plans, or their con-sciences – during the famine, the dividend on shares increased from 11 to 12.5 per cent. The total annual amount sent home by Company employees from their own private speculation stood at £79,000 in 1756, the year before Plassey. Between then and 1784 it averaged £500,000 per annum. But in the years of the famine, it rocketed to £1,086,255 (£100 million today). Jawaharlal Nehru, who would become India's first prime minister, while serving a jail sentence for daring to suggest India might be better off ruling itself, wrote: 'The corruption, venality, nepotism, violence and greed of money of these early generations of British rule in India is something that passes comprehension . . . It is significant that one of the Hindustani words which has become part of the English language is "loot".'

Half a world away on the east coast of North America, another bunch of colonists under British rule identified with the Indians. The 'most powerful Trading Company in the Universe' was selling them tea with a swingeing tax rate attached. This Company, 'well-versed in tyranny, plunder, oppression and bloodshed', became a symbol against which the colonists could rally. 'Their Conduct in Asia, for some years past, has given simple Proof, how little they regard the Laws of Nations, the Rights, Liberties, or Lives of Men.' Inevitably, the dumping of Company tea into Boston harbour became the flashpoint for the American War of Independence.

In 1774, a sick Clive, back home in England, committed suicide. Dr Johnson, ready as ever with a well-chosen word or two, noted that Clive had 'acquired his fortune by such crimes that his consciousness of them impelled him to cut his own throat'.

The problem with worrying about next year's shareholder dividend and nothing else is that it tends to keep your eye off the longer-term ramifications of your actions. Having raped Bengal, leaving the huge region bankrupt and impoverished with up to half its population dead and its vast wealth gone, the Company was surprised when it was saddled with huge administrative costs and no revenue. Having made obscene profits for years, it now faced collapse and begged the British government for financial help.[43]

The government did save the Company, but massively curtailed its power, finally realizing that single-minded obsession with profit may not be the best qualification to govern. The post of Governor General was introduced, based in Calcutta, with authority over the presidencies of Bombay and Madras.

Clive wrote that Calcutta was 'one of the most wicked Places in the Universe', full of Company servants who 'by frequent bad examples have grown callous, Rapacious and Luxurious beyond Conception'. And yet, a few decades later, Frederick Shore found society there very much like that of 'a country town in England'. Calcutta was a blank canvas on to which the English could project whatever they desired. Perhaps these two men each saw what they wanted to see – a reflection of their own character.

In the nineteenth century, religious fundamentalists would come here and find themselves able to give freer rein to their evangelical urges than they ever could at home. But late eighteenth-century London was a city of unbridled excess, a non-stop procession of feasting, boozing and whoring. For those who found their desires unquenched, who came to view London's fleshpots as a little tame, Calcutta promised a widescreen, uncensored version. Even after Prime Minister Pitt had reined in the worst of the corruption, Bengal was a place to get rich quick, and have the time of your life while you did so. Young blades and adventurers bought their

---

43. Hmm . . . greedy, rapacious companies making themselves rich off the back of the poor, squandering that wealth, then having the bare-faced cheek to ask the government to bail them out. It's a good job we've learned the lessons of history. If anything like that happened today it might cause a global financial crisis or something.

passages out in droves. They were in high demand, because now, as well as merchants, Bengal needed lawyers, accountants, clerks, administrators, clergymen and shopkeepers. And soldiers: always more soldiers. While being an enlisted trooper was still arguably a worse fate than ending your days in Newgate prison, an officer's commission was a guarantee of wealth.

As soon as all these lusty, ambitious men arrived, they immediately began sending home for creature comforts, and drink was at the top of the list. Arak was suitable only for the lower classes and the military. The new nabobs could afford the best from home; they wanted it here, and they wanted it now. On the Company ships and around the Company docks were shrewd men only too happy to supply them, so long as the price was right.

CHAPTER FOURTEEN

SAILAWAY

I heard Barry before I saw him. There was a forceful clattering, louder and more aggressive than the soft slump of all the previous bags that slid down the conveyor and on to the baggage carousel. I was standing about twenty yards away from the chute, and I looked up in time to see a red lump streak down and hit the barrier at the side of the carousel with a loud *thunk*! The impact made him rear up on his hind wheels, as if he really were alive, trying to head-butt the man standing at the bottom of the chute, who skittered backwards nervously. Another man darted forward and gingerly pushed Barry back on the belt.

We'd zipped him inside a brand-new red wheelie bag. Two hundred yards across the concourse at Heathrow, the internal skeleton of this bag yielded to his bulk, wheels splaying out sideways, the fabric on the bottom already fraying and splitting.

'Well, that's twenty quid down the drain,' said Liz, who had bought the bag.

'Twenty quid? The poor thing never stood a chance against him,' I said, nursing the saucer-sized bruise on my bicep.

When we checked him in, he tipped the scales at 31 kilos. 'That's half my body weight,' whispered Liz.

'What's in there?' asks the check-in attendant. 'It's so *small*.'

She charged us sixty quid excess baggage, which I was happy to pay – I'd been worried for weeks that they might not allow him on the plane at all.

We were joining *Oceana* in Vigo, northern Spain, her first stop since leaving Southampton two days before on her way to the Canary Islands. As she left port in the UK, I was doing readings and beer tastings at a food festival, so I'd had to compromise and fly Barry the first few hundred miles of his journey. After spending so long thinking about sea travel, I felt guilty about flying. It just seemed so . . . crude and clumsy. Not proper travelling at all. A cop-out. But I didn't have any choice.

Now, after a two-hour flight to Madrid, I could tell Barry had been in the wars. One of the bag's side-pockets was torn. Greasy black scuffs and scars lined the top and sides. The orange 'heavy' sticker he'd gained at check-in was half gone. The retractable carrying handle was warped, stuck half in, half out, mutilated with the bag's shattered spine.

For the onward flight to Vigo, we decided to bring him down a peg or two. We had him condomized, wrapped in a thick, tight layer of cellophane. The red fabric of the bag glaring through this new phlegm-green wrapping gave him a furious hue, and as he rolled away on the check-in conveyor he pitched and rolled and clanked, attacking the barriers at the sides of the belt.

By the time we collected him in Vigo, Barry had shrugged his shoulders out of the cellophane, but was still held by it. We'd also strapped his shattered bag to a wheelie trolley. It wasn't perfect, but I could now manoeuvre him without serious injury.

As we hoisted him off the belt, my mobile rang: Souheila, my Iranian visa agent, told me that Tehran were refusing even to give a reason why they had denied me a visa. 'This has never happened before,' she insisted. Great. I was breaking new ground in my inability to travel to places I didn't even want to go.

There was nothing I could do now until I boarded the *Caribbean* in six weeks' time. Urs at Station Weggis advised that there might be something the captain of that ship could do, perhaps employing me as a steward. The alternative was to leave the *Caribbean* in Khor Fakkan, get myself across the United Arab Emirates and waste a week admiring the footballers' wives chic of Dubai before boarding another container ship that would take me to India without going through Iranian waters. The choice between these two alternatives was entirely at the discretion of the *Caribbean*'s captain. I might as well enjoy our brief stay on the Canaries Carousel.

The Peninsular and Oriental Company began life as a steamer service delivering mail and passengers from London to Spain and Portugal. Later it won a contract to deliver to Egypt, and through most of the nineteenth century it took passengers to Cairo and, after the Suez Canal was built, all the way to Bombay. So in a roundabout way, boarding a giant P&O cruise liner in northern Spain felt like a legitimate and fitting part of my voyage – or so I tried to persuade a visibly horrified Liz as we joined the security queue to board the ship.

Few of our fellow passengers looked under seventy. A third of them couldn't walk unassisted. Most people don't even think about coming on a cruise like this until post-menopause, and yet here we were. And it wasn't just an age thing: weren't cruises for people who were too scared to visit these destinations without being chaperoned? The unadventurous, who get frightened even watching Judith Chalmers?[44] Who refuse to eat the local 'foreign muck' and flee back aboard for fish and chips? The size of the queue seemed to suggest so. It was midday, and judging by the volume of people eager to get back on *Oceana*, Vigo's attractions were fleeting. Meals on the ship were included in the fare, so the town's many celebrated seafood restaurants had received short shrift.

I scanned the security queue, seeking to reassure Liz.

---

44. I mean because of the places she visits, obviously.

'Look, there are some young people,' I said, pointing at some attractive girls who looked like . . . dancers. I surrendered to the realization that everyone younger than us was only on board because they were being paid to be there.

But you'd have to be very cold-hearted indeed to be blind to the good points once you've been struck dumb by the scale of this floating city and then welcomed aboard. It may not have been to our tastes, but it *was* tasteful. I once described a cruise as Blackpool-on-Sea, but the element of artificially flavoured tackiness this was meant to imply couldn't be more wrong. Liz's dad is in his eighties and fought in the war, and used to play rugby for Pontypool. He's a man with standards and expectations, and his main comment about his own cruise experience was, 'everything is done proper'. I could see exactly what he meant.

As Liz and I came aboard, porters disappeared with our luggage, and an officer guided us to a table while she checked us in. A waitress appeared instantly, with a drinks menu featuring decent wines as well as both Bass ale and Marston's Pedigree, sold by the bottle at prices cheaper than my local would have sold it if it stocked them in the first place. Barry was in good company, and somebody in P&O had a fondness for Burton ales. It felt like a good omen.

We sat with our drinks and gazed up into the vast atrium, unable to believe we were on a ship. Steps lined with runway lights curved down towards a sinuous waterfall sculpture. The soft lighting and golden rails reminded me of the very finest hotels I've ever stayed in while travelling on business, but this place was designed purely for pleasure.

We spent our first afternoon exploring. *Oceana* is fifteen storeys – or decks – high. There are three restaurants, two theatres, a pub, a casino, a nightclub and seven bars; a shopping mall, a library, a gallery exhibiting toe-curlingly bad art, a cyb@study – yes, a cyb@study – a driving range, four swimming pools, football and cricket pitches, tennis courts, and various salons and spas. It sucked us in.

We decided to skip the Challenging Arthritis seminar, and while Liz headed off for a facial I went to the cyb@study to catch up on the last bit of work that refused to die. After a quick visit to the gym, while Liz was still being pampered, I sat at the Terrace Bar at the stern of the ship with a bottle of Pedigree. The sky was grey and overcast, and a chill wind I hadn't felt for months blew through craggy peaks worn down and splintered by an often vicious North Atlantic. Those peaks sheltered Vigo Bay, a natural harbour so long and broad it's claimed it can accommodate the combined fleets of the entire world. It was the perfect place for a large industrial port, and we had a good view of it from the twelfth floor of our floating skyscraper. Pontoons, piers and jetties lay in ranks at various points around us. The skyline over the city and port was crazed with mustard-yellow cranes, and the sound of industrial jack-hammers rose and fell like a tide on the wind, sometimes drowning out the soundtrack of eighties pop hits completely.

I was at the start of the voyage proper. A week after picking up Barry from Burton, I was more dog-tired than I could ever remember ever being. A cold sore had appeared on my bottom lip. I'd been drinking too much, and my kidneys ached dully. My lips were chapped. My shirt was too tight. And my nose was peeling. I needed a holiday, badly, and wondered if any part of what lay ahead would be restful.

At five o'clock the captain briefly interrupted Duran Duran. 'I'm pleased to report that you've all been very good and you're all on board on time, so we'll be leaving a little early,' he mollycoddled. We were going to push off past the clam and mussel beds that surrounded us, following a south-westerly course into the Atlantic, across the Iberian Basin to Madeira. There was wind and rain at sea, of course, but the weather was forecast to improve as we headed south.

As soon as the captain finished his address, DJ Matthew slipped on 'Something Tells Me I'm Into Something Good' and thoughtfully turned his mike up so we could still hear him over the music. In his cheery South Wales accent, he hoped we'd all had a cracking day in Vigo, because he'd had a cracking day, and he hoped we were going to have a cracking time here at the Sailaway Disco.

Vigo's stonewashed buildings and ochre roofs began to rotate past the bow as the ship described a slow arc to face the open sea.

'We're turning round now,' shouted DJ Matthew over Billy Ocean's 'When the Going Gets Tough, the Tough Get Going'.

The bar had become crowded, and there was no space between people leaning over the rails. It struck me that most of us can't help feeling reflective when we leave port, even if we've only been there for a few hours. Watching the shore twist and shrink, leaving a place at this stately pace made me feel a melancholy I don't think you get when leaving anywhere by plane.

The wind whipped the pages of my journal and my discarded sunglasses slid across the table. The waves seemed curiously dense from this height, the porridgy pattern of woodchip wallpaper and the colour of molten lead. The sea grew mottled and patchy in the distance, and out near the horizon it held a band of hazy silver that made me think of Tolkien's elves, sailing into the west.

DJ Matthew told us about the day's drama on the quoits and shuffleboard courts over the top of 'Surfin' USA', until both his voice and the music were obliterated by three long blasts of *Oceana*'s horn. In the age of satellite navigation and digital communication I had no idea whether this horn served any real purpose. But it didn't matter. Neither did the kind of ship it was, or who else was on it. This was it, the start of a sea voyage halfway around the world. And as DJ Matthew introduced 'the song "Stuck in the Middle With You" from the film *Reservoir Dogs*' I decided I wouldn't swap this for a resurrected Concorde transatlantic flight, or Virgin Upper Class, or any other more celebrated means of international travel. For the duration of those horn blasts, there was nothing but a sweet, painful yearning to spend the rest of my life at sea.

CHAPTER FIFTEEN

PRIVATE TRADE

In 1773, Warren Hastings was appointed the first Governor General of all British India. Like his peers he made his fortune there, and would later face an exhausting trial for corruption. But Hastings was a deeply thoughtful man, genuinely fascinated by his host country, which he felt did not need the dubious benefits of European rule. He studied Hindu scripture, founded colleges to advance the understanding of Muslim law, and attempted to involve Indians in the administration of Bengal. He was no saint, but few other Imperial rulers would have argued: 'If our people, instead of erecting themselves into lords and oppressors of the country, confine themselves to an honest and fair trade, they will everywhere be respected, and the English name, instead of being a reproach, will be universally revered.'

Between his influence and that of their Indian wives, the Company merchants became a curious mix. They hankered after home comforts, and at the same time smoked hookahs and bhang (cannabis), ate curry, drank arak, wore lightweight nankeen jackets, white linen waistcoats, and sometimes even loose Indian pyjamas. They were neither British nor Indian, but Anglo-Indian, a tribe William Dalrymple refers to as the White Mughals.[45]

---

45. Only in 1911 did the term 'Anglo-Indian' start to be applied to people of mixed British and Asian parentage. Until that point, they were known as Eurasians.

Officially these men were paid miserly wages. A President's annual salary was £200; a factor's a mere £5. It was impossible to live in comfort, let alone make your fortune, without indulging in a little personal speculation. The Company tolerated this private trade because it meant they could continue paying a pittance and still attract the kind of hard-bitten, self-sufficient people who could survive on the wild frontier of its operations. Everybody did it. For the most part the Company turned a blind eye, but should someone fall out of favour, everyone could pretend outrage, point to the man's corruption and bring him down. This encouraged a sense of ruthless opportunism. Hastings stood little chance of dissuading his men from acting like 'lords and oppressors', particularly when demands from London for more respectable behaviour were invariably accompanied by ever-higher profit targets.

The self-styled 'nabobs' expected to stay in Calcutta for around five years then return home with their fortunes. So despite their Indian affectations, it was important not to lose touch with the gossip, fashions and customs of London. As the remodelled Company finally managed to curb the worst excesses of corruption, the prospect of instant riches dimmed. You could still get stinking rich, but you had to pay your dues in years of long service. The nabobs were keenly aware that, in caste-conscious India, they may be the new rulers, but they were still seen by many of their subjects as lower-class traders, and this stung them into becoming ever more extravagant. If they couldn't go home and live like the nobility, they would stay in India adorned in the trappings of kings.

This was a lifestyle that required both the riches of India and the comforts of home. There was no bigger symbol of the transfer of wealth between Asia and Europe under Company rule than the fact that ships bound for India had hold space to spare on departure from England, returning the following year low in the water, heavily laden with textiles, garments, tea and exotic treasures.[46] Profits from the returning cargoes covered the cost of both the outward and return journeys. The Company didn't really care about what the outbound ships carried, so long as they came back full. In 1674 they granted ships' captains and officers a personal allowance of 5 tons of cargo on the way out, and 5 per cent of the total tonnage on the way home. In 1772, with bigger ships, this had grown to 25 tons outward, and 15 home. Eventually, to varying degrees, these privileges extended to the entire crew.

They took out whatever they liked, and bought precious stones to trade back home. An East Indiaman captain could make as much as £30,000 on a triangular voyage from London, to India, to China and back to London again. A typical trade would be to sell beer, shoes and hunting guns in Bombay or Calcutta, reinvest that profit in raw cotton, which was sold in Canton, and buy tea and Chinaware to take back to London. By 1784 it was customary (though illegal) to sell a captaincy of an East Indiaman for up to 7,000 guineas.

In late eighteenth-century Calcutta, these sea-going entrepreneurs catered to an insatiable thirst. The captains of the East Indiamen used their hold allowances to bring in glassware, stationery, hats, and surprisingly modern-sounding food such as salad oil, olives, Italian capers and white wine vinegar. But more than anything else, they ferried in booze. Without the civilizing influence of English wives, the nabobs made an artform of feasting and boozing. In one month in 1774, Mr Francis of Madras and his guests got through seventy-five bottles of Madeira, ninety-nine bottles of claret, seventy-four

---

46. In 1700 India accounted for an incredible 22.54 per cent of global GDP, and Britain a mere 1.8 per cent. By 1870, Britain's share had grown to 9.1 per cent, while India's had plummeted to 12.25 per cent. Yes, I know wealth and GDP aren't the same thing – I did economics A level, you know – but you see the point.

bottles of porter, sixteen bottles of rum, three bottles of brandy and one bottle of cherry brandy. It was an expensive business getting drink to India, but the new wealth of the nabobs meant the days of going blind on arak in seedy taverns a few decades before were forgotten.

There was an increasingly bitter rivalry between the army and the 'civilians' of the Company who lorded it over them. The officers were at pains to show that they could party just as hard as the nabobs. An evening in the mess would begin with sherry or Madeira. Claret would accompany the meal, and then the tablecloth was removed and toasts drunk. A course of hard drinking would commence, and any officer who left early would be chased out of the door with cries of 'Shabby fellow', 'Milk sop' or 'Cock-tail' ringing in his ears.

During the hot season there was little trade to be done. The heat laid people low, or sent them scurrying to the hills in search of cooler temperatures. But around November, when the cool season began, the entertainments in town sprung to life, and a healthy demand sprang up for beer, wine, cider, perry, cordials, spirits, ham, cheeses and pickles.

In 1785 the *Calcutta Gazette* was published for the first time. Essentially a mouthpiece for Company business, it was laden with advertising. Nothing beats the state of a country's advertising as a window into the collective soul of its people. Writing this in Britain in early 2008, every product from margarine to luxury cars is trumpeting its green credentials, showing that concern over the environment had finally gone mainstream.[47] At the same time in East Africa, every other billboard features an ad for a cell-phone company, as the introduction of affordable mobile telephony transforms both the social life and the economies of countries like Kenya and Tanzania.

---

47. And twelve months later, green messages had been swept away by thrifty credit-crunch chic.

In the Bengal of the 1780s and 1790s, three-quarters of newspaper ads were for booze. The *Bombay Courier* of 28 September 1790 offered a full price list for goods on sale at the Tavern Warehouses, fresh from an East Indiaman captain:

	Rs
English Claret by the chest, per dozen	20
By single dozen	24
French Claret 1st quality per dozen	9
Old Hock, per ditto	34
Champagne per ditto	30
Port wine per ditto	20
Constantia per ditto	30
Perry per ditto	18
Cyder per ditto	10
Cherry and Raspberry brandy	12
Madeira in Pipes of the first quality, per pipe	400
Ditto in bottled per doz.	15
Pale Ale in Bottled per ditto	8
Porter per ditto	7

This was a range of drinks any modern bar would be proud of. Pale ale, as well as porter, had its place. But that place was the bottom of the list, cheaper than anything else, including 'Cyder'. Madeira was clearly the most popular drink, and one estimate suggests the annual consumption of all wine in Calcutta stood at well over 3 million bottles.

In 1813, Charles D'Oyly wrote *The European in India*, a guide for the increasing number of people coming out to Bengal, which finally suggests the beginnings of a move away from the fashion of drinking yourself to death:

A young person of good health, disposed to moderation in general, avoiding the sun during the great heats, may expect to live as long in Calcutta as in any part of the world. On the other hand, it is found, that such as do not touch wine, especially as they advance in years, are not only more subject to disease, but to go off more suddenly than those who take a few glasses at their meals. Claret is in general use, as is also Madeira; of which, though it be excellent, much should not be drank; [but] Spirits, in any form, are baneful. In a warm climate persons are subject to great drought, and one glass follows the other but too rapidly . . . when the inconsiderate tippler speedily passes through the various stages of disease, avoided by society, and his demise is scarcely noticed but by those who may be benefitted by the vacancy.

Beer is not mentioned anywhere in the book as an alternative. But it seems clear that there was a gap in the market for a drink that was less intoxicating than wine or Madeira, but still offered the perceived health benefits of alcohol. With the Napoleonic Wars coming to a close in distant Europe, and a burgeoning sense of English superiority over the natives in India, there was a strong whiff of jingoism in the air. We've always chosen what to drink partly because of what that choice says about us. D'Oyly had overlooked a drink that was not only suitable to the climate, but could also be a symbol of dyed-in-the-wool Englishness. Beer's day in the sun was about to dawn.

CHAPTER SIXTEEN

A DROP OF MADEIRA

It was William Hickey who first introduced me to Madeira, both the place and the drink. The volcanic island, four hundred miles off the coast of Africa, is believed by some to be the remains of the lost continent of Atlantis, but then those people also believe Narnia is real. Archaeological evidence suggests that while the Phoenicians knew of it (they seem to have known about everything), Madeira was first colonized by Portugal's Prince Henry the Navigator in the fifteenth century. Vines and sugar cane were planted on the steep slopes, and in 1453 Aviso da Mosto visited and claimed 'really good wines are produced here'. Merchants made their way here from across Europe, and by the late seventeenth century it was an essential stop for British shipping bound for the East and West Indies. Fresh water, fruit and vegetables were taken on board, but the main priority was the wine. In 1782, Hickey was making his way to India for the second time in his life.[48] His ship stopped to pick up a cargo of Madeira wine, which took three days to load. Hickey was unhappy about the excessive cargo – 240 'pipes' – which made the ship sit low in the water and roll violently. In one storm two men were killed as pipes came loose and crushed them.

This unusual wine was for many years the drink of choice

---

48. He'd been sent there in disgrace as a teenager, after embezzling hundreds of pounds from his father's firm, to become an army officer. He decided he didn't like it, and came straight back.

across British India. Following in the rake's distant wake, I was looking forward to finding out why. What I wasn't expecting was the huge insight into India Pale Ale I was about to discover along the way.

In Hickey's time, the journey from the South Downs to Madeira took two or three weeks. *Oceana* made the same journey, at a leisurely pace, in four days. The night before we docked in Funchal, Madeira's capital, I left the Plaza restaurant, pushed open the heavy storm doors and walked out into the darkness of the Sky Deck. It was like leaping to another dimension, being hit around the face by the fresh breeze of the open sea after the heavy, damp party air within.

We'd been on board for two days, and had settled into the routine of the ship. Reluctantly, Liz was starting to warm to the idea of cruising. 'I have to say, if this is your kind of thing, there's nothing better. It's fantastic,' she'd said over dinner in the Plaza. We'd tried one or two of the other restaurants but this had become our favourite. *Remus*, big as s/he was, would have fitted into the Plaza as little more than an extravagant table decoration. It was a buffet, and they had specially themed nights. Tonight was Indian, and as most of the staff were Indian the food was excellent. 'I might have been a bit snobby about it when we got on, and it is definitely not for me, but for a lot of people it's the holiday of a lifetime, and you can't knock it,' continued Liz. She was enjoying herself, and fighting with all her might against admitting the fact. We were both succumbing, being lulled into a second childhood. It was like being sedated and slowly eaten by a giant, warm marshmallow.

I came out on to the deck to clear my head while Liz disappeared to the cyb@study to make sure work was OK in her absence. I went to the railing and stared out to sea. At first the sky was a thick blanket, but as my eyes adjusted I picked out the horizon and one or two stars. Fifteen floors below, the sea was a bruise, inky black, glittering purple and dark green. Our wake hissed and fizzed boisterously, larking with *Oceana*'s flanks.

As the lights of our floating Las Vegas illuminated the surf, it struck me as the most bizarre profligacy that there were hundreds of people on this ship for no other reason than the pure pleasure of being here, simply to enjoy the journey and eat and drink as much as possible. In Hickey's day this journey – even this modest section of it – cost lives as well as money. How strange the old sea dogs must have found it when people first started doing this just for a laugh, rather than because they had to. How unimaginably different it was from when James Lancaster laid the template for my voyage over four hundred years ago. I didn't know what to do with thoughts like this, so I decided to go down the pub for a pint instead.

The Yacht and Compass occupied a fat chunk of deck seven, but there were no seats free because the Fabulous Fascination Band was on. I imagined the meeting where they decided upon the name. 'Come on, lads, it does what it says on the tin! We're fabulous, aren't we? And fascinating?'

'Well . . . yes, we are. But I'm just a tiny bit worried that it might send out the wrong signals. Do you really think the serious music papers will go for it?'

'Course they will! We'll be supporting Radiohead by this time next year!'

'Well, you're the manager. But I'm telling you now, if we're not talking to Thom Yorke about global warming on the tour bus by this time next year, and instead we're, I dunno, playing Beatles covers on a cruise ship or something, I'm going to be really upset.'

'Guys, trust me . . .'

After the Beatles covers, the Fabulous Fascination Band launched into a spirited version of 'Let's Stick Together' by Bryan Ferry. I thought this was a bit brave of them, possibly a little racy for the Yacht and Compass crowd. And then, something extraordinary happened. When they reached Chris Mercer's sax solo – the dirty, sexy, smudged mascara squall that really makes the original – Mercer's Fabulous counterpart decided he could improve on it . . . by segueing into the *Benny Hill* theme.

It was fascinating, I'll give them that. But not in a good way. Somewhere over northern Europe, Bryan Ferry was preparing an Exocet missile for launch. I didn't want to be in the room when it hit: I broke into a run on my way out of the door.

We were woken the next morning by a soothing voice on the Tannoy telling us we'd docked in Funchal, and coach tours of the island were leaving soon. The day was gloomy and overcast, the island's sheer, green slopes disappearing into writhing tendrils of cloud. Despite this, Funchal still called out an alluring welcome to holidaymakers. Yachts and catamarans idled at anchor. Palm trees lined all the main boulevards, and the whitewashed, red-roofed buildings tumbled down the hills. The ship's port guide recommended Cabo Girão, at 1,932 feet the world's second-highest sea cliffs, or Camacha, the centre of the wickerwork industry. But we already had plans.

Rupert Ponsonby, a man with fingers in more pies than Sweeney Todd, does an awful lot of work with wine as well as beer, and numbers among his clients the firm of Henriques & Henriques, the largest independent winemaker on Madeira. The firm has been around since 1850, and was now run by John Cossart, an Englishman born on Madeira, whose father, Peter, entered the business in 1938. At Rupert's request, John had very kindly offered to show us around.

He met us on the quayside, weaving his saloon car through the shuttling minibuses in the shadow of the giant cruise liner. John Cossart was in his early sixties, immaculately dressed, the kind of man you could spot as an English gentleman in any port in the world. As one journalist said of him, 'in blue blazer and old school tie, he's as English as steak and kidney pudding'. Liz was swept away immediately by his charm and manners, and I sat in the passenger seat aware of how completely inelegant I was as he drove us up into the hills.

Our first stop was the new vineyard and *adega* (winery) in Quinta Grande, high on the slopes of a steep, south-facing valley. Most producers don't own their own vineyards, but this one was planted in 1995 and designed to be accessible to machinery. 'We do things our own way,' John explained in his deliberate, sometimes painstakingly slow manner. 'Madeira is very traditional. There was a big upset when we started using spectrometers to analyse the sugar level and likely alcohol content. People felt they were being taken for a ride by science. One guy pulled a knife and held it to the throat of someone trying to use one.'

We watched as grapes from the vineyard were loaded into a hopper that noisily stripped off the stalks, broke the skins, and propelled them into a vinifier beneath our feet. These were Verdelho grapes, strong and sweet with a real sharpness at the end. A powerful smell of fresh fruit filled the area.

The vinifier is temperature controlled, and fermentation takes place with the natural yeast on the grape skins. So far, so typical of winemaking. Originally, wine made on Madeira was the same as that made anywhere else. But thanks to the voyages of the East India Company, something very unusual happened. Shipments that followed the route around the Cape and into Asia were changed. The wine oxidized, acquiring a slightly burnt, caramelized flavour that shouldn't have been there, but proved very moreish. The early merchants in the factories had prized Shiraz wine, originally from Persia, above anything else. But war between Persia and the Mughals made it harder to obtain, and Madeira took its place. Compared to everything else that came off the ships, it was striking how it had kept its quality. The Anglo-Indians soon figured out that the temperature and movement of the voyage had improved the wine, and believed it continued to improve in India's sultry climate. It was sent inland, up-country to Cawnpore to continue to mature. In Madras, Colonel Martinez hung pipes of Madeira from his cellar roof and would regularly set them spinning, as he put it, to 'give them a voyage around the Cape'.

In the mid-eighteenth century the winemakers began fortifying Madeira wine with brandy to improve its already remarkable keeping qualities, and it became virtually indestructible. As the fame of this unusual wine spread, it soon became profitable to take cargoes of Madeira on the round trip to India and sell them back in Europe. Company servants returned home with a taste for the wine, and as the ships only stopped at the island on the outward leg, Madeira reached England via India in every sense.

This was all great, but shipping the stuff halfway around the world and back to get the taste people wanted was an extravagance. By trial and error, the islanders developed a system of *estufas* (literally, 'saunas') to reproduce the conditions of the voyage. Because they weren't sure what the heat did and what the motion did, some also replicated the motion of the ships by following Martinez's example, hanging pipes from the ceiling and giving them a regular spin.

At the Henriques *adega*, the wine was piped into carefully controlled *estufas*, of which John Cossart was very proud. Like the spectrometers, this new *estufa* didn't follow traditional design, and not everyone was happy about it. But John had been credited with playing a major role in the revival of Madeira. To get his point across, he once held a tasting for journalists in a London sauna. Coils carrying hot water encircled the storage tanks. Traditionally, Madeira wine is heated to between 35 and 60 degrees Celsius. This creates the burnt caramelization, which can be quite harsh if it's done too quickly, so cheaper varieties are treated to higher temperatures, while the best quality are heated slower and more moderately. 'We've got the most sensitive one on the island,' said John, showing us how the wine was circulated. 'We put electric motors in here in '94 to replicate the movement of the voyage. The best wines went to the South China Sea and back, around 35,000 miles. The temperature partially pasteurizes the wine, and with the movement you get the oxidization and the heating without baking the wine and losing that fine spine of acidity.'

I was amazed. The legend of Madeira wine was identical to that of IPA, but production of the two drinks had evolved in completely different directions. Beer critics and brewers alike are perfectly happy to declaim about how important the voyage was in creating the character of the beer, and here was dramatic proof that it really did have a profound effect. An entire industry on Madeira has devoted itself to replicating that effect, and continues to find better ways to do so even today. The proof is in the difference between the virgin wine at the start of the process and the wine it creates. 'It's perfectly good wine,' insisted John, 'very nice, but it's not Madeira.' Beer brewers have gone the other way, watering down and bastardizing the style itself, talking about the voyage, but doing nothing to recreate it. Even robust, hoppy American IPAs, I now realized, tasted nothing like the beer that was drunk in India. How could they? Along with every other hop-head on the planet, I had in a sense been drinking only unconditioned 'green' beer. It was very nice beer – my favourite beer. But I had just arrived at a new standard for what constituted 'real' India Pale Ale. And I suspected I was carrying the only barrel in the whole world of what would hopefully, one day, become truly authentic IPA. It only seemed right then, given my bruises, that Barry now carried a great weight on his shoulders.

Next we visited Henriques's lodge in the village of Câmara de Lobos. The lodge was a south-facing, glass-fronted building that let in the sun's heat to bake the ranks of wooden pipes. This was the expensive, vintage stuff, aged naturally over a longer period than the cheaper stuff in the pipe-lined tanks. I'd read so much about 'pipes of Madeira' I couldn't wait to see them. They were barrels like an elephant's torso, fat and round in the middle, holding up to 120 gallons. Larger and exotic-looking compared with beer barrels, I simply couldn't imagine two hundred fitting into a ship's hold.

We toured the building, a spicy, sherry-like smell filling our noses as soon as we came through the door. Names and years were stencilled on the ends of the pipes: *Verdelho 1999*; *Terrantez 1996*; *Bastardo 1927*. These are all varieties of grape that age here for at least twenty years before being bottled as vintage wines, or blended with younger varieties.

With the help of oxidation, gentle pasteurization and fortification, Madeira wines keep an extraordinarily long time, with vintages of up to a hundred years regularly appearing in fine-wine shops. As we finished our tour in the tasting room, I wondered if, just a week after drinking the Ratcliff Ale, I'd get lucky. Would our host would be so generous as to offer us – a holidaymaking couple he had never met before and knew nothing about – anything that could compare to that experience?

Oh, yes.

We started off with Rainwater, allegedly so-called because someone left it out in the rain and quite liked the resulting taste. It was thick and golden with a honey stickiness, a warm alcohol glow and a short, pleasant finish. John, who was obviously far better at this than me, pointed out that it was 'the colour of straw after rain' and that the taste was 'as soft as rain water'.

Rainwater is very popular in the United States – the early American colonies loved Madeira at least as much as the Anglo-Indians did. The seizure of a cargo of Madeira wine was, just like the Company's tea, a flashpoint to the War of

Independence, causing riots in Boston. George Washington was reputed to have enjoyed a pint a day, and when the Declaration of Independence was signed, the founding fathers toasted themselves with Madeira.

We moved on through the caramelly five-year-old, sweet Single Harvest 1995, and the floral, perfumed ten-year-old Verdelho. The fifteen-year-old Malvazia was amazing: thick and warming, the colour of chocolate, full of caramel, coffee and dried-fruit flavours with a tingling, sweet finish. But we were only just getting started.

There are four main types of Madeira: Malvazia (known as malmsey in English), Bual (or Boal), Verdelho and Sercial. They need to be matured in cask for twenty years before they can be bottled as vintage wines, and must then mature in the bottle for a further three. 'It's not a fair playing field. Port only has to be matured for a year before they can declare a vintage,' said John, reaching past the common varieties we'd just tasted to something a little more special.

Terrantez is another variety, increasingly rare these days thanks to phylloxera. According to the encyclopaedic website, www.madeirawineguide.com, 'the total harvest of Terrantez does not even fill a complete cask of wine.' John poured us each a taste of Terrantez 1976 vintage, musty, cheesy, earthy and sweet, with a fine thread of bitterness throughout. It was what I would expect from an old vintage, based on the scant experience I have of tasting old wines and beers. I assumed that the mature, musty flavours would intensify the older we got. I was wrong – Madeira doesn't play by the rules.

Next up was a 1964 Sercial. It was drier and fresher, a little sour, but sweet and juicy like a late summer. The 1954 Boal was the colour of Guinness, its rich polished leather transporting me to an old stately home. It partied on every part of my tongue: sweet at the front, acidic down the sides, with a long, dry bitterness at the back.

And still there was more. The Solera 1900, or Century

Malmsey, was a dark, inky brown that crawled down the sides of the glass as if it were warping time, and climbed straight back out in a magic-potion vapour. There was no mustiness, just a taste of fresh honey that was impossible to reconcile with a century-old wine.

And then, the finale.

Four near mythical vintages of Madeira are referred to by buffs as 'the heavenly quartet'. These wines have no specific vintage date, but were already being referred to as 'old wines' in 1852. The W. S. Boal is widely considered the best of the four, but as the author of www.madeirawineguide.com writes wistfully, 'Due to their very limited stock they are rather expensive. Unfortunately it is no longer possible to taste wines of the "heavenly quartet" in Câmara de Lobos.' Our host made an exception. 'We think the W. S. Boal is about two hundred years old,' he said, pouring out three small glasses.

It looked and tasted clean and alive. It was meaty and sweet, tart and bitter, spicy and quenching, and utterly remarkable. For anyone, it was a taste experience to remember for a lifetime. For me, it had even greater significance. This wine was bottled at the height of the IPA trade. I wasn't just tasting the style of drink that once went to India; I was drinking *the same wine* that people like Samuel Allsopp, Campbell Marjoribanks and William Hickey might have drunk.

Somehow believing he hadn't already been generous enough, John invited us to lunch just up the road, at a cool, smart fish restaurant overlooking the harbour of Câmara de Lobos, where Winston Churchill spent many happy hours painting watercolours. I could see why, as small fishing boats bobbed, sheltered by a rocky charcoal arm flung out from the beach by some ancient volcanic eruption.[49] All the fish in the restaurant had been caught and landed down there that morning. On John's recommendation I had the sea

---

49. Or maybe it's a remnant of Atlantis. What do I know?

bass. 'You mustn't forget the cheeks,' he insisted, showing me where they were and how to dig them out. As I did so, I noticed the action of my knife was making the dead fish's jaw move. After the morning's Madeira tasting the idea of a spontaneous ventriloquism routine with a dead fish struck me as potentially the funniest thing the island had ever seen, but from somewhere I dredged up the will to resist.

We were starting to look at our watches and think about what time we needed to be back on the ship when John insisted on taking care of the bill. He dropped us off back by the harbour. Hopefully, the sincerity of my gratitude wasn't compromised by the very slight slurring of speech I seemed to have picked up. Liz, I could tell, was smitten by him. 'Do come back again, and stay for longer,' he said as we climbed out of the car.

We promised we would.[50]

---

50. Later, while filling in the background research for this chapter, I Googled John Cossart and was horrified when the first hit returned was his obituary. He died in February 2008, at the age of sixty-three. I knew nothing about him the morning we met, but his obituaries describe a legend – a real gentleman, a great character, a brilliant raconteur, and a controversial businessman with an unrivalled passion for his product. He was loved by the entire wine industry, and is credited even by his competitors with modernizing and popularizing Madeira wine. Liz and I feel privileged to have met him.

CHAPTER SEVENTEEN

HODGSON'S INDIA ALE

The biggest problem with the history of India Pale Ale is that no one actually started calling it India Pale Ale until it had been going to India for at least half a century. At one point there was something in England called pale ale. Later, in retrospect, there was a style of pale ale that was brewed specifically for the Indian climate and the journey there. What happened in between is, to some extent, conjecture. Beer books and websites usually suggest that George Hodgson sat in his East London brewery one day and had a eureka moment, realizing what needed to be done to create a beer that would survive the voyage, brewing it and crying, 'My ale is pale, and it is perfect for India. I shall call it . . . India Pale Ale!'

If only history really did work the way it does in children's books! I'd have been able to spend a considerably smaller proportion of the last two years stuck inside the British Library.

Just as we don't know when IPA was 'invented', neither do we know exactly when pale ale of any description was first brewed. The *Flying Post* or *Post Master* of London carried an ad in 1700: 'At a Vault, next to the Weavers Arms in Duke Street in the Old Artillery Ground, will be sold Pale Ale, Nottingham, Derby &c by the Winchester Gallon, in great or small Quantities, and that cheaper than any sold in town.'

In the mid-eighteenth century, the *Weekly Journal* reports on a court case where a cooper's daughter was suing a man for breach of promise when, on his stag night, he met another woman and married her instead the following day. Apparently he was 'making merry with some other young Sparks', and they 'Liquor'd him well all Night with Punch and Pale-Ale, the common Slabber of Porters and Car-men'.

The question is, how pale was pale? In the early eighteenth century the emerging commercial or 'common brewers' were trying to make a profit while being heavily taxed to fund whatever war was happening at the time – usually a spat with the French – and their beers were often adulterated with cheaper adjuncts. The private houses of the wealthy had their own breweries and created paler beers that not only looked more appetizing in the glass – then something only the privileged could afford – but were also much harder to adulterate without being spotted. Pale ale therefore emerged as a more refined drink, brewed in country houses and drunk by the upper classes. Commercial brewers began to replicate this for when the gentry came into town on business.

The colour of beer is determined by the malting of the barley. When this was done over a wood fire, it was imprecise. Coal was more exact, but it contained gases that would contaminate the barley. There would have been times when a maltster succeeded in producing a pale malt, but it's not something he could guarantee.

In 1603, Sir Henry Platt charred coal to create coke, a fuel that had none of coal's noxious gases. Coke fires were easier to control, and coke was used to malt barley in Derbyshire in 1642. The location, plus the *Flying Post*'s allusion to 'Pale Ale, Nottingham, Derby &c', strongly suggests that Burton brewers would have been among the first to produce beers that were described at the time as pale ales. They may have been nut-brown, or red, or golden. We simply don't know. But they were paler than what had gone before, and were prized as premium beers. In 1709 Adam Darby created a new process for coke smelting in the iron industry – again based in the Midlands, not far from Burton

– which had the happy side-effect of making pale malt much more accessible. The popularity of pale ale began to spread.

We already know that pale ale and Burton ale were being exported to India as early as 1716. But it was going out in tiny quantities, probably more as favours for friends than as any official cargo. Ships used it as ballast, the same as a load of bricks. Beer exports doubled over the first half of the eighteenth century, but the total represented only a drop in the mash tun for any of London's burgeoning porter brewers.

Porter was thick, dark and rich, a forerunner of stouts such as Guinness, and was taking England by storm, but it wasn't necessarily the ideal drink for hot climates such as India. India had no choice. Brewers had little idea how yeast worked and no control over it. Even in Britain, brewing could only take place in the cooler winter months, when wild yeasts lay dormant. In India, a century before refrigeration was invented, brewing was out of the question. It was technically possible in the foothills of the Himalayas, but the logistics of getting beer from the remote hill stations back to the lowlands around Calcutta, Madras or Bombay made shipping it 18,000 miles around the Cape of Good Hope seem like a gentle Sunday-afternoon pedalo ride in the pond of a particularly genteel and picturesque park. If beer had to be imported, and porter was the dominant beer in port cities like London, it made sense that porter would be the beer exported from English ports along with other drinks, such as port. All clear? Good.

The IPA legend usually states that porter arrived in India flat, sour and undrinkable, hence the need for a new, miracle beverage. The problem with keeping beer in good condition is hinted at by a passage in *Moby-Dick*, where Starbuck, the chief mate of the *Pequod*, is described by the narrator in admiring terms. So strong was he that 'transported to the Indies, his live blood would not spoil like bottled ale'.

In fact, while spoiled beer and ullaged casks were a

constant reality, they were by no means the norm, and porter continued to be imported until the late nineteenth century. What's more likely is that it simply didn't suit the sweltering climate. Beer remained relatively unimportant compared to claret, old hock, and particularly Madeira. Early ads refer to ale, and porter, and sometimes small beer generically, with the brewer's name deemed unimportant. In 1785, the *Calcutta Gazette* advertises 'London Porter and pale Ale, light and excellent, 150 Rupees per hogshead'.[51] In 1790, the first ad naming a specific brewer appears: Captain Douglas of the Queen, 'which is daily expected', had 'Small Beer and Porter' and 'Bell's Beer and Pale Ale' for sale. But a few years later, one name dominated the beer ads. And it wasn't Bell.

Burton-on-Trent is so synonymous with IPA, it's easy to forget that the beer that created the first benchmark for the style was brewed in London. George Hodgson opened a brewery on the banks of the River Lea near where it flowed into the Thames by the East India Dock at the Old Bridge, Bow, in 1751. Hodgson's was one of the smaller London breweries, rarely mentioned in the same breath as famous names such as Whitbread and Barclay Perkins, but brewed porter like those giants (Hodgson's was still shipping porter to India as late as 1823). No documentary evidence of his decision to focus on brewing for India exists, but we can assume certain things. George Hodgson would have met the captains and crews of the East Indiamen in the Bombay Grab, the nearest pub to his brewery.[52] He would have been aware of the need for a beer that suited the tropical climate. Just as the Burton brewers had done with the Baltic trade, Hodgson used the economics of shipping. Freight charges to India were the same as charges from London to Edinburgh.

---

51. A hogshead was a large barrel holding 432 pints.

52. Probably named after a type of Indian fishing boat rather than being a comment on how the Company made its money.

Sitting so close to the dock, Hodgson was in pole position for a lucrative trade. He offered generous credit terms to the ships' captains, and they began to come to him for their beer.

But trade still wasn't easy. Most beer was sent out in hogsheads, but would be shipped along with crates of bottles and corks so it could be bottled and sold on arrival. This, plus insurance, could add 20 per cent to the cost of shipping. And with a time lag of up to a year between orders being placed and delivered, trading conditions could completely change while the beer was en route.

The pale ale downed in Madras in 1716 was undoubtedly different from the pale ale advertised in the *Calcutta Gazette* a century later. But the fact that there is no sudden ta-dah! moment in the pages of the *Gazette* suggests India Pale Ale evolved gradually, by trial and error. Hodgson would have known that high alcohol levels help preserve beer, but many porters were just as strong as the classic IPAs. He would also know that beer was likely to oxidize on the long sea journey, like Madeira did. As well as helping to preserve beer from bacterial infection thanks to their resins, high hop levels would help mask the stale flavours oxidization could produce. Hodgson most likely turned to October beers – the strong, heavily hopped ales produced in country houses and cellared before being drunk – like the one Hickey tried from the Marquis of Rockingham's estate. If you wanted a beer that survived, you'd start with one that was designed to age for years. Much later, the *Calcutta Gazette* carried an ad for 'Hodgson's prime picked pale ale of the genuine October brewing' confirming that this was his template for what would become India Pale Ale.

Hodgson's Indian adventure is often thought to have begun in the 1780s, but this is because that's when the first ads appeared in the *Calcutta Gazette*. The main reason there were no ads before then is not that the beer wasn't going to India, but that the means to advertise it didn't yet exist. The fact that 'pale Ale, light and excellent' was advertised in very early issues of the *Gazette* suggests there was already a decent beer business by the time the paper was launched in 1785. But events around that time did have a dramatic effect on the amount of beer being shipped to India. And Hodgson was perfectly positioned to capitalize.

In the 1780s, amid the scandal over corruption and enormous profit in Bengal, the Company came under pressure to free up private trade on its outbound routes. The size of the Company's ships had grown dramatically, because tea was now superseding spices and even fabrics as the Company's major import (the Boston Tea Party had happened only a few years before) and it was a bulkier commodity. A new generation of East Indiamen was built with displacement of 1,200 tons, twice the size they had been. The Company jealously guarded the monopoly that kept these ships half-empty on their outward journeys, but when its charter was renewed in 1793 clauses were added, which guaranteed that:

> The company shall, in the proper season of every year, provide and appropriate 3000 tons of shipping, at the least, for the specific purposes of carrying to the East Indies such goods, wares and merchandize, as may be lawfully exported thither by individuals . . . and if said tonnage shall be found insufficient . . . the Company shall, from time to time, provide such an additional quantity of tonnage . . . for the carriage of the said private trade.

With far more hold space freely available, export of bulky items became even more economical. Shipments of beer to India grew tenfold in the space of twenty years, and ales went from the bottom of the list in a captain's auction to having large display ads of their own.

Brewers' names such as Harper & Bell and Begbie & Murray appeared. But when Mark Hodgson took over the

brewery from his father, he attacked the Indian market with
youthful vigour and determination. Hodgson's pale ale is
first mentioned by name in Calcutta in 1801. Gradually, by
trial and error, he adapted the initial October-ale recipe,
listening to feedback from his customers, creating a beer
specifically to suit Anglo-Indian tastes. IPA recipes from later
years suggest it became paler, hoppier and more refreshing. By
1809, an ad for 'HODGSON'S very best Pale Ale, Brewed
for this Climate, and warranted of a Superior Quality', ran
across three columns of the *Calcutta Gazette*'s front page. The
prices were higher than for any beer before, the attention
given to it far greater than anything devoted to claret or even
Madeira in previous decades. Ultimately, Hodgson's status was
confirmed by that most embarrassing of nineteenth-century
habits – immortalization in bad verse:

> 'Take away this clammy nectar,'
>   Said the King of Gods and Men,
> 'Never at Olympus' table
>   Let such trash be served again.'
> Terror shook the limbs of Bacchus,
>   Paly grew his pimpled nose,
> And already in his rearward
>   Felt he Jove's tremendous toes.
> When a bright idea struck him: –
>   'Dash my thyrsus! I'll go bail,
> For you never were in India.
>   That you know not Hodgson's ale.'
> 'Bring it,' quoth the Cloud Compeller,
>   And the wine god brought the beer.
> Port and claret are like water
>   To the glorious stuff that is here.
> Then Saturnius drank and nodded,
>   Winking with his lightning eyes,
> And amid the constellations
>   Did the star of Hodgson rise.

At the negotiations to renew its charter in 1813, the East India Company was stripped of its monopoly on trade, and private firms entered the market properly. Ships' captains still took their personal allowances, but these were now bolstered by large-volume cargoes from a new wave of shipping lines. By 1815, the beer trade was almost entirely in the hands of free traders.

Attitudes in British India were changing. In 1785 Warren Hastings retired as Governor General to be replaced by Cornwallis, who claimed that 'every native of India, I verily believe, is corrupt', which was a bit rich coming from an employee of the East India Company serving in Bengal. Cornwallis was succeeded by Richard Wellesley, whose younger brother Arthur, later the Duke of Wellington, followed him to India in 1798. In 1799 Arthur defeated Tipu Sultan, an ally of France, finally ending French claims in India. He then crushed the troublesome Marathas, the last obstacle to British expansion. By 1805, a large swathe of the entire subcontinent, including the ancient cities of Delhi and Agra, was under direct British rule, or was controlled indirectly by a British resident in the local nawab's court.

As rulers (who, remember, were mere merchants in the eyes of their subjects) the British felt the need to establish their supremacy. In 1817 James Mill (father of that advocate of personal liberty, John Stuart Mill) wrote a six-volume history of India and close study of Hindu civilization that would ultimately change the way the country was run. He claimed that India was barbarous and primitive, that Hindus possessed a 'general disposition to deceit and perfidy' and a 'total absence of moral feeling'. They were incapable of progressing from this sorry state on their own, and needed the British to look after them. The fact that Mill arrived at this conclusion without ever visiting India or meeting a single Hindu was neither here nor there. His writings helped instil in the British the sense of superiority they craved.

An attitude of official racism was encouraged. 'Nigger' became the common term of reference for Indians, and those vast armies of servants were seen as subhuman.[53] Elihu Yale, the nice man who went on to found the university, once had a servant hanged on trumped-up charges of piracy simply because the man left his employ without giving proper notice. It became unfashionable to have any interest in what was increasingly being spun as a primitive, barbaric culture, and the delights of Persian poetry and Hindu metaphysics were conveniently forgotten. In 1810, Captain Williamson noted that 'Europeans have very little connexion with natives of either religion', and Mrs Graham regretted that 'Every Briton appears to pride himself on being outrageously a John Bull.' Clothes began to follow London fashions more closely, and Indian food became scarce outside the taverns and punch houses. The memsahibs arrived from Britain and the Indian wives and mistresses were shown the door. As the number of Britons and the breadth of British society grew, so did the ability to pretend that this really was Britain.

And nothing was more British than beer. The more freely available it was, the less anyone had to drink arak, the drink of the niggers. With the Prince Regent's words 'Beer and beef has made us what we are' ringing in their ears, beer became a necessary piece in the armoury of the new rulers. In 1810, V. M. Williamson wrote of Indian society that 'porter, pale-ale and table-beer of great strength are often drank after meals'.

Hodgson's ale played a significant role in William Makepeace Thackeray's *The Tremendous Adventures of Major Gahagan*, the tale of a Hickey-like army officer who, during his service

---

53. William Dalrymple asserts that the ideas of racial purity that scarred the twentieth century had 'roots that can be traced back to developments in European thought a century earlier, and at least partly to developments in British India'.

in India, had 'been at more pitched battles, led more forlorn hopes, had more success among the fair sex, drunk harder, read more, and been a handsomer man than any officer now serving her Majesty'. Gahagan claims to have drunk 234 dozen bottles of Hodgson's pale ale during his first year in India (1802). His superior, Colonel Jowler, actively encourages him to drink deep:

> 'What! Gagy my boy, how do, how do?' said the fat Colonel. 'What! run through the body? – got well again – have some Hodgson – run through your body too!' – and at this, I may say, coarse joke (alluding to the fact that in these hot climates the ale oozes out as it were from the pores of the skin) old Jowler laughed: a host of swarthy chobdars, kitmatgars, sices, consomahs, and bobbychies laughed too, as they provided me, unasked, with the grateful fluid.

And Gagy promptly drinks six tumblers.

Other London brewers sought to emulate Hodgson's success. In 1799, Barclay Perkins, the inheritor of the old Thrale brewery, copied Hodgson's ale but couldn't force their way into the market. Later, *The Times* carried ads from the 'Imperial Brewery, Bromley Bow [which] brews superior ales . . . excelling in flavour and quality Burton or any other ales ever offered in the trade . . . Captains and Merchants supplied with Pale Ale, prepared for the East and West India Climate', and Drury, Thompson and Neale, near Southwark Bridge, offered 'Ale, Pale Ale and Porter always ready for exportation'.

But while supplies were growing, they were still highly irregular. Conditions at sea and the rigours of the voyage may have been partly to blame, but Hodgson's, now being run by Frederick Hodgson and business partner Mark Drane, began turning the screw.

In 1829, Tulloh & Co., then the leading Calcutta trading

house, published a 'Circular on the Beer Trade in India'. Looking back over the first few decades of the nineteenth century, the circular explained:

> Previous to the years 1816 and 17, the demand for Beer in India was nothing compared to what it has become during the last seven or eight years, the pressing calls of 1821 for an increased supply, led Hodgson, of London, to enlarge his brewery, and induced some to enter into arrangements for monopolizing the market: this, as usual in such cases, ended in severe losses to all concerned. Beer has for many years been an article of extensive consumption in Bengal, and it is highly probable that a greater increase would take place, were it not for the very high price to which it has frequently risen: this, however, could not be guarded against, so long as Hodgson exclusively had the supplying of the market.

Whenever other brewers tried to enter, Hodgson flooded the market to drive prices down, forcing fledgling entrants to suffer a steep loss. The circular tells us that: 'Having effected this, the following years he had the market to himself, and the prices rose occasionally under the short supply, to 180 Rs, and even 200 Rs a hogshead. He thereby made up for the sacrifice of the previous year, and effectually deterred others from prosecuting their speculations in this market.'

Maybe it's understandable that young Frederick Hodgson got cocky. Maybe he felt he no longer had to put up with the risk and uncertainty of the delay between shipping the beer and receiving the revenue from it. He must have thought his position was unassailable when he began to throw his weight around with his customers – either that, or he'd forgotten who most of them worked for. Either through arrogance or sheer stupidity, Hodgson upset the most powerful corporation the world has ever known. The Company may have been reduced to a mere anomalous administrative arm of the

British government by this time, but the nabobs were still influential, and were not going to allow an upstart London brewer to hold a gun to their heads.

And so, we come back one final time to that rainy night in 1822. Was Campbell Marjoribanks of the Honourable East India Company a personal friend of Samuel Allsopp? Had he been burned in dealings of his own with Hodgson? As head of what was now an arcane administrative body, did he yearn for the days of speculation and private trade he enjoyed as an East Indiamen captain fifteen years before? Was he simply heeding 'the pressing calls of 1821 for an increased supply'? We don't know. But when the dinner plates had been cleared, he finally came to his point. 'We are now all dependent upon Hodgson, who has given offence to most of our merchants in India. But your Burton ale, so strong and sweet, will not suit our market.'

If there were any doubt that this seemingly casual conversation had in fact been carefully orchestrated, it was dispelled when Mr Marjoribanks rang a bell for service. Instantly, his butler appeared carrying a bottle of Hodgson's India Ale.

Mr Marjoribanks poured out a glass for Mr Allsopp, who held the pale, sparkling beer up to the light appraisingly. 'Is this the India beer? I can brew it.'

'If you can,' promised Mr Marjoribanks, 'it will be a fortune to you.'

CHAPTER EIGHTEEN

A LOVELY NIGHT

Twenty-four hours after the three horn blasts signalled our departure from Madeira, we repeated the ritual once more off the shore of its smaller neighbour. Pulling away from the port of Santa Cruz de la Palma the broader coastline came into view, the whole sky clear apart from the clouds that clung to the island's peaks. The view reminded me of childhood stories about pirates or castaways – tropical islands were always like this, a tall peak shrouded in cloud (though usually with the crown of the volcano peeking out of the top) against a crystal blue sea and sky. Our sea was a steely blue-grey, liquid metal, white scratches scarring its surface.

Sipping a Dorada – the beer of the Canaries, a crisp, golden lager at 5.5 per cent – I took stock of my injuries. From the top:

- Right arm numb with occasional shooting pains from elbow to shoulder if held wrongly. Too weak to bend arm while picking up 1.9kg laptop. Possible carpal tunnel syndrome.
- Left arm still bruised and tenderized across whole bicep from manfully carrying 30kg beer barrel on shoulder.
- Left knee too painful to put any weight on from being smacked against metal hull of narrowboat while falling in canal.
- Now, right ankle sprained and swollen from running back to cruise ship along cobbled road after going into town for day carrying no money or credit cards.

Less than two weeks into a journey that was meant to toughen me up, I was an invalid with not a healthy limb left. And these were supposed to be the easy stages, activities the elderly did with ease. In just over a week, I was supposed to be helping to crew a tall ship. Many of these ships have been adapted with disabled people specifically in mind, but *Europa* wasn't one of them. On my current trajectory, I was worried that I would end up having to dictate this book using one eyelid, like the man in *The Diving-bell and the Butterfly*.

So it was good to be back on the ship, leaning back with fresh drinks brought to us whenever our glasses were empty, watching the island recede.

A few minutes passed, the sun dipping to kiss the top of the peaks.

Liz said, 'I don't want to get off the ship.'

I was glad she said it first.

From being Liz's worst nightmare, the cruise had become something special. It wasn't just laziness; it was the sense of being taken care of, something that, as an adult, you only ever experience if you're ill unless you do a holiday like this. For the first day or so there was a sense of guilt – we had to be 'better' than this somehow. But sod it: the world is big and frightening, and we make our way through it every day. Liz and I live in a fast, loud, impersonal city. We're both very independent: she runs her own business, and I consult on a freelance basis and write, unsure at any point where my next cheque is going to come from. We have a six-figure mortgage – who in their right mind would lend me that much money? Don't they know who I am? What I'm like? And what about my pension? Will it be sufficient to provide for me when I'm old? And does any of this even matter when global warming is about to hit tipping point and we're facing imminent global shortages of oil, food and fresh water? I was tired of struggling and fretting all the time. What was wrong with being looked after, with being mollycoddled? Just for a few days, or even the full two weeks of the cruise? We didn't even need to carry money with us. If we wanted to, we could have spent whole days eating and drinking during which the only movement we needed to make was raising our right arms: first to summon the waiter, then to sign the chit, then to bring the food and 'special' pink cocktails to our mouths. And so, on our final night on *Oceana*, we found ourselves embracing the cruising life with no hint of irony or self-consciousness.

After dinner, we drifted to the Starlights theatre, for *What's My Line?* 'with your Cruise Director Gary', trying to guess the occupations of our fellow passengers (an animal husband, an exam invigilator and a prison warden). We stayed on to watch Julie A. Scott, a former winner of one of those Saturday-night talent shows that were the distant ancestors of *X Factor* back in simpler, less-knowing decades. She covered everything from opera to the Doors, a real pro. Being from Liverpool, she was fixated on Cilla Black, dropping in a passable impersonation at the start of one song before reverting to her own, far superior voice. Between songs she joked about her weight, her sex life, what her career might have been if she were younger, and the life-affirming powers of gin. As a genre of entertainment it may have been painfully out of fashion, but it was supremely entertaining for anyone who could stop worrying about what was and wasn't cool for longer than half an hour.

Towards the end, Julie announced she was going to sing 'Time to Say Goodbye', a 'modern opera song' that was a big hit for Sarah Brightman and Andrea Bocelli in the nineties. With that less-than-promising intro, she proceeded to silence, stun, paralyse and transport everyone in the room, Liz and I included. Go on, laugh. I would too if I hadn't been there, wide-eyed and spellbound.

The next morning, as Liz, Barry and I stood on the hot, white concrete quayside in Santa Cruz de Tenerife, anxiety and stress were back. And they'd brought reinforcements, in the shape of regret and longing. I felt so stupid having left the ship, like someone who makes a big deal about leaving a party early just to get everyone to persuade them to stay, and instead everyone says, 'Oh, bye then.'

I looked down at Barry, his red bag and green plastic glowering, and felt a flash of intense hatred. Between the cabin and the quayside he'd managed to scrape off most of the paint from his trolley. What a *twat* he was. The porter had appeared at the bottom of the lift seemingly wrestling with him, sporting a wild-eyed look that was becoming familiar. I gave him a generous tip.

We heaved our luggage into the shuttle bus to the harbour entrance and took our seats. We didn't look back, didn't think about the sailaway and the three long blasts from the ship's horn, didn't reflect on how far away we would be from *Oceana* when she pulled away into another star-studded night.

*

When nineteen-year-old William Hickey first saw Tenerife from the deck of a Madras-bound East Indiaman on the first of his three voyages to India in 1768, he was enraptured by its beauty:

> On my arrival [on deck] a sublime scene presented itself to my sight. We were close inshore, under the island of Teneriffe. The sun, which had not risen to us, was shining upon the upper part of the peak, giving the most luxuriant tints to the snow-capped summit of that stupendous mountain, and varying the colours as its light descended downwards, until the glorious orb appeared above our horizon, when a thousand new beauties were displayed. The sea was serene and smooth as a looking-glass.

Admittedly, he had been confined to his cabin by chronic seasickness for the month since he left England, strapped to a bunk with little to eat or drink. I imagine the sight of any land would have looked beautiful to his eyes. Nevertheless, it had a remarkably restorative effect. Cheered by the sight, he popped below for half a boiled chicken washed down with a cheeky early morning pint of wine, and felt much better. 'From that hour my sickness ceased, and I began to enjoy myself; I entered into all the fun and joined in all the tricks that went forward in the ship,' he assures us.

Two hundred and forty years later, Tenerife is synonymous with the package holiday. But Liz and I were doing things differently.

Despite arriving on a cruise ship – the only holiday option that wraps you in more cotton wool than a package holiday – we stepped off the shuttle bus and found ourselves alone at the edge of an unfamiliar port, laden with heavy luggage. In the harbour in front of us sat two other cruise ships, which *Oceana* could easily have hidden beneath her skirts. Outside – in the bit offshore that seafarers used to and perhaps still do call 'the roads' – half a dozen container ships lay at anchor, waiting. Behind us, a few commercial buildings fronted an unprepossessing town that clambered up the scrubby, volcanic Canarian slopes.

I had a week to kill before *Europa* departed this same port. Liz was staying with me for the weekend before going home and back to work, and I had to pop back myself during the week to attend a conference, arriving back here the night before *Europa* sailed. I didn't want to lug Barry around any more than I had to, so the simplest solution seemed to be to rent an apartment.

We found the place on a building site at the end of an hour-long cab ride to the windiest corner of a very windy island. The wind howled through the corridor outside. It shrieked under doors and groaned through the plumbing. Liz, Barry and I sat in an empty room, midway between two small villages, with no bars, restaurants or shops within walking distance, and no means of transport. We could see the sea, slightly, over the top of the high garden wall and beyond the car park. I opened the sliding doors on to the small garden. Within minutes, every object and flat surface was covered in fine brown dust. Even Barry now looked dejected rather than furious, lying sullenly next to the sofa, silently and half-heartedly trying to break his trolley. This was as far away from *Oceana* as you could get.

The next morning, with the sun in a cloudless sky and a newly hired car outside, there seemed no better idea than to explore the resorts for which Tenerife is notorious. Coming off the motorway into Los Cristianos, rows of billboards promised we would be able to eat at McDonald's and Burger King in just a few minutes' time. But when we got into the centre of the town, we were surprised. Los Cristianos may be many things, but it wasn't the dump we'd anticipated. It was neat, prim and gleaming, all white buildings, palm trees, carefully planted beds and trellises in pretty, tiled town squares. It reminded us of Portmeirion, the eccentric and unnaturally ordered Welsh 'village' in *The Prisoner*.

We parked on the seafront, near the ferry terminal. Immediately, we noticed a crowd of people lining the harbour wall, more climbing the steps to join them, all staring out into the bay.

Anchored a hundred yards out was a tall ship.

Three masts stood against a creamy blue sky, sails furled in the most neat and elegant fashion. Gunwales were open along her sides, and at the stern an ensign flew, a blue cross on a white background. Only her twin radar domes betrayed the fact that she was real, sitting here in the twenty-first century. She was magnificent, arrayed as if she were on some kind of parade, daring any onlooker not to be impressed.

'Is that your ship?' whispered Liz, clutching my arm.

'No. See how the hull's blue? *Europa*'s is white.'

We stared at her for several minutes, speechless, until Liz suddenly said, 'Oh, my God. I can't believe you're actually

going to sail across the Atlantic to Brazil on one of *those*!
You're not just sailing around the coast of Tenerife, saying
"Look at us, we're on a tall ship" you're actually going to sail
out across the horizon. To Brazil.'

I smiled, thrilled at the note of awe in her voice. 'I know.
Do you think I'm brave?'

'Not at all!' she laughed, a little hysterically. 'I think you
haven't thought through the consequences of what you're
doing yet.'

And I realized this was true.

I've always imagined that true bravery is feeling the fear
and doing it anyway. Looking at this ship, I was experiencing
a total absence of fear, in fact an absence of any emotion at
all. The work I still needed to finish on my brief return to the
UK was keeping my brain occupied. I'd not had a second to
think about what the voyage meant for me personally, about
my experience of it. And now here it was, already two weeks
in. I needed to stop worrying, and start living the journey.

Liz went home the following day, and although I would
be seeing her again in a few days it was a difficult departure,
suffused with a sense of the bigger goodbye that was coming
in less than a week. I spent my days in the apartment,
working and casting sidelong glances at Barry, who seemed
to be trying not to be noticed. Perhaps I should have realized
then that he was up to something, but I thought he was
merely settling down, resigned to his fate.

I spent the evenings slumming around the nearby coastal
village of El Médano, a quiet place in the shadow of Mount
Roja, seemingly a giant pile of slurry that had been shovelled
up and had set in frozen, rippling layers before it could flatten
out again. It was a strange little town. In the middle of this
volcanic desolation, it looked like it had simply been dropped
there, an artificial place built from giant pastel-coloured Lego
bricks. I felt as if I were on the hastily constructed set of a
cheap soap. I suspected the entire place could be dismantled

and flat-packed at the end of the season. And yet, I kind of liked it. The feeling of transience suited my mood – I too was transient now, in perpetual motion.

I'd enjoyed canal boating, despite my best efforts, and I'd enjoyed cruising. And now I really quite liked Tenerife. Finally, after a couple of days of quiet reflection, I was ready for my adventure. I ate dinner and watched the sunset, and when it was dark, the moon appeared, almost full now. There were cabs in the square, but I walked back along the beach, across the scrubby skirts of the mountain, alone, guided by moonlight, reassured that my immense watch agreed that the moon was just about full, and completely at peace. The next morning I left Barry locked in the apartment, packed the smart clothes I'd brought along for the cruise and no longer needed, and headed home for the final time, oblivious to the catastrophe I'd just set in motion.

CHAPTER NINETEEN

COALS TO NEWCASTLE

So I think Samuel Allsopp was being a bit disingenuous when he said of the India trade, 'I never heard of it.' Of course he'd heard of it. He was still heading what had been the biggest brewery in Burton, even if the industry were a shadow of its fleeting glory. He took one look at Hodgson's ale and said, 'I can brew it,' confirming that, as records of his correspondence and advertisements show, he already had an understanding of the techniques needed to create pale malt for pale ale. His recent fire sale had included 'a quantity of rich pale ale', and Bass recorded the use of pale malts in 1819.

By the time of the dinner with Marjoribanks in 1822, Bass had surpassed Allsopp to become Burton's dominant brewer. Michael Bass had focused on the domestic trade after Benjamin Wilson and Allsopp had shut him out of the Baltic party. Now, Bass and his son, Michael Thomas, who started work in the brewery in 1818 as a teenager, were reaping the dividends. Although they were only growing slowly, they were growing. In 1820 their order books show that much of their beer was going to London and Liverpool, and many of the customers in these busy port cities were not publicans, but merchants. Beer was leaving England through the same ports as sugar, rum, tobacco and cotton were coming in. By 1799 Bass was exporting small quantities of ale to America, encouraged by a report from a satisfied Antipodean customer. Michael Bass noted: 'I should myself have despaired of it proving good after so long a voyage had not Captain Raven informed that he took some of my ale to the Colony in New South Wales which was found to be of good quality on arrival.'

The other remaining Burton brewers were also exporting where they could. In 1769, the *London Gazetteer and New Daily Advertiser* offered: 'Burton Ale &c., in the utmost perfection, both for exportation and home consumption; will stand good to the East and West Indies.'

We already know that Burton ale played a major role in the debauchery of the public tables at Bencoolen and Madras early in the eighteenth century. In 1790, Bell's, a long-forgotten Burton brewer, was advertising their 'Beer and Pale Ale' in the *Calcutta Gazette*. So Burton brewers were making something they called pale ale, and shipping it to India, long before Campbell Marjoribanks intervened.

So perhaps when Allsopp professed his ignorance about the India trade, he was waiting to see what opportunity would be offered him, shrewdly playing his cards close to his chest. Or maybe I'm paying too much attention to an alleged conversation not written down until thirty years after it happened, recounted by a man who wasn't there to another who was apparently in love with Samuel Allsopp, and had his own motives for displaying him in a good light.

Whatever – irrespective of who was selling beer in India, or what that beer was like, Hodgson's pale ale, 'Brewed for this Climate', now dominated the market. While Mark, and then Frederick Hodgson, may have cemented their position through commercial skulduggery, they could only get away with this because the Anglo-Indians loved his brew. Frederick Hodgson's position seemed unassailable, but this was something the Company appeared intent on changing. And while the Company's influence may have declined by this stage, it was still an organization you really wouldn't want as an enemy.

Some days after his intriguing dinner with Campbell Marjoribanks, Samuel Allsopp was back in Burton when a mysterious package arrived. He was in his counting house at the time and irritated by the interruption. A hamper was brought in and laid on the table in front of him. It had been sent from London, and when he opened it he found a dozen bottles of beer, labelled 'Hodgson's India Ale', compliments of Campbell Marjoribanks.

'Coals to Newcastle!' he harrumphed, 'a present of ale to Samuel Allsopp at Burton!' But Allsopp was no fool, and only a fool would fail to act on such a heavy hint from the chairman of the East India Company. Allsopp summoned his chief maltster, Job Goodhead.[54]

Goodhead was the key witness in the story of how Samuel Allsopp came to brew India Pale Ale, and it was he who recounted the whole tale to J. Stevenson Bushnan in 1853. We might need to indulge him a little in his seemingly word-perfect recollection of all these conversations thirty years later, but it seems as though Goodhead, like Allsopp, was a remarkable man. Bushnan claimed that his informant had been working at the brewery for fifty years by the time of the interview, and yet was 'still alive, as if to laugh to scorn what some have endeavoured to make out – the fatal consequences of drinking too much Burton ale'.[55]

'Job, can you dry your malt to that colour?' asked Allsopp.

'Yes, sir,' answered the maltster. He raised the beer to his lips, took a mouthful and immediately spat it out again, the intense, hoppy bitterness at odds with the sweeter, darker ales he was accustomed to.[56] 'But sir—,' he spluttered.

---

54. A man who later went on to father a dynasty of Bond girls.

55. St Modwen, Steve Wellington, and now Job Goodhead, all showing signs of extended youthfulness and vigour, all closely connected with Burton well water. There's definitely a pattern forming here.

56. It's sometimes claimed that Hodgson's beer had been to India and back to improve the flavour. This is almost certainly untrue, and probably derives from the fact that Madeira often made the round trip before being

'Never mind the taste, Job. Can you dry your malt to this colour? Are you sure?'

'Quite sure, sir.'

'Then do so.'

And so the two brewers set to work, creating the first batch of the beer that would revolutionize the drinking habits of the world. They made several small test brews, and finally pronounced success with a brew created in a teapot.

Having brewed the beer, the obstacles facing Allsopp were still considerable. There was the problem of the canals. Hodgson's brewery sat right by the East India Dock. To get his beer to the same dock, Allsopp would have to pay 60 shillings per ton; at the time the charge for freight from London to Calcutta was only a third of that. Liverpool was slightly cheaper, somewhat more reliable, and that's where the first consignment was sent.

Then there was the sheer strength of Hodgson's brand in the Calcutta market. Monopolistic trading practices aside, the London beer had a formidable reputation. According to the 'Circular on the Beer Trade in India': 'Another thing in his favour, and which operated for a long time, was the high repute in which his name stood for beer; so much so, that no other of a good quality was bought by the retailers, as they could not dispose of it.'

And that was the fate for good-quality beer – even to get

---

sold in London. Madeira is far more robust than beer, and it's extremely unlikely that beer would survive both legs. And while it filled empty hold space on the way out, those holds were crammed full of tea and cotton on the way home. In addition, beer brewed for export qualified for a drawback on the swingeing rates of duty being charged on British beer. If it were reimported, these taxes would be reapplied, making such a move completely uneconomical. The fact that Goodhead spat the beer out suggests it was still young, with a strong spike of hop bitterness, which would have disappeared completely in a beer that had spent anything up to a year at sea.

to a point where your beers could be rejected in favour of Hodgson's it would have to be passed by 'the tasters' in the Indian ports, who declared it fit to drink – or not – and sold off beer that didn't make the grade at public auction,[57] at prices that wouldn't even cover the cost of transit.

But Allsopp was a determined man. Bushnan, warming to his theme, describes the brewer as having 'the head to conceive . . . the hand to execute . . . having entered upon an undertaking he never failed to carry it out'. He wrote to people at Gainsborough and Fennings Wharf on the Trent, asking them to watch out for his cargo, and the beer arrived safely at port. Twelve butts and fourteen hogsheads were loaded on to the *Bencoolen*, which set sail for India on 27 December 1822. A second consignment of ten butts and twelve hogsheads followed on the *Seaforth*.

The India Office records in the British Library have details of every single voyage made by any East India Company ship over the course of the Company's 264-year existence. You can look up the exact dates of departure and arrival, where they stopped on the way, what the weather was like, who the captain and ship's officers were, and every detail of the cargo.[58] So it was with some anticipation that I dived into the records to discover what happened on Burton India Pale Ale's first ever voyage. There was just one problem: the *Bencoolen* and the *Seaforth* were not Company ships. After the Company lost its monopoly in 1813, the India trade had been opened up to all. The *Bencoolen* was owned by Cropper

---

57. In search of a dramatic flourish, many writers of the IPA story conjure up a scene of hard-mouthed clerks pouring unfit beer into the river at Calcutta. This hardly ever happened. Nothing could be wasted in India. The *Calcutta Gazette* is full of ads for unfit beer, which had many uses – as we'll see later.

58. One nineteenth-century voyage – and I swear this is true – was captained by a certain 'Jackson Sparrow'.

Benson & Co., who went on to become agents for the Black Ball Line, which later pioneered transatlantic steam packets. She was built and launched in Liverpool in 1818. Rigged as a ship of regular type, 416 tons with a length of 114 feet 2 inches and a beam of 26 feet 8 inches, she was licensed for private trade to India, and is advertised as 'The fine ship *Bencoolen*' in the *Liverpool Mercury* in 1824. In 1832 she was bought by the Company, but completed only one voyage for them before being released in 1833. She was broken up in 1844. But of her voyage to Calcutta carrying Allsopp's ale, there is no bastard trace whatsobloodyever.

But she went – we know that. And with her sailed the sum of Samuel Allsopp's hopes, his fate as a brewer lying in her hold.

It would be twelve months before he knew what that fate was.

CHAPTER TWENTY

A VERY BAD DAY

Almost two hundred years later, my own waiting game echoed Allsopp's. I'd brewed a beer very similar to his just a few hundred yards away from where he created it, and I'd carried it on the first 2,000 miles of its journey. Luckily, I only had another two and a half months to wait before discovering whether or not my venture would be a success. Would that be long enough for the beer to undergo its alteration? What was happening to Barry's innards? Being separated from my barrel made me anxious, but I kept telling myself that nothing could happen to him in an empty apartment on a deserted building site.

Forty-eight hours back in the UK felt like about four. I floated through my life, disconnected from it, revisiting it like a ghost, finishing off everything I could. And then it was Friday morning and I had to say goodbye to Liz, knowing I wasn't going to see her for two months, and for most of that time I wouldn't even be able to talk to her. We'd been building up to this point of departure, dreading it, arguing over it, for weeks. And here it was, upon us.

I'd screwed up. Men who love their wives are not supposed to make them cry, especially when they're Liz. Upsetting Liz should be a criminal offence. But here we were.

'I can't just cry tears. My whole face has to get involved,' Liz choked as we said goodbye. At least, I think it was Liz. I couldn't see anything by this point.

'You have the best, the most wonderful time,' she sobbed. 'It's going to be amazing. It's going to be the experience of a lifetime. Promise me you'll have the best time. Because you're never fucking doing anything like this ever again.'

But that was it. At least all the variable stuff, the potential for upset, was behind me. Now it was simply a case of Barry and me getting on board a ship tomorrow morning. It was finally happening.

Looking back on that day and what happened, I realize that, thinking like this, I was tempting fate. I just wish that fate didn't have to give in to temptation *every single fucking time*.

During the flight I was lucky enough to catch the third *Pirates of the Caribbean* movie, the latest Hollywood exploration of the cycle of diminishing returns. I started to cheer up with the shocking realization that all my research for this voyage had turned me into something of a nautical nerd. The villains of the piece were the East India Company, which made me smile because, for once, there was some justification in the choice of plummy English accents for Hollywood baddies. But they'd invented an East India Company flag that was totally fictitious, probably because the real Company flag looked so similar to the Stars and Stripes, and was almost certainly the inspiration for it, and that wouldn't do at all. When we reached the climactic battle, I scoffed because the Company never had that many ships in service at any one time. Then I caught myself, and realized that if I were going to start picking faults with the historical accuracy, there were bigger targets, such as a giant squid, ships crewed by dead men including one with tentacles growing out of his face, and Keira Knightley having perfect skin and all her own teeth despite living at sea in the eighteenth century. They should have made her up to have wooden dentures and authentic-looking smallpox scars. It would have been a much more rewarding film, I'm sure you agree.

By the time I was waiting for my rucksack at the baggage carousel, I was reasonably happy. Just one more evening back at the apartment – the keys of which I suddenly pictured very clearly in the front pocket of my laptop bag, my big, black laptop bag that I'd taken home and swapped for a more 'travelly' green canvas bag, and left in my study. Like a corny movie flashback, I saw myself checking every pocket of this laptop bag, transferring everything I needed. I saw my fingers reach for the front-pocket zip, and then the phone ringing, and me putting the bag down, and not picking it up again before I left.

The sky had turned to velvet by the time I'd contacted the landlord and had dinner in El Médano while I waited for him to drive all the way down from Santa Cruz with a spare set of keys. As midnight approached, I returned to the apartment.

About four years after I moved to London, I was burgled. It happens. I was living in a ground-floor flat with my then-partner, Jill, and she arrived home before me. She saw the broken window, clocked that my CD collection had all but disappeared, and observed that the contents of our wardrobe were strewn across the floor. And her immediate conclusion was . . . how strange. The boy next door must have kicked a ball against the window and broken it, which must have taken some doing with that hedge in the way. And at the same time Pete must have been home early because he's been roped into going on a business trip at short notice. He must have had no time at all to pack, and that's why it's so messy. Gosh, he's taken a lot of CDs with him – it must be a long trip. And how bizarre – the boy's ball must have bounced back off the window as it broke, because it's not in the room.

She then noticed that some of her smarter clothes were missing, along with all my suits.

Oh dear, she thought. The stress of this trip must be getting to Pete. He's started to experiment with cross-dressing. Fancy that happening at the same time as the boy breaking our window with his ball.

It took her twenty minutes to realize she was looking at a break-in. Burglary is such a huge, traumatic idea that the brain simply doesn't want to deal with it, and throws up all manner of muddy bollocks before being dragged to the stand and admitting the truth.

When I got back to the apartment, it hadn't been burgled. But I was about to go through a strikingly similar process of denial.

My last thought before I put the new key in the door was that someone had been very enthusiastic with the air freshener in the hallway. Inside, I expected the place to be muggy – it's a south-facing apartment with big windows that had been closed for three days. But there was something more than closeness in the air. There was something . . . meaty.

I'd been fearing a rotting-garbage smell, but not this. I opened the cupboard under the sink where the rubbish bin stood. No, it wasn't coming from there – a faint mouldering vegetable whiff, but it was a different smell, and safely confined.

Then I noticed that the soles of my shoes were sticking to the floor as I walked. I could see a moist residue shining between some of the floor tiles.

I checked the ceiling for leaks from the noisy apartment above, then examined all the taps in the kitchen and bathroom and the fridge for exploding food and drink. I went back and looked at the bin again, checked the toilet and bidet for cracks.

I was in the apartment for ten minutes before it occurred to me that Barry might have anything to do with it. My brain slowly caught up with my nose and identified the 'meaty' smell: it was the smell of stale beer. Oxidized beer. *Spilt* beer.

Even now, denial was still fighting a furious rearguard action. A little drop of beer must have come out of the top. That happens sometimes when live beer is fermenting in the cask: a little bit comes out of the top.

A little bit? whispered a voice in my head. *Yeah, that'll be right, just a few drops . . . that have covered the entire floor of poor old David's apartment, reached into the kitchen and the bedroom, and driven somebody to fill the corridor outside with air freshener.*

I picked up Barry by the scruff of the neck. His dead weight had disappeared. 'Oh, that's nice,' I thought, 'he'll be much easier to get on and off ships.' Even now, I still hadn't realized there was little point in taking him on board any ships.

As I dumped him on the patio, the truth was finally starting to push through. Using my brand-new Swiss Army knife I sliced Barry free of his bonds, and peeling away the thick, suffocating cellophane. I unzipped the bag. Stale beer and wet hops sloshed around as I lifted out the barrel, so light now, so insubstantial.

The bung from the barrel was swimming in a hop-filled puddle. The bunghole had been facing the floor. When the bung came out, the entire contents of the barrel had drained away.

The other voice in my head – which I now recognized as the disembodied narrator who often accompanies me on my travels, especially in times of great stress – piped up, maddeningly clear over the whirlpool of rising panic: *Well, this is not ideal, but it's great material. Barry's taken this whole idea of humorous anthropomorphism of inanimate objects to its logical conclusion by actually committing suicide. Heh heh, I hadn't realized our relationship had deteriorated quite so far.*

'Are you fucking insane?' replied my own tired, stressed, paranoid voice (missing the fact that, by having an argument with myself in this way, I was making my question rhetorical). 'That's it. Gone. The whole POINT of this trip! There's no beer. And that means there's no point.'

For all that it was funny to imbue Barry with a personality (until he started doing it on his own) the truth is that he was a living, breathing entity. The yeast inside the cask was fermenting slowly, creating carbon dioxide. Warmer temperatures create a more vigorous fermentation, meaning a more rapid build-up of CO_2. With the apartment closed up for three days, it obviously got quite warm – especially, I now realized, as I'd forgotten to close the metal shutters over the south-facing glass doors. Excess gas must have built up and forced the bung out. For no reason, I tried to force the bung back in, pounding it with my fist, and couldn't. The pressure to push it out must have been immense.

'I should have been here!' I wailed.

There was nothing you could have done, said the other voice. *It's what he wanted.*

'Oh, shut up.'

You've got less than twelve hours to get rid of the stink before David the landlord arrives to inspect the apartment and give you your deposit back.

'I know.'

And you've got to repack everything.

'I know.'

What are you going to do?

'I don't know.'

I cradled Barry's still-damp corpse in my arms, looking down at the lipstick lettering of his name, faded after being washed away by his own insides. 'You stupid, stupid fucker,' I said, unsure which of the three of us I was talking to.

PART FOUR

EUROPA

CHAPTER TWENTY-ONE

THE TALL SHIP

'*Fuhgeddaboudit!*'

'Brazil, man, fuhgeddaboudit. You know dere are twenny girls to every guy over there? Beautiful blonde girls with the . . . with the curves, man, fuhgeddaboudit! And girls that are dark, like me. You tell them girls you're from England, you're gonna be like, geddaway from me, I can't move, fuhgeddaboudit! But you gotta watch 'em, man. They so friendly, but they all HIV.'

Musing on the miracle of speech, I realized I'd been right to take an expensive cab from El Médano to Santa Cruz. If I'd saved seventy euros and dragged my rucksack, duffel bag, computer bag and what-the-hell-am-I-going-to-do-with-this-beer-stinking-empty-keg-and-now-redundant-trolley bag on to the bus instead, I wouldn't have met Alberto.

Alberto was a Colombian who grew up in New York, was very good friends with a world-famous novelist whose name he couldn't quite remember ('Anne Somebody'), was kidnapped, freed, then sent to prison for a crime he didn't commit, escaped, and fled to Europe. He now owned a chain of restaurants across Tenerife, and I was lucky to catch him behind the wheel of a cab. He was only driving it that day because he was dying of pancreatic cancer and couldn't stand up for very long. As we spoke, he was waiting to have the tumour removed, which would also entail him having his entire stomach and oesophagus replaced. (They were growing him a new stomach in a tank.) Oh, and he had a Sicilian grandfather, which is why he said 'Fuhgeddaboudit' all the time, exploring all its forms. Having dropped these heavy hints, he surprised me by saying nothing at all about any Mafia connection.[59]

I drifted in and out of Alberto's life story as we tore up the coastal road. I was tired but not sleepy, stress-adrenalin reminding me of what life used to be like when I relied on coffee and ProPlus to pull me through advertising's eighteen-hour working days.[60] I'd spent half the night cleaning the floor of the apartment, again and again, all the windows open, until merely a faint farmyard whiff remained in the corner near the settee where Barry had spilled his guts. If David the landlord smelled anything unusual when he arrived to check the apartment he didn't mention it, and he handed back my deposit without complaint.

'I work fourteen hours a day, man,' Alberto was saying as we traced the smashed-rubble coastline back to Santa Cruz, 'I only keep thoidy-five per cent of what I take, the rest goes to the owner of the cab. I make fiddy euros a day, just to buy myself a little hole in da ground so that when I die my beautiful children don't have to pay for when they bury me, fuhgeddaboudit. But I never complain. Never. That hole in the ground, that's all I can afford. Nothing else.'

I know what you're thinking, reader. You're thinking, hang on, what about the income from the chain of restaurants across the island?

'And I just bought my kids a huge apartment right on the sea,' said Alberto.

Ah, there we go.

'But I never complain! I'm happy, ya know? I laugh, I joke, I sing all the time. Fuhgeddaboudit!'

---

59. But then, the real mafiosi don't, do they?

60. I've since found out that every other person who has ever worked in advertising, ever, relies on a substance known as 'cocaine', which is apparently far more invigorating than coffee or ProPlus. No one ever told me about it at the time. Maybe *that's* why my advertising career stalled.

A tide of speech flowed around me and washed me down past the primary-coloured power station into Santa Cruz, through the harbour, and past the ferries and cruise ships. Even the wildest reaches of his story could distract me only briefly from the fact that my whole enterprise was now quite monumentally screwed. There seemed little point in carrying on.

And then we pulled up alongside *Europa*, and even Alberto was lost for words.

When I say lost for words, I mean he was silent for about five seconds – the longest he's stopped talking while awake for forty years. 'Aw, man, fuh-gedd-ab-OUD-it! You're going to Brazil on *that*? Jeez, aw, come on, man, take me with you, *please!*'

Pancreatic cancer, crocked stomach, fucked oesophagus and inability to stand all momentarily forgotten, Alberto leapt from the cab like a steroid-crazed Russian gymnast and insisted on hauling my heavy bags aboard the ship. Long after I'd paid him (both the fare, and a little extra for his bravura performance) he was still standing on the dockside staring, open-mouthed and glassy-eyed. The hope and long-ing in those eyes confirmed that there was far more than rope and wood in *Europa*'s soaring masts and spider-web rigging.

She was exquisite. She stood there in defiance of cynicism, a fairy tale, a dream of a ship that could surely never be as good in reality, and yet here she was.

Even for those who would never dream of leaving port on one, tall ships are stunning to look at, and a steady stream of people came to the quayside to gawp. A sandwich board stood next to the gangplank, giving the vital statistics of the ship, pictures of her on a glamorous photo-shoot in Antarctica, and contact details if you felt like booking a voyage rather than just staring at her star-struck, as if she were a visiting Hollywood legend. A few months previously, I'd had an email from The International Travel Writers

Alliance advertising an event in Aarhus, Denmark, where you could go and see the vessels (*Europa* included) that were taking part in the Tall Ships' Race. Going all that way, just to look at them! It made me cocky to actually be boarding one, calling it home for a month.

Much of our perception of beauty has to do with proportion, and I guess that's what's compelling about tall ships – the clue is in the name. *Europa*'s three masts reached into the cloudless blue, the yards on which the sails lay neatly furled reminding me of trapeze artists with arms outstretched, perfectly poised. Towards the stern the mizzenmast, smallest of the three, rose from the poop deck between the large, spoked wheel that I would soon be on such familiar terms with and the wheelhouse, the nerve centre of the ship. Steep steps descended to the main deck. We would eat most of our meals here, in the shadow of the tall mainmast with the star-spangled European flag at its tip. The deckhouse – where the bar was – squatted in front of the mainmast, with more stairs leading to the sloop deck on its roof. In front of the deckhouse was a cramped space where the foremast stood, almost a twin to the main behind it. A walkway ran overhead from the sloop to the raised foredeck, which tapered to the bowsprit, a long beam stretching like a ballerina up and forward from the bow, a safety net strung beneath. Every foot of the ship seemed to be laced with rigging. 'No winches, but an infinite number of lines, at first glance, completely indistinguishable', the brochure had read.

She was breathtakingly beautiful, there was no argument about that. That was the first thing that struck me. But close up – close enough finally to touch – another observation demanded to be heard.

I hadn't realized how short 149 feet is.

Maybe 149 feet sounds generous to you, sitting there in your house or flat, wishing the rooms were a bit bigger. But when this is all the space you have for several weeks, and when you're looking at sharing it with nearly fifty other people, bobbing upon the open sea, it really doesn't feel like very much at all. Surely she was far too small to sail to Brazil in?

Nervously, I stepped aboard. I was slightly disturbed to see that, while the hull was painted gleaming white, the walls and doors of the deckhouse and wheelhouse were the same hot-dog condiment hues as *Remus*. There must have been all sorts of practical sea-going reasons for this, but I never found out what they were.

A young man in a harness slid down the mainmast and helped me aboard. 'I'll find someone,' he said, looking amused. I wondered if everyone coming aboard had the same look of nervous wonder I obviously had plastered across my face.

A tanned blonde woman in her mid-twenties, Scandinavian looking, pretty yet overwhelmingly practical, direct from central casting for an advertisement for healthy living on the ocean waves, appeared and said, 'Hi, I'm Val.'

'Pete.'

'Ah, you're English Pete, yes?'

'Yes!'

This was great. Already, I had a pirate name. English Pete – it suited me.[61]

This was it. The full impact of what I was doing finally hit home. I was an adventurer, an explorer, embarking on something few ordinary people would ever dare. Wasn't I?

'You'll be sharing your cabin with a couple of men in their late fifties.'

---

61. Unfortunately it turned out to be a pretty useless pirate name. In fact this would be the only time it was ever used, because the other Pete on board was English too. Given that the other English Pete had been on the ship since she was in Amsterdam, I've no idea what possessed Val to raise my hopes so high.

OK, maybe not as adventurous as I thought.

'I've put them on the two lower bunks if that's OK with you. You can have the upper bunks for yourself and your . . . extra baggage. What are you doing with all this extra baggage?'

'Well, for me it's a very long trip.'

I explained about my quest, and the fact that one bag was a beer barrel.

'Ah, well, you'll have to put that on our form of effects – you must declare it for customs.'

'OK. Right. It's just, you see – it's an empty beer barrel.'

'Oh. OKaaaaay . . .'

First the smirk. Now the OKaaaaay. I worried that I wasn't creating a great first impression with these hardened seafarers.

I dumped my bags, stashing Barry's corpse in the bottom of the wardrobe. There were three of us in a four-berth cabin. We each had a drawer under one of the beds, a cupboard, a shelf, and we shared a wardrobe. The snug, satisfying use of space in the cabin reminded me again of *Remus*, and I could hardly believe it was only three weeks since I'd boarded our oversized, gender-confused canal boat. It seemed like years ago.

I'd arrived early, so I wandered off to spend a fitful, restless afternoon in Santa Cruz. As you might appreciate, I was a little preoccupied. I'd boarded the most exciting, authentic ship on my journey, carrying an empty beer barrel.

When I'd discovered Barry's remains I'd phoned Rudgie. It was late and he was drunk or asleep, possibly both. I wasn't sure what I expected him to do, short of driving into Burton, breaking into the brewery, putting some more beer in another cask, driving down to the airport, buying a last-minute overnight flight and getting here before I boarded the ship. I can see now that this was perhaps beyond the call of either duty or friendship. But I had to share the disaster with him. My brain had shut down, and I needed someone to tell me what to do. Rudgie told me to get on the ship anyway. He told me he'd look into getting another barrel flown over to meet me in Brazil. This replacement would miss the most authentic leg of the journey, but if I could meet it in Rio it would still travel 12,000 miles with me, through tropical waters and, most importantly, around the Cape. It would spend weeks rather than months at sea, but it was still travelling most of the route. Would it make any difference to the beer? I didn't know. But I had to cling to something. For now, I held on to Barry's corpse. I didn't know what else to do.

When I returned to *Europa*, other people were arriving and beers were being handed out. One young, bespectacled man came on with his wife and when asked who he was replied, 'Oh, I'm not sailing. I'm just here to look at the ship and say hello to one of my clients.'

I turned to him. 'Urs?'

'Pete!'

It was so great to meet him, the man without whom I wouldn't have been here. He was younger and altogether more normal than I'd expected. He was on holiday in the Canaries, and couldn't resist visiting the ship with which he, too, was in love.

'So, you are safely on board?' he asked.

'Yes.'

'And the beer?'

'No.'

'No?' His eyes grew wide in shock. It was nice that so many people seemed to have a genuine concern about what I was trying to do.

'It exploded. I'm carrying an empty cask.'

'But the whole point of your journey has now disappeared!'

'Yes, I know. Sort of.' You can go off someone quickly, I thought.

Urs works full time booking passengers on ships. *Europa* sails a vaguely regular route across to Brazil, down to Ushuaia on the southern tip of Argentina, round the Antarctic, to Cape Town and back up to Europe each year. Urs sailed the leg from Cape Town to Ascension earlier this year. He must have seen my email only weeks after the end of his voyage, which may explain his interest in mine.

I asked him about the market for this kind of travel. Demand had grown exponentially after 9/11, with new fears about flying, but security fears meant new shipping regulations weren't far behind. The Athens Convention came into force in 2004, and has made it much more difficult for ships to take on passengers.

'Isn't there any growth from people wanting to travel in a more green or slow way?' I pressed.

'Not really. The people who are interested because of green issues don't really have the money for it. They talk about it, but they never do it.'

I asked about routes.

'Some become very popular for a few years because they are interesting. From Europe to Cape Town for example. But the one you will be doing in the container ship, they rarely have passengers.'

Urs had really come to revisit the ship rather than see me, and I allowed him his communion with her. After he left I drifted through introductory conversations that reminded me of Freshers' Week at university. Dieter, a tall, lanky German, had been with the ship since Amsterdam and obviously yearned to be part of the permanent crew. 'Ah, another English,' he said through his teeth when we were introduced. 'There is a nest of you somewhere, yes?'

'You'll probably be able to flush us all out with alcohol,' I smiled back, taking another beer and walking away from him. Once the ship was under way he would rarely emerge from the rigging. He liked being aloft. I liked him being aloft too.

Others made a better first impression. Margriet, from Friesland in the north of the Netherlands, was embarking on her third voyage aboard *Europa* and her reaction at being reunited with the ship was one of relief more than anything else. 'Three weeks of not having to think about what to do, what to wear, what to eat, how you look. It's great to be back,' she smiled.

A family smelling of immense wealth emerged from a shiny black SUV with darkened windows, all draped in the special kind of uncreasable white linen that only very rich people seem to find. I was alarmed when, after ten minutes, three of them climbed back into the SUV and drove away, leaving behind a pretty blonde girl in tight white shorts who looked no older than sixteen. As she introduced herself to Margriet and me, I felt a fatherly instinct to make sure she was going to be all right, rather than a younger man's involuntary urge to check her out.[62] I needn't have worried for her: Laura was eighteen, came from Munich, and belying her chic, slender beauty, drank beer like a bastard. By the third day, every male member of the permanent crew aged twenty-five or under was trailing in her wake like a poodle, acting on her every whim.

As the shadows grew longer, the captain made his appearance. You could tell he was the captain.

From first appearances, it was hard to tell whether Klaas Gaastra lived on the sea or in it, but he definitely lived for it. He was somewhere within touching distance of his mid-fifties, tall, lean and weathered, long salt-and-pepper hair hanging

---

62. This started happening to me with Keira Knightley. Whenever I see her some gender memory tells me I should be going 'phwoaar', but instead I think, Ooh, you're thin – are you sure you're looking after yourself? And you should wrap up a bit warmer, you'll catch a chill wearing that. This undoubtedly makes me a better man, but at the same time I feel *diminished* somehow.

kinked and chaotic like exotic seaweed around his shoulders. With his wind-lined face, thick Santa Claus beard, two piercing eyes the colour of an equatorial sky and what looked like a spare one dangling from one ear, you could have spotted him at a Parisian cocktail party or Manhattan gallery opening and you'd still say, 'Oh, look, that man's the captain of a sailing ship,' even if he were wearing full evening attire, which I doubt he ever would.[63]

Captain Klaas welcomed us aboard with a sandpapered voice, and told us that we were aiming to sail at noon the following day. We would have safety briefings in the morning, but for now it was time to relax.

Dusk settled in, and I noticed a group of English lads had formed around Padraig – thirtyish, irrepressibly Irish, taking the piss out of everyone seconds after meeting them. You could tell the others were English from the way they gripped their cans of beer and hunched over them protectively. We have a way of finding each other out in mixed company, and soon a group of us were planning an expedition into Santa Cruz for more focused drinking. I was delighted when both Laura and Margriet decided to join us, each matching us beer for beer and holding it as well as any of us, and better than some.

Later, as I climbed into my bunk for the first time, my two roomies had already retired, drawing the curtains across their bunks for privacy. I realized then that *Europa* resembled *Big Brother*. We were a random, diverse collection of people thrown together in a confined space, to be assigned a series of tasks between which there would be long periods lazing under the sun. The difference was that anyone evicted here would have to walk the plank.

---

63. In the three weeks I spent aboard *Europa*, the only time I ever saw Klaas in anything other than a sleeveless T-shirt, shorts and flip-flops was when a storm was raging.

And there it was – the format for a new reality-TV show.

But this was the kind of thinking I was hoping to escape from during my time at sea. Out on the ocean there would be no telly, apart from the occasional evening DVD. It would be a world without reality TV, *Heat* magazine, newspapers, Oyster cards, CCTV cameras and 'solutions'. Just 149 feet of wood and metal, 300 ropes, 30 sails and 40-something people. I had no idea what to expect but, finally, there was no ambiguity or extraneous concern. So I was carrying an empty beer barrel and somehow had to get a full one to meet me in Brazil. So what?

Whatever happened, I was in love with this ship. And, finally, I was with her.

CHAPTER TWENTY-TWO

BEER AT SEA

Talk about a bad omen.

Late in 1792, when George Hodgson's beer was gathering a reputation in India and Benjamin Wilson was still building his fortune in the Baltic, an armed ship left Spithead, just off Portsmouth, and slipped into a querulous English Channel on a peculiar mission. The orders were to head for the Society Islands, a tiny archipelago in the distant South Pacific. The ship was to pick up breadfruit, which grew in abundance there, and bring them back to His Majesty's possessions in the West Indies, where they might 'constitute an article of food [that] would be of very essential benefit to the inhabitants'. After waiting for days with the wind against them, the ship finally set sail on 23 December, bound first for Tenerife.

She ran into trouble almost immediately. That night, according to the captain's log, 'the wind increased to a strong gale with a heavy sea'. It moderated on Christmas Day, but returned with a vengeance and battered the ship for days, washing away the spare yards and spars, and – worse – breaking the bonds that lashed the ship's supply of beer to the deck, sending the barrels tumbling overboard, never to be seen again. The ship's name was the *Bounty*. The captain, who supplied the account of the journey, was William Bligh.

Having to endure a voyage all the way to the South Seas without beer was perhaps not enough to spark the most infamous naval mutiny in history, but it can't have helped. As historian Peter Matthias notes, 'afloat as ashore, beer was the national drink'. The fact that an English sailor might be thousands of miles away from home in the middle of uncharted waters didn't stop him from demanding something that was, in his eyes, a right rather than a privilege.

Beer had been a staple onboard ship since Tudor times. In 1620, the Pilgrim Fathers landed earlier than they had planned, explaining in the journal of the *Mayflower*, 'We could not now take time for further search or consideration; our victuals being much spent, especially our beere.'

Every English ship hoped to have beer among its supplies, but for His Majesty's Navy it was a matter of fundamental importance. Brewers in port towns such as London, Liverpool and Bristol received a sudden, sporadic windfall every time a naval fleet docked. In times of war – which became more frequent as Britain began to argue with her close neighbours not just over centuries-old grievances at home but also over land-grab claims in distant colonies – they simply couldn't brew enough beer to meet demand. The navy set up its own breweries, and by the eighteenth century the three royal victualling yards at Deptford, Gosport and Plymouth all boasted massive brewhouses, bigger than any other brewery in the country save those of the London porter giants.

Back in 1588, the year of the defeat of the Spanish Armada, naval rations essentially consisted of beer, biscuit and salt meat, and the Lord High Admiral of England, Lord Howard, reflected that 'Nothing doth displease the seamen so as sour beer.' But sour beer was a real and constant danger. The navy would eventually employ both the finest scientific minds and the most famous adventurers of the day to solve the problem of maintaining a steady ration of drinkable beer for men at sea.

Ships left port with both beer and water stored in wooden barrels. While Bligh had his lashed to the deck, the common practice was to stow it in deep holds. The barrels containing water were often recycled – some had recently contained oil

– and the water soon became stale and started to grow algae. Given a choice between beer and water, sailors went for beer every time. It was usually pretty bad beer – small beer that, in the now beautifully archaic words of John Masefield, was 'of poor quality, not at all the sort of stuff to put the souls of three butchers into one weaver'. But at least it didn't have stuff growing in it. Ironically therefore, the water would remain untouched until the beer was finished, by which time it really had grown foul. In 1781, sailor Silas James's account of a journey to India reveals that when a water cask was broached it 'stank so much, that when the steward broached a cask, and applied the lighted candle to the bunghole, it burnt blue like spirits: this was the Thames water . . .'

At a ration of a gallon per man per day, the beer would last for a month before running out, but small beer would often go sour even in this time. For longer voyages on tropical missions, stronger beer would be provided because of its better keeping qualities. The problem was, the quality ingredients supplied to make decent beer were often appropriated by corrupt brewers, meaning that, according to a Parliamentary Committee investigating 'frauds and abuses' in 1710: 'the sailors had their full proportion of Drink, but the strength and Heart of the beer was left behind in the Brewhouse cellars'.

In hot climates, the daily gallon of beer was switched for a pint of Spanish wine or a half a pint of spirits. The Admiralty believed a simple solution to the prospect of ships full of drunken sailors was to issue half the ration twice a day, never stopping to consider that seamen may be bright enough to save it up for a party after sundown.

But there was a more serious problem with these arrangements: if the country weren't at war with the Spanish (thereby losing the wine supply) it was squabbling with the French (thereby losing the brandy supply). This dilemma was eventually solved by the capture of Jamaica in 1655, after which rum was issued instead, soon becoming synonymous with the image of the Jolly Jack Tar. But its supply was unofficial and unsanctioned by the Admiralty at first, for good reason.

Among the squadrons in the West Indies drunkenness became endemic. Captain Hall wrote, 'I really do not think it an exaggeration to say that one-third of every ship's company were more or less intoxicated, or at least muddled and half stupefied, every evening.' Admiral Edward Vernon, nicknamed 'Old Grogram' by his men on account of the waterproof boat cloak he always wore,[64] despaired at how 'the pernicious custom of the seamen drinking their allowance of rum in drams, and often at once, is attended with many fatal effects to their morals as well as their health'. He proposed mixing rum with water, sugar and lemon or lime juice. In his honour, the potion became known as grog, and was made official in the revised *Regulations and Instructions relating to His Majesty's Service at Sea* in 1756. But the Admiralty was not entirely convinced that grog was the answer, and beer remained the recommended ration. Grog was not to be issued until the beer had run out.

Those same 1756 regulations also proposed the introduction of a tipple with the alluring name of 'British Malt Spirits', which sounds like vinegar, but was probably more akin to cheap, unmatured whisky. The document insisted that: 'The introduction of malt spirits into the Victualling was intended to enable HM Ships . . . to lengthen their Cruizes, they not being able to stow a proportion of Beer answerable to their other provisions.'

The evidence suggests the sailors spat it back at their superiors. Because a few years later, the navy thought again, and hit upon what seemed like an ingenious solution.

It had long been a scam to vary the strength of beer to

---

64. Grogram was a coarse fabric of silk mixed with wool or mohair and stiffened with gum.

defraud the excise. Brewers would create an extra-strong beer, pay the duty on it, then dilute it to create greater volumes. But if water could be added to beer, it could also be taken away. The scientists of the eighteenth century were fascinated by distillation and had finally mastered the art. If beer could be concentrated into a higher-alcohol syrup by 'freezing out' excess water, and then diluted when needed, it could cure both of the Admiralty's headaches: it would take up less space, and would last longer. The Admiralty's victuallers drafted in members of the Royal Society to explore the possibilities.

In January 1772, Henry Pelham, Secretary to the Commissioners of Victualling, declared a breakthrough. In a letter to the Admiralty he described how beer might be made at sea from 'inpissated Juice of Malt'. Incredibly, the images this term conjures up didn't put anyone off, and they read on. It sounded straightforward enough: make the beer, simmer it down until it is 'thick and viscid', then 'this Juice might . . . be afterwards made into Beer at Sea without any other Trouble than the mixing it with the necessary quantity of warm water and letting it stand to acquire a proper spirit and Briskness'.

The Admiralty immediately ordered a trial batch to be made and issued it to the sloops *Resolution* and *Adventure*, which were being fitted out for an expedition under Captain Cook 'for remote parts' – it was the perfect trial. Mr H. Jackson, a chemist, was put in charge. Early on, he was incredibly bullish: 'Being so much convinced of the Practicability as well as the Usefulness of the scheme . . . I am determined to attempt its introduction to the Public as a new branch of Commerce.'

The trial was a storming success. The beer was reconstituted and sampled as far away from Britain as it were possible to sail: around New Zealand, at Kamchatka, and off the west coast of America. Not only did the men seemingly agree to drink it, Cook proclaimed the concentrated beer to be one of the best anti-scorbutic sea medicines yet discovered, and credited it, along with the 'sourkrout' (salted cabbage) that was also being tested for the first time, for a near-total absence of scurvy on the voyage.

But one of Jackson's rivals had pushed the envelope even further. In 1778, Robert Thornton revealed beer that he had managed to reduce to a solid block that, when reconstituted, had 'the genuine pure flavour of the malt and hops' and was 'remarkably agreeable to the palate'. This seemed too good to be true: an end to scurvy, and beer that tasted as good when it was reconstituted anything up to three years after brewing. Apart from giving Britain the fittest, healthiest navy on the planet, it made English beer potentially a tradable commodity as efficient and desirable as tea, coffee, or anything else. In 1779 the Admiralty ordered all ships to be issued with beer concentrate, 'as a wholesome beverage at the rate of ¼lb of essence in lieu of a gallon of Beer, which will save the Beer, preserve the health of the Men and not increase the expense of victualling them'.

So at this point, you're thinking: well, where is it then? Instant beer – just add water! It's the answer to any reasonable man's dreams! Why don't we have it now? No more carrying heavy slabs home from Asda. You could take it camping and everything. You could even have beer in space! Not to mention making this whole fabled IPA voyage completely unnecessary.

The answer came two years later, when the Commissioners of Victualling grudgingly admitted to the Admiralty: 'We find from repeated trials that the said essence, though universally acknowledged to be extremely salutary for the purposes recommended [a remedy against scurvy] will not be accepted on board HM Ships but as a medicine.'

The officers may have loved the idea, but the men refused to drink it. They didn't know what this ... substance was, but it wasn't good English beer. And that's what they demanded. You ask for beer and get foul-tasting scurvy medicine instead? Where's that copy of *Mutiny for Dummies* got to?

The ration was scaled down to ¾lb a month and dispensed as a medicine. It came with instructions, almost apologetic in tone: 'The Essence is very pleasant to eat and very probably many modes of taking it may be thought on, which by way of change may be both agreeable and useful.'

So while malt essence briefly became the leading antidote to scurvy in the navy, the original idea of dehydrated beer died an embarrassed death. In 1798 the Admiralty discovered a far more efficient anti-scorbutic, and began using lemon or lime juice instead.

So that was scurvy sorted. But there was still the basic question: how can we keep beer at sea in good condition? Surely there must be a happy medium between tasty but short-lived beer, and undrinkable goo that lasted for ever?

Further compromises were attempted. On his South Sea travels, Cook tried arak on board before swiftly moving on to brewing 'spruce beer' with ingredients picked up at the Cape of Good Hope. A small amount of rum and brown sugar was added to the beer, which allegedly created a beverage that was refreshing and healthy. When stirred vigorously it tasted 'rather like champagne'. Yeah, right.

In 1797 a publication called *The Seaman's Guide: Shewing How to Live Comfortably at Sea* suggested that the daily ration of a gallon of porter be boiled down to two quarts of extra-strong beer. Sneakily, with the brew having been halved in volume, the sailor was then expected to treble rather than double the quantity to get his beer:

> To every quart of porter, add two quarts of water, moderately warm. To every quart of this mixture add a tablespoonful of brown sugar, or a wine glass of syrup, or

> molasses. Put the whole into a tub; beat and whisk it with
> a bundle of rods for at least half-an-hour; bottle and cork
> it and tie the corks down with strings ... in the East
> Indies, fermentation is so quick that what is made in the
> evening is ripe the next day.

If you think that sounds revolting, I think you're probably
right.

Beer was gradually replaced by wine and spirits, and the
general issue of beer to the Fleet ended altogether in 1831,
when the rum ration finally knocked it off its official perch.
Beer was still brewed in the naval victualling yards for shore
use, and as late as 1870 it was supplied to troop transports as
'medical comforts'. Even in the twentieth century, Terence
Lewin, Admiral of the Fleet from 1973 to 1982, recalls that
in his time as a midshipman in the Second World War, 'it
was clear from the eagerness with which they offered to swop
a tot of their rum for a bottle of my gunroom beer that not
all sailors considered rum to be the only desirable drink'.

Beer's troubled history at sea would make me more
appreciative of the beers available on each of my ships as the
choice of available brands dwindled and worsened. But more
than that, it validated the legend of India Pale Ale. Hodgson
had developed his beer at the same time as these experiments
were happening. That he spoke to East India Company
captains about it rather than the navy tells us a great deal
about the Company's stature. That it often reached India in
perfect condition tells us volumes about the quality of the
beer, and the sheer good fortune of the brewer who first
thought of sending it to the Indies. But as every IPA brewer
would discover, it wasn't always plain sailing.

CHAPTER TWENTY-THREE

LIFE ON THE FLAT SILVER DISC

We breakfasted at eight as the sun rose over the sea. I loved this about Tenerife – they'd even set the clocks a little differently than the rest of Europe so that the sun rose late – no holidaymakers were interested in the early morning – and set late, allowing slow, golden evenings that seemed to last twice as long as they should.

After breakfast Val briefed us on the basics of ship safety, and gave us our first lesson on how to be sailors. It begins and ends with rope. Just as trainee chefs might spend six months making nothing but stock, so trainee sailors start with learning how to coil and belay rope. Not that I was complaining – if you put your fingers in the wrong place when a sail is being raised or taken away, you can easily lose them. We moved on from coiling to a few simple knots, and I was impressed that I still remembered from Scouts twenty-five years ago how to tie a bowline incorrectly.

We were due to sail at midday, and at eleven the anticipation began to build. Those of us who had just come aboard retreated into corners and huddled over our mobile phones, saying goodbye and promising to call as soon as we sighted land again.

The gangplank was raised and lines were cast off. The ship's horn blared three times, and we used the engine to power away from the dockside, past the huge catamaran ferry, which *Remus* could have sailed beneath without scuffing his/her paintwork, past the cruise-ship berths, where another vessel now stood in *Oceana*'s place, and out of the harbour, into the strait between Tenerife and Gran Canaria.

Frank Brookesmith was a crewman on the last working tall ships in the 1920s, after the steamers had taken over, when the only work the sailing ships could get was ferrying coal or guano. In his book *I Remember the Tall Ships*, he reveals a poetic heart that the romantic suspects lies within any sailor:

> 'Nothing I have ever experienced is more filled with promises than that curtsey of a ship leaving port to the first of the deep sea rollers. Then, if at no other time, a ship takes on personality. She greets the sea with a buoyant gladness and she shakes from her the bewilderment of the land, and she spreads her wings to the wild wind and the ever distant horizon.'

There was no wild wind, no deep-sea rollers to greet us, thanks to the bulk of El Teide, Tenerife's highest peak, at our backs. There was the gentlest of swells, a rhythmic, stuttering hiss as we cut through the slight waves and created a wake. But while our departure lacked the drama of Brookesmith's maiden voyage, it was good enough for me. I searched my mind for the perfect word to describe the colour of the sea, and I'm afraid the only word that fitted the bill was 'blue'. But to borrow from Billy Connolly, this wasn't just blue; after so much variation in the sea on *Oceana*, this was BLUE!!!! If you scooped out a glass of it, it would be opaque, like watery blue paint; luminous, solid, infinite, neon blue, scattered with twinkling fairy lights where the sun caught the ripples.

There were around fifteen permanent crew and twenty-five passengers or 'trainee crew' on *Europa*. We trainees were expected to play our part in the running of the ship, and were divided into three watches: red, white and blue, the colours of the Dutch flag that flew from the mast alongside the stars of Europe. Our duties would be light compared with those of the permanent crew, but nevertheless essential – or so Val insisted.

I was on red watch and we were first up on the rota. Frank Brookesmith described how on watch his crew 'took our tricks at the kicking wheel or we dreamed of home and beauty on lookout at the focsle head'. Our duties weren't described quite like that, but broadly they were the same. My first shift was bow lookout, and I realized immediately that I was going to love being 'the eyes and ears of the ship'. 'The area between nine o'clock and three o'clock is your responsibility,' said Val. Well, mine and the ultra-high-tech radar equipment's, I thought. The watch person's duty was to look for any other shipping, and for debris such as containers that may have fallen overboard, which, to be fair, may not be picked up by radar. When I realized that the people on the bridge couldn't see anything in front of the ship, it did make sense. We were also to keep our eyes and ears peeled for dolphins, whales, or anything else the rest of the crew might be interested in seeing. There was an intercom to report back to the bridge, and I was sure the urge to press it and yell 'Iceberg, dead ahead!' would recede quickly. Sure enough, it did – as soon as I remembered that *Europa* spends a lot of her time in the Antarctic.

At 2 p.m. three bells rang, announcing the captain's daily address to the ship. We gathered on the main deck, and Klaas emerged from his cabin. 'Good afternoon. We are running south-south-west, three or four miles off Tenerife on our starboard side, that is, our right-hand side,' he smiled at the novices, 'and Gran Canaria a little further away off to port. The island, these peaks, they mess up the weather. We need to power out from between them, hopefully by early this evening, and at that point we should catch the north-east trade winds. We're then heading for the Cape Verde islands, where we should be able to go ashore for a while. It's 840 miles away, so about six, seven days.'

'What's the long-range weather forecast?' asked Padraig.

Klaas looked at him nonplussed. 'North-east trade winds,' he repeated, in a voice that made it clear that, when you're on a tall ship at sea, wind is the only weather worth mentioning.

After the briefing we were shown how to put on harnesses and we went aloft, into the rigging. On the big ships Frank Brookesmith sailed, teams of men would hang from the spars punching and wrestling solid, wind-filled wet sails till their knuckles bled. We had it relatively easy. On a ship of *Europa*'s size, the sails can be set and taken away down on deck. But once sails are away, they need to be properly tied so the wind doesn't catch them again. And that means going aloft.

The first thirty feet or so was fairly straightforward, like climbing a ladder. Then you reached the level of the first yard, from which the main sail hung. Here was a small platform, and climbing up from the deck, you were underneath it. For about three feet, you had to climb out, hanging underneath the platform before hauling yourself over the lip and on to it. Once you'd made it, then you could clip on your safety harness, so you didn't fall to your death.

'What do you do about safety on the way up to the platform?' someone asked.

'Um, don't fall off,' replied Val.

'Can you imagine doing this on a British ship, with health and safety?' said Padraig standing next to me. 'They'd be stapling you to the mast.'

I took my turn. I'd been looking forward to this. I scrambled up the rigging easily, but when I reached the underhang to the platform, I realized there was a point where I had to let my arms take my whole weight. My right arm was still some way from recovering from the ordeal on *Remus*, still giving a twinge if I lifted anything with it. I didn't trust my limb, worried that it had its own agenda, and motives that I couldn't know. I made it on to the platform, clipped on and refused to go out along the yards like the others, or go any higher. It was great up there. I have no fear of heights. But if my arm went, the chances of an unpleasant death were pretty high. I descended gratefully, promising myself I'd get up into the rigging later in the voyage, when my arm had had more time to heal. It was a promise I never kept.

Gran Canaria was a pale silhouette, but as is always the case when you leave anywhere, Tenerife was enjoying the most perfect day I'd seen. The merest smudge of cloud blurred the mountains, and as we pulled away further we saw this was only hanging around the shoulders of El Teide in a single air-brushed sweep, leaving the 10,000-foot peak clearly visible for the first time since I arrived. Out here, looking back from twenty or thirty miles away, it was obvious how it would interfere with the weather. The warm sea wind hits it and cools as it rises. As the afternoon wore on the mountain's faint gauze shroud became a sheet, a blanket, then a nice thick duvet of cloud as we continued to crawl away, denied the wind.

After five hours at sea we cruised past El Médano, now an indistinct smudge beneath the dark mound of Mount Roja. In the distance, planes full of tourists were tiny white midges descending under the peaks towards the airport.

It's sixty kilometres from Santa Cruz to El Médano. It took me an hour to get up there in the taxi yesterday with Alberto, five hours to come back to where I had started. So what? I challenged myself. But it was very difficult to overcome a nagging feeling that we should be going faster, even though there was nothing to go fast for. Surely that was the point? But I was struggling to take my mental foot off the gas. The feeling that I should be doing something – anything – to try to replace my dank, empty beer barrel with a foaming full one refused to leave me.

We reached the southern tip of Tenerife. The island scrolled out to starboard and behind us, and finally began to diminish. As the sun sank and cooking smells wafted up from the galley, a group of dolphins broke the surface, about seventy yards off to port, a rollercoaster of arced backs and dorsal fins swimming in the same direction as us, but coming no closer.

Later, out into the open sea, the other English Peter, a grizzled but remarkably fit man in his late sixties, was on bow watch with his wife, Janet. He spotted a whale's tail rise and then submerge. While this was obviously amazing for him, it meant the rest of us were just too late: whales come up to the surface for about ten minutes to get some air, and that tail fin means they're going back down, for anything up to forty minutes, to resurface who knows where. As we scoured the silvering surface, a shoal of large fish, probably tuna, broke and began jumping, really leaping from the water. 'They're being chased,' said Peter, clearly keen to establish his credentials as the sea-life expert. 'Being herded. By dolphins probably.' It seemed the whole sea was suddenly alive.

And now here came another school of dolphins. They broke the surface much closer than the last lot, and began heading directly for the ship. They came up under the bow and spent about half a minute jumping and diving alongside us, or just under us, before falling away again one by one. I stood at the bow, grinning, staring at the water for ten minutes after the last one had peeled away.

It had been an extraordinarily eventful hour, and it was crowned by the first in a series of stunning sunsets that sent people scurrying for their cameras. As the sun dipped below the horizon it threw out thick orange shafts, three or four searchlight beams stretching back up into the sky.

I scribbled in my notebook.

'Don't forget to write about the whale,' said a voice behind me. Anton, the tall loner from Luxembourg who was one of my cabin mates, was grinning at me in a satisfied manner.

'Oh, yes, the whale. Thanks for reminding me, I'd have let that slip my mind.' I suspected this might become tiresome.

We took our watch again at eight o'clock. During my first stint on the wheel, attempting to stick to the bearing given to us by Klaas, the stars began to appear. I'd been looking forward to this possibly more than any other part of the voyage, and I wasn't disappointed. The stars came out, and there was no light pollution at all, and I thought, Hurray, just as I expected. I haven't seen stars like this since camping in the Scouts. And then they just kept coming, more and more, until it was impossible to make out individual constellations because the clusters of light were so thick. I thought I'd seen the Milky Way before, and now I realized I hadn't, not properly. Now, I saw that the Milky Way gets its name because when it's fully visible, it's like someone has airbrushed a thick, creamy path, straight and wide down the middle of the sky. Behind the ship, the sea lit up with phosphorescence from the plankton, exploding like submerged camera flashes.

When I emerged from my cabin the next morning the Canary Islands had finally vanished, and we were alone. The horizon seemed to be trying to pretend they had never been there at all. 'Islands, mate? What, big rocky things up to 10,000 feet in height with loads of people and buildings on 'em? Nah, sorry. Never heard of 'em.' Now, it no longer mattered how far or how fast we went: we were always smack in the middle of a flat silver disc. There was no way of judging our speed, and, finally, with no alternative, I began to relax into the rhythms of the ship. We were fully under sail, the engine off, and we were really rolling. I had to think carefully about walking – it was impossible to move anywhere in a straight line.

The configuration of sails on a tall ship depends entirely on the strength and angle of the wind. On that morning – the least autumnal 1 October I'd ever witnessed – there was a gentle breeze blowing directly from our stern, and every sail was out. And then, we bettered that.

Poles were hoisted and strapped on the ends of the yards

on the foremast, stretching them to an implausible degree. And on these extra yards we hoisted an extra set of sails, the stunsails. It felt almost like cheating, but as the wind filled them and created a solid wall of canvas at the front of the ship, it looked magnificent – as good as anything in any library picture of any sailing ship I had ever seen. As the ship rolled, the ends of the yards were mere inches from the waves, never quite making contact. *Europa*'s stately pace, and the simple pageantry of the stunsails, made me understand why those who have known her for a while call her the 'Grand Old Lady'. I saw Klaas gazing at the stunsails with what could only be love, and realized this event was something special, even for an old sea dog.

The watch system was four hours on, eight hours off, except between noon and 4 p.m., which was split into two two-hour watches, meaning everyone moved around one slot each day. The watches, combined with the rules of sunrise and sunset and the moods of the wind, meant the days blurred into a dreamy routine. I felt foolish remembering my Captain Bligh-lite discipline on *Remus*, thinking I was being organized. This was how a proper ship ran. We may have been moving at jogging speed, but we were moving relentlessly, as only ships can.

Dog watch quickly became my favourite shift. I was shaken awake in my bunk at 11.45 p.m. Fifteen minutes later, armed with a cup of black tea, I'd climb the steps to the foredeck and take my place at a seat on lookout. For the first few nights, I donned long trousers and a sweater for this duty, but as we pushed south this became needless. With nothing to see save the lights of a distant container ship every other night, I spent most of the time looking at the sky. The moon rose around 3 a.m., so for the first few hours the Milky Way remained fully visible. Every few minutes, if I didn't blink, there'd be a shooting star. Eventually, after a few nights, I learned to stop scanning the heavens for movement, for action, and simply gazed at the sky for its own sake, drinking it in.

Above the sound of the bow ploughing through the hissing waves rose the occasional series of skipping plops as a shoal of flying fish skittered out of our way. Sometimes the dolphins visited again. In *Moby-Dick* the narrator, Ishmael, writes of dolphins: 'Their appearance is generally hailed with delight by the mariner. Full of fine spirits, they invariably come from the breezy billows to windward. They are the lads that always live before the wind. They are accounted a lucky omen. If you yourself can withstand three cheers at beholding these vivacious fish, then heaven help ye; the spirit of godly game-someness is not in ye.'

As soon as they appeared we'd all feel a yearning, a communion with them, desperately wanting them to stay. And the most amazing part of it was that it seemed mutual – they genuinely liked frolicking with us, showering in the spray where *Europa*'s bow cut the waves.

Half an hour's rest in the deckhouse and it would be time for a stint on the wheel. The team we relieved told us the course, and we'd take over. Like bow watch we always did this in pairs, which I think was more a matter of psychological than physical expediency. At night, in the middle of the ocean, your imagination can easily have its own little party. The sea or the rigging would make random noises – a sigh or an exclamation – that could be disconcerting if you were on your own.

I did most of my shifts with Slovenian Denis. The whole crew agreed that Denis was really, really nice, and he was. But he didn't say much, which gave him a dark, brooding presence. He was very tall and well-built, powerful and languorous, like a big cat with a number-one crop. He told us he was a 'police judge' at home, though a couple of my new friends decided he was an Eastern European spy. When we asked what laws he upheld, he replied cheerfully that he made them up as he went along. When he smiled and laughed – which he did a lot, to be fair – it was the laugh of someone who finds you amusing, but might choose to snap your neck like a twig if you ceased to be. Neither Denis nor I minded being together, out there on the wheel in the dark. I think we both appreciated the peace. Apart from the under-lit compass, the only light was from the wheel-house, a hub of modern technology with our position, speed and course, a scarlet line tracing across a black screen.

After dog watch I slept through breakfast, dozing to the sound of the waves rinsing the hull, inches from my head, until the day's heat penetrated and my head began to burn where it touched the pillow. After a cool shower I'd head out on deck, and find the sun high in the sky.

There was always somebody working: Erik the barman would be sanding and varnishing the wheelhouse. With his gentle seriousness and greying surf-bum hair, he looked like a hippie undertaker. Combining Zen calm and gravitas, he made the perfect philosopher–barman, and sanded and varnished every minute the bar was closed. Dieter would be in his harness somewhere above, sanding blocks. Someone else would be repairing the sealant between the planks on deck. Frank Brookesmith reckoned that 'half a voyage is spent in making a ship ready for sea and the other half in getting her ready for port', and this seemed as true on *Europa* as it was when he sailed the guano ships.

When there was no work there would be lectures on sails and sailing, man-overboard procedures, the locations of ropes. We were listed on the ship's manifest as trainee crew, and that's how it felt most of the time. Some joined in as fully as possible, desperately wishing they were full-time crew. Others chipped in between reading and sunbathing. Only one or two did nothing at all. Sleepy Hans, a hamster of a man with a surprisingly furious voice, took up permanent residence in a hammock on the foredeck, and we had to climb around him to get to our seats for bow watch. And American Debbie spent almost the entire voyage too seasick to move. But for most of us, this was not a holiday. It was wonderful, but in every possible meaning of the phrase this was no pleasure cruise.

I had to recalibrate sights and sounds quickly. I'd see someone sending a text message, then realize they couldn't be, that they must be looking at a compass. I'd hear a mobile phone ringing, and it would be a random noise from the rigging or the hull. I did overcompensate, it has to be said – at one point I heard a sea lion honking from the foredeck, before realizing it was the noise of a vacuum toilet flushing.

The highlights of my mornings were my encounters with Cosmic Joe. Joe was my other roomie along with the mysterious Anton; a Polish walnut aged somewhere – it could have been anywhere – between 50 and 108, who had lived in Notting Hill for decades but still spoke like someone whose relationship with spoken English had yet to get past the polite introductions. Rumour had it that he was a very successful graphic designer, that he'd run his own company in London for years. On the ship, he wore nothing but a pair of tight red running shorts, a permanent beatific, blissed-out grin, and occasionally a vest. For night watches he had a fabulous gold quilted jacket that was about as different from something you'd find in a camping shop as it's possible to get. It was the kind of coat Shirley Bassey might have worn if she were obliged to take the helm of a ship at 3 a.m. having woken up ten minutes before.

Joe's strategy for getting through life was simply to ask random people lots of questions about whatever was bothering him. He'd ask Erik where someone was, or ask me when the ship's clock was due to change, or Padraig what was for dinner. Invariably, we would direct him to someone else and he always seemed to get to the right place in the end.

By the fifth day, I'd obviously established myself as the
ship's reader, plundering the shelves in the deckhouse for
useful material or the odd thriller for the middle of the night,
when I was too spaced to concentrate on anything else. Joe
approached me, and our first-ever conversation went like this:

'Pete, do you know if there are any books on the fiction of
science?'

'I'm not sure, Joe, I haven't looked at all the shelves yet.'

'You know the kind of thing. Stories about when you go
with a woman, and you do not know if the woman is a robot
or if she is real.'

It was out before I could stop it. 'I've known some women
like that in real life, Joe. But I'll keep an eye out for you.'

'Yes.'

And he was off to ask someone else about the weather.

Eventually we got the hang of the helm, learned to read
both rudder and compass together, homing in on the right
course by feel and instinct: the rudder slightly to port to
compensate for the wind hitting from starboard, a variation
of a couple of degrees, a slight turn of the wheel by a spoke
or so – and that was it, you were steering a tall ship, fighting
the urge to sing like Jack Sparrow. It was perfect. And then
Klaas would walk towards you and the whole delicate balance
of wind, sail, wave and current you held in your hands like a
miracle would sproing and make cuckoo-clock noises and the
compass would spout steam and start spinning crazily like in
those made-for-TV films about the Bermuda Triangle.

The afternoons were lazy, with reading broken up by a
spot of sail-mending or the occasional pulling on ropes when
Klaas decided a sail had to be set or taken away. We searched
for the small patches of sunlight where the deck wasn't
completely shaded. I tanned quickly. I'd bought some big
outward-bound sunglasses that kept out the glare from the
sea, and when I took them off I looked like a negative image

of Bono – dark face, with big, pasty white goggles. Dieter invariably lay prone, eyes closed, iPod in, arms aloft. *Air-conducting.*

Around five in the afternoon, Erik would put down his varnish brush and lower a stereo speaker on to the deck from the deckhouse-bar window. Gentle Latin grooves filled the main deck, the bar opened and plates of anchovies, meat and cheese appeared. Two beers in, there'd be another sunset sparking the western sky alight for us, and then it was time for dinner. And as darkness completed its takeover of the sky, it was watch time again. The schedule had moved around, and if it were dog watch the night before, it was first watch tonight, eight till midnight followed by a full night's sleep. As the week wore on and the weather got hotter, we'd drag our mattresses out from the stifling heat below decks and sleep on the sloop deck, under the stars, and that was another day done.

In the middle of all the stress of my journey, with so much more hassle to come and the prospect of failing in my quest to take a barrel of beer to India by sea, I was enjoying the first of the happiest three weeks of my life.

CHAPTER TWENTY-FOUR

PALE ALE'S PASSAGE TO INDIA

The skeletal masts loomed high over meek, bowed terraces. Where the streets ran directly towards the river, the hulking hulls of the ships lurked at the end like overgrown delinquents. Closer in, you could make out sailors climbing in the rigging, dodging the flapping pennants and St George flags. These were the East Indiamen, each one a floating parcel of England, possessing both the finery and brutality this entailed. As John Keay describes: 'From the stern they looked like quaint tea shoppes, leaded Tudor casements, maybe a lace-curtained bow window to the roundhouse, the most sought-after accommodation on board. But move round to the side and quaintness turned to menace: rows of cannons gleamed.'

At this point in the journey, all was optimism and elegance. According to one traveller, the East Indiaman at rest was one of the most compelling sights in London, rivalled only by that of 'St Paul's great church', a little further back from the riverbank.

Small craft buzzed around the hulks like birds around hippos, loading cargo and provisions. The whole focus of the enterprise may have been on the riches that were being stripped from India and brought home, but that doesn't mean there was nothing on the way out. Bullion, 'in the form of Spanish dollars', was the main export, to pay for the goods being acquired. After that came slightly less precious forms of metal – iron was the only ore that had been discovered in India, so imported copper was in heavy demand. Also, by the second half of the Company's life, it had such might in India that it managed to do by force what it had failed to do in open commerce during its first century: after strenuous complaints that the importation of beautiful fabrics and garments from India was damaging the domestic textiles industry, British textiles and clothing became one of the most exported articles back to India.

After bullion, metal and fabric, the greatest item of export was booze.

In the early decades of the nineteenth-century beer accounted for around a fifth of total drinks imports into Bengal. Madeira, claret, port and spirits were all welcomed by a thirsty populace, and most of it came via British traders. As the decades passed, beer gradually increased, while Madeira in particular fell away, a symbol of an earlier, more hedonistic age. But when Allsopp's ale made its maiden voyage, beer was a luxury, as expensive as good wine, bulky and difficult to transport on a journey it may not even survive.

Being extremely heavy, beer was stowed in the lowest decks of the ship as ballast. It was certainly useful in this role, but there wasn't really anywhere else for it to go. The East Indiaman was cargo ship, passenger ship, troop ship and warship rolled into one brooding, stunningly beautiful whole. As well as the bullion, metal and textiles for India, the ships were crammed with supplies for the journey. A typical voyage might carry a dozen passengers, a few officer cadets and a couple of regiments of soldiers. As the Company's Indian territories increased, so did the number of clerks, lawyers and administrators required, and by the end of the eighteenth century Company ships were carrying a thousand passengers a year. With a full complement of crew, there could be anywhere between a 150 and 400 souls on board, all needing to be fed and watered for between three and six months. Live cows, goats and poultry were caged on deck – they wouldn't last long, but they'd make the first few weeks' eating reasonably pleasant, delaying the inevitable diet of dried beef and biscuit.

The captain was free to supplement his private trade income by charging passengers steep fees for cabin accommodation: £250 for a general, £110 for a subaltern or Company writer. Special accommodation for ladies might cost £500 or more for each berth. These private berths were spaces in the 'tween-decks, screened off with canvas and furnished at the passenger's expense. The only place anywhere near comfortable was the captain's cabin, where passengers longed to be invited to dine.

For these passengers, bound for a mysterious land that was rumoured to be a passport to the lifestyle of the nobility, this was the journey of a lifetime. William Hickey is merely the most eloquent and entertaining of dozens who recorded their impressions of the voyage for friends and family back home, then thought, 'You know what? This reads really well. I bet people would pay good money to read this. Didn't you once tell me you had a mate in publishing?'

One such passenger was Fanny Parkes. Her work is still in print today, not because she's as rollickingly entertaining as Hickey (she isn't), but because she sees the world with wide-eyed wonder and enthusiasm, and communicates this as clearly and engagingly as the best modern-day travel writer. By the time she arrived in Calcutta the English PR war against Indian culture was in full swing. Parkes found the older Anglo-Indians happily enchanted by an ancient graceful, beautiful culture, while her own generation took a much harder line. With a stubbornness you soon start to love her for, as the British establishment went one way – towards a forcible Westernization of India – she went the other, becoming fluent in Urdu, making friends with Indian noblewomen and learning how to play the sitar.

Parkes sailed for India on the *Marchioness of Ely* in June

1822, about six months before the *Bencoolen* set off from
Liverpool with the first consignment of Allsopp's Pale Ale,
with her husband – a minor civil servant – and four troops of
His Majesty's 16th Lancers.

Departure was often an uncertain affair: cargo-laden ships
slipped out of the Thames only to hang around in the English
Channel, waiting for the wind. They would then sail in packs
of up to twenty, parading down the Channel in double line,
flags and bunting streaming above the three masts of full sails,
an escort of Royal Navy frigates around them.

Passengers usually joined their ship at Gravesend, twenty
miles down the Thames, a few days before she sailed. Parkes
joined the *Ely* in the South Downs, several days after she
left London, and was lucky to get away reasonably quickly.
On one voyage Hickey was on his ship as she sailed down
the Thames, got bored, went ashore, rode south, enjoyed a
slap-up dinner and rejoined her as she crept along the south
coast. On his second voyage he was stuck in Portsmouth for
three weeks, waiting for the wind.

As we already know, the Canaries and Madeira were
regular stops (which Fanny Parkes found 'most charming').
Then, it was out into the wide ocean, where Fanny soon
adapted to life on board: 'The stern cabin, twelve feet by ten,
at first sight appeared most extremely inconvenient; but now
it seemed to have enlarged itself, and we were more comfortable. Still sleep would scarcely visit me, until a swinging cot
was procured. From that time I slept calmly and quietly,
whatever pranks the old *Ely* might choose to play.'

Out at sea, the working day for a typical crewman would
begin at 5 a.m., when the 'fresh' water was served out. It
seems that this was one aspect of the voyage that never
improved, with Parkes commenting, 'The ship water [is] very
black, and it smells vilely. I knew not before the value of good
water.'

At six-thirty the decks were swabbed, and by seven-thirty

all hammocks had been stowed. Breakfast at eight was burgoo
(a thick oatmeal gruel), and in the first couple of weeks maybe
a beer. And then there was the infamous ship's biscuit. Hickey
found this 'uncommonly bad and flinty', and difficult to break
with his teeth. On his first voyage one man accepted a wager
to try to eat one biscuit in four minutes, without the aid of
liquid. He almost choked to death twice 'by which he lost
several seconds', but made it with four seconds to spare. The
grog ration was served at midday, and later salt beef, salt
pork and pease pudding rounded out the diet.

Life was always busy for the crew. Divided into two
watches with four hours on, four hours off, sails had to be set
and taken away, ballast might require shifting, sails had to be
repaired and leaks stopped. On Wednesdays and Saturdays
the 'tween decks were cleaned with sand and stone.

Passengers tended to be quiet until the ship had cleared
the Bay of Biscay and the inevitable seasickness had receded.
Once they found their sea legs, they amused themselves with
boxing, chess, games of pitch and toss, gambling and drinking. At the captain's table, rations were significantly better
than for the rest of the crew. Things would kick off with a
three-course lunch, after which the ladies would retire while
the gentlemen enjoyed the port decanter being passed around
the table, how many times depending on the humour of the
captain. Anne Barnard, a passenger on board the *Sir Edward
Hughes* in 1797, noted that the menu for dinner for sixteen
people included pea soup, roast legs of mutton, hogs' pud-
dings, two fowls, two hams, two ducks, corned round of beef,
mutton pies, pork pies, mutton chops, stewed cabbage and
potatoes, followed by 'an enormous plum pudding and
washed down with porter, spruce beer, port wine, gin, sherry,
rum etc.'. A band would often play while they drank loyal
toasts, and the claret went around briskly. Once the plates
were cleared away, the serious drinkers – including Hickey
whenever he was at sea – gathered in the roundhouse and

drank burgundy and champagne, singing songs until one in the morning.

But these were special occasions – every Saturday on Hickey's voyage – and most nights saw a simple dinner of soup, cheese and cold meats, just one round from the decanter, and candles out by 10 p.m. 'for the Preservation of good Order on board the Company's ships'.

Most accounts of India Pale Ale's journey wave vaguely at the Atlantic and claim the East Indiamen sailed down the African coast. If you consult your mental map of the world, there's no reason to believe otherwise. But sail the Atlantic, and you start to see things differently. For one thing, the map of the world we think we know is entirely wrong. Get around the western cape of Africa, and Brazil is almost due south rather than the thousands of miles west we imagine it to be. Secondly, as I was beginning to realize under Klaas's laid-back tuition, sailing is about three things: wind, wind and wind.

Out at sea, weather systems tend to be fairly consistent over time. You don't get to a particular latitude and think, 'Ooh, it's not normally this calm round here.' The winds in the Atlantic are stable, and they mean that you'd have to be extraordinarily lucky to sail down the coast of western Africa, particularly as the South African current pushes north. The North Atlantic trade winds[65] blow you towards Cape Verde, as I was about to discover. From there, they take you into the Doldrums, the area of fitful pressure and moody waters that could wreak disaster on the voyage of an East Indiaman. You could be racing along, hit this weather system a couple of hundred miles north of the equator, and stop as surely as if

---

65. Trade winds got their name from the medieval expression 'to blow trade', which meant to blow true, or straight. But since the eighteenth century most mariners have assumed they were so-called because of their importance to seaborne trade.

you'd hit a wall. Dead calm, stifling heat and a sea like glass, with not a puff of wind, could ground you here for weeks, even months. It moved Fanny Parkes to quote 'The Rime of the Ancient Mariner':

> Day after day, day after day,
>   We stuck, nor breath nor motion;
> As idle as a painted ship
>   Upon a painted ocean.

And because no wind doesn't mean no ocean swell, Fanny Parkes's ship was 'rolling and pitching most unmercifully . . . as if she would send her masts overboard', all in stifling heat with no comforting sea breeze.

When the ship was becalmed, it was time for another popular pastime of the English gentleman: slaughtering any living thing that crossed his path. Fanny Parkes describes how in one calm spell, the captain allowed 'the jolly boat' to be lowered, and her husband and some of the lancers went out shooting:

> This day, the 28th of August, was the commencement of the shooting season; game was in abundance, and they sought it over the long heavy swell of the glasslike and unrippled sea. The sportsmen returned with forty head of game: in this number was an albatross, measuring nine feet from the tip of one wing to that of the other; a Cape hen, a sea-swallow, with several pintado and other birds.

All this time, the beer sat in the hold, slowly changing. It's common sense to assume that the lowest holds would be the coolest places on the ship, but my experience on *Europa* was suggesting otherwise. Down below, the still air was slow-baked by the heat of the equatorial waters. And apart from the temperature's peaks, there was also the fact that it was steadily fluctuating. For the first few weeks the surface water temperature would have averaged around eleven degrees. At

the equator it got as high as thirty. Around the Cape of Good
Hope it would drop back to around twenty, then start to
climb again across the Indian Ocean, back over the equator
for a second time, exceeding thirty once more.

This would have had a huge effect on any yeast left in the
beer. Above twenty-two degrees ale yeasts start to misbehave,
leading to the formation of esters (acidic compounds) and
undesirable flavours. At the bottom end of the scale the yeast
would be too sluggish to do anything at all. And as I'd
discovered on Tenerife, high temperatures can simply make
the beer explode. Casks were built to very strict specifications
to withstand the pressure of the journey, and had vent plugs
made of red oak, 'almost as porous as cane' to allow gas to
escape. But on an average shipment, between 5 and 10 per
cent of casks would explode. Years later, Horace Brown,
Worthington's famous chemist, would comment: 'The system
was only commercially possible with high gross profits to
carry such risks and all other expenses incidental to it ...
under such conditions great financial losses occurred at times
through spoiled beer.'

All this led William Tizard, a Professor of Brewing in
London, to give a piece of advice about the keeping of beers
for export in his 1843 book *The Theory and Practice of Brewing*
that may come as a shock to the present-day real-ale fan,
but makes perfect sense to a writer who has spent a night
mopping up the residue of twenty litres of beer from a
stinking floor: 'It is imperatively necessary that all extraneous
vegetable matter which forms the yeast, lees &c. be removed;
because the agitation during the voyage would otherwise
produce extreme fretting, leakages and premature acidity.'

OK thanks, Bill, for telling us now.[66] But this was crucial:
in the UK we view cask-conditioned beers – where live yeast

---

66. OK, I suppose he told us almost 170 years ago. But I really wish I'd
read the book sometime between 1843 and September 2007.

is still in the cask, undergoing a slow, secondary fermentation – as our traditional beer style. And so it is. But true IPA – one of the most beloved beer styles of the hardcore real-ale fan – was not technically real ale. And that meant that Steve Wellington and I had packaged our beer wrong, following a tradition that wasn't even invented in IPA's heyday. There may have been some residual yeast if filtration techniques weren't up to scratch, but the intention was to get it all out. James Herbert, a Burton brewer and author of *The Art of Brewing India Pale Ale and Export Ale* in 1865, makes it very clear that a secondary fermentation is undesirable, something caused by 'bad management and inferior materials' that gives the beer 'a disagreeable flavour to the palate . . . and there is no remedy for the evil after it once takes place'. As well as filtration, the long heat during months in the hold may not have been enough to pasteurize the beer in the strictest sense (pasteurization starts at 60 degrees Celsius), but if you've ever slow-cooked at much lower temperatures you know you can get the same effect as higher heat over time. IPA was more similar to a modern filtered and pasteurized beer than it was to traditional cask ale.

With no wind the equatorial current carried ships west, so that when they emerged from the Doldrums they were not far from the South American coast. And if there were good wind, the trade winds blew you this way too. Whenever I'd told people about my journey, my stop-off in Brazil had confused them. Wasn't it in the wrong direction if I were trying to get to India? Was I going around the wrong Cape? At first I said there was simply no choice – I had to cross the Atlantic twice, or not go at all. But as I learned more about the history of my voyage, I realized I was following the Company's route more accurately than if I'd succeeded in going direct to Cape Town. The reason Brazilians speak Portuguese while the rest of South America speaks Spanish is that the mentalist Vasco da Gama's countrymen stumbled across the country while trying to sail to India., not west like Columbus, but simply trying to get round Africa. Portuguese traders were responsible for introducing chilli peppers to India, having discovered them in Brazil.

So India-bound ships would often call in at Rio to take on fresh water, fruit and vegetables, particularly if they'd had a bad run through the Doldrums. Clive of India himself ended up here for a few weeks on his third and final voyage to Bengal in 1764, confined to port by savage storms. Typically Clive, he idly amused himself by working out how he would take the city with a single battalion of men inside twenty-four hours.

And now I was following in Clive's wake, in da Gama's wake, in Allsopp's wake. My journey had turned out to be more historically accurate than I could have imagined.

CHAPTER TWENTY-FIVE

CAPE VERDE

Cape Verde is made of compacted cigarette ash, is covered in flies and the beer tastes of wet cardboard.

That's all you need to know.

No, really.

OK, I'll expand a bit.

In weeks to come, the thought of a mere six days out of sight of land would seem like nothing but a brief hop. But at the end of that first week on board, the excitement of seeing land again was enormous. We all loved being on *Europa*, but the idea of some other stimulus – different people, different food, something new to look at and hear and smell – made us giddy.

There's always a faint haze where the sea meets the sky, even on the clearest days, and land doesn't just peek gradually up from under the horizon. It suggests itself as a grey outline, a rubbed-out sketch, and you dismiss it as cloud if you notice it at all. Then you look again minutes later and it's there, a silvery-olive hulking lump full of possibility.

There were two islands rearing up before us, and as they gradually took on definition, developing like a photograph, revealing cliffs and rocks and beaches, our mobile phones came out of hibernation. I was pleasantly surprised by how few people rushed to grab them when they realized we had a signal. I was one of two or three who did, desperate to call Liz; anxious to see if there had been any progress in getting a replacement barrel shipped to Rio.

There hadn't. Rudgie was optimistic, and had an entire

team of people at Coors – one of the largest brewers on the planet – working on it. It was all going to be fine, they assured me. They just hadn't quite figured it out yet.

We sailed between the islands, ragged and volcanic in close-up. We were making for São Vicente, the biggest island. Ruined, biblical houses perched high on its grey cliffs, flat, square and monochrome with windows like eyeless sockets. Eventually the cliffs and houses gave way to Mindelo, a wide harbour dotted with rusting container ships and Second World War motor-torpedo boats dragged from retirement to serve as coastguard vessels. Incongruous beside these, a few luxury yachts dawdled nonchalantly.

We moored at the very end of the concrete harbour wall, as if for a quick getaway. Ten minutes later, every surface on the ship was covered in a fine grey dust, which must have been volcanic in origin, but looked and felt exactly like cigarette ash. Sheltered from the sea breeze, the air was suddenly hot and sticky. Workers rushed to help with ropes and then stood staring at the masts. It seemed to take an inordinate number of customs officials to clear us, and once everything was in order they hung on, as unwilling to leave as Alberto had been on Tenerife. This is what it must feel like to be going out with a supermodel, I thought – men staring at her wherever you go. I was proud that I was with her, accepting that I was invisible to others who desired her.

We went for beers, to a succession of bars that we soon drank dry. The town seemed only just awake on this, a Saturday night, and the waitresses seemed surprised to see us. Different groups – split mainly down watch lines – criss-crossed the town before converging on the inappropriately named yacht club, the only place with a pulse.

Inside, Dieter, wankered off his tits after two small beers, decided it was time to demolish the myth about Germans and their sense of humour once and for all. He approached Margriet and me and announced, 'A man fell down a flight

of stairs. He turned to his wife and said, "I've lost my hat."
She said, "Oh, I thought you said you had lost your head." '

We waited a few seconds to see if there were any more of
the joke, but that was it. I thought I must have misheard, or
missed some of it, but a few days later somebody else told me
they'd had the same joke inflicted on them too, and that was
definitely how it went.

After we'd drunk the yacht club and therefore the whole
town dry, we returned to the ship. With no watch necessary,
most of us went to bed for a full, uninterrupted night's sleep.
Or so I thought.

I woke up at 4 a.m. unable to breathe. The air was so hot
it felt like the oxygen had been burned out of it. I staggered
up to the deck and collapsed on to a seat in the deckhouse,
where I was a little cooler. I dozed, and woke up three hours
later covered in flies.

By the time we were ready to cast off at midday, a thirty-
knot wind was barrelling between the islands, sending
breakers crashing over the sides of a battered old cargo
freighter anchored out in the strait. When we were clear of
the protective harbour wall *Europa* heeled over, every sinew
straining, singing in the wind. This time getting the sails up
was a serious, tightly controlled operation. While I was
working on the main deck, a wave hit me square in the back
and swept me across the planks, and we all realized we
needed to be careful.

In front of the wind we shot forward, peaking at eleven
knots, only two below *Europa*'s maximum recorded speed.
Our jet-propelled escape seemed to lift the spirits of everyone
on board. We all felt dirty. Everyone wanted a shower.

The air was thick and steamy, and as the sun sank the
light took on a solid hue. The whole sky turned a pale, golden
straw colour, and the sea was purple.

It took a week to get rid of the flies from the deckhouse.

CHAPTER TWENTY-SIX

IN THE DOLDRUMS

We'd come to expect traffic-stopping sunsets but even by the standards of the mid-Atlantic this one was special. The sky was beautiful and threatening, a jumble sale of different clouds, every formation you've ever seen all scattered and piled: wisps, cumulonimbus, hazy sheets, towering thunder-heads – whatever your taste in clouds, this sky had something for you. It meant the sun was obscured for the last fifteen minutes of its descent, and just when we'd forgotten about it and resigned ourselves to night, the western horizon blazed a hot, fiery crimson, while the north of the sky showed us just how many different shades of peach and apricot there are in the world. One big, solid anvil of cloud just where the sun had disappeared became an IMAX cinema screen. One minute it depicted a mushroom cloud, the next the face of God, the next a giant whale's tail descending into the sea, all picked out in red, orange, yellow, purple and green against a backdrop of boiling fire.

We were heading almost due south now, chasing the sun into the southern hemisphere as the north hunkered down for winter. Travelling under sail, it was satisfying that 'climate change' had taken on a different meaning from the one airlines are becoming increasingly defensive about. Each day was a little warmer, a bit more humid, a slow, gradual change that, without our navigation instruments, would have been the only evidence of our progress.

I was enjoying travelling slowly – finally. There was integrity to it. Knowing that Cape Verde sits between Tenerife and Brazil, and that it's a bit rubbish, seemed very important. I needed to know how the world fits together, where all the different bits go in relation to each other. I decided that, no matter how much travelling you might do, if you went everywhere by plane you couldn't truly say you were seeing the world.

All of this was wholesome and satisfying until I tried to go to bed. The temperature below decks was becoming unbearable. Even popping down to the cabin to retrieve a book or a tube of sunscreen left me coated in sweat. The sea temperature was up to thirty degrees, from twenty-three a week ago, and below decks it surrounded us, warmed the metal hull and slow-cooked the still, dead air. As we entered the Doldrums the threat of rain made sleep under the stars a risky option. If a sudden downpour soaked your bedding before you got inside, you'd really find out how miserable a night at sea could be.

I felt that Barry was somehow still with me. This may have been because many of my possessions still had a whiff of stale beer. But if he had survived Tenerife, he would definitely have blown here. And I may have been made to walk the plank if I'd managed to fill the ship with that meaty smell of stale, oxidized beer. My new beer, if it ever arrived, was going to be in a modern keg, built to withstand ninety pounds of pressure per square inch. We were taking no chances with this one – apart for the chance that we may not be allowed to fly it into Brazil. I was able to send and receive emails – for a cost – over *Europa*'s satellite connection, but updates were rare and inconclusive.

These were the scurvy latitudes, the spirit-sapping belt that could fill you with slow, heavy despair if it didn't kill you. It was fortunate then, that for all the terrible majesty of the 4,000-ton East Indiamen, our modest ship had one thing they lacked: a great big Caterpillar engine. We soon needed it.

Klaas told us these sultry latitudes are also the cradle

where tropical storms are born; starting here innocently enough, they head west, picking up power with which to batter the American coastline. We had to take care with the currents. 'If we head west we get into strong currents in the Caribbean. Get caught by them, and the only thing you can do is follow them back to Europe and start again. We don't want to do that.'

This point was stressed in the history books I'd brought with me. The East India Company's third voyage – the one carrying Surat-bound William Hawkins – left the South Downs on April Fool's Day 1607, too late to catch the trade winds. They made it to the Brazilian coast in June, but by August they were back off North Africa, waiting for wind, unable to press across the equator without it. It was Christmas by the time they reached the Cape.

The Doldrums complete their reputation as a complete pain-in-the-arse by being unpredictable. Yeah, you might get stuck for weeks, rolling at a standstill. Or you might not. It might be unbearably hot. Or then again . . . not. The days when we had to use the engine felt a bit like cheating, but no one minded, least of all me. But most of the time we had a decent wind. It fretted and changed about, but still blew from the north-east.

At the end of our second week, the meaning of 'weather' grew to encompass more than 'wind', and I journeyed through my own personal Doldrums.

I had a dreadful night's sleep, and was due on day watch at 4 a.m. I couldn't sleep in the cabin, couldn't risk the rainy sloop deck, and in the deckhouse Dieter was chatting incessantly at the table opposite mine. I wanted to yell, 'STOP TALKING IN GERMAN!' at him. I realized this was unreasonable, but his voice was a horrible noise.

The air had grown thick and soupy. Even though we had a cloudless sky and new moon, the Milky Way wasn't visible.

The dawn, when it came, presented a phlegmy, grey and yellow shell above us, and a pressing sense of foreboding. The barometer on my seafarer's watch was bumping along the bottom of the graph. Sleepy Hans sat up sideways, blinking at the world, his huge Croc-shod red feet dangling. He contemplated the situation for a few minutes, then disappeared back inside his hammock. He wasn't going to be able to stay there long. It was going to rain, hard.

We could see it in the sky off to the north-east where our wind was coming from, a grey curtain shutting out the horizon. We heard it before we felt it, a hiss racing across the sea, getting louder, and then a second later water was bouncing off every surface and running in rivers off the decks. There was wind in it too; an unexpected and ironic chill as the sea boiled under the onslaught. I sat staring out to sea, soaking.

I was grateful to get below for breakfast, but had one more stint on the bow before the watch changed at eight. The ship heeled before the wind, unrelenting, and soon we were walking steeply uphill from the counter to the seats, and couldn't be confident that any liquid was going to stay in bowls or glasses for very long. I heard the thudding of running feet over our heads. I went out, and some of the crew were stripping off T-shirts and putting on harnesses as quickly as they could, the first time I'd really seen the chilled-out Dutch rushing over a task.

Rain was trying to strip the decks, its wind hitting us at a ninety-degree angle, pushing us over, and our starboard rail was level with the thrashing waves. We had too much sail out, and suddenly being such a tall, beautiful ship seemed like a liability. Panicking, I looked for Klaas. He seemed calm, monitoring the crew as they took sails away. And as I read his expression I felt perfectly calm too. I realized casually that I trusted this man with my life. That reads more melodramatic than it was – he was the captain of the ship, and in the middle of the ocean, I had no choice but to trust him. It was simply his job to keep us alive.

Back on watch, I pulled myself up to the foredeck and looped my arms through the railings to hold on. The rain was a constant drum roll on my hood, joined by the occasional splash cymbal of a wave of spray breaking over me. Looking to the east I could see that the rain had almost spent itself, and sure enough it soon faded out. But the wind was still there. We were still heeling at around thirty degrees. A couple of the crew were climbing into the rigging to tie up sails. Whatever angle you're heeling at on deck, whatever roll there is, you feel it much more when you're up there. The first climb into the rigging was now more across than up. No one was going to ask me to do the climb, but in any case I realized it was beyond the limits of my bravery. I may have no fear of heights, but throw in a storm, thrashing, fighting waves and a wrong, unnatural angle, and there was no way I could ever do that.

The sails were soon away and *Europa* gradually righted herself. Twenty minutes later the morning watch emerged blinking from their bunks, saw our waterproofs and the hair plastered to our faces, looked at the dry decks and the bright sun and, confused, asked, 'Has it been raining?'

Later, at his lunchtime briefing, Klaas informed those who weren't awake to witness it that we'd had 'a little shower' and 'a nice breeze'.

I went to bed for a few hours and re-emerged to discover that the stroppy Doldrums wind had flipped round to blow weakly from the west. The sea was calm, a light swell and gentle crêpe furrow, with no trace of the earlier storm. The sun burned fiercely, directly overhead. Most of us had long since followed the crew's example and gone barefoot, but now the deck scorched the soles of our feet and we had to scurry for flip-flops and factor 30.

I took the helm after lunch, and *Europa* was being tricky. When Frank Brookesmith was at the wheel of a ship, he felt she was at her best in front of a good blow. 'She seems to know that the grip on the spokes is to help her and she behaves like a lady. You know that she's just a complicated fabric of steel and timber, canvas and rope, but the breath of heaven has put life into her.' Well that's fine for you, Frank, but *Europa* seemed to be running on Satan's halitosis. 'She is behaving most of the time, but every now and again she goes off at a tangent,' said Erik, who enjoyed his half-hour stint on the wheel when lunch was served, allowing the watch to eat. 'This is why we call ships "she". They are high maintenance, and expensive to keep.'

Soon I was cursing her as she resolutely refused to stick to the bearing. She'd be happy to remain steady ten degrees either side, but refused to stay still within five degrees of our desired course. 'She doesn't respond well to bad language. She is a lady,' chided Klaas, possibly in response to me using the kind of language that would have prompted my mum to remind me that I'm not too big for a clip round the ear.

We lay on the deck, poaching in our own sweat. Cosmic Joe was being particularly far out. He was wearing a pair of bright-yellow shorts, three contrasting necklaces swinging above a round, sunburned belly, a broad-peaked baseball cap with a stray barcode sticker on the peak and a chin strap over one eye. He was creating a new way to belay rope, because the way it had been done for centuries didn't suit him.

In the middle of the afternoon the engines were turned off, the door on the side of the main deck was opened, and we plunged in for a swim. I jumped from the rigging and sank into deep, warm water that felt like a heated swimming pool until I surfaced and immediately swallowed a salty wave. I'm not a strong swimmer. I've known how to swim since I was a kid; it just seems to take me much more effort than other people. I tried to tread water for a bit, but the swell, far deeper here than it looked from the deck, made it difficult. One second we were level with the portholes, the next we were below *Europa*'s waterline, where her white hull gave way to a rusty red you never see in port. I was breathing heavily, and decided to make my way back to the rope ladder dangling from the side of the ship, but each time I reached for it the swell rose and pushed me ten yards back away. Just as I was starting to worry, I finally grasped the ladder and clung to it, knowing only that whatever happened, I wasn't letting go. Now the swell battered me against the unforgiving, barnacle-encrusted steel hull, boosting me effortlessly up a couple of rungs then leaving me dangling, graceless, in mid-air. I could only think of holding on, and ignored the concerned voices from the sea asking if I were OK each time my body smacked against the metal. When I finally dragged myself back on board, my feet were bleeding. It had been fun for ten minutes, and I envied the stronger swimmers still diving from the foredeck and swimming circuits of the ship. But for the first time I realized that if I fell overboard, I'd have about twenty minutes before I went under. And this was in a calm, warm sea.

The sun was still strong as we grabbed our towels and the engine grumbled back into life. But we could see three separate storms on the horizon, grey curtains hanging from low clouds, swishing along the ocean. Five minutes later it was dark and then the sea was fizzing once again, and we closed the windows to the deckhouse against the rain, and sat inside, and sweated.

I tried to write up some notes, but the heat, the storm, and the people openly reading my screen over my shoulder and reminding me to mention the sodding dolphins meant that Solitaire was the limit of my intellectual capabilities. Everyone looked unhappy, and there was a fractious mood in the air. The weight of the clouds and the rain and the heat pushed down on me, darkening my mood like the unnatural sky outside.

By dinnertime the rain was heavy and constant, and for the first time we all ate crowded gloomily inside the deckhouse. It was dark, and felt like winter. Crewmember Ron brought out his guitar and white watch produced bottles of wine. Soon a modest party was in gentle swing, but I was back on watch in an hour and couldn't join in.

Padraig and Paul, my main drinking buddies, sat down and we started talking about onward plans after reaching Brazil. 'So what do you think you'll do about Iran?' asked Paul.

'Well, the man at the agency said the captain might pull some strings to allow me to stay on board. Maybe enrol me as supernumerary crew or something like that. Otherwise I have to get off in Khor Fakkan and I don't reach India till the twelfth of December. So I'm hoping I can make friends with the captain.'

Paul looked sceptical, and Padraig was shaking his head. Paul had travelled by ship before, and Padraig had to deal with commercial shipping as part of his job. I'd been waiting for an opportunity to sound them out about what might happen.

'Why would the captain do that?' said Padraig. 'There's nothing in it for him. It's far too big a risk these days.'

I was starting to worry about my whole quest falling apart. It had been over a week since I'd last emailed Rudgie over the ship's satellite connection about arrangements for getting a replacement keg to meet me in Brazil, and I'd heard nothing back. There were ten days left on the ship, maybe a week after that in Brazil. If the beer didn't make it by then, was there any point carrying on?

After my first stint back on the bucking wheel in the battering rain, I felt I couldn't bear to go back to the deckhouse.

The ship was closing in on me. There was no privacy anywhere on board, and I needed to be alone. Joe would be sleeping in the cabin if the temperature permitted it. The crew were everywhere, always working, never allowing a moment's peace.

I found myself hunched on the sloop deck. The rain was sheeting down, the lights were off. No one knew I was here. I could fall overboard and no one would know. It would be at least an hour before anyone realized I was missing. I felt absurd, rain drumming off my waterproof coat, unrelenting, pouring off plastic trousers, puddling around my flip-flops. Who wears full wet-weather gear with flip-flops?

I'd drifted quite far out into depression. I wanted off this ship, now. I wanted to go home. I didn't know what I wanted to do when I got there. People would be sympathetic to my face, and would ridicule me behind my back. I would have to take it. It was time to grow up. I simply wasn't the kind of person who could do this, even if it had been a good idea in the first place, and I was no longer sure it was. I had made no checks about customs and immigration. Not that it mattered, because I hadn't taken into account what might happen to the beer. And even if I had been successful, so what? Who would have actually cared apart from a handful of blogging beer geeks? What was I going to do?

I did nothing. I drifted. The sound of the rain on my hood, like peas on a drum, slowly lulled me into a catatonic state. After ten minutes I wasn't worrying, I wasn't angry. I simply felt nothing at all.

Half an hour later it suddenly felt like time to move. I'd been too busy thinking about what had happened before, and what would happen after, to truly appreciate what I was experiencing now. It wasn't too late to start. I'd take my fate as it came, and enjoy the moment in the meantime.

The unsettled weather had brought the phosphorescence back for the first time since before Cape Verde. Lime-green flashbulbs were going off furiously behind us, as if *Europa* were on the catwalk. The sea frothed white around her bows, and we were leaving a long, defined wake. As I headed back to the deckhouse to rejoin my shipmates, I wished I could see her from the air – a collection of lights inside a white chevron, leaving a trail of stars in her wake.

CHAPTER TWENTY-SEVEN

IN THE COURT OF KING NEPTUNE

Ron strums his tuneless guitar, nervously trying to croak out any lyrics he can conjure up. Nervous, perhaps, because he's wearing a blindfold and is harnessed to a bosun's chair strung ten feet above the deck, spinning slowly in the stiffening wind like a serial killer's Christmas bauble. He's probably regretting bringing the guitar on board now that everyone understands it's more of a prop – something to complete the image created by his floppy blond hair (which he is about to lose) and his collection of death-metal T-shirts – than something he can usefully play.

Beneath Ron's dangling feet, three more of the permanent crew members sit on a bench while Val, dressed in a traditional blue and white Austrian dirndl, fag hanging from her mouth, laughing, demented, sprays them with something evil and brown, something that contains stale beer and fish guts and reeks so foul you know the ghost of it will still be under their noses days from now. Behind them sits one of *Europa*'s zodiacs, a big black dinghy half full of soupy brown water. At their feet, with a wide strip newly shaved down the centre of his head, crewmember Ewout sits tied to a metal tray full of old food, a huge Brillo pad strapped to his arse. Every time he stops shuffling in the pan, he's berated and told to keep going by Klaas, who controls the proceedings from his throne, resplendent in a pair of trunks and a sarong around his shoulders. Others of his crew are sporting long, filthy dreadlocks, eye patches and tattoos. They're the lucky ones, and they're enjoying it as much as you would if you knew you were all right, that having been through this on some previous voyage, you were already a shellback. They roar and slap pollywogs with the flats of their swords, or threaten them with scissors.

There's no escape for passengers either. After all, technically we're 'trainee crew'. So up on the sloop deck, trainee crew members Annalies and Martine are nervously trying to assume yoga positions while Ilonka, renowned for being the nicest person on the ship, screams foul abuse at them in three different languages.

Welcome to Neptune's Court, now in session.

I think I first became aware of sinister goings on around the equator when I was about thirteen. The British Task Force was sailing for the South Atlantic and the Falklands War, and I remember news footage of 'Randy Andy', a young Prince Andrew, being ducked and shaved when his ship crossed the line. But it's a ritual that goes back much further than that. In 1822, 'having beaten about the line for a fortnight, with a contrary wind', Fanny Parkes's ship finally crossed. 'Letters were received on board from Neptune and Amphitrite, requesting to be supplied with clothes, having lost their own in a gale of wind.' Neptune subsequently came aboard to inform the captain of a visit the following day, before vanishing in a cloud of flame and water. The next morning, the Sea King and his retinue processed across deck before calling the ship to order. The crew were tried, and all those who had not crossed the line before were shaved and ducked. After this, 'In the evening the sailors danced, sang, recited verses and spliced the main brace (drank grog), until very late.'

This implies that Parkes managed to escape the proceedings herself. William Hickey, travelling half a century earlier, reveals how: 'Upon crossing the Line, all those who had never done so before paid the customary forfeit of a gallon of rum to the ship's crew, except Mr Smith the Scotch cadet, who not being overstocked with money to purchase the spirits, preferred submitting to the ceremony of ducking and shaving, which he went through to our infinite amusement.'

Unfortunately, neither I nor the rest of *Europa*'s trainee crew had thought to bring a barrel of rum with us, and Klaas didn't drink that much anyway. A few days before we were due to cross the equator, Neptune's trident banner appeared at the top of the main mast, inviting the King of the Sea to board. Pictures appeared on walls and doors below decks of crew members with Photoshopped bald heads, and Val started cackling, 'Heh heh, Pollywogs!' at random. Graffiti was chalked everywhere – 'Neptune's court is coming' – with pictures of scissors.

I began to fret about the likelihood of having my head shaved. They wouldn't, would they? They were acting like they would. I've never fancied a close crop because my head is so lumpy. What would I do if they tried? Would I fight them off? There'd be too many of them. In 1801, when a Mr Maw arrived in India he brought an action against the captain of his ship for having permitted the ceremonies known as 'Neptune's Rites'. The Bombay court upheld his complete lack of a sense of humour and fined the captain £400. I decided that I would have to go along with whatever happened.

Unlike Mrs Parkes's voyage, a firm wind took us gliding across the equator. It was exactly like a New Year celebration. Thanks to our GPS, we had been counting down the degrees for days, and as degrees break down into minutes and seconds, we were literally counting down the seconds at the end. We crossed the line around 12.20 a.m. on 15 October 2007, a Monday morning. Everyone on board had gathered around the wheelhouse, and when we crossed, the ship's horn was sounded. It was deliciously liberating – so FUCKING LOUD in the middle of the night. But with no one else within a couple of hundred miles to hear it, there was no environmental-health officer; no threat of an ASBO. Then we drank some cough mixture, which the Dutch pretended was some fancy liqueur for special occasions.

And then . . . it was a bit of an anticlimax. We all stood around, uncertain what to do next. It was our turn on dog watch, and soon it was time to head up to the bow as the other watches drifted off to bed. As I said, just like New Year. As the gathering broke up, Klaas said softly, 'That is the quietest equator crossing I've ever experienced.' Those of us on watch kept popping into the wheelhouse to watch the numbers on the GPS start to climb again. Crossing the equator had made us all quiet and reflective. We were in the southern hemisphere. How good was this? People smiled to themselves and shook their heads in disbelief.

If the crossing itself had been quiet, we made up for it twelve hours later.

We were doing seven knots against a fresh wind and a clear blue sky. The ship was on a permanent heel to starboard, and you had to think carefully about how you were going to make every step of a short journey: OK, now I'm going over to the tea and coffee. I'll need to put my book down. I'll need a hand free, which I can use to grab that belaying pin just over there . . . This was 'good' sailing weather. What am I doing with those inverted commas? It was fantastic. Not the best weather for lying on deck and reading a book, but we were here to sail.

It began after a suspiciously early lunch. As soon as we finished eating, we were ordered below decks, into the lounge opposite the galley where we usually ate breakfast. Strange, alarming sounds came from the deck. The air was stifling. After half an hour the room smelled of very ripe, expensive French cheese, which was curious as there was none within at least 500 miles of us.

When we were finally released, into the sweet, fresh air, *Europa* had been transformed. The zodiac took up half the main deck. A long bench ran in front of it, next to which was a cauldron full of the leftovers of every meal we'd had while on board. I suddenly wished I'd eaten more.

Everyone who had not been in the lounge with us stood in some kind of improvised costume – demented creatures of the sea. Sleepy Hans was one of them: he'd kept quiet about that. But then, he was quiet about everything – he was usually asleep.

At the head of the proceedings was Klaas. At first I thought he could have made a bit more of an effort. After reading Fanny Parkes's account, I was expecting Neptune to be resplendent in robes and masks, an elaborate costume with . . . with what? Long, stringy hair like seaweed fronds? He had that already. A mighty beard? Ditto. Unlike his young crew, Klaas didn't need a costume to be a denizen of the deep. He already was Neptune.

The permanent crew were the first to be tried. They were brought blindfolded, one by one, from the library. A list of crimes was read out for each person. Ron was first, accused of being pretentious with his guitar.[67] He was duly hoisted and remained dangling for the rest of the proceedings. Swedish Sofia got violent when she thought her long blonde hair was for the chop, but it was only the male crew members who were shaved, just enough to turn each barnet into that of a lunatic, stripes here and patches there, before Klaas would say, 'OK, that's enough.'

There were many of us to get through, and punishments were set in train to continue while others were tried. Soon the whole deck was a riot of demented behaviour.

---

67. As well as other things, which I'll remain discreet about, in case Ron ever falls in love, gets married, settles down and has children, and that life is perfect until the day his loving wife discovers this book in a charity shop, leafs through it and thinks, 'Hey, that's the ship Ron once worked on. I wonder if he's mentioned? Why, yes, here he . . . oh.'

When it was finally my turn, I got off lightly. Red watch was tried as a group, and I realized that each of the trainee crew who had been pulled out for special treatment had been on the ship since Amsterdam. They were better known to the permanent crew, both in terms of their crimes and their ability to take a joke. By contrast, I was accused of 'playing Solitaire on my laptop'. While not strictly untrue, I hardly felt Solitaire had defined my voyage so far. If that's all anyone had noticed, I'd kept well under the radar, which struck me with a mix of relief and disappointment. On the other hand, Dieter, our glorious watch leader, had captured the imagination of the crew with his attempt to build a model of *Europa* in a bottle. So our punishment was to make a model of the ship ourselves, using only our bodies and clothes, which I have to say we achieved very well. We took the bench, had slop ladled over our heads and flung in our faces, and took our ducking. We were blasted clean with a high-pressure seawater hose and that was that. I'd survived, and so had my hair.

Once we had all been tried and punished, trays of drinks were passed round for a toast. The glasses were cool and filmed with condensation, the liquid crystal clear. 'Half of them are jenever, half are salt water,' said Neptune. 'If you look closely, you should be able to tell which is which.' Now this was something I was good at. I looked closely, chose a glass, and knocked back a mouthful of freshly chilled salt water.

And that was how we spent Monday afternoon.

Later, we each received a certificate. More than a nice souvenir, we were advised to take this on any future voyage to prove our shellback status and avoid having to go through this again. 'To all sailors wherever they may be', it began:

Know ye that on this 15th day of October the BARK EUROPA entered into our Royal Equatorial Domain at longitude 27°44, 19'W.

Having been tried and tested in KING NEPTUNE'S ROYAL COURT Peter Brown was found worthy to possess the Royal document awarded to those duly initiated into the solemn mysteries of the Ancient Order of the Deep.

At the bottom, as proof of this, it declared my new sea name.

That night, as those who had been shaved helped each other finish the job, hair pooling on the deck to be hosed over the side as an offering to Neptune, I wrote an email to Liz informing her of my new status:

> I've come through a centuries-old initiation process as a real seaman. From the ceremony, I take with me a passport confirming that I have crossed the equator and been tried in Neptune's Court – as well as a new name. It's a secret name, a seagoing name, one that reflects my new status as a veteran of the oceans, that will act as a secret sign to those who have been through what I have, so that we can nod meaningfully to each other over hard liquor in dockside bars, and so that I can generate instant respect among Pollywogs and landlubbers everywhere, who will look at me and say, 'There goes a man of the sea – a man who has done things I can only dream of.'
>
> I love you,
>
> Oscar the Oyster
>
> xxxxxxx

CHAPTER TWENTY-EIGHT

EUROPA OVERTAKES THE SUN

Cosmic Joe was reading *Daughters of Fire* by Barbara Erskine. He was enjoying it. He hadn't enjoyed Don DeLillo. 'The man can't write. He doesn't know what he is talking about.' But *Daughters of Fire* was an inspiration. 'You should read this,' he said, waving it in my face, 'then you will write a book about someone writing a book, about people coming from the past. You need to hear voices. You need to put yourself into a trance, otherwise what you are writing is no good.'

After three weeks on board I was drunk on sleep, sedated by the sun. The thought of putting shoes and socks on again was alien. But idyllic though on-board life was, I had an occasional but increasingly frequent longing for a sea-view restaurant, a table with white linen cloths, fresh green salad, a seafood platter, and a glass of cold white wine, condensation frosting the outside, all blown by a soft sea breeze. I didn't want to see a ham and cheese sandwich again for some time.

But most of the time, I didn't want my voyage on *Europa* to end. For the past two nights there had been pools of light on the horizon, watery gobbets of pale yellow bleeding and washing into the midnight blue. The real world was just over the horizon, bearing a large and urgent To Do list, at the top of which was getting a barrel of beer into the country at some point over the next seven days. Three weeks since Barry exploded, and still there was no solution in sight.

My biggest regret was that I hadn't mastered the principles of sailing. 'It might all look a blur, but by the end of your voyage, you'll know all the sails and ropes,' said the blurb that arrived in my inbox when my booking was confirmed. Not me. There were twenty-four sails, not including the stunsails. As sailing has developed, it's been a case of sub-dividing sails to get more control, and this means greater confusion because the names of sails often seem to go in the wrong place. The foremast and mainmast each have six sails. The bottom sail is the main or course sail. The second from bottom sail is the lower topsail. See my problem? It's the topsail (admittedly the lower topsail) and it's one from the bottom. Next comes the upper topsail (they used to be one sail). Above the topsails are the topgallant, or t'gallant, the coolest-sounding sail, then the royal and then the skysail, each progressively smaller. On the rear mast are the splendidly named spanker and gaff, and between each mast are the triangular staysails.

Each one of these has a halyard for hoisting, a sheet for setting the sail properly to the wind, buntlines, which furl the body of the sail, bringing the foot up to the yard, and clewlines, which bring the corners of the sail up to the yard. When you're hoisting and taking down sails, it's important that people are on the end of every rope, and that everyone knows what to do when. Done properly, it's beautifully simple: the sail goes up and opens out to catch the wind simultaneously. Get it wrong, and you've got a very heavy sail full of wind that's not secured in place and a tough job ahead, or even the prospect of damaging sail and/or rigging.

I simply couldn't work out the pattern of what lines went where, or what they did. We had an inter-watch pin-rail race three days from the end, where someone would shout the name of a line and we had to race to find the wooden pin it was coiled around, and correctly identify it. I got every one of mine wrong. I didn't do as badly as Cosmic Joe though. When it was his turn, racing against Debbie the American, who hadn't taken part much in the sailing of the ship, the shouted instruction was not 'find the clew for the foremast main sail'[68] or something like that, but simply, 'Find the pointy end of the ship!' Joe stood rooted to the spot, rotating slowly, deep in thought, before ambling hesitantly forward just as Debbie's shrieks of triumph reached us from the bow.

A few days before the end, Klaas set another challenge. We were heading south, chasing the sun into the southern hemisphere and its summer, our winter. *Europa* might only be moving at a fast jogging speed, but the sun takes six months to make its southward journey. A prize was offered for the closest estimate for the time and position where we would pass beneath the sun, where it would be directly overhead. We were due to reach Salvador some time on Sunday, 21 October. The day before, as anticipation built, a notice appeared on the deckhouse blackboard:

> At 22.30 on 19th October, at 10° 08' 7s, *Europa*
> caught up with the sun.

I can't remember who won.

On the morning of our final day at sea, the wind had dropped and shifted round to the north. A strong current carried us forward, bringing its own waves, which cross-hatched with those whipped up by the wind, two wave systems hitting each other at right angles. These weather systems have changed little over the centuries. Maybe the Portuguese were borne into land by these same currents. Maybe that's why Salvador, the first Portuguese settlement in Brazil, grew up where it did. I was following in ancient footsteps.

Our night-time arrival in Salvador was inglorious and shambolic. The permanent crew wanted to finish in style, sailing across busy shipping lanes and navigating through buoys and shallow-water markers into the harbour rather

---

68. It's a trick question – there *is* no clew on the foremast main sail! Oh, how we laughed.

than powering for the last few miles. Klaas was asleep. Sails were taken down and put back up again, tempers frayed, the other watches got pissed and went to bed, and were woken up again to coil ropes that didn't need coiling any more. The lights of Salvador grew closer and resolved themselves into the shape of a city. Halogen spotlights lined what was clearly an ocean boulevard. Skyscrapers hung in an eerie black void, suspended in darkness thanks to a sheer cliff face that separated the harbour from the city. Behind these, ruby-studded tower blocks rose into the dark like a petrified forest. With a couple of miles left, the smell of the coast – seaweed and diesel seasoned with a hint of sewage, the smell landlubbers think of as the smell of the sea – wafted out to our ship. Finally, around midnight, we dropped anchor in Salvador harbour, surrounded by the hulking bodies of container ships, bats chip-chipping across the still water.

And, finally, the next morning, we went ashore for chips etc.

Salvador was confusing and a little frightening. It was too big. There were too many people. There was too much space to walk in, and with no wind the heat flayed our skin. We explored in downbeat packs, changing currency and finding web cafes from which to make hotel reservations and send emails about beer barrels.

The chips were good though. We ate them at a restaurant on top of a small cliff overlooking a strip of brilliant white sand, and watched Brazilian kids being rubbish at surfing and absurdly good at football.

After a few hours we were back at the yacht club where *Europa* was anchored. She stood a hundred yards out in the bay, breeding inferiority complexes among the rest of the boats and dark envy among their owners. Barra is an 'exclusive suburb' of Salvador, and that became clear now. Ninety-eight per cent of Salvador's population is black: this was obviously where the other 2 per cent hung out – in every imaginable meaning of the phrase. We were served bottles of Bohemia lager in silver buckets full of ice. I spend a great deal of my professional life telling people that if you serve beer too cold it masks the flavour, but sometimes it's not about flavour. I took photos and video film of my first bottle. I caressed it. I stroked it. I drank it quickly and ordered another from the passing waiter. If he had told me this bottle of beer cost a hundred dollars, I would have paid happily.

The sun sank and we could see that fairy lights had been strung across *Europa*'s decks. Three beers to the good, it was time to go back aboard for our farewell party.

The flip-flops and shorts had disappeared. Make-up had been dug out from the bottom of canvas bags, 'dress to impress' written on the deckhouse blackboard and on the cerebral cortex of everyone who had spent time flirting with each other over the last three weeks. It quickly became obvious that there was more going on than simply every male crew member under twenty-five being profoundly in love with Laura. A web of flirtations either fizzled like hot coals chucked in the sea, or moved to Def Con One.

But this was a special occasion all round. Everyone had dressed up. Well, almost everyone. Klaas stood in the corner, quiet and out of sorts. Still dressed resolutely in his shorts, vest and flip-flops, he seemed diminished somehow, standing on the cusp between his world and ours.

The fabric of the boat had altered. As soon as we neared land, it started to feel different. When there were other people – no, the *possibility* of other people – the relationships on board changed. People became more open and honest in the final few days, knowing we weren't going to be in confinement together for much longer. Gulfs had split open between those who merely tolerated each other and those who actually liked each other.

Matt, a tall, handsome English dentist I hadn't really got to know during the voyage, was on great form, talking to

Cosmic Joe in a voice that was soft and soothing, professional and kind.

'So what are you doing now, Joe?'

'Eeh, I stay in Salvador until Friday.'

'And what then – back to Mars?'

Joe wandered off, and Matt told me a story about Dieter. They'd both joined the ship in Amsterdam, and a couple of days out Matt had been up in the rigging, doing something with the sails that required him to lean out at an awkward angle. His balance depended entirely on a slight foothold he had on a wooden block. He was halfway through his task when there was a clink of harness below him. He looked down to see Dieter, staring determinedly at the block.

'I must varnish this block,' said Dieter.

'Sorry, mate, I need it just now. It's the only thing carrying my weight.'

'Yes, but I must varnish this block.'

'Well, you'll have to wait. I'm standing on it, and we're forty feet up.'

'But I must varnish the block. I have the varnish and the brush here.'

'If I move my foot from the block I will fall. Wait!'

'I must varnish the block.'

And Dieter proceeded to varnish the block. He left a tiny spot for Matt's foot.

So Matt waited until a week or so later. Normally, Dieter displayed the toothy grin and gentle manner of a country vicar. One time, he was on the sheet, bringing around one of the yards, and Matt saw his chance. Every time Dieter pulled, Matt pulled the corresponding sheet on the other side instead of letting it run through. Dieter pulled harder and harder, until finally he turned, saw what Matt was doing, and completely lost it. 'YOU FUCKING BASTARD ENGLISH!' he screamed, the mask slipping wonderfully.

After a while, I went to the bow. I had no idea why. I

wanted to do one more bow watch, to coil one more rope. Sleepy Hans was, of course, asleep in his hammock. Denis was there too, but after a few minutes he left me alone.

I made myself think about where I was, and why I was here. I'd finally stopped worrying about both the past and the future, and simply luxuriated in the moment. This was something I might never do again, and I wanted to drink in the last few hours. I was floating off the coast of Brazil, weeks after leaving home. Everyone on the ship was unusual in that respect, in that they all had their reasons and motivations for being here. All of us had, one way or another, escaped the usual stricture of 'Here are your two weeks' holiday, your brief window of recovery from endless drudgery – enjoy'.

I wasn't sure I would ever be able to go back to that.

I thought of Frank Brookesmith again, and the mixture of longing and desperation that seemed to characterize the tall shipmen of his time. Conditions were often so bad that crew would jump ship, forfeiting their pay. One minute Frank is complaining that life on board 'entails so much of wet and hunger, cold and misery, and back-breaking, brutalizing toil, which cannot be justified'. The next, he's coming into port and as he looks at the houses on the shore, he thinks of 'the people who lived their secure lives there and I envied them not'.

The tall ships couldn't compete economically once the steamers arrived. Time was money, an ironic contrast with today, when slowness is one of the selling points for the privileged few who get to sail the surviving ships. Captains were torn between driving their ships as fast as possible, running close to the wind and with as much sail out as they dared, weighing the cost of losing sail and rigging against the money to be gained by shaving off a little time. They had all but disappeared by the 1930s. The handful that remain today cast spells wherever they go, making all who see them wish they could live like Frank Brookesmith, or at least write like him. I felt that tomorrow they would have to prise my fingers one by one from the hull of the ship.

Then, I went on to the sloop deck and gazed down at the main deck. My watch-mates Peter and Janet and another middle-aged couple, Maiike and Daniel, were the only people apart from Klaas who were wearing the same clothes they always did. Peter seemed to be morris dancing to the Chemical Brothers.

We all have to move on when it's time.

PART FIVE

CARIBBEAN

CHAPTER TWENTY-NINE

RACING JEFF

The most famous beach in the world is not a place you readily associate with feelings of stress and anxiety, but here I was – the least relaxed person in Copacabana since a girl called Lola – she was a showgirl – got a bit freaked out when a bloke with a badly highlighted mullet and the biggest nose she'd ever seen wouldn't stop staring at her.

Music and passion did indeed seem to be the fashion here, but I could enjoy neither. My brain was full. My nerves were shot. My nails were a shrivelled memory. A large concrete block sat in the middle of my skull, and I'd developed a distinctly unappealing nervous twitch that made my whole top lip try to jump up my nose whenever I held any unbroken train of thought for more than thirty seconds.

I had thought my personal journey was going to be about slowing down and learning how to escape from the pressures of modern life. Instead, all I'd done in nearly a week in Brazil was take those pressures to unfeasible new heights. I was fetishizing my replacement mobile phone and convalescing BlackBerry as never before. I'd cajoled an army of people into trying to helping me, and still ended up spending days mired in administration and bureaucracy.

I hadn't seen much of Brazil apart from a hotel room in Salvador. I sat for three days, phoning and emailing in an attempt to get a replacement keg or cask of Calcutta IPA into Brazil before my next ship sailed. I spoke to Rudgie, to Steve Wellington, and to the Coors export department. I spoke to Liz, who showed the forbearance of a saint,[69] who in turn spoke to the Brazilian High Commission in London, the British Consulate in São Paulo, several airlines, the Brazilian Tourist Board, two different Brazilian beer importers, DHL and FedEx, none of whom would touch it. We spoke to InBev, the world's largest brewer, which is based in both Europe and South America. No one could help. The beer had to be checked by customs and receive appropriate clearance, and that would take about two weeks. In addition, they may well open it to taste it, which would mean the beer would be exposed to the air and would be dead by the time I reached India. I checked with Station Weggis about delaying my journey: this was the last time the *Caribbean* was making the stop in Rio, and her sister ships didn't carry passengers. If I weren't on the sailing in five days, there was no possible way of completing the journey. We spoke to the DTI and the All-Party Parliamentary Beer Group to see if we could get it in via a diplomatic bag. Nothing doing.

I stayed in Salvador for three days, unsure whether I would be travelling to São Paulo next, where the beer was most likely to enter the country if I could make it work, or Rio, where the *Caribbean* was sailing from. My plan had been to get from Salvador to Rio by bus, a twenty-four-hour journey along beautiful, jungle-lined coastal roads, my barrel stashed safely in the luggage compartment. But as the days slipped past, I realized I couldn't risk being out of circulation for so long.

With a heavy heart, a churning stomach and no idea what to do when I got there, I booked a flight to Rio. I repacked my belongings: clothes, books, laptop and accessories, wet weather gear . . . empty beer barrel. I stared at Barry. I'd imagined him as the hero of my story, the central character.

---

69. Admittedly, after also showing the colourful grasp of the bad language of a sailor.

He had caused me more stress and pain – both physically and mentally – than I could ever have imagined on the sunny early autumn day we left Burton-on-Trent together. He'd only made it the first 2,000 miles before blowing, and I'd hauled his sorry corpse all the way across the Atlantic. He'd sat in the bottom of the wardrobe, smelling slightly, and I'd hardly been able to bring myself to look at him. If I did get a new barrel, there was no way I would be able to carry Barry too. If I didn't get a new barrel, I was never going to want to see a beer barrel again for as long as I lived. It made no sense to take him any further.

I checked out of the hotel. 'I left something behind,' I told the owner. 'An empty aluminium beer barrel. It's a long story. Would it be OK to leave it for you to dispose of?'

'Of course,' the owner replied, as if people left things like this with him every day. Wheeling my luggage to check-in an hour later, I felt incomplete. Naked. But no lighter. I followed Robert Clive's dead tracks down to Rio.

By the time I'd landed, crawled into town through a rainy, sodium-lit murk and checked into a cheap hotel near the beach, nothing had changed on the beer front.

It wasn't going to work.

I thought again of Barry: posing with us on the back of the Coors dray; sitting in the galley on the barge; glowing sullenly, intimidating anyone who entered our cabin on *Oceana*; clanking down the airport luggage carousel and nearly chinning the man at the bottom of the chute. The airport. Where we had taken him through as personal luggage. Where no one had raised an eyebrow at the contents of the small, very heavy bag.

Fine. If that's what it took, then fine.

I opened my email and in the 'To' box typed the name of everyone I knew who might be desperate, unhinged or kind enough to help:

Subject: Fancy a few days in Rio – or know anyone
who does?

I'm looking for someone who would be prepared to
fly out to Rio at my expense – this weekend – with a
very special piece of luggage – a keg of very special
beer.

I explained what had happened so far, continuing:

Our only chance is to have someone bring it in as
personal luggage. There is a small element of risk
involved in this – you'd have to come through
nothing to declare and hope not to get stopped. If you
did get stopped, there would be duty and a fine to
pay, or the beer would be confiscated. However,
foreigners are hardly ever stopped coming into Brazil
– they're usually after natives returning with
contraband. The journey time out here is tortuous,
between 14 and 18 hours with one or two changes
(Lisbon, and maybe São Paulo) with the final
destination being Rio. Once you get to Rio, I'm in a
hotel two blocks from Copacabana beach which still
has rooms free at the time of writing! I'd meet all
expenses.

You have all been selected for admirable qualities
such as steely determination, general derring-do or
simply having the flexibility and attitude to be able to
say, 'Fuck it, why not?' I'd say flying Friday or
Saturday night would be the best idea, have a few
days on the beach, fly back maybe Weds or Thurs.

Do we have any interested parties?

And I waited.

And Jeff wrote back. Jeff Pickthall is a beer writer and
former speciality-beer bar owner, a cantankerous curmudg-
eon whose catchphrase is 'They make my blood boil', 'they'

usually being the Campaign for Real Ale. His blood wasn't boiling now. But it was certainly up:

> ME ME ME!
>
> Brazil! Blimey, my top fantasy location (that doesn't have a particular beer connotation).
>
> I lurv Brazilian music! I was hoping to go there for my 40th birthday earlier this year (almost Carnival season) but finances wouldn't allow it.
>
> What are Brazilian jails like?
>
> Jeff

That was Thursday evening. By 11 a.m. the next morning, everything was sorted. Jeff would drive from his home in Barrow-in-Furness, first thing Saturday morning, to Burton. Steve Wellington had agreed to give up his Saturday to go in, prepare the beer, buy a bag for it and hand it over to Jeff, who would then drive down to Heathrow and board an overnight flight (booked by Rudgie), arriving in Rio on Sunday morning. Sorted. All I had to do was book Jeff's hotel and make one final phone call. Then I could enjoy the best part of a week in Rio de Janeiro, wandering around on my own to get a feel for the city, so I'd be familiar with it by the time Jeff arrived. Once he was here we'd visit the *Chopperias* together, and then the bars where live music was played. We'd explore everything the city had to offer.

By 11.30 a.m., chaos ruled once more.

That final phone call was a simple, routine task. A call with no possibility whatsoever for further stress and upset.

'Mr Peter, thank you for calling. My name is Wagner, I am the agent for CMA CGA in Rio. Now let me check the schedule . . . ah yes. Your ship is arriving in Rio on the 28th. That's Sunday. She leaves in the evening. You must be on board as early as possible. We will board you at 1 p.m.'

'I thought she left on Wednesday. The latest information on your website says she leaves on Wednesday!'

'No, definitely Sunday. She is ahead of schedule. We will come to your hotel to collect you at midday, maybe 1 p.m. I will phone you tomorrow to confirm.'

'There's no possibility of boarding the ship a little later?'

'No. All has to be completed as early as possible.'

I hung up. Jeff was due to land in Rio on Sunday morning, around 9.45 a.m. When I arrived it took me almost two hours to get off the plane, get my luggage, get in a cab and make it to the hotel. And I was coming in from a domestic flight, without customs or passport control. If Jeff's flight landed on time, and it took him the same length of time as me, he would be arriving at the hotel with the beer possibly fifteen minutes before I had to leave. After all this work, on everyone's part, it was going to be a photo finish.

So I now had a day and a half – not five days – to see Rio de Janeiro. There was nothing else to do. I figured I should start with the beach.

Stepping on to Copacabana beach, I was happy that such a fabled, clichéd location easily lived up to its billing. Copacabana is the king of beaches. If you're another beach reading this, and you fancy yourself as something special, you're deluding yourself. Just give up. There's no point.

Copacabana beach is big enough – about four kilometres long. It's parenthesized at each end by humped green islands, low, lone mountains rising from a haze of surf. The Statue of Christ the Redeemer blesses the scene from on high, behind the unbroken massif of beachfront hotels. Copacabana beach is the perfect width – about a hundred-and-fifty yards from the umbrella-shaded cafes and *Chopperias* on the palm-lined road, via the football goalposts and beach-volleyball pitches, to the steep slope down to the surf. The sand is the perfect shade of whiteness. The perfectly proportioned breakers – big enough to dive under and make a dramatic crash, not big enough to sweep you away – are the perfect shade of lemonade-green. The only strange thing was down at the shoreline, where huge brown-winged insects, like sunburnt bumble bees on steroids, crawled drunkenly in broken ranks. I laid out my towel a little further up the sand from them, and tried to relax.

People dived into the rolling breakers, or simply walked along the shoreline, checking each other out. Container ships glided slowly landward, sneaking between the peaks. I grew paranoid that each one was the *Caribbean*, having shaved yet another day off her schedule. That was impossible – she would have had to double her speed over the last twenty-four hours – but it was no use. I couldn't relax, so I went for a walk.

Strolling along the front, I was never more than a minute's walk from one of the umbrella cafes selling chopp (draught beer), ice cream, fresh green coconuts and an astonishingly comprehensive menu of main meals that seemed to appear from nowhere after being broadcast through a bingo caller's microphone.[70] It was at one of these that I sat, hugging a beer, trying to make my head slow down, trying to appreciate where I was. Hawkers flitted constantly between the tables, selling sarongs, jewellery, sunglasses, baseball caps, T-shirts, maps, replica football shirts, fake 'RIO 2007' American licence plates, temporary tattoos, and handbags made entirely out of zips. A new one approached me every thirty seconds, not too pushy, moving on as soon as I smiled and shook my head.

The next day I went on a tour of the favelas, the independent, self-built communities that cling to the hillsides

---

70. In fact, many of them have dumb waiters leading to underground kitchens – a use of space that is ingenious, but nevertheless made me imagine sweltering subterranean caverns populated by evil, bad-tempered little goblin cooks.

the city deemed too steep to build on. Martha our guide gave us strict instructions about where we could walk, when we could and couldn't take photos, and what directions we were not allowed to take photos in. Tourism is one major source of income in these places – the other is drugs. The favelas are run by private armies, each with their own turf, financed by drug money. The police do not intervene, and so, under the casual rule of the drug armies, these communities govern themselves. The ones we saw were happy and thriving. Martha showed us the school that tourist fees had built, and told us proudly that 65 per cent of Brazilians do some form of charity work. 'Have you seen anyone begging? Anyone at all? No. These are proud people. They will try to sell you anything, but they will not beg for money.'

I remembered this back on the beach later that evening, when a man approached me with a world map. I didn't want one, but I bought it anyway. The only problem was, this alerted every hawker on the beach that here was a guy who buys stuff. I had to retreat to my hotel to get away.

Sometimes when you cry, you don't know if the tears are happy or sad. As I watched the sunset from the rooftop pool bar of my hotel, I thought about how to make the most of my last night of luxury before setting sail again. Maybe I felt like crying because I was missing Liz. Maybe it was the raw emotion brought on by travel. Or maybe it was because sunset over Copacabana beach was being soundtracked by Phil Collins singing 'Sussudio' from very well-hidden speakers.

Most people can't step off the treadmill that leads from school to career to mediocrity. But Christ, I thought, just look what happens when you do. After the gap year, is it really only trust-fund kids, the damaged, the deadbeats, eccentrics and dropouts who get to experience a life of travel like this? What prevents the rest of us? A belief that we 'can't' just ditch everything and go out and see the world? The commitment of having children? The millstone of 'career'? The

approval of other people we secretly hate anyway? I scrawled
in slurring block capitals 'HOW CAN I EVER STEP BACK
INSIDE AN ADVERTISING AGENCY AFTER THIS?'
and then, wisely, closed my notebook.

I was awake early the next morning, blissfully unprepared
for the new peaks of stress the day had in store for me.

My phone beeped around 8 a.m. Jeff had landed in São
Paulo. I panicked – he was late. Then I told myself that the
fact that he'd sent a message meant he hadn't just landed;
he'd taxied in and got inside the terminal. I phoned, and he
confirmed that he was at the gate for the Rio connection. I
relaxed, went to the restaurant to try to eat some breakfast,
gave up, went back to my room.

While I was packing, the room phone rang. 'Mr Peter.
This is Wagner from CMA CGA. We are coming to pick you
up from your hotel at eleven o'clock to take you to the ship.'

I looked at my watch. It was now 10.20. 'Eleven? I
thought you said one!'

'No, no. We must go to the ship at eleven.'

'Is there any chance that we could board at twelve o'clock
instead?'

'What? You want to board at Salvador instead?'

'No, no. I need a little more time. Can we go to the ship
at twelve, not eleven?'

'You would like to board the ship today?'

'Yes. Yes.'

'Then we will see you at eleven o'clock. Goodbye.'

I paced the room, making a low keening sound. I hit the
buttons on my mobile with trembling fingers. 'Jeff! How are
we doing?'

He replied in a low voice, 'Just in the green channel now.
Oh. Gottagobye.' Click.

An ululating moan rose from the back of my throat and
eventually resolved itself into words, 'This cannot be happening this is not happening oh God oh fuck oh fucking Christing

twats this cannot be fucking happening this will not happen this will not happen this will not HAPPEN!' I felt as if I should be crying, only my tear ducts were so stressed they were too tightly contracted to allow anything to come out.

I couldn't phone Jeff back in case he were talking to a customs official. I knew he knew the situation. I knew he'd get in touch as soon as he could. And there was no point talking to the shipping agent again.

There were only two options: fall to the floor like a puppet with severed strings, or blind, pointless, futile hope. I chose the latter.

I finished my packing slowly and methodically. Half past ten came and went. Twenty to eleven. Brazilians were always late. Weren't we half an hour late on the favela tour yesterday? But if they were late because of traffic, wouldn't the same traffic delay Jeff? Oh, fuck.

10.50.

Maybe I could direct Jeff to meet us at the port. Only I had no idea where it was. I searched through my papers and found a Google Earth map with the port, Corcovado, and the Sugarloaf pointed out. There were directions to the port – printed in German. But it looked like it was near the airport. I'd get Jeff to go straight there. He was probably still waiting for a cab.

My phone beeped:

> In a red cab going very fast. Emerson Fittipaldi
> driving. Jeff.

Too late to send him to the port. He was on his way here.

10.56.

I shouldered my rucksack and picked up my other bags. I walked out to the lift and went down to check out. A porter relieved me of my bags and asked me if I needed a taxi.

'No. No, someone's coming to pick me up, thanks.'

11.04.

No sign of Jeff. No sign of the shipping agent.

'Did you have anything from the minibar?'

I told the receptionist what I'd had, and she phoned room service and asked them to check my room. I didn't know why she didn't believe me. I didn't care.

A grey people-mover pulled up outside. My heart lurched. A valet opened the back door and an elderly man stepped out with some luggage. The people mover pulled away. I breathed again.

'I'll just print your bill for you to check.'

'Thanks.'

11.07.

I gave the receptionist my credit card. She slipped it into the reader, which chattered away.

'Peter Brown?'

'Yes.'

'I am Cesar from the shipping company. I'm parked just outside.'

He walked away, climbed back into the car and pulled it closer to the door of the hotel, the engine idling.

I moved away from the desk, phoned Jeff. 'I don't know where we are but I can see the sea,' he said. 'Unfortunately there's no way I can ask the driver how long we're going to be. Sorry.'

11.15.

We were so close. We were already fifteen minutes late. Surely a little more delay would be no problem? I walked out to the car. The agent got out to help the porter load my bags into the boot.

'Wagner sends his apologies,' said Cesar. 'He is ill. He has, how you say, stomach problems. He is sitting on the toilet all morning.'

I'd only had three short conversations with Wagner, but this news made me absurdly happy. I had no idea why, but at that moment I knew everything was going to be fine.

'I have a problem . . .' I began.

Two minutes later, after I'd phoned Jeff and arranged a brief conversation between his driver and the shipping agent, after which the shipping agent had said, 'They are ten minutes away. We can wait, it is no problem. The ship does not leave until late tonight,' I thanked a God I resolutely do not believe in for interfering with Wagner's bowels, and stood in the warm honey of Rio's sunshine, grinning at the road.

Precisely ten minutes after the phone conversation, a red taxi pulled up. A porter was at the boot instantly, taking out a red rucksack and a suspiciously heavy-looking wheeled bag. The back door opened and Jeff Pickthall, beer writer, cantankerous CAMRA-baiter, possessor of one of the finest beer-tasting palates in the UK and now international beer smuggler, stepped out, tired and bewildered.

'I never thought I would be so happy to see you!' I said, which possibly wasn't the best form of words, but I think he got the sentiment as we fell into a questionably passionate embrace.

Jeff was, at best, only half hearing me. 'What am I doing here?' he said, looking frightened.

'I recommend the favela tour. I did it yesterday. I'll send you the number. And the beach is down there. Room is booked under your name on my credit card. Breakfast is included. Bye!'

The heavy wheeled bag Jeff brought was already in the boot of the agent's car. I climbed in while Jeff stood uncertainly on the pavement, then turned and went inside the hotel. Sixty seconds after he arrived, twenty-five minutes after the time I had been told I must be ready to leave, we set off for the container terminal, carrying twenty-odd litres of contraband India Pale Ale.

I'm glad to report that, at the time of writing, neither Brazil's economy, its beer industry, its eco-system nor the health of its population seem to have suffered as a result.

CHAPTER THIRTY

EMBARKING ON THE *CARIBBEAN*

The customs officer leafed slowly through my passport then stared up at me suspiciously. He looked back down at the passport, spitting quick sentences in Portuguese, not making eye contact with anyone in the room. I could follow enough of the meaning, through both familiar-sounding words and body language, to tell he was dubious about my motives for being here.

'Do you have your ticket?' Cesar the shipping agent asked me in English. 'He does not believe you are a passenger, because he has never seen a passenger on this route before. What is usual is that people are trying to work on board pretending to be passengers. Also, he is looking for a bribe.'

I handed over four stapled A4 pages of ticket. More discussion ensued. A second agent, who we'd just met outside the terminal, leaned over the seated customs official and pointed out my name, my passenger status, and the price I had paid for the ticket.

'*Tres mil euro!*' exclaimed the official, staring at me long and hard now, no longer suspicious, but with a look that conveyed his unwelcome epiphany that I was clinically insane. He shrugged and handed back my passport and ticket. Nabbing someone for trying to work a passage illegally was one thing – a source of good revenue, both officially and personally. But a madman with documentary evidence of his insanity, that was something else. There was no profit to be made here. The fight left him.

Through a vacant, expectant new passenger terminal fresh

with cellophane and the smell of sawdust, we stepped out on to the port side. A car and driver appeared to take me, the customs man and the two ship's agents three miles along a cobbled dockside scored with veiny, forgotten railway lines. We clattered past rusting hulks and proud oil tankers, and a sense of anticipation about meeting *Caribbean* gathered inside me.

Past signs reading 'A Dock 2km', under giant cranes, alongside walls daubed with caricatures and graffiti, *Caribbean* suddenly loomed up, a blue hull with neat white writing, a large white superstructure, and a walkway climbing about twenty feet up to the main deck. Filipinos in greasy yellow overalls and white hard hats nodded to me when I reached the top, saying, 'Welcome aboard, sir' and 'Hello, sir'. I signed a logbook, writing 'passenger' in the column requiring my reason for being aboard. They repeated the word curiously to each other as I followed the agents up to the poop deck, and into the ship's office.

'NO ONE TOLD ME ABOUT A PASSENGER,' boomed a voice from the corridor leading into the innards of the ship. A few seconds later, a man carved from ancient oak emerged. He was well over six feet tall, a long, bushy ponytail reaching halfway down his back, two large, sweeping brushes creating a moustache. He looked at the four figures in his office, saw the rucksack on my back, and loped towards me like a curious wolf, smiling. I just had time to notice the tattoo of a voluptuous, naked woman curving up his forearm before he took my hand – my writing hand – and crushed it, quickly and cleanly, into a soggy bag of gristle and bone fragments. 'WERNER,' he rumbled, grinning.

'P-Pete,' I winced back, holding my whole face down by the corners of my mouth to disguise the rictus of agony.

'WELCOME, MR PETER! WELL, WELL, A PAS-SENGER. *HAR! HAR! HAR!*' The pictures of *Caribbean*'s sister ships, fixed firmly enough to the walls of the office to withstand the storms of the Cape, rattled as he laughed. 'WHICH PORT ARE YOU TRAVELLING TO?'

I explain the situation with the Iranian visa, leaving it hanging.

Werner glanced at the customs man, smiled, and said, 'AH, WE TALK ABOUT ZIS LATER. NOW, WHICH CABIN WOULD YOU LIKE, MR PASSENGER?'

'Er, I think I'm booked into portside aft?' With my remaining good hand, I drew out my thick book of tickets and itineraries, flipped to the right wallet and took out my confirmation. 'Yes, look. Portside aft.'

'AH, GOOD! PORTSIDE AFT. ZIS IS THE BEST CABIN. FOLLOW ME, MR PETER. I HOPE YOU LIKE STAIRS. HAR! HAR! HAR!'

After two months of living out of a rucksack and holdall, it felt good to be able to spread my stuff out. Despite Werner booming, 'BUT YOU HAVE TOO MUCH LUGGAGE FOR ZIS SMALL CABIN!' when he showed me in, past the wild-eyed panting of the poor Filipinos who had carried the bags up five flights of stairs, there was space to spare. Kevin the Keg nestled in the bottom of the wardrobe. My washbag unpacked into the cabinet above the bathroom sink. My books stacked neatly in a shelf above the bed, and another next to the TV, and everything else went into more drawers and cupboards than we have in our bedroom at home. The empty bags went under the banquette seat in my living room, laptop on the table. I placed Liz's photo in the corner, my map of the world above the bed, and it felt like home.

And then, for four hours, nothing happened.

I was hungover, hungry, and suffering a severe adrenalin crash. I wasn't sure where I was or wasn't allowed to go on the ship, but I needed to go and find out. Back down the stairs to the poop deck, I bumped into Werner coming the other way. 'I wondered if I could get some water . . . or something?' I asked.

'YOU WANT A CASE OF WATER?'

'A case? Well, I just wanted a drink, but, yes, if there's a case, I guess . . .'

'IS THAT ALL? YOU WANT SOME BEER AS WELL? I ALSO HAVE WINE, TWIXES, MARS BAR, ZER PRINGLES?'

This was brilliant. There was a fridge in my cabin, and by gods I was going to stock it. Werner took me down to the captain's slop chest, his private shop for relieving his crew of a little of their earnings. 'CANS OF AMSTERDAM BEER OR BOTTLES OF CASTLE?'

'Er . . . I've not had Amsterdam beer before, could I try that?'

'NO. YOU CANNOT DRINK BEER FROM CANS. ONLY BOTTLED BEER IS GOOD. I GIVE YOU A CASE OF CASTLE AND A CASE OF WATER.'

My cabin was now complete. I was ready to go. I doubt I'll ever forget leaving Rio de Janeiro aboard the *Caribbean*, late that night.

I got over the shock of meeting Werner. While he still had the physique of a decathlete, he no longer seemed to tower above me. His ponytail no longer seemed several feet long. And while his voice still sounded as if it issued from a vast, dry torch-lit cave, he was no longer speaking in capital letters.

At 10 p.m. the phone in my cabin cheeped. 'Peter, zer pilot is aboard. Would you like to join us on zer bridge?'

Oh, go on then.

One thing that hasn't changed since the days of the East India Company is that big ships need a pilot to take you in and out of port. There may be marker buoys and you might have charts and radar, but the pilot knows the rocks and the currents intimately. In his way, the pilot can be as heroic a figure as the captain himself (but don't let Werner hear you say that). So it took me aback a little when I clambered up another two flights of stairs, past the red light glowing at the bottom of the final flight, and up on to the bridge to see a round old man in baggy jeans and a baseball cap, issuing commands to Werner.

But I didn't even notice him at first. I was transfixed by what seemed to be the bridge of the starship *Enterprise*. Arrayed in an angular arc, the bridge console glowed with radar screens and computerized charts and a satisfying number of dials, switches and little red lights. Above our heads, digital read-outs displayed the course and speed of the ship. Observation decks stretched out on either side of the main bridge, exposed to the wind but with a roof overhead. On each stood an auxiliary control centre. Werner was outside on one of these, peering down at the main deck eighty feet below, barking commands through a walkie-talkie.

There was a growing rumble like the approach of stampeding buffalo as the engines came to life. The whole ship was vibrating, and I was awestruck by its humbling power. Some 180 metres of containers stacked six high, seven wide, began to move. I pictured how big each of these containers seems when it's on the back of a lorry, and my brain simply couldn't match that with the dainty movements of the ship as stevedores cast off ropes thicker than my thigh and we inched away from the dockside.

Werner directed the ship as if he were doing this on some PlayStation simulator, touching a tiny lever, taking two steps to peer over the side down to the churning water far below, then dancing back and tapping the controls again. Incredibly, the leviathan moved to his bidding, inches at a time. With thirty feet between the ship and the dock we started to rotate, and I was terrified, properly scared, with my breath coming in short gasps and my heart punching my Adam's apple. I wasn't scared of drowning, or capsizing, or plummeting from the bridge to certain death on the decks below – just scared of the sheer power of the vessel.

We finished turning through 180 degrees. Now facing the

sea, we picked up speed and headed out towards the red and green buoys winking in the bay, always keeping one colour on either side. The pilot had total command of the bridge, and Werner would obey his orders without question until the old man saw fit to give the ship back to its master.

Rio's port is quite far inside the bay, and it was a while before the city slid past our starboard side. High above the floodlit strip of Copacabana beach and the kaleidoscope of downtown, the favelas were suspended on the dark hillside, tumbled and tangled golden spots like dense clusters of fairy lights.

Above one such cluster an astonishing firework display leapt and danced in the sky, seeing us out of the port. Until the day before, this would have filled me with delight – both a sense that this was a good omen for my journey, and the simple, innocent pleasure that fireworks have always represented. There are not many of these pleasures left. And now, there was one fewer.

On the favela tour yesterday, a Canadian couple had asked Martha, our guide, about the significance of a similar firework display they had witnessed. They were staying in a B&B on the edge of a favela, and the fireworks had gone off around them for half an hour, just like those I was watching now. When the starbursts and flares had finished, the bangs and pops had continued, the sound of gunfire filling the night air. 'The armies in the favelas use fireworks as signals,' explained Martha. 'Either another army is invading the favela, or a large new shipment of drugs has arrived. But no one invades at night.'

'Why not?'

'It would be suicide. The army who occupies the favela knows its alleys. They know how to cut off the invaders and surround them. Invasions only happen in the daytime, so fireworks at night, it must be the children sending signals that a large consignment of drugs has arrived.'

As I watched the celebration of this new shipment recede, Christ the Redeemer stood luminous and disembodied, floating over the city. His spreadeagled arms seemed less like a benediction now, more like the action that goes with a cry of 'Ta-dah!' when a magician invites applause. 'And for my next trick, I need a volunteer from the audience. How about it, boys and girls? Yes, you – don't be shy. Come on now, little children of the favelas – suffer, and come unto me . . .'

Dark hulks of islands slid briefly in front of the view. Out past the last outcrop, and floodlit Copacabana beach was peeling away behind us, a bright, expensive pearl necklace garlanding the city above.

I felt exhilarated. But there was one question nagging me: how was the pilot going to get off? Did we stop somewhere? And wouldn't that defeat the point, because then we'd need guiding safely back to sea again? I peered over the side. The red and white pilot boat that had been waiting for us by the furthest buoy was now circling behind us and approaching our starboard side. My gaze fell to the side of the ship, where the gangway was being carefully lowered. I looked at our speed: we were doing six knots. No, I thought, He's not going to . . . he can't . . .

I turned around to see the pilot putting on a baseball cap and life jacket. Werner shook his hand warmly, and a crewmember escorted him from the bridge. Werner sent a warm smile after him, turned to me and said, 'Good pilot. You know they have no retirement pension in Brazil? He had a hard time coming up to zer bridge. That man, still working as a pilot at sixty-nine years old.'

'Sixty-nine? Um, how is he . . . how does he get off the ship?'

'Oh, he is so old we make special arrangements for him.'

'Oh, right! Sorry, I was being very stupid. I thought he was going to go down the gangway and jump from there on to the deck of the pilot boat! While both boats were still moving!'

'Ja, that is the arrangement we make. Normally we would not slow down to six knots, and he would have to use zer rope ladder. But he asks us to do zis for him, because of his age.'

I tried to convince myself that I was horrified by this . . . Bollocks, I was enthralled by it. I rushed back to the observation deck in time to see the pilot emerge shakily at the top of the gangway, a couple of the crew helping him on to the steps. I'd found those steps tricky to walk up in bright daylight with the lower end resting reassuringly against solid concrete rather than bouncing in black air. The pilot boat came alongside us, and was soon matching our speed exactly. A younger man (at least I hoped he was younger) emerged on the pilot boat's deck and moved forward, one hand sliding along silver railings that circled the centre of the boat. The pilot made his way unsteadily down the gangway steps, stumbling every now and again, holding the side rails as tightly as he could. As he reached the bottom, the small red boat was almost underneath him – almost – bouncing across the luminous surf of *Caribbean*'s wake.

When there was nothing left for anyone else to do, the pilot took his right hand from the rail nearest the ship, flung it around . . . and had it grasped immediately by his companion on the pilot boat deck, who swung him aboard, where he clung to the rail for a few seconds before disappearing below, even as his boat roared and arced away, skipping across the waves, barely giving him time to make sure of his footing.

Back in my cabin, the movement of the ship was strange and jerky, free of the stabilizers employed by namby-pamby cruise ships. This was going to take some getting used to. The vibration went through everything. As I wobbled off to sleep, I imagined what it might be doing to the contents of Kevin, my new keg.

CHAPTER THIRTY-ONE

AN EVENING WITH THE SLUDGE LADY

'So, you are going ashore in Santos?'

We were approaching Brazil's biggest port, three hundred miles south of Rio. It was just Werner and me at breakfast. Plates of sickly orange cheese and pink, spongy cartoon meat sat untouched, scaring me through their cellophane. I was having eggs with a few strips of plywood that had been softened, soaked in red dye and then deep-fried. Werner was eating muesli, and I decided that would be the best option from now on.

I'd never be able to match the captain in the magnificent, manly act of eating it though. His bowl overflowed with cereal, lapping over the sides. He poured almost a pint of product-derived-from-milk over it, and wielded his spoon like a weapon. Not like the image this sentence has conjured up in your brain, like he might chafe someone's skin with it or, at worst, depending on the vividness of your imagination, do a bit of gouging. No, Werner could use an ordinary, bendable spoon to club a man to death with. Never before had I seen anyone fill the universal, everyday necessity of eating with so much machismo. And eating muesli at that.

'I might go ashore, I don't know. What do you think?'

'Ah, it is dangerous here. I don't know. Tonight we are anchoring, and in zer night before we go into port, we must be on guard against pirates. And when we go ashore we will be robbed. It is zer children, thirteen, fifteen years old. You can kill maybe two or three of zem, but zen . . .' He tailed off, shook his head and fisted more muesli into his mouth. I wondered if he were joking. He didn't look like he was joking.

I had my safety demonstration after breakfast. The main lifeboat looked almost exactly like *Thunderbird 4*, bright orange and poised on a ramp high on the deck, sloping towards the sea at a forty-five-degree angle. I wished there were some other way to have a go in it without the ship having to sink. It didn't seem fair somehow. If I ever were to experience it, I'd be too terrified really to appreciate it. I had to be shown not just how to get into the boat and strap myself in, but also how to operate it, 'In case you are the only one who makes it.'

Despite this, having been shown immersion suits, the back-up lifeboat, the other two life rafts with special, pressurized locks that release and inflate automatically if they are submerged below five metres, the flares in the cabin, the chest with two or three life jackets for every man aboard, the back-up life-jacket store in case we couldn't reach the main chest for some reason, the emergency beacon, and the good old orange lifebelts, I felt safer than I do in my own bed at home.

Safe, that is, from everything except pirates.

There was a mess for the crew and one for the officers. Passengers, if there ever were any, ate in the officers' mess. 'MASTER, CHIEF ENGINEER, ELECTRICIAN, YOU,' Werner had said when I came aboard, jabbing his finger at each seat in turn from the top to the bottom of the table. I'd expected everyone to sit down at once, but it soon became apparent that people just popped in when they could, or maybe even preferred to dine when others weren't there.[71]

Later that afternoon it was just me and the chief engineer, another German, who looked like Klaus Kinski's slightly seedier older brother, an adult Stewie Griffin. Over what

---

71. In five weeks on board there was only one mealtime when everyone ate together. No one said a word through the whole meal.

might have been a lamb chop, with carrots swimming in grease and defeated potatoes, we talked about Santos. Within about a minute, he was saying, 'Ja, the pirates. At night we must lock all the outside doors. This is a very dangerous place. And they are well equipped here.' The captain hadn't been joking after all.

Two months ago I'd been playing a Pirates game on Facebook, laughing at the idea of attacking ships and throwing bombs at my friends. At the last fancy-dress party I went to (I don't make a habit of going to them, but it was New Year) about a third of the revellers were dressed as pirates. The idea of them existing now can't help but raise an involuntary chuckle. There's no denying it – the image of men wearing eye-patches and stripy shirts and carrying cutlasses in their teeth assaulting a modern ship is a funny one. This is why today's pirate sometimes relies on an AK-47 instead, having found it a brilliant way to stop seamen taking the piss and saying 'Aarrrrrr' at him.

Piracy is simply large-scale thieving at sea, backed up with heavy weaponry. Pirates were always after cargo rather than anything else, and as cargo vessels have evolved, so have they. The International Maritime Bureau sends warnings and details of attacks to shipping. A week after we left Santos, the bridge's printer chattered and the latest report came through, detailing four incidents. The third one down caught my eye:

27.10.2007: SANTOS OUTER ROADS ANCHORAGE
NO.4, BRAZIL
ROBBERS ARMED WITH GUNS BOARDED A
CONTAINER SHIP AND FIRED THEIR GUNS AT
THE APPROACHING CREW MEMBERS. FOR
SAFETY CREW MEMBERS LOCKED THEMSELVES
IN A SAFER PLACE. ROBBERS OPENED 8 REEFER
CONTAINERS AND STOLE CARGO CONTENTS
AND ESCAPED. NO ONE WAS INJURED.

Three days after this incident, although we had no idea at the time, we anchored in the same place. We arrived in the evening, with berthing scheduled for the following morning. There was nothing to see apart from the smudges of lights of other ships studding the horizon. I shut and bolted my cabin window in case there were any pirates fit enough to climb up the five flights of stairs outside to get to it, and slept soundly through the midnight watch I'd agreed to do from the bridge while the crew patrolled the decks beneath bright floodlights.

The next morning I counted nineteen other ships anchored, waiting, like us. Squat peaks sulked at our stern, and I could make out the faintest suggestion of a city in the low charcoal murk. Santos is almost exactly on the Tropic of Capricorn, and it was the Southern-hemisphere equivalent of the beginning of May, but the chill and pall in the air were all too familiarly English. I could almost see my tan leeching away. Around lunchtime, the pilot vessel sped towards us. After a brief moment of alarm (when Werner spoke quickly the words 'pilot' and 'pirate' were indistinguishable) the pilot boarded the ship, took control of the bridge and guided us into port. Santos is the busiest, most important port in South America. If you have coffee, sugar or oranges in your kitchen, there's a fair chance they passed through here. Werner worked on the juice ships coming through Santos and signed off here twenty years ago. His face softened for the first time as he remembered it. He seemed very excited to be back.

The whole of Brazil existed in microcosm along the bay and up the banks of the river into the port. The seafront was a wide, white gold strip separated from the land by a wall of creamy buildings that looked like a phalanx of giant beehives. To the sides were low green hills, giving way to a thick band of rainforested mountains, greying in the distance. The main city was on the left bank. On the right, snuggled just inside the river mouth, was a yacht club – it seems every port should have one – crammed with sleek, arrowhead-shaped erection substitutes. A few hundred yards further on, the riverbank became a boggy shantytown. Many of the buildings closest to the water leaned drunkenly on stilts, like they might stumble over into the mud any second. Children buzzed around the shore in swarms of tiny black dots, kicking homemade footballs through the mud. Here and there were half-submerged sets of goalposts, football pitches relegated to the few places on which the residents daren't build. Ferries criss-crossed in perpetual motion from the shantytown to the city. I watched a squat one, like a yellow box file with a little tower on top, moor on the Santos side of the river and burst, emitting a hundred cyclists into the city.

And then we were in the port, although we were still only halfway to our mooring. Warehouses and silos, shiny juice tankers and ancient rust-buckets, and monstrosities three times the size of *Caribbean* loaded with enough containers to keep the M25 in permanent gridlock for a year all rolled past for miles. Beautiful, old colonial-style buildings with turrets and columns stood incongruous amid the industry, an old town swallowed up as the port expanded, abandoned as it receded. Finally, we saw two giant blue cranes looming a hundred feet over an empty berth. Time again for those tiny joystick movements, and the massive ship turned on its axis and nudged smoothly home. Stevedores stood on the dockside, communicating with the crew by whistles and waves. When we were close enough, guide ropes were thrown from ship to dock. The stevedores caught them and pulled, and cables snaked through the water like giant sea serpents before being hauled out and secured around huge metal stanchions. Motors whirred on the deck, taking up the slack, and we were secure.

'So have you decided about going ashore?' Werner asked.

'I don't think so,' I replied, 'not after everything I've heard about how dangerous it is.'

Werner waved contemptuously at this, as if he hadn't been

the principal doom-monger. 'The lady who is emptying our sludge promised me that next time I was in port, she would show me the town. You must come with us.'

Out with the captain? Well, that was a different matter. Bullets would probably bounce off his moustache. And we were going around this dangerous town full of pirates with the Sludge Lady. Who could say no to that?

Rosimeire the Sludge Lady was both literally and metaphorically an Amazonian, a woman only someone like Werner could even think about crossing. She was beautiful once, but was now simply impressive, a woman you could imagine ruling the country. At first I'd assumed the worst about what ship's sludge might be, but it turns out that it's the by-product of our fuel, a water-and-oil mix. It's no longer of any use to the ship, but Rosimeire's people separate out the water, break it down and reuse it or sell it on. The lower the water content, the higher the price. In cash. No questions asked. But there was no money this time: there had been too much water in the sludge. Werner protested he didn't know why that should be, but Rosimeire insisted. The tension needed to be laughed away over alcohol.

Rosimeire took us to the beach. Dusk had just fallen and left only a faint pinky-blue glow on the horizon, and floodlights bathed the sand. Tiny kiosks lay scattered under the beachside palm trees. Less slick and shiny than their Rio cousins, each was a cheerful jumble of chest freezers, white tiles, burger buns and cachaca bottles, serving drinks to be sipped at fat concrete tables and stools facing the ocean.

Rosimeire bought ice-cold cans of Brahma. 'Brazilian number one,' she said proudly, and Werner showed his gratitude by keeping his grumble that you cannot drink beer from cans to a level where she could only just hear it.

After the first beer Rosimeire treated us to caipirinhas. They were excellent, but delivered an immediate icy fist to the head, and they must have been served by the half pint.

At four real a pop, I couldn't resist comparing prices in a London cocktail bar. For a drink half this size at a hotel bar you'd be paying nearly ten quid, or thirty-five real. Rosimeire instantly had to convey this to the barman who was amazed, then amused. He held up a large plastic bucket, and I knew what he was saying even before Rosimeire translated. 'He'll make you a thirty-five real caipirinha if you like – would this be OK?'

We talked about travel and the price I had paid for my voyage. Werner was continually processing figures. It's what he does. He worked out what I was paying per day, and decided it was too much. 'Don't go through the travel agents. They're just trying to make money. Go direct to the shipping companies. They'll take you to places the travel agents won't.' He insisted I would have been able to get a ship from South Africa to India if I had gone straight to the ships themselves. Any ship would take passengers if they felt like it, he insisted. Most ships from Europe to South Africa had passengers on board, and ships crossing the Caribbean were also popular. But I was the first passenger ever to sail this route, as far as he knew.

'But best of all is the trip up the Amazon,' Werner continued. 'You can get a cargo boat up to the city of Manaus. That is number one in the whole world.'

'For the women! I bet, that's why he likes it,' hooted Rosimeire.

'No!' Werner was suddenly solemn. 'No, you go for the journey. The river journey up to Manaus, where the Amazon meets the Rio Negro and the water changes colour from yellow to dark brown, just like that, on the line . . .' He kissed his thumb and forefinger, the international gesture for a gorgeous meal. 'Number one. Number one in the whole world. You must do this.'

After our second caipirinha, it felt like time to move on. 'We must show Pete the sailors' paradise!' ordered Werner, and we drove back to the port area, along narrow cobbled streets full of dark warehouses, until we reached one block where bright light spilled out on to the shiny round stones.

'Twenty years ago when I signed off here, this whole strip was full of bars,' said Werner fondly. 'Now they are all gone. About seven or eight barfronts in one strip – this is all that is left.'

'These are bars just for the sailors?' I asked.

'Yes. Sailors, drug dealers and whores – these are the only people who ever drink here. Shall we go in?'

It would have been rude to say no.

The ABC Bar was a nightclub with a raised dance floor in the middle and small round tables radiating around it. Three Filipino sailors were dancing together to Wham!, flinging their arms around and giggling. More giddy men sat at some of the tables, glancing at the groups of women sitting at others. These ladies came in all shapes and sizes, all ages, all dressed up, all in single-sex groups watching the room keenly, expectantly.

Most of them seemed to know Rosimeire and a group of them joined us, sizing up Werner and me but not making any advances. We were drinking with a friend of theirs, and this seemed to be protecting us, at least for now.

We had two more caipirinhas, and then I had to switch to beer. I was enjoying the numb buzz crawling across my skin, but just watching the caipirinhas being made gave me tooth-ache. The barmaid seemed to have worked out precisely how much sugar it was possible to dissolve in 250ml of liquid, using whole bags in one drinks order.

One of Rosimeire's friends, a round, shiny latte-skinned woman who looked as if she'd be more likely to charge you a fee for making sure you were eating properly and wrapping up warm against a chill rather than having sex with you, handed me a limp balloon. Her friends giggled, but they were all blowing up balloons too, so my paranoia about a practical joke seemed unfounded. I blew it up, tied it and handed it to one of the girls who, smirking, tied it into a chain of green and white balloons. Immediately I was handed another from a large packet on the bar. I shrugged, handed one to Werner, and we stood there for twenty minutes, helping prostitutes blow up balloons. It was nice, companionable work, until Werner grew bored and began bursting them manfully with huge exhalations of pure, gaseous testosterone. I carried on until the packet was empty. It gave me a purpose, a role, and as I had absolutely no idea what kind of conversation to attempt with these women, I clung to this role like a lifebelt.

The balloons disappeared, replaced on the bar by plates of potatoes and pastry parcels, which we were invited to tuck into. This was very jolly. When the food was finished, we were pulled over into a dark corner. By this time, the idea of this being a transition to anything improper did not occur to me, and rightly so. Our balloons garlanded curtains that shut out the dark reality of the port, framing a table that supported a huge birthday cake, candles glowing. And here came a young woman in a tiny skirt with a blindfold over her eyes, led to the table by two of her friends. The blindfold was whipped off, and we sang and clapped the local equivalent of 'Happy Birthday'. And with that, my first-ever evening getting drunk with a group of prostitutes became, somewhat unexpectedly, one I couldn't wait to tell my wife about.

In the library I'd brought with me, I had a volume called *Vagabond Voyaging*, a how-to book from the 1930s about travelling as a passenger aboard freighters. As I weaved back to my cabin very early the next morning, one particular passage stuck in my mind: 'Of one thing you can be sure: you're more likely to get fair prices and certainly more likely to see the towns with a clear eye when you arrive via freighter than when you come to a city that is all keyed up to collect the month's rent from three hundred world trippers.' Whatever else had changed in the intervening seventy years, this was still wonderfully true.

CHAPTER THIRTY-TWO

LIFE ABOARD THE *CARIBBEAN*

The towns and ports shrank as we made our way south down the Brazilian coast.

At each port a pilot came aboard to take us in and out. I saw now what Werner had meant when he described the antics coming out of Rio as a special arrangement for the septuagenarian pilot there. The normal routine was for the launch to come alongside towards the front of the ship, and for the pilot, clad in life jacket and crash helmet, to get himself from the launch on to a rope ladder, and up to the deck, all while we were doing twelve knots.

Once he was on board and heading our way, Werner would reluctantly cover his bright-red vest with the shirt signifying his rank and tuck it into his drawstring trousers, ready for his favourite bit. As the pilot's head appeared, several minutes after he boarded, the captain would switch back into upper case and boom, 'WELCOME, MR PILOT! WELCOME TO OUR ONE HUNDRED THIRTY STEPS! HAR HAR HAR! WOULD YOU LIKE COFFEE OR SOMESING?'

'Co-cold drink. Water . . . water or soft drink,' the pilot would gasp, arms braced against the windows at the front of the bridge, his back heaving as he sucked in sweet breaths. As soon as he recovered, he took the bridge. Werner hated to yield control of his ship, but the steps were his consolation.

Also on deck was Ron, a tall, doe-eyed German officer cadet barely out of his teens. He spent most of his day in the same paint-spattered overalls as the Filipino crew but, perhaps because it was valuable training, and perhaps because Werner hated to demean himself by taking direct orders from the pilot, it was Ron who took charge of the toy-car steering wheel as the pilot stared vacantly out of the window, firing off tiny changes in the heading.

'Two-three-zero.'

'Two-three-zero . . . heading two-three-zero,' Ron replied in crisp, professional tones. There was no room here for ambiguity or mistakes. Electronic read-outs displayed the heading in red LEDs, together with dials showing engine revolutions and rudder angle.

'Two-three-two.'

'Two-three-two . . . heading two-three-two.'

'Steady as she goes.'

'Steady on two-three-two.'

It made a mockery of our ham-fisted attempts at steering *Europa*, pleased with ourselves if we managed to get within five degrees of the course we had been given.

As soon as those fat, snaking ropes had secured us in our berth, blue-overalled shoremen joined our yellow-clad crew on deck, and the giant cranes rolled towards us on rails I'd once mistaken for disused train tracks. Trucks queued along the causeway, sometimes big, muzzle-nosed Macks to take containers straight out on the road, but mostly skeletal yellow port lorries to cart them a few hundred yards and add them to the primary-coloured corrugated city blocks in port. Hours later, laden lorries would queue to repeat the procedure in reverse, the whole ship occasionally shuddering when new cargo landed a little too abruptly.

In idle moments, the crew made crude fishing equipment by wrapping twine around empty plastic bottles, and casting off from the back of the ship. 'Is that to catch something extra for dinner?' I asked. They nodded seriously. In the days to come, I would understand why.

A week after I boarded we came to Rio Grande, a

thousand miles south of Rio de Janeiro. We entered a vast river estuary with a narrow opening, the viridian sea striped with khaki swathes. It was cold, and even Werner wore a coat and woolly hat on the bridge. The chief engineer and I went ashore into what I would call a one-horse town if there weren't several, grazing freely at the side of the road. We were looking for food to stock up for the eighteen uninterrupted days at sea ahead, mistrustful of the cook's abilities to keep us alive unassisted. But I forgot all about fresh fruit when I saw a range of brews by Eisenbahn, a Brazilian craft brewer trying their hand at German beer styles. This was more like it! I loaded up with samples of rauchbier (smoked beer), weissbier (wheat beer), dunkel (dark beer), a proper pilsner, and a strong barley wine. 'This is work for me,' I said apologetically to the chief engineer as we clanked back to the ship, he carrying one of my bags for me. We didn't know each other very well, so he smiled politely rather than heaping jealous abuse on me the way friends do whenever I trot out this lame excuse.

Then, just as waiting at anchorage, having pilots aboard and shifting containers were becoming routine, there was suddenly no more Brazil left, and we turned and headed for the open sea.

Before this trip I'd always assumed the Cape of Good Hope and Cape Horn were roughly level with each other. In fact the Horn is a good twenty-odd degrees further south, with Good Hope about level with the border between Brazil and Uruguay, the whole length of Argentina stretching south below it. Ask anyone who has sailed, and they'll not be disrespectful to Good Hope, but it's surviving the journey around the Horn that makes you a true Old Salt. So from Rio Grande we sailed more or less east, at a steady twenty knots per hour, back across the Atlantic towards the Cape of Good Hope. It would be almost three weeks before we stepped on land again.

Halfway through that first night of the Atlantic crossing, I woke to a riot of crashing, grating, grinding, sliding and banging, as everything in my cabin that wasn't on an anti-slip mat relocated to the floor. I'd expected a big ship like this to be more stable, and the next morning when I looked out of the window the sea wasn't even that rough – it was just a normal swell. Then I thought of *Europa*, and being up the mast. Any movement at deck level was exaggerated up there, and I was seven floors up from the main deck. Sure enough, down on the poop deck for breakfast I could hardly feel the movement. It became harder to walk normally as I went back up each flight of stairs. Cruise ships have expensive stabilizers to reduce this movement. It seemed there was no call for that here.

I wondered about Kevin, my new travelling companion, and the effect this movement might have. I remembered a conversation I'd had with a prominent home brewer earlier in the year, an undisputed expert on Victorian-era recipes for India Pale Ale. I explained to him what I was hoping to do, and to my astonishment, he waved the air contemptuously and said, 'Been done.'

My heart fell through the floor. 'Done? When? How? Who?'

'I did it myself a couple of years ago.'

'Really? But I never heard—'

'Of course, there was no point in actually taking it all the way to *India*. I merely kept a cask on my small boat in the English Channel for six months. The temperature change on the journey doesn't make any difference. The rolling is what matters.'

Sitting in my cabin, feet braced against the legs of the desk so I didn't fly across the table and through the TV screen, I speculated that, even if he were right about the temperature change (thereby disproving not only the whole premise by which Madeira is made, but also challenging everything biochemistry tells us about the behaviour of yeasts), you don't get rolls like this in the English Channel.

At lunch the chief electrician, a Ukrainian who had scowled into his flour, chicken and sweetcorn soup opposite me until I asked him a question, and then lit up, becoming the most talkative crewmember apart from Werner, offered another explanation for the movement. 'We are now loaded with one hundred sixty reefers – refrigerated containers. With that weight, we roll deeply.'

This was the moment for a question I'd been dying to ask someone. The link between the East India Company, India Pale Ale and my own journey was the flow of international commerce. And so it was very important to know what I was crossing two oceans with. I knew what the Company ships carried, what travelled with IPA. I needed to complete the story. What could be going from South America to the Middle East and India? What significance, what parallels would there be between my journey and the historic voyages of the East Indiamen?

'Chickens.'

'Chickens?'

'One hundred sixty reefers full of frozen chicken for our Arabian friends. Every day I must check them all, make sure they are kept at minus eighteen degrees.'

'It's all chicken?'

'All chicken.'

I love chicken. But, somehow, this cargo seemed less profound than I'd hoped.

When Liz and I first talked about this voyage toughening me up, this long container-ship leg was the part I always had in mind. Since leaving Burton two months ago time had become malleable. Some days had to be planned down to the last minute, with the precision of a wedding day, while others I'd simply lost, bobbing past unnoticed on the waves. Now I had two and a half weeks of unstructured, shapeless hours to fill, I was about to find out just how much I liked my own company.

Everyone else was busy, and I was expected to keep out of their way. They had a routine, with fixed hours of work. I needed a routine too, something to define the days. I had a book to write, and there was a new urgency to complete as much of the book as possible: when I disembarked in Mumbai, there was a good chance Werner would shake my hand again.

The first planks in the schedule were meal times. Breakfast was 07.00 to 08.15; lunch 11.30 till 12.15; dinner 17.30 to 18.15. Between these I slotted in times for writing up notes, for writing the book proper, for reading the shelf of historical tomes I'd brought with me, for a slog on the exercise bike and for meditation. I allowed myself a few hours free in the evening. By the third week, when I was no longer capable of even looking at it, I'd got a schedule that worked.

The problem was, it nearly all took place in my cabin, and after a few days I began to feel unusual. I started talking to myself out loud after only a week. I had to break things up more, but there wasn't really anywhere else to go.

Towards the end of our first week on the open sea, Werner revealed the foredeck to me, a five-minute stagger from my cabin. Everything was painted blood red. The stanchions that the massive mooring ropes went around were the height and width of pub tables with black and yellow striped tops, but the ropes were all now stowed away. The holes they fed through in port were now windows on to the racing blue sea. There was no engine noise here, no rumble of power, but the groans, grunts and roars coming from all around as she cut through the waves made her seem like a giant animal. Every few seconds there was a deep belch, and water fountained up from the wells into which the anchor chains disappeared. Over the top of the prow, blue crystal ocean surrounded us. Occasionally a huge wall of water reared up at the front of the ship, making me flinch, but the curve of the bow meant that by the time I could even see it, it was arcing away from me. The only other noise was the waves, hissing like cheap plastic bags caught in fences. It was a wonderful place.

Werner gave me a tour. The engine room was three storeys of engineering that made the propeller turn. The gears connecting the little wheel to the massive rudder were a towering cylinder of brushed metal. The pistons that drove the propeller were each bigger than Werner, and needed complex cooling systems and hydraulics to stop their power shaking the ship apart. Behind a glass wall, Chief Engineer German Stewie watched banks of computers and flashing lights.

The cargo hold inside the ship was eleven containers wide and five containers deep, and they could be stacked six high on the deck. That really is a colossal amount of chicken. We went up into the cockpit of the crane, almost level with the bridge. It was only used in small ports, where they don't have the mobile superstructures of the dockside cranes. 'Being up here when zere is a big swell, when zer ship is pitching forty degrees . . .' Werner made his thumb and forefinger kiss again, 'zat is zer best feeling in zer world.' Well, it would be if you were a hundred per cent testosterone.

After that, I spent every afternoon on the foredeck, from lunch until sunset. The sunsets were always spectacular, the highlight of my day. Between a gunmetal sea and a steely blue sky, the red glow at the horizon was a welder's torch, trying to fuse air and water together. As the sun disappeared the water turned black. It jumped and danced at the side of the ship, mazed with the delicate white lace of surf, like the sea of Japanese Ukiyo-e art.

In the evenings, the crew retreated to their cabins. There was a common room with a bar just down the corridor from the messes, but no one ever used it and plastic still covered the seats. This was a private ship. Occasionally I would hear a couple of guys talking behind a closed door, but there was no evidence of any real social life.

'If you want to retire to your cabin to sit and think, or just to sit, there's no dissenting voice raised,' read *Vagabond Voyaging*. 'No dapper young man in white pants with a carnation in his blue coat will grab your arm and plead with you to act as jockey in the horse race, no bustling purser will annoy you with requests to join in a fancy-dress ball.' Well, great, but as the days wore on, the cheery excesses of the cruise ship no longer seemed like such an irritant. 'Two or more officers are always off duty, so there's someone around nearly all the time to make a fourth at bridge, or to challenge you to a chess match,' continued the section headed 'Your Friends the Officers'. I cursed myself for not bringing a chess-set with me – it could all have been so different.

And then one night, it was. On the Saturday at the end of the second week, I was leaving the officer's mess after dinner and contemplating another long, lonely evening. The door to the crew's mess was wedged open, and cheesy disco music blasted out. I popped my head around the door to offer a watery smile, and the crew cheered and urged me to join them.

'Mr Peter! Can we get you beer? Wine?'

I asked for some wine, and one man sent another to the fridge to get it. I took a seat and they beamed at me. Most of the crew were in here, but no officers. Everyone was drinking, and a laptop had been hooked up to some speakers. A couple of guys were grooving in the centre of the floor, everyone else occasionally cheering them along.

One man, maybe twenty-five, shaven-headed with a goatee and huge liquid-brown eyes, moved his chair over to me and started talking. After a few pleasantries, he smiled and said, 'We're so honoured that a rich man such as you has come to drink with us and join our party. When you came aboard – we thought you were the new captain!'

Everyone roared with laughter, me included. 'But I'm not rich!' I protested.

We talked about my trip, and they confirmed that I was the first passenger they had ever seen on this route. I said I was starting to find it a little difficult on board. My companion smiled. 'Yes, it does get hard eventually. We come on board for ten months, leaving our families behind. It is . . . difficult. But then we get two months off, and go home and see them again. In the ten months we're on ship, we go round this journey, from Brazil to the Middle East, three times. The only time we have a night ashore is when we reach Santos. Tonight is special. In port, some of us have to work all the time. Out at sea, we can have the night off.'

'So why do you do it?' I asked, mentally scrolling out my notebook about the relationship between men and the ocean, the lure the waves have for a certain kind of person, the restlessness of *Europa*'s permanent crew as we neared land, the long history of discontented seekers running away to sea.

'It is really good money.'

'Oh. Really?'

'Yes, there are very few jobs at home. Certainly none that pay as well as this. We get twelve hundred US dollars.'

'Twelve hundred dollars a month? Wow, that's . . . not bad.'

'No!' he laughed, 'you are a rich man! No, twelve hundred dollars for ten months. For one tour.'

'You get paid one hundred and twenty dollars a month?'

'Yes. This is good money.'

I had paid more than double for my cabin for five weeks than they were paid in a year.

The rich man and the crewmember were interrupted in their conversation by the arrival of the steward and the cook, who had just finished in the kitchen. I hadn't seen the cook before, because the steward always brought our food into the mess. The cook was a small man, bald, with little round glasses, and a huge potbelly. He had a sweet, beatific smile, and took a seat the others had been saving him. As soon as he sat down they urged him to perform what was clearly a party piece. He made a reasonable effort of trying to wave them off, but the chant grew louder. The music was turned off, and he straightened in his seat. Everyone fell silent. And then, this small, spherical man launched into a pitch-perfect cover of 'I Can't Live (If Living is Without You)', as sung by Mariah Carey. His voice was high and pure as a mountain stream, every note perfect, right down to the diva's mad meandering up and down the scales.

After whooping and hollering my approval when he finished I was too stunned to say anything else. My glass was filled whenever it was more than half-empty. More crew members came to ask me if I were enjoying my time aboard the ship, and if I liked their little party. I nodded and grinned like a lunatic.

It must get lonely being away from your family for ten months, on a giant ship with seventeen or eighteen other men. The prostitutes in Santos made perfect sense now. It seemed impossible to find anything wrong with the scenario – one night every three months or so, and although money changed hands, it obviously couldn't have been much. I learned that while the old adage might refer to a sailor having a girl in every port, those girls also had a sailor on every ship. They knew when each vessel came in, and would be waiting for their guy when it did. While his ship was in port, she would be faithful only to him, and she expected the same in return. There are plenty of sailors with steel-comb scars across their cheeks from the night they decided they fancied a bit of variety.

But that was only three nights in every ten months. Now, with the alcohol flowing on a Saturday night, things started to get a bit fruity.

The disco music came back on, and a couple of guys

would get up and dance. Eventually I worked out it was a game, a sort of 'chicken' based around who was most comfortable with their sexuality. Their moves would gradually become more suggestive, more overtly sexual, until one of them would scream, freak out and run for his seat, and everyone would declare the other man winner. He'd stay on the floor, waiting for challengers.

The steward was the undisputed champion. For starters, he was a natural dancer, combining the druggy abandon of Madchester monkey dancing with the flair and grace of a choreographed idol. On top of that, he had no shame or fear. And, finally, he had a really cute arse. I hadn't appreciated how cute until he dropped his trousers, pulled his Y-fronts up his arse-crack to create a thong, and began grinding his tight, round chestnut-coloured buttocks into his latest rival for the throne. This guy withstood the treatment for about five seconds before running from the room.

And then it was midnight. I didn't know where the time had gone; I just knew that it had been a fantastic party. It was still in full flow when I left, and they gave me a loud cheer. I felt calmer than I had for months. Finally, I had my barrel on board and India in my sights. I was back on Samuel Allsopp's trail. I decided to treat myself to a Sunday break from writing and looked forward to the same time next week, unaware that this would be the only such party while I was aboard.

CHAPTER THIRTY-THREE

THE ARRIVAL OF THE *BENCOOLEN*

After Rio, once they were far enough south, the East India-men could pick up the westerly winds and turn to face the Cape of Good Hope.

They might stop at St Helena, the remote colony that served as a staging post, prison for Napoleon Bonaparte, and later a concentration camp for captured Boers, and then came the Cape itself. Following the establishment of Cape Town as a permanent colony by the Dutch, it became a pleasant district of guesthouses, bright flowers and coach rides. As Kincaid observes, the 'undreamt of reserves of gold and diamonds' here could have 'bought more cottons and spices than all Europe could consume', but on the way out it was light relief, where 'outgoing crews took a last bracing breath before plunging into Asia's malarial miasma', and on the way back was a place where 'returning wanderers dared to dream again of cool green pastures and dank ale houses'. An early English visitor complained that he could find 'but 3 Houses in the Town that sell strong Liquor', but this situation was quickly remedied. Soon a Dutch governor reprimanded the colony for its 'excessive cultivation of the vine', and an English clergyman was shocked that travellers 'Revel, bouze and break Glasses, what they please'. The town earned the enduring nickname, the 'Tavern of Two Seas'.

Navigation of the stormy Cape of Good Hope followed. After the Cape the Indian Ocean was potentially even more dangerous, with the constant threat of pirates, privateers and French attacks, and inadequate protection from the English navy – on his third journey to India Hickey was captured and held for some time by the French – and, eventually, arrival in Madras or Bengal. Fanny Parkes arrived in India in November, five months after she had left the Downs.

According to Hickey, the first thing to do upon arrival was often to demand satisfaction in the form of a duel over disputes that had simmered on board for so long that no one could remember what had kicked them off in the first place. And while the passengers brawled and brandished letters of introduction and the lancers hit the taverns and toddy houses with a vengeance, the beer was unloaded along with the claret and Madeira and hats and sideboards and engravings and hams and 'prints of droll and political characters', and adverts were placed in the *Calcutta Gazette*. The liquid in these casks was not the same as it had been when it left London months ago. Ads would refer to the finest beers as 'ripe' or 'well up', and ready to drink, proving that the 'green' beer that had left England was still in need of conditioning. Now, months after brewing, in an alien climate, it was time to find out whose beers made the grade. Here on the steamy Calcutta dockside, fortunes stood to be won or lost.

Given the Bencoolen factory's historic reputation as a disease-blown, drink-sodden last-chance saloon that convicts would rather hang than be posted to, and its censure by John Company over its enthusiasm for Burton ale, it's perhaps fitting that Samuel Allsopp's first consignment of strong beer for India went on a ship of the same name. But much had changed in the century since the Bencoolen public table's legendary binge. Affairs in the east were more organized, more civilized now. Beer had become a respectable drink, a sign of good standing, drunk by people who were creating a New England that was different from home in only a few key respects: it was much hotter, a bit more dangerous, and they were able to live like lords rather than clerks.

But an exotic world still lay outside the window. Fanny

Parkes, arriving only a few months earlier, painted a vivid picture of the sight that would have greeted the *Bencoolen* as she made her final passage up the Hooghly River:

> Passing through the different vessels that crowd the Hoogly off Calcutta gave me great pleasure; the fine merchant-ships, the gay, well-trimmed American vessels, the grotesque forms of the Arab ships, the Chinese vessels with an eye on each side of the bows to enable the vessel to see her way across the deep waters, the native vessels in all their fanciful and picturesque forms, the pleasure-boats of private gentlemen, the beautiful private residences in Chowringhee, the Government-house, the crowds of people and vehicles of all descriptions, both European and Asiatic, form a scene of beauty of which I know not the equal.

A further key difference is that here beer was still a luxury rather than the centuries-old staple it was back home. The market Hodgson dominated was not huge. John Bell, who compiled trade figures for the Bengal authorities, estimated the average annual consumption of beer at almost 7,000 hogsheads, a quarter of which went to Madras, the rest to Bengal. 'There is reason to suppose that the demand would increase if the price was steady', he wrote, 'but while it fluctuates from six to fifteen rupees a dozen it is not likely that the consumption will be increased.' On the contrary, 'thousands would be compelled to give it up and take to drinking French clarets, which are and have been selling at from three to eighteen rupees a dozen'. French clarets? Less than a decade after Waterloo? No, we couldn't have that. The supply of affordable beer had to be stabilized.

The fact that pale ale occupied a very similar price range to French claret speaks volumes about the quality of the beer and the demand for it in this climate. That quality was strictly upheld by the import agents. Some historians wax dramatically about how rejected beer was poured away into the harbour. This did sometimes happen – W. H. Roberts heard from a correspondent in 1845 of eighty hogsheads being poured away – but it would have had to have been incredibly bad beer to warrant such measures. Even beer that couldn't pass muster had its uses. It might have molasses pitched in, the sugar giving it an additional fermentation, then be watered down and mixed with spices to disguise the rank taste. If it were too bad even for that, it could be used to form the base of ketchup: one of the first recipes for 'catsup' was devised by Hannah Glasse in 1747 'for the Captains of ships'. It could keep for up to twenty years, and consisted of stale beer, anchovies, mace, cloves, pepper, ginger and mushrooms.

But there was to be no Samuel Allsopp's ketchup after the tasters had done their work. The Burton pale ale was approved. The cargo went to the city's auction houses, and the *Calcutta Gazette* filled up with beer ads.

Hodgson was clearly at the swamp-the-market phase in his protectionist cycle. He must have got wind of Allsopp's intentions, because 11,500 hogsheads of beer were imported in the 1822–3 season, double the amount of the year before, four times the amount of the year before that, and double anything that would be achieved for the rest of the decade. The ads in the paper became increasingly lyrical in their praise. In April the front page boasted 'prime picked' Hodgson's pale ale, which 'surpasses in superiority of quality, any of the former season's . . . as fine Malt Liquor as ever was drunk'.

The price of ale plummeted. Hodgson's beer was selling for twenty-five rupees per hogshead – the price of Allsopp's ale was set at twenty. It was a good start, but it wasn't great – twenty rupees a hogshead when in some years you could get fifteen for a dozen quart bottles was not the basis for a profitable business. John Bell wasn't happy:

The enhanced scale of importation which took place in 1822–23 was both unwise, and attended with great loss to those immediately concerned with the trial of monopolizing the Indian market; and the sorrowful winding up of that speculation, by forced sales of unsound beer ... evinced a want of proper discrimination on the part of those whose time would have been more properly and advantageously employed in the immediate exercise of their calling.

Allsopp's second consignment fared better, helped by a fortunate bit of circumstance. When the second ship, the *Seaforth*, came in, Tulloh & Co. as usual offered 'the finest stock of HODGSON'S ripe PALE ALE to be met with in India', but further down the page sat the following notice:

REJECTED BEER

To be sold by Public Auction, by Messrs Taylor & Co, on the
CUSTOM HOUSE WHARF, by permission of the Collector
of Sea Customs, at eleven o' Clock precisely, on Saturday
next, the 28th Instant, 48 HOGSHEADS of Hodgson's
BEER, and 17 empty HOGSHEADS, landed from the ship
Timandra, and 30 hogsheads of Hodgson's BEER, landed
from the ship Seaforth.

A good portion of Hodgson's beer had spoiled. Allsopp's beer, on the same ship, had not. This time, it fetched forty rupees at auction.

With a journey of up to six months each way, brewers in England often had to wait a year to learn how their business had gone. But slowly the letters began to arrive back in Burton. Mr Gisborne, a customer of the first order, wrote to Allsopp in July 1823 asking if the trade in Burton ale could be expanded, recommending that he be given the authority to bottle the ale for retail on arrival. In November 1824, Mr J. C. Bailton wrote from Calcutta:

I have watched the whole progress of your ale ... With reference to the loss you have sustained in your first shipments, you must have been prepared for that, had you known that market as well as I do; here almost everything is name, and Hodgson's has so long stood without a rival, that it was a matter of astonishment how your ale could have stood in competition; but that it did is a fact, and I myself was present when a butt of yours fetched 136 rupees, and a butt of Hodgson's only 80 rupees at public sale.

Captain Chapman wrote that the ale had turned out well, that a bigger shipment should be sent the following year, and that even then it might be scarce. In the same month, Messrs Gordon & Co. wrote:

After bottling off a portion, which was approved by our friends, the demand for this article has since been very great, and we now have orders to some extent for this ale. We would, therefore, strenuously recommend Mr Allsopp to make further consignments of it; and we have every reason to believe he will have a fair competition with Messrs Hodgson & Co.

The trickle of orders coming in via agents in Liverpool and London turned into a steady stream. Allsopp increased his shipments, and received assurances that 'many who had been long in India, declared it to be preferable to any they had ever tasted in the East'. Soon his price was matching Hodgson's, and auctioneers Tulloh & Co. (who would go on to write the highly critical *Circular on the Beer Trade in India*) began to rhapsodize over it in their advertisements. They still sold Hodgson's beer of course, but now there was a worthy rival the copy seemed a little less effusive. As Tizard put it, 'the spell had been broken'. In four seasons, Allsopp shattered Hodgson's grip on the market.

In the face of seemingly insurmountable odds, there was

something about Allsopp's beer that was powerful enough to supplant the established, dominant market leader that seemingly held all the cards. Of course some of this success was due to the vision and determination of Allsopp himself, a man who 'saw no difficulties which time, perseverance, resolution, consistency, and steady, unswerving honour could not overcome'.[72] But there was more to it than that. What Campbell Marjoribanks couldn't have realized when he decided to court Allsopp is that he was approaching a brewer who possessed a very special ingredient.

We now know that the water of the Trent valley is the best water for brewing ale anywhere in the world. Write a spec for the perfect composition of salts and minerals to brew a bright, sparkling bitter beer, and there they are, in water that's trickled through beds of sand and gravel anywhere up to sixty feet deep. The strong, hoppy beer devised by Hodgson was given a whole new dimension when brewed in Burton. It was a phenomenal stroke of good fortune, bringing a style of beer that suited the Indian climate to a place that would never have had good reason to brew it, but was, in the words of a Bass historian, 'The one spot in the world where the well-water is so obviously intended by Nature for kindly union with those fruits of the earth, to give beer incomparable.'

In 1828 a senior partner at George's, a porter brewery in Bristol that had decided to experiment with pale ale, suggested that Hodgson's beer simply didn't match up to the new brews from Burton. Writing to Willis & Earle in Calcutta, he said of Hodgson's ale, 'We neither like its thick and muddy appearance or rank bitter flavour.' Two years later, when George's joined the golden beer rush to Calcutta, the same partner explained, 'We made a slight alteration to the Ale by brewing it rather of a paler colour and more hop'd to make it as similar as possible to some samples of Allsopp's

---

72. Yeah, Bushnan again.

ale.' But still, it didn't have the magic ingredient. Even if Hodgson's recipe was recreated exactly in Burton, with the only difference being Burton instead of London water, the Burton version would have been superior in quality and character when it reached India.

And Frederick Hodgson was simply his own worst enemy. Having already pissed off the East India Company to such an extent that one of its directors went out of his way to find someone capable of putting up a fight, Hodgson, surely expecting to rout Allsopp from the market, changed his terms of business in 1824 and shut out the very people he relied on to get his beer to India. The captains and officers of the East Indiamen had been Hodgson's best customers thanks largely to the generous credit terms he extended to them. Hodgson's ale was 'one of the principal articles in their investments' until, in 1824, he not only raised his prices to them, but also refused to sell on any terms except for hard cash. According to the *Circular on the Beer Trade in India*:

> Hodgson & Co . . . sent the Beer out for sale on their own account; thus they, in a short time, became Brewers, Shippers, Merchants, and even retailers. These proceedings naturally and justly excited hostile feelings in those engaged in the Indian Trade at home; while the public here, seeing at last the complete control which Hodgson endeavoured to maintain over the market, turned their faces against him, and gave encouragement to other Brewers who fortunately sent out excellent beer.

That 'encouragement' took many forms. Happy customers were eager to advise Allsopp not just on how to brew his beer, but also when the best time was to send it. Then, as now, one of the things that mattered most was that the beer was served cool, which wasn't easy when the temperature rarely dipped below 30 degrees Celsius and refrigeration wasn't going to appear for another fifty years. Happily, one of India's main manufactures provided the answer. In 1828, when young Henry Allsopp was working for Gladstone & Co, a Liverpool shipping agent, he received a letter for a Mr Lyon in Calcutta:

> I would advise your father to ship his Beer in the month of November or latter end of October, to arrive here in March or April; it is then our hottest season, and the quantity of Beer then consumed is tremendous. Your Beer is certainly a most delightful beverage during the hot season; it is always cooled with saltpetre before it is drank; we can make it by this article as cold as ice.

'F.E.W.' reminisced in a newspaper article years later that for beer, being cooled with saltpetre when everything else was lukewarm was 'a point very much in its favour'.

A bottle or flask of ale would be immersed in a solution of saltpetre. Water was added, and as it mixed with the saltpetre it would cool within a few minutes. It was an effective method but fiddly and expensive, especially given that a more lucrative use of saltpetre was in the manufacture of gunpowder, which some believed the Company still needed even more than cold beer.

Gradually, an even more ingenious cooling method came into use. Bottles were hung outdoors, inside a cage or cradle and covered with a wet cloth, the edges of which sat in a trough of water at the bottom of the cage. The hot wind evaporated the water, and the evaporation cooled the bottle. The cloths sucked up more water, creating a continuous cooling process.

Michael Bass soon noticed what was happening over at Allsopp's. He'd already experimented with pale malts a few years previously, and now, shut out of the Baltic trade by Benjamin Wilson twenty years before, it was time for his revenge. Forced to turn back to the domestic market after the Baltic fiasco, Bass had built far better trading links with important cities such as Liverpool, London and Manchester.

Now, his network was more developed than Allsopp's, and he knew the canals better. From 1823 there was a sharp increase in Bass sales to London agents. By 1828, 41 per cent of Bass' output was going to London and Liverpool, much of it in large consignments for export. In 1828 the *Calcutta Gazette* was advertising 'Hodgson's Allsopp's and Basse's Beer in wood, and in bottle, of different ages, some all perfection, others approaching it', and most auction houses continued to promote all three brands over the next few years. In 1832 Bass exported 5,193 barrels to Calcutta – slightly more than Hodgson and Allsopp's combined shipments. Although Michael Bass didn't live to see it (he died in 1827, leaving the brewery to his son, Michael Thomas) his victory over Allsopp's was decisive. The two would remain rivals for another century, each far bigger than any other Burton brewer, but Allsopp would never again quite challenge the Bass supremacy.

In 1835, John Bell noted that the beer trade had fallen off again, and that 'the most remarkable deficiency is in supplies from Hodgson; on the other hand, Bass and Allsopp have shipped more extensively.'

Tizard revealed a crucial aspect of this victory in his advice to brewers on how to succeed in India:

> The first point of consideration is Quality ... The ale adapted for this market should be a clear-light-bitter-pale ale of a moderate strength, and by no means what is termed in Calcutta heady; it should be shipped in hogsheads which, we need scarcely observe, should be most carefully coopered ... Another point is, that by frequent consignments, you acquire a name, which, as you may be aware, is everything in India.

While it would be a long time before the word was used freely in commerce, in order to succeed, these beers had to be strong brands. This was Hodgson's legacy: his name became synonymous with quality. To beat him, you had to beat him not only on quality, but also on sheer brand awareness. It's no coincidence that, fifty years after establishing itself in India, Bass would become the UK's first registered trademark.

As well as the triumvirate of Bass, Allsopp and, to an increasingly lesser extent, Hodgson, by 1833 brewers such as Ind and Smith, Worthington, Charrington and Barclay Perkins of London and Tennent of Glasgow were sending pale ale to India. By 1837, Bell notes the arrival of beer from the United States and 'Cape Beer', but these were to make up a tiny amount of the beer drunk in India – as Tizard states, it was 'clear that England must furnish the supply'.

Imports doubled through the 1830s. The competition and regularity of supply stabilized prices, allowing the taste for beer to spread throughout Anglo-Indian society, right through to 'the poorer classes of British inhabitants, which having once acquired, they will continue to indulge as long as prices remain moderate'. Allsopp's 'Burton India Ale' lost out to Bass in sales, but was still considered by many, including Tizard, to be 'the most salable', thanks mainly to its 'superior lightness and brilliancy'. Soon, according to Bell, 'no less than twenty brewers now send out Beer from England, where one occupied the field a very few years ago'.

Beer now quickly supplanted other drinks. Sales of Madeira collapsed from 85,204 rupees in 1829–30 to 21,632 rupees in 1833–4, with Bell observing that 'this once-favoured wine stands . . . as an example of the effects produced on trade by the caprice of fashion . . . the sudden distaste for Madeira would almost lead us to believe that some magic influence had been at work'. As for the oversupply of claret, 'we hope that the French have at last seen the folly of driving such a ruinous trade'. As Bushnan remarked in 1853, thanks to the many fine qualities of Samuel Allsopp: 'Since the year 1824 no Englishman has been reduced to the sad necessity of drinking French claret for the want of a draught of good, sound, wholesome, and refreshing English Burton beer.'

CHAPTER THIRTY-FOUR

LOSING IT IN THE INDIAN OCEAN

In many ways, freighter travel has moved on unimaginably since the publication of *Vagabond Voyaging*. Vessels are bigger, faster, and can go further. They're cleaner and better organized. They stick to their schedule more closely, and are therefore more reliable as a means of transport, my close shave in Rio notwithstanding. But when you're aboard a modern container ship and you're reading *Vagabond Voyaging* at mealtimes, one aspect of change strikes you as the opposite of progress, to quite a distressing degree.

'The food on this vessel is shit,' Chief Engineer German Stewie said, looking even more despondent than usual. He pronounced the last word with a satisfyingly expressive little kiss of the teeth. 'Before this job I travelled with five different lines, and this is the worst for food.'

According to *Vagabond Voyaging*, the Chilean freighter *Angol* served the following as a typical 1930s breakfast: fresh fruit, oatmeal, cornflakes, ham, bacon, eggs, boiled or fried potatoes, toasted bread, jelly, marmalade, coffee, tea. *Caribbean* served cornflakes, a sawdust compound masquerading as muesli, some watery scrambled eggs if you could find the steward, and long-life white bread that you could toast yourself and smear with Flora, and wash down with instant coffee.

In *Vagabond Voyaging* a 'regular dinner', served on the *Javanese Prince*, was – well, just look at it:

TOMATO JUICE COCKTAIL
STUFFED OLIVES

CONSOMMÉ CELESTINE
FRIED SOLE   TARTAR SAUCE
BREADED PORK CUTLET
BEEFSTEAK AND KIDNEY PUDDING
ROAST MUTTON   RED CURRANT JELLY
COLD PRESSED BEEF HAM
BAKED OR BOILED POTATOES
MARROW BEANS VICHY   SUGAR CORN
GOLDEN PUDDING AND SYRUP
CALIFORNIA FRUIT SALAD
CRACKERS   CHEESE   FRUIT
COFFEE

Nixon, the author, rubs it in by boasting that this is 'nothing out of the ordinary, but typical of the service on that particular ship'.

Following this dinner, eighty years passed. There were advances in refrigeration and the preservation of food. A revolution in global cuisine.

Dinner on the *Caribbean*: two fried eggs, gritty spinach and a potato that had been boiled so violently that only starchy willpower held it together.

A typical 1930s drinks list had, as well as a fully stocked cocktail cabinet, Johnnie Walker whiskies, an extensive wine list including Margaux Sauternes, Pilsner lagers and Bass ale.

We had cans of lager even I had never heard of before, a few half-decent bottles of South African Sauvignon blanc, a very, very cheap brand of whisky, and Brazilian red wine that tasted like melted cough sweets.

'This sausage – it is the cheapest sausage,' pouted the chief, prodding the spongy, synthetic slices that looked exactly like meat does in a *Tom and Jerry* cartoon. 'Always the same for five months. The owners are always trying to save money. The budget for food is six euros per man per day, but they try to save money even from that.'

We'd been at sea for about two and a half weeks, travelling

due east for a week or ten days. I was losing count, and my note-taking was grinding to a halt. I was starting to find the voyage an ordeal, and not just because my gums had started bleeding when I brushed my teeth, leading me to worry about scurvy.

Every few days Werner's voice would boom from speakers in every part of the ship, 'INFO. INFO. TONIGHT, SHIP'S TIME, FORWARD ONE HOUR.' We moved time zones not at the exact point at which we crossed lines of longitude, but when Werner said we did. 'Remember each boat is a different world of its own and each captain a dictator with a dictator's right to rule,' Nixon had written. 'But then he's a good chap, even if a bit of a fuss-budget.'

When passengers on the East Indiamen drew near to the Cape they were feverish with anticipation of the prospect of stopping to sample some of the famous grapes. For many it meant fresh fruit and the possible relief of scurvy. But if the wind were right, and conditions on board were not too bad, the captain might decide to press on, shaving as much as a month off the journey. This is what happened to Hickey on his first voyage out to Madras. It would have been agonizing to watch the coast slide past, so close you imagine you could swim the distance.

I sympathized. As I knew only too well, neither *Caribbean* nor any other container ship stopped in South Africa on its eastward journey. Up on the bridge the radio blared out a local station talking about what a great summer it was going to be in Cape Town. My mobile picked up a South African network, allowing me to talk to Liz briefly, before losing touch again. I stood outside on the bridge, holding mobile phone and BlackBerry to the heavens, praying for just one bar of signal – just enough for another few minutes' conversation or a flurry of emails. I accepted then that my experiment to see if I could live without modern communication had failed utterly. I retired to my cabin and a tin of Brazilian lager, after a meal consisting of some strips of pork fat on rice with an egg beaten into it.

Rounding the Cape was going to be one of the key moments. This stretch of water, this place where oceans meet, had claimed the lives of countless sailors. Everyone I spoke to raised their eyebrows at this prospect. It was the point in the journey that defined India Pale Ale, the extreme end of the conditions it had to endure, and I felt that it was a defining point for me too, the point at which I would face my greatest test and, hopefully, sail through it. How would I fare? Would I measure up? Was I truly a seaman?

The sea was like glass. There was no wind. We moved at speed, and without incident.

We followed Hickey's wake up the Mozambique Channel, between Madagascar and Mozambique. Hickey's ship stopped at the Comoro Islands at the top of the strait, just off the coast of what is now Malawi, for water and provisions. He was quite taken by the place, writing, 'It affords one of the most luxuriant and picturesque scenes it is possible to conceive.' But the captain advised that if they did go ashore, they should go by day and be back on board by night to avoid being attacked. They did at least find time for the favourite pursuit of the day. After a wonderful picnic under a beautiful tree whose branches were full of flying foxes. 'My companions, who had guns with them, shot several.'

By this time I was going stir-crazy and beginning to understand the restorative power of murdering a few defenceless animals to break up the monotony of life on board. But again, we pressed on. To be fair, there's no port in the Comoros, so we couldn't have stopped anyway. But the afternoon we spent sailing a course among them, gazing through binoculars at blue-green slopes scored through by thin columns of wood smoke rising straight into the windless blue, made me yearn to be on land, to feel sand between my toes and something natural – tree bark, grass, dirt, anything – in my hands.

I'd been drinking too much cheap, nasty beer during my evenings alone in my cabin, watching DVDs. To remedy this, I moved my hour on the exercise bike to seven, was back in my cabin doing sit-ups and the murderous plank until eight, which left only a couple of hours to fill before I could think about turning in. My drink problem was solved a day or so after the Comoros, when the captain's slop chest ran dry. I had a couple of bottles of decent South African white left, and an abundance of the undrinkable Brazilian red, and just over a week to go before the next port.

And then, I ran out of DVDs to watch.

One night, after my exercises, I realized I'd been ... elsewhere, not really in my body. I was talking to myself again, but this was different. I was lying on the floor of the cabin, babbling, and the sentient part of me that now felt closed off inside my brain had no idea what I was saying. I decided to tune in and listen, and immediately wished I hadn't. I think it had started as a stream of motivational goading to finish the last few crunches, but it had carried on long after the crunches were completed, becoming a stream of hysterical bile and vitriol, obscene, filthy, furious, and directed at myself. Eavesdropping on it, I realized I obviously meant it. I'd effectively been in solitary confinement for weeks, and now there were two of me in the room. I wasn't sure which one I was, and I was clearly tiring of my own company. This wasn't just irritation; it was outright hatred. As I managed to take back control of my vocal cords, pull myself off the floor and get into the shower, I saw with a strange mixture of alarm and detached relief that an introduction to psychotherapy awaited me back home. Stir-craziness had flourished to the point where we no longer needed to bother with the word 'stir'. In that cabin on the Indian Ocean, a straight foamy highway behind us and nothing on the horizon in front, with around twenty minutes of human contact each day, I was going insane.

Looking back, I'm disappointed at how mundane my madness was. Apart from chattering to myself constantly and engaging in the odd bout of Olympian self-abuse (no, not that kind – those urges disappeared completely), I took endless photos of myself on my mobile phone, transferring them to the laptop and flicking through them, scrutinizing the face to see if I could recognize it. My hair, sun-bleached and grown-out to the point of bouffancy, looked like it belonged to 1984-era George Michael. My beard had grown bushy in the journey across the South Atlantic, pouching under my chin and making me look like a very old bullfrog. I became obsessive about it. I began to hack at it with the tiny scissors on my Swiss Army Knife, returning obsessively to the bathroom mirror every time I found a clump that was longer than the rest. I grew paranoid about the chopped whiskers, purging the tiny bathroom of them, hunting down every last one, wondering how so many had found their way behind the toilet seat.

I lost whole days to Solitaire and Minesweeper, deleting game after game until only the really crap ones I had never played before were left, and then I got addicted to those too. I spent one day playing something called Spider Solitaire for an uninterrupted eight-hour stint before deleting it in floods of tears. Then, I tried to recreate it with the deck of cards I was carrying with me, chuntering to myself and making up songs to the rhythm of each card thwapping the banquette.

Kevin the Keg kept an embarrassed silence. I felt that Barry's anthropomorphism had contributed to his demise in some way, allowing him the will to act. I wasn't going to give this one the chance.

I wondered if the beer were changing, and how it might taste. With no other booze left, the temptation to open it should have been terrible. But I'd come too far, gone through too much to get it to this point, so close to India. The thought of broaching it never even crossed my mind.

My afternoons on the foredeck grew similarly less productive. I'd do a bit of reading before jumping up and pacing the deck, looking over the bow at the sea below. It was the most inviting body of water I'd ever seen, as deep and smooth and shiny as a newly waxed car. I longed to jump in for a swim, but the absolute certainty of death prevented me from doing so. Air travel may be dangerous, but the danger is entirely man-made, like the danger involved in driving or DIY. And air travel is quick – the longest journey on the planet is around twenty-four hours. Even a long-haul flight is a one-night stand, a brief flirtation with death, whereas a sea voyage is more of a long, drawn-out affair, with fatality something to be constantly negotiated and bartered. It's far less certain, far less black and white, much more shades of greeny-grey: a flight either lands safely or you die quickly and violently. There's no in between. At sea, the options are endless.

The world map I'd bought from the hawker on Copacabana beach saved me. I'd taped it to the wall next to my bed, and it was the first thing I saw every morning and the last thing every night. It was crowded with information: I memorized the flags and currencies of nations. I realized that Brunei, with its famous sultan, is nowhere near the Middle East, but in fact shares an island with Borneo, between the Philippines and Indonesia. I wondered if it were possible to sail the North West Passage, as the forerunners of the East India Company had once tried.[73] I traced the paths of the trade winds through the Atlantic, stared at the lines of longitude and estimated where in the endless blue we might be. It kept me connected to the world.

There was no ceremony, not even an announcement, when *Caribbean* recrossed the equator.

---

73. It never used to be. But while I'd been somewhere between Burton and Tenerife, the European Space Agency declared that the polar ice cap had shrunk to such an extent that it was now navigable for the first time since records began. Anyone up for it?

One morning, when we were about four days out from our first Arabian port, the sea was flat and waxy under an eggshell blue sky, and the captain tipped me off that we were going to have a man-overboard drill. Did I want to take part? I consulted my calendar, saw that I had a bit of a window between appointments, and said yes. At 10 a.m. an alarm sounded. I grabbed my hard hat from where it hung on my cabin wall, and ran down to the deck where the lifeboat was kept. A chest had been thrown open and we all donned life jackets. The steward helped me tie mine.

'Hmm . . . you need to go on a diet perhaps,' he said, loosening the straps.

I was very put out. Thanks mainly to my obsessive commitment to the exercise bike, I'd already lost a stone since leaving home. And if anyone were to blame for me not losing more, it was him and the bloody cook.

Five of us climbed into the lifeboat – I'd been offered the chance to go along and wasn't going to miss it for the world. The sea stretched flat and glittering until it merged with the horizon, somewhere lost in the heat haze. A winch ground into operation, and the cables holding our dinghy tautened. We swung out, a little crazily, over the side of the ship, and we were dangling fifty feet above the sea. I gripped the cable above my head as we started a jerky descent, relieved when we finally hit the water with a heavy splash.

Via walkie-talkie from the bridge, the captain directed us to do a circuit of the ship. We cruised forwards, beneath her prow, and I marvelled at her curves, at the way the sunlight reflecting from the waves made her royal-blue paintwork flicker.

And then we were on the weather side of the ship, and here it wasn't as calm as it had looked from the deck. Cadet Ron, who was in the boat with us, stripped down to his shorts and dived backwards from the side of the boat. We lurched violently from side to side for a few seconds, and I slipped from my bench into the central well. I liked it down there. Things seemed to wobble less, and it was quite cosy. The waves were further away.

'Mr Peter, would you like to come and sit here?' asked the first mate, moving up on the bench to make room for me.

I thought for a few seconds. 'No. No, I don't think so. I really like sitting here, thanks.'

We 'rescued' Ron and hauled him back on board – when I say 'we', of course I mean 'they' – and spun around *Caribbean*'s stern, past *Thunderbird 4*, back to the winch. We hadn't done it right, and Werner ordered us to go round again, all the time with me sitting in the bottom of the boat. And then we couldn't reattach the winch. The heavy metal block swung over our heads and clanged against the side of the ship. Finally, Werner ordered them to come alongside and a rope ladder was dropped for me to come back aboard, leaving my crewmates to get a walkie-talkie bollocking until they sorted it out.

We carried on up the coast of East Africa, passing just a few hundred miles from Zanzibar, where Liz and I had honeymooned and enjoyed fresh seafood and fruit and spices and really, really nice wine, and where I had had my lifetime's perfect beer moment.

A day or two later Werner appeared with a solemn expression. 'Peter, from tonight after dark you must close your blinds over your windows. Tonight we switch off the navigation lights and keep all doors and windows closed. We are two hundred miles from zer coast, but zer last attack was over two hundred miles out.'

As with the old adage about one man's terrorist being another's freedom fighter, historically the term 'pirate' depended largely on your perspective. Spanish history still refers to 'the pirate Francis Drake', but to an Englishman Drake was a hero, knighted for his actions. Similarly, when the Company arrived here in the Indian Ocean, it pursued for many years a policy described by Nick Robins as 'trade where necessary and plunder where possible'. Ships would be seized on the flimsiest of excuses, their cargoes rarely returned when a dispute had been resolved. In later years Company ships, with their superior gunnery, were given specific orders definitely not to attack shipping, under any circumstances. But then a big, fat trading vessel would sail past, low in the water, just asking for it, taunting them, *deserving* it. The East Indiaman captain would invariably give in, seize the ship and its cargo, and receive a wink and a weak slap on the wrist from his pretend-angry superiors.

But the Company were not the only pirates. Their monopoly angered those who wanted a share of the trade, and interlopers and privateers made the shipping lanes of the Indian Ocean busy and treacherous. Captain Kidd was sent by the British government to India to catch pirates, and allegedly the first thing he did was attack a Mughal convoy under Company protection. Legend has it that he then became the most notorious gamekeeper-turned-poacher ever to cry 'ah-harr!' in the Indian Ocean. Stripped of the myth that surrounds him, the facts suggest he wasn't really a particularly good pirate – he spent most of his time trying to persuade his pissed-off crew not to mutiny – but he was hanged and gibbeted above the Thames all the same.

Now, we were the modern equivalent of the Company's tall ships, while Kidd's successors were the Somalis. Somalia, riven by tribal and religious divisions, has had no effective government since 1991, with various warlords declaring independence or autonomy within a federal state. Its coastal waters are lawless. Pirates approach shipping in trawlers and launches, capturing cargoes and holding crew members to ransom. And, according to Werner, they were growing bolder.

Somalia's 1,800-mile coastline is the longest in Africa. In April 2008, the *Observer* called it the most dangerous strip of sea in the world, with thirty-one attacks there in 2007, 'making the notorious bandits operating in the South China Sea and Malacca Straits look almost lazy by comparison'. It explained how larger hijacked ships now served as mother ships, towing launches well beyond the 200-mile limit, before releasing men armed with AK-47s and rocket-propelled grenades.

For two nights I sat in my cabin, tense and nervy as we ran silent, shocked that we were in very real danger. We heard and saw nothing. We were lucky.

In the end, there were no pirates on the *Caribbean*.[74]

As we neared the bottom of the Arabian peninsula the water became busier, and not just with commercial shipping. One afternoon, a school of dolphins came and frolicked off our bows, and I felt a return of the exhilaration I'd experienced on *Europa*. I had no one to share it with – when I mentioned them to Werner later he couldn't have cared less – but that just made it more intense, my own private communion with them.

And finally, we reached Oman, and the nondescript port of Salalah. We berthed overnight and unloaded, and I was back in touch with the world. I phoned Liz, and Rudgie and Steve, talking for ages, not caring about the bills, just glad to be back in contact. The end of the journey was in sight. Sharing my hopes and anticipation was like drinking fresh water after days in the desert, particularly given that, after omitting to mention to Werner or anyone in the shipping company that I was carrying twenty-odd litres of beer, I now felt it would be a bad idea to bring it up onboard ship.

Then we were on our way again, towards the Gulf of Oman and the Straits of Hormuz. As we left the port, passing our neighbours, I realized with a sense of dread that the *Caribbean*, at 180 metres, was pretty damn small for a con-

---

74. Sorry. But how was I meant to resist that?

tainer ship. The *Kirsten Maersk*, in front of us, carried a load nineteen containers wide by eighteen long, and ten high. It was simply impossible to imagine that much cargo.

Khor Fakkan is a popular tourist destination and deep-water port in the United Arab Emirates, and I was happy to see it for two reasons. Firstly, its strategic location meant we didn't have to enter the Persian Gulf itself. I don't know why, but I just wasn't keen on that idea. And, secondly, there was a world-famous duty-free shop in the port. You know you've been travelling a while when your brands of toiletries have become unfamiliar. I had to stock up on a flavour of Colgate I'd never seen before, with Arabic script down its tube, and a brand of deodorant that was completely new to me. The brands of malt whisky on offer were more universal. I bought a bottle of something good to leave the crew for the next Saturday party, whenever that might be, and a thank-you present for Werner, as well as making my cabin far more comfortable for the last few days on board than it had been in recent weeks.

A new chief engineer came aboard in Khor Fakkan, a bearded Russian giant who was obviously half-insane, growling and muttering to himself over meals. He wasn't happy with the state of things on the *Caribbean*. On his last ship there had been 2,500 DVDs to choose from and a sailors' mess with a full disco, karaoke machine and huge plasma TV screen.

'But where did all that come from?' I asked.

'Sludge money!' he roared. 'All from sludge money! Other captains put it back into the ship. This one keeps it. I was talking to your old chief engineer. He was angry about this. That's why he cut the stuff in your last visit to Rio with so much water, to teach the captain a lesson.'

I said nothing. I couldn't criticize Werner, not with my fate in his hands at our next port of call.

The Persian port of Gombroon was universally disliked by

Company-era mariners, but it was a vital part of their operations. Control Gombroon, and you controlled the Straits of Hormuz – and the shipping that passed through it. But as James Douglas, a Bombay historian, wrote in his book *Bombay and Western India* in 1893: 'You cannot get too excited about Gombroon. It would be difficult to select a place less known or less calculated to awaken an interest of any kind in the reader.' In the 1980s it was renamed Bandar Abbas, and now houses most of the Iranian navy. This was our next port of call – the place I didn't have a visa for.

I didn't know what Werner was going to do, but I knew the penalties would be high if he failed. What if I were arrested? What if they searched my cabin and found the beer? How stupid would I look if some kind of international incident occurred?

The night before we docked, Werner counselled me in a low voice. 'You must stay in your cabin tomorrow. Do not go out on zer decks. Zey mustn't see you.'

I remained in my cabin all day, waiting, out of sight, hoping. I popped downstairs only for lunch, and wondered whether the cook was taking the piss after arriving in an Islamic Republic by serving pork fillets for the first time in five weeks. As dusk fell curiosity got the better of me, and I crept down the stairs. I met Werner coming up the other way.

'Ah, hello! Do you want to go ashore?' he boomed.

This was a joke, obviously. 'No,' I laughed.

'There is a seaman's club! They serve soft drinks and non-alcoholic beer. Go and have a look at pictures of Khomeini! HA! HA! HA!'

'Is everything all right? What about my visa?'

'Yes, everything is fine! Some cigarettes and whisky, and it is not a problem.'

I almost crumpled with relief.

Out on deck the covers to the storage hatches had been removed, and an illuminated chasm yawned all the way down to the bottom of the ship. We were offloading the last of our chicken, ready for whatever it was that would be going back to South Africa (they stopped at bloody Durban going the other way – of course they did) and South America. On the next ship, Thais were fishing off the back with nets. I went ashore and made my way carefully along uneven paving stones that had shattered under enormous weights, towards the building Werner had pointed to, the seamen's mission. I passed a spray-painted mural depicting a huge temple and the words DEAR SEAFARERS WELCOME TO THE ISLAMIC REPUBLIC OF IRAN. I couldn't hear anything from inside the building, and as I got closer I realized it consisted of offices, with no bar visible. Two men approached me, smiling, cradling machine guns.

'I'm looking for the sailors' mission? Bar? Drink?'

They were very friendly. They each shook my hand, grinning. And gestured with their guns back along the avenue of containers, back towards my ship. I smiled, turned around, and was back on board the *Caribbean* two minutes later. And that was my visit to Iran.

There were only two days left of my voyage. Sometime in the middle of the night, seven hours earlier than the earliest estimated departure time we'd been given, we pulled out of Bandar Abbas, bound for Nhava Sheva. This was great. I woke the next day and went to the foredeck, for what I thought was the last time. And then the ship broke down.

We drifted at sea for a day, listless. I couldn't believe it. I went to the bridge to find Werner vacillating between furious and scared. He blamed the new chief engineer – I really hoped I would be off the ship before the inevitable flare-up between these two – and fretted over justifying the delay to Mr Ritscher, the ship's owner. A new part had to be brought by courier from Europe, and until then we had a patched-up engine that could only make two-thirds of our normal speed. We limped slowly towards India, and two more days passed.

When I woke up the next morning, we were at anchor. We stayed there for a full day, waiting for a berthing in one of the busiest ports in the world. I couldn't see land through the dirty snot-coloured haze, but I knew it was there. Flat fishing boats with canvas roofs puttered past us. Shoes – always shoes, never any other kind of human rubbish – bobbed by in the water. I spent a final afternoon on the foredeck, reading my Lonely Planet guide, fantasizing about curry.

Hopefully we would dock sometime tomorrow. And, finally, for the first time since the start of the voyage, I had no worries, no stress. I could just look forward to my remaining brief time on board and then India. The spectre of Bandar Abbas had been removed like a tumour, the final concern from my set of worries about visas and exploding beer barrels finally erased.

How could I have known then that all the worry, all the stress, had been directed at the wrong port?

PART SIX

KOLKATA

CHAPTER THIRTY-FIVE

GLORY DAYS

The 1784 East India Act banned further territorial expansion by the Company at a time when they controlled a mere 7 per cent of the subcontinent's land mass. Nevertheless, by 1856, the Company controlled 62 per cent of India. As William Dalrymple writes, 'for the first time there was a feeling that technologically, economically and politically, the British had nothing to learn from India and much to teach . . . it did not take long for Imperial arrogance to set in.'

Karl Marx, writing in the *New York Daily Tribune* in 1853, seemed a tad put out that the Company had stripped India of its wealth, dismantled its economy, provided nothing in return, and yet was still skint. He attacked the court of directors on the grounds that only one of these policymakers had ever actually been to India, and that was by accident. 'There exists no government by which so much is written and so little done,' he railed, calling the Company a government of 'obstinate clerks and the like odd fellows'. He claimed the Company's charter consisted of nothing more than 'a permanent financial deficit, a regular oversupply of wars, and no supply at all of public works, an abominable system of taxation, and a no less abominable system of justice and law'. But that's Lefties for you – always finding something to moan about.

John Stuart Mill – the champion of liberty – disagreed, which had nothing to do with his position as a clerk at East India House. The man famous for arguing that 'the only purpose for which power can be rightfully exercised over any member of a civilized community, against his will, is to prevent harm to others' maintained that the Company's way of doing things was 'a legitimate mode of government in dealing with barbarians'. Barbarians? Well, that's all right then.

This climate of 'Imperial arrogance' helped many Anglo-Indians to forget they'd left the mother country – well that, and possibly the fact that many were so drunk they simply thought they were having an uncharacteristically warm summer in Bedfordshire. One diarist quoted by Kincaid fondly paints a typical scene following a Sunday-morning church service in Calcutta, which the actual location only just manages rudely to interrupt:

> And now as the carriages rattled down the Mall in the blinding sunshine, red-coated peons majestic on the box, a cloud of white dust springing up under the wheels, the ladies eagerly criticized Mrs Brown's extraordinary hat and the very unbecoming colours which Mrs Smith saw fit to wear at her age. And the gentlemen sat back and thought with pleasure of a bottle of iced beer and the Sunday lunch of roast beef and Yorkshire pudding, horse-radish sauce and baked potatoes, and a long sleep after-wards with the heavy punkah stirring overhead, the glare of the Indian noon shut out by bamboo-splinter curtains.

While still fond of its ale, this was a more genteel, refined India now. The illusion had been completed, Jam and Jerusalem rebuilt in perfect replica. Beer had survived the earlier ages of excess because it was, like the roast beef and Yorkshire pudding, evidence that the Anglo-Indians didn't actually have to leave England at all inside their heads. Stability and settlement meant wives could come out from England, complete with the latest fashions. Dinner-party invitations bore the discreet instruction 'no hookahs', and meals were served on Wedgwood china imported from Staffordshire, just like the beer.

Pale ale became ubiquitous in Anglo-Indian society. In the

1850s, if you wanted to exchange courtesies with a dinner-table guest, particularly in the provinces or at the mess table, you would invite him to 'drink beer' with you. Two tumblers were brought to the invitee, who would split a bottle equally between them and have one sent over to the guest he had invited to drink beer with him.

It would have been thought a serious affront to decline the invitation, even though one might have had beer with half-a-dozen people already,' recalled 'F.E.W.' in 1882. 'The quantity of beer, otherwise bottled India pale ale, which people drank in those days was something almost incredible. I have known a man to drink his dozen quarts a day, and I have often seen ladies take four tumblers, or two quarts, at dinner alone. To be sure there was this safeguard against intoxication, that the liquid ran out of the pores of their skins almost as fast as they imbibed it.

One returning civilian from India shared his travel stories with English newspaper readers in 1854, claiming:

I fear when the genuine Cockney carelessly reads the words 'Allsopp's India Ale' in going through the streets of London, he seldom realizes to himself the delight with which the weary traveller in India or Ceylon sees these words on the outside of a full bottle . . . Champagne is an excellent drink if you don't anticipate a dinner after it; but for a breakfast after a hard ride,[75] or a luncheon in the jungle, there is nothing equal to the sparkling glass of cool Allsopp. The frame is perhaps on fire, this is the potation to extinguish the flame; exhausted with physical oriental fatigue, with a thermometer ranging between 80 and 90

---

75. I love the simple matter of factness of this quote. You've probably seen the range of humorous, faux-retro postcards and posters with grinning 1950s-style illustrations and slogans such as 'Beer! Helping ugly people have sex since 1952!' When they came up with the one that runs 'Beer! So much more than a breakfast drink!' they thought it was a *joke*.

degrees, nothing is half so gently inspiriting as the white-capped draught of Pale India Ale . . . it must be quaffed, not hurriedly but without pause; be the quantity large or small, it should not remain in the glass a minute.

Up in the hills, out in the stations in the mofussil, the comforts of home were less apparent. But there were compensations: here, where the air was cooler, the Indians knew how to make ice. In 1828 Fanny Parkes's husband was put in charge of the ice pits at Allahabad. In the cooler months an old abdar (water cooler) would pace up and down, judging the conditions. If he smelled frost in the air, tom-toms were beaten to summon the coolies to work, filling vast fields of shallow pans with water. As night fell, ice would form on the surface, growing to maybe an inch in thickness. At 3 a.m. the abdar would emerge from his hut, decide when the ice formation had reached its peak, then beat the tom-tom again. Now the coolies, shivering with cold, chipped the ice out of the pans and ran to the icehouse. Armed with blankets, shoes and a mallet, they descended four at a time into a large pit and beat the ice flat, working in relays for as long as they could stand. The compacted ice was then covered with mats and buried under a layer of straw.

This would happen through January and February. The pits then remained closed until April or May, when clubs were formed and people subscribed to cover the costs and were given an allowance of 24lb of ice per day. At this rate, there was usually enough ice to keep the beer cool until August.

Then, in 1833, some Americans sent a trial shipment of apples to India. To keep these from rotting, the merchants cooled them below decks with ice from the Great Lakes. On arrival in Calcutta, the ice sold for more than the apples. The coolies employed to haul it off the ship complained that it 'scalded' their backs. Soon, regular shipments of ice were arriving from America.

The extraordinary import of this event deserved special mention in John Bell's account of trade that year.

The truth of our Indian palates being refrigerated with American ice, will be treated by many well-informed people at home with ridicule,' he wrote, 'and despite of testimony from the most respectable, it will be quite as little credited by old women "north of the Tweed", as the story of the flying fish was to the sailor's maternal aunt ... the success of this speculation, which exceeded the most sanguine expectations of the projector, will no doubt lead to a further, and in time regular, supply of ice.

The Sunday-afternoon beer could now be perfectly chilled, though in fact the Europeans themselves never had to worry about how it was actually done. It was common for dinner parties to have as many as twenty-two servants waiting upon a table of eight. The abdar would arrive at the house hours before such parties began in order to chill the water, champagne, Madeira, claret and pale ale, and some guests would even bring their own abdar with them, just to make sure everything was done to their own high standards.

Dining and entertaining were vital to maintaining your position in society, and the tight corsets, stiff attitudes and sniffy disdain for 'foreign' food were – at least until the middle of the nineteenth century – loosened a little after the sun went down. Balls were still a popular form of entertainment, and while the raucous affairs of Hickey's day had gone, veteran Anglo-Indians still enjoyed dancing till dawn. One of the anonymous authors of *The East-India sketch-book*, published in 1832, tells us:

Two or three ultra-fashionists, just imported from cold and icy Europe, stared, and turned a little pale as they inhaled the steam arising from the various 'savouries' – swallowed a jelly, and a biscuit, and a glass of wine; but the rest of the party addresses themselves valiantly to the work of devastation. They drank beer in huge tumblers, men and women; they ate of the beef, and the mutton, and the pork, and the turkeys and the fowls, and they closed with real Mussulmauni curries.

These entertainments were often exclusively English, but some fraternization with the natives occasionally took place. A few Indian nobles were adopted almost as pets. George Atkinson, the author of *Curry and Rice on Forty Plates*, gives a typically charming account of what a rollicking time was had when one local nawab threw a nautch, a lavish entertainment to impress his rulers:

> 'Our Nawab' invites us to supper; and there we find our tables groaning with the productions of Sticker and Doss's Europe shop, for which 'Our Nawab' has given unlimited orders . . . the wines and beers have been properly cooled, and considering they came from Sticker Doss's, are not so bad. . . . We drink his health the three times three, which gratifies him intensely. Then we adjourn to witness the fireworks, and a troop of fifty pariah-dogs let loose, each with a lighted squib at its tail, is pronounced to be great sport.

Another nawab, who called himself Nana Sahib, didn't fare as well, causing amusement among his European dinner guests by serving their drinks in unsuitable receptacles. 'The cool claret I drank out of a richly cut champagne glass,' chortled one, 'and the beer out of an American tumbler of the very worst quality.' Maybe Nana Sahib resented being patronized. Because a few years later, he was slaughtering British civilians rather than offering them a top-up of sherry in a humorously inappropriate fashion.

The British holiday in India ended abruptly in 1857. Amid growing resentment on a great number of issues, a (false) rumour began to circulate around sepoy ranks about the introduction of a new type of rifle cartridge that had been greased with cow or pig fat. As these cartridges had to be primed by the rifleman biting down on to them, this would have been sacrilegious, an unacceptable insult. The resentment and frustration against people who had arrived as merchants and mutated into avaricious, racist oppressors finally boiled over. The Company's own army rose up against it, with Nana Sahib leading the sepoys, and was soon joined by huge swathes of the civilian population. Depending on your point of view, the Indian Mutiny or the First War of Independence had begun.

The fighting lasted two years. As is always the case in violent disputes where resentments run deep, each side used the atrocities of the other to justify its own. In the initial uprising the Indians slaughtered European women and children wherever they found them. When the English took Cawnpore – the scene of one vicious massacre – captured rebel sepoys were made to lick the blood from the floor before they were hanged. One officer roving through the countryside boasted, 'we hold court martials on horseback, and every nigger we meet we either string up or shoot'. At the end, when the Company finally retook Delhi and deposed the last Mughal emperor – a gentle poet who had been used as a figurehead by the rebels – they turned the surviving inhabitants out of the city, locked the gates and left them to starve.

It was open season for the bigots – the racists and Christian fundamentalists – who crowed in their vindication that the barbarian scum could not be trusted. The *Englishman* newspaper was full of letters like the one from 'Britannicus', who claimed: 'The only people who have any right to India are the British; the SO-CALLED Indians have no right whatever.' Those who were not stark-staring mad argued that the loss of life – on both sides – was unacceptable. Everyone agreed – sane and sociopath alike – that the Company had really screwed up this time.

John Stuart Mill did a barnstorming job of trying to

brazen it out, a virtuoso performance akin to standing in front of a blazing building with a box of matches and a can of paraffin in your hand shrugging your shoulders and going, 'What?' The author of the sentence 'rulers should be identified with the people; that their interest and will should be the interest and will of the nation' presented a lengthy petition to parliament, a work of black comic genius that actually had the front to describe the Company as 'the most beneficent [government] ever known among mankind'.[76]

When parliament regained its breath and wiped the collective tears of laughter from its eyes, it stripped what it called the 'corrupt', 'perfidious' and 'rapacious' Company of its administrative powers in India and transferred them to the crown. Queen Victoria was named Empress of India, not because she or even her armies had won it, but because the other guy, John Company, was disqualified for foul play.

The aftermath saw an influx of new civilians to India, men trained at Haileybury College specifically to be rulers of India. One, John Beames, took a P&O steamer through the Bay of Biscay into the Mediterranean, pausing at Malta and alighting at Alexandria. Here, he took a train to Cairo, met the passengers from another steamer from Marseilles (you could pick up this one after crossing the Channel and getting the train down via Paris if you didn't fancy stormy Biscay) then took another train into the middle of the desert, met a caravan that took them and their luggage to 'dirty Suez', where they boarded another ship to Bombay. Even before the Suez Canal opened, the journey to India had been reduced from several months to a mere six weeks, and Europe felt much closer.

Many more British troops arrived too. Since the Company's earliest days, it had made sense to recruit sepoys, with just enough English men and officers to preserve order and

---

76. To be fair to him, he didn't actually spell out *to whom* it was beneficent.

discipline. With these English-trained men now in revolt, entire battalions of British-born troops were needed.

The circumstances in India were still little better for Our Boys than they had ever been. After spending five months on board ship with four troops of lancers, Fanny Parkes remained aware of the conditions in which soldiers lived. The mortality was terrible, owing, she believed, to 'the cheapness of spirituous liquors, and exposure to the sun'. Polite society may have anglicized, but imported luxuries were out of reach of the average squaddie, who turned to tried-and-tested lethal alternatives. Parkes felt for them: 'What can be more wretched than the life of a private soldier in the East? His profession employs but little of his time. During the heat of the day, he is forced to remain within the intensely-hot barrack rooms; heat produces thirst, and idleness discontent. He drinks arak like a fish, and soon finds life a burden, almost insupportable.'

After the Mutiny, the army took action and placed orders for oceans of beer with British pale ale brewers. After an invitation to supply 36,000 hogsheads of pale ale for troops in India saw 'only only about half the quantity competed for, and that portion chiefly by London brewers', Allsopp's built a new 'Leviathan brewery' to meet demand. Over the next ten to fifteen years the orders from the India Office to supply troops serving in the subcontinent became epic. Bass received a single order in 1872 for 16,000 hogsheads of pale ale, as well as 7,000 hogsheads of porter.[77] Beer finally became cheaply available in the wet canteens, displacing toddy and arak.

In 1860, *The Times* told the story of one soldier who, while helping put down the Mutiny, was told he had inherited a

---

77. Clearly the old dark beer still had a role to play. The opening of the Suez Canal meant drastically reduced journey times and fewer temperature fluctuations on the voyage, improving the chances of the beer reaching its destination in good condition.

substantial fortune, and was asked how he would like to take
it. He replied that he would take the value in pale ale. While
accepting that this created some amusement in the camp, *The
Times* editorial felt this was a sound business decision: 'Beer,
in short, is the natural support of British soldiers in the East.
It keeps them in condition, not only by its proper virtues, but
by driving other liquors out of the field. If the men can get
sound ale or porter they are not disposed to resort to arrack,
and consequently there is less drunkenness and more general
efficiency.'

The importance of beer in this respect is emphasized by
the attention to detail in the orders issued by the India Office,
with detailed specifications running to four, sometimes six
pages. A typical tender issued to Bass in 1874 stated that the
beer must be 'of a strength to obtain the excise drawback of
5s 9d per barrel', that it should be brewed using only 'good,
sound barley malt (no sugar of any kind whatever), with 20lbs
of the best new hops per quarter of malt' and 'new dry hops
in the proportion of 1lb per barrel'.[78] Even the dimensions of
and quality of the cask staves were clearly specified.

With such careful specifications, it seems extremely
unlikely, as is often claimed, that this beer was then watered

---

78. I discussed this recipe with a couple of brewers, who speculated that
the resulting beer would have been around 7 per cent ABV and would
have had around sixty units of bitterness, which is extremely high, but has
since been superseded by the more extreme modern American IPAs. Then,
while finishing this book, I worked with Leicestershire brewer Everards to
recreate the beer exactly, as the Leicestershire Regiment were the longest
serving in Bengal. The first beer we brewed topped out with a bitterness
rating of ninety-two and was completely undrinkable until we modified and
blended it. Everards's brewer Mark Tetlow believes this is because we get
much more utilization out of modern hops than they would have in the
1870s. The dry-hopping rate is also extraordinary – around eight times
higher than a typical dry-hopped bitter today. This would have been an
incredibly aromatic beer.

down on arrival. The journey time was now only six weeks, so there was less of a need to brew to this strength in order to survive the rigours of a five-month trek around the Cape or the temperature extremes of the equator: the beer was brewed like this because that's how they wanted it to taste. It wasn't to everyone's taste – some individuals preferred to water it down with a mixture of toddy, brown sugar, ginger and lime peel – but in the main IPA was sold as it was brewed.

In 1886, *Hobson-Jobson*, a guide to the language of the Raj, had a great deal to say about beer. It had been 'a favourite in India from an early date', and after the initial popularity of porter, 'pale ale' had become so ubiquitous that the 'expression has long since been disused in India, and beer, simply, has represented the thing'. By the 1870s the name of Bass had also become synonymous with beer in India. Bengal import figures for 1877–8 show that they dwarfed Allsopp, Worthington and the emerging Scottish pale ale brewers, accounting for a whopping 64 per cent of the total Bengal beer market. The beer was immortalized in verse and prose. But nothing can beat the endorsement in one short story that ran in *Cornhill Magazine* in March 1891. Let's ask the narrator of 'Eight Days' – how's the beer, sir?

'The drinking of a glass of Bass's pale ale, iced, in India in the hot weather, is an orgasm!'

Come again? Let me rephrase that. I'm sorry, a what?

'An orgasm! How it diffuses itself through you! How it revives and re-invigorates you! It would produce a soul under the ribs of death.'

Perhaps we should look at this quote in its full context. In the story, the characters are being chased by a mob when they reach a house that promises temporary safety. The mob is not far behind, and will surely kill our heroes if they catch up. But 'the ladies are faint', and refreshment is necessary if the party is to go on:

'Bring us plenty of cold water,' says Hay.

'And some beer,' says Hamilton. 'I suppose you have some cooled?'

'Plenty.'

'Quick then – quick.'

After a while the old man returns, accompanied by a khidmutgar (literally, 'serving man'), and they carry two big trays, on which are cold meat and bread and butter and biscuits, and other eatables, and they bring down several bottles of iced water and several bottles of iced beer. How delicious is the fragrance of the latter as the old man draws the corks! I have drunk many a tankard of cool ale in this our native land with a sensation of great delight, but the drinking of a glass of Bass's pale ale, iced, in India in the hot weather, is an orgasm! How it diffuses itself through you! How it revives and re-invigorates you! It would produce a soul under the ribs of death. The clean, wholesome, hoppy perfume! What bouquet of what wine ever equalled it? And as you hold the glass lovingly up before you, what ruby or purple of what wine ever equalled that amber tint? The 'beaded bubbles winking at the brim' of a glass of champagne, what are they compared to that tender froth? Many of our poets have celebrated the praises of this our national drink; to what a height would their strains have risen had they ever enjoyed a glass of it at the end of a long hot day in India?

So let's get this straight: here's a party of Victorian Anglo-Indians in mortal danger, running for their lives, but out comes the beer and all worries of a violent death vanish instantly. *That's* how good this beer was.

Incredible then, that ten years after this story was published, it had all but disappeared from India.

CHAPTER THIRTY-SIX

WELCOME ASHORE

I woke at 5 a.m. Sickly yellow light stained the curtains. I opened them and looked out on to tall red cranes loading a wide container ship under bright floodlights. It was flying an Indian flag. Finally, twelve weeks to the day since picking up *Remus* at Rugby, my sea voyage was over.

Like a child who's woken up too early on Christmas morning, I couldn't get back to sleep. I was suffocated by the ship and desperate to dive into Mumbai, and yet already I couldn't help feeling a twinge of regret. I suspected I would soon forget how dire the food had been – or at least the actual taste of it.[79] Instead I'd remember the Saturday-night party, the afternoons on the foredeck and the evenings when I had DVDs to enjoy after a successful day's writing. The later weeks – isolated, in solitary, seeing other people for only a few minutes a day – I'd soon forget. The nausea of sitting in front of my keyboard yet again, the obsessive playing of Solitaire for eight hours straight, the prospect of watching the first season of *Family Guy* for a fourth time, the taste of the last bottle of Brazilian red wine when all the other booze had run out, the shock at finding myself lying on the floor of my cabin jabbering disgusting insults at myself – it might take therapy, but I'd forget all this one day.

While researching my journey I'd found a book called *Supercargo*, in which Thornton McCamish sets out to travel

---

79. I was actually wrong about that bit. Eight months later, I still woke up screaming after nightmares about cartoon-like meat.

the world's ports, places he sees as the fringes of the land, the home of deadbeats and people escaping shady pasts. He thinks he glimpses this life in the Eritrean port of Massawa, and sets out to try to find 'portiness': 'I would keep company with dissipated missionaries, exiled Anglophiles, sea dogs, pimps and saints. The whisky would be vile rotgut. There would be a piano in the corner with keys sticky from spilt absinthe . . . it would be a purely whimsical trip, an attempt to find a culture that may have already disappeared.'

By the end of the book his conclusion seems to be that this culture has in fact vanished – he doesn't seem able to find it anywhere. But travelling five years after him, when regulations have tightened and squeezed the potential for random adventure even further, I felt as though I'd glimpsed what he'd been after. Certainly it was still there in Santos. Even though it has faded from what it was in Werner's heyday, the very cobbles on the dockside whispered of adventure and lawlessness. Our encounters with corrupt customs officials, near misses with pirates and the general way business was done out here made what most of us regard as the real world feel like life in a bubble where every surface has been wiped down with Dettol. And Werner's choice in wine and beer as well as whisky certainly ticked the 'vile rotgut' box. I'd gone mad, I'd been bored beyond belief, but it had been a true adventure.

I'd realized that the world is not shrinking, as we so often say – it's our perception of the world that's narrowing into a web of metal cylinders between the key nodes we're interested in. The real world, the world of the ports and beyond, remains vast and inexhaustible, unknowable and ungraspable.

Caribbean aside, I was heartbroken to be leaving the sea behind. Or, at least, I told myself I was. But I didn't really feel it. Not because I was relieved to be back on land. Deep down, lower than actual thought, I knew I wasn't saying goodbye to the high seas; just 'see you later'.

But I was glad to say hello to telecommunications again. Of all the various aspects of my journey, my attempt to live a simpler comms-free life had been the most abject failure. I know that there are people who can build happy, successful lives without modern technology – people who live in crofts and communes and make things and sell them at markets – and I really envy them. But I knew now that, for the time being at least, I wasn't one of them. My trip would have got no further than Tenerife without 3G, quad-band mobile telephony and high speed Wi-Fi Internet access. I wouldn't have been able to write about it the way I have without my laptop computer, or record such good-quality still images and movie clips without my HD 4.0 megapixel 80x digital zoom 16GB camcorder. I couldn't have done the research that enabled me to book the trip in the first place, or meet the people who have helped me in various places, without the World Wide Web.

But there has to be a better balance. It had been liberating to be forced to accept and fully engage with the here and now. Until it drove me insane, of course.

Now there was just the small matter of getting my beer off the ship and into India. The tasters who had greeted Allsopp's beer were long gone, but I was about to meet their replacements.

Nhava Sheva sits on the other side of Mumbai harbour from the main city. It's the largest port serving one of the world's most rapidly expanding economies, and it surrounded our berthing. Tree-covered islands dotted the estuary, many connected by long, low bridges. The sky was a silver haze dissolving at the edges into the sea, the sun shining in soft-focus. The city's high-rise skyline was a faint shadow that slowly gained definition as the sun rose higher. By midday it stretched into infinity, as if Manhattan had been copied and pasted. It was a view to make you gasp. The problem being, by midday I was still staring at it from the bridge of the ship.

When I read Paul Theroux's *The Great Railway Bazaar* the week after boarding *Caribbean*, I filed away his constant references to baksheesh – the bribes he had to pay while travelling in India seemingly every single time he encountered anyone acting in an official capacity – alongside hippies and the fact that he felt he had to explain what a samosa was under the heading 'Stuff That Shows This Book Was Written in the Seventies and Reflects How Much Things Have Changed Since Then'. I'd read so much about how India had changed, how Mumbai was one of the most modern, dynamic cities in the world, and how the country was thriving. So my encounter with the shipping company's agent took me completely by surprise.

Given that I was paying sixty euros a day for my voyage, consuming food that cost less than six euros a day, paying for drinks and snacks, doing my own laundry and cleaning my own cabin, I thought that some of what I'd paid might go towards getting me off the ship smoothly. The agent had collected me at my hotel in Rio; I was sure his counterpart here would drop me off at my hotel in Mumbai. It's the shipping company's duty to make sure crew members get home safely after they sign off, so they arrange and pay for transfers and flights. When the agent arrived on board, I hauled my bags down stairs, ready for a quick goodbye and a drive downtown.

'We have no record of a passenger signing off here,' said the agent.

'I VILL SHOW YOU ZER EMAIL I SENT FOUR DAYS AGO! I SPOKE ON THE PHONE ZIS MORNING AND ZEY SAID ZEY KNEW ALL ABOUT IT AND YOU WOULD TAKE CARE OF ZER PASSENGER.'

My ears rang. My fillings rattled.

The agent wobbled his head. 'This is very difficult. We know nothing about this. You will have to stay on board and disembark at the next port. Where is the next port?'

'DURBAN!' Werner's ponytail looked like it wanted to strangle the agent. His eyes burned holes through the man's clothing.

'Oh, this is very hard. Maybe I could take you. But it will be expensive. There is the agency fee, and the people I will have to talk to, customs and immigration charges and . . . let's see . . .' He did a very physical but not quite believable impersonation of someone calculating figures in their head. 'I can allow you off the ship for two hundred and seventy-five dollars American.'

'Two hundred and seventy-five dollars? To get off the ship? Why do I have to pay an agency fee when it's your agency that's screwed up? AND SURELY THERE'S A RECORD OF ME DISEMBARKING HERE FROM WHEN I BOOKED MY VOYAGE IN THE FIRST PLACE!' Being around Werner was starting to affect me.

'I know nothing about this. What is your decision?'

I glanced at Werner. He was looking at me, waiting for me to make my decision. 'You can stay on until Durban, pay nothing, and fly home from zere?'

The master wasn't arguing.

Werner didn't break the agent's back over his knee, tear him to shreds, throw the remains out of a porthole and bellow at the crew to clean it up. I could tell he loathed this man even more than all the other agents, customs officers, immigration officials and anyone else who tried to impinge upon his kingdom. If he weren't doing anything, that meant there was nothing that could be done. This was routine. Baksheesh. If I hadn't read the book I may have been more indignant, asked what would happen if I simply walked off the ship on my own and went to the gate wielding my passport. But I knew it wouldn't do anything, apart from maybe push up the price. Besides, what he didn't know was that with Kevin and my luggage, I was only capable of walking two hundred yards unassisted without collapsing.

'Fine.'

I was lucky I had 275 sodding dollars. I'd taken out 500 before leaving home, thinking 'just in case'. Just in case what, I couldn't say, but I was relieved now at my caution. I handed over the wad of notes, hoping I was setting in motion a morality play, and that he'd spend the money in a way that would bring about his downfall, leaving him destitute and friendless.

'Then I come back and collect you at fifteen hundred.'

Fifteen hundred. I wasn't going to be in Mumbai before nightfall. Another day lost.

Once the corrupt, thieving, venal bastard had left, Werner shrugged. 'In zis port it is always zer same.' He opened a cupboard, almost empty apart from a carton of cigarettes and two bottles of whisky. 'We have to give something in every port, to the customs guys – a bottle of whisky, cigarettes – for nothing. *Nothing*. The customs man here this morning, he came in with a second little man. This man's only job was to carry zer whisky and cigarettes. They took everything!'

To be entirely fair to the larcenous little scrote, it turned out he was only personally stealing about half the money he'd extorted from me. After I had an affectionate and surprisingly pain-free farewell handshake with Werner and headed into the port, I watched as chunks of my dollars were handed to officials at regular intervals.

We drove first to a large, pointless-looking building where my bags were unloaded and taken into a dingy office piled high with worm-eaten ledgers and box files tied with string; paperwork as furniture. Here my bags were tied shut with string and dripped with wax to seal them. 'You must be careful not to break the seal before we are out of the port,' said the agent, suddenly the nearest thing I had to an ally.

'They are asking if you have any cigarettes?'

I shook my head, trying to look nonchalant and sincere, knowing what was coming next.

'Any bottles?'

'No,' I said truthfully.

And then, one of them tried to lift Kevin.

'What is in this bag?'

I could answer their questions economically, but I couldn't lie. Even after all this way, all the work everyone had done, it wasn't worth it. 'This bag? This one here? Ah, that's beer.'

'Beer.'

'Yes, a large keg of beer.'

The customs men looked at each other. I'd stopped breathing. They shrugged, bent and sealed Kev's holdall with wax. Maybe I'd bought something worth while with my dollars after all.

'They may ask you at the gate to pay more money,' said the agent. 'Normally, you shouldn't bring in so much beer.'

'OK,' I said, smiling and civil. So long as they didn't confiscate it, I didn't mind. So long as they didn't arrest me for smuggling. Because now I thought about it, that's exactly what I was doing.

We loaded up the van again. As the agent went to close the door, a hand appeared and stopped him. A man in a khaki uniform and green beret, who we had never seen before, was standing with one hand holding the door open, his other hand outstretched.

'But we already paid all the bribes!' shouted the agent in English.

The man said nothing, just waited with his hand out. The agent screamed protests in Hindi and the man stood, immobile, until finally our driver put the van into gear and sped off, tearing the officer's hand from the door, which swung wildly until the agent pulled it closed.

We didn't stop again until the outside gate where we joined a queue of lorries. We were pulled over and told to get out of the van. Yet another uniformed official walked slowly towards the rear of the van, casually tossing a mean-looking truncheon from hand to hand. He asked for the back door to be opened. Then more officials called me to a desk by the barrier. Caught between indignation at being ripped off, and the small matter that I was in fact smuggling something they should be on the lookout for, it took every last ounce of will to walk casually, yet respectfully, towards the desk. They asked me to sign a paper, and then gave me back my passport. The truncheon man gazed at my bags, eventually decided there was nothing in them that was worth his while, and wandered off.

We got back in the van, and seconds later we were through.

Relief, anger and guilt fought briefly, then decided there wasn't much point. I had a legitimate visa and had every right to disembark in this port, and yet I'd been robbed of 275 dollars by an employee of the shipping line who was there to help me do so. But I'd smuggled in illegal contraband, which customs officials had caught, and let go. Was this karmic balance? Or just a typical encounter with people who have no motivation to do their jobs properly? It didn't matter. After three months – a reasonably quick journey by the standards of the 1830s but not record-breaking – I'd landed in India with my India Pale Ale. Yes, I'd failed in the strictest sense. Kev had flown halfway round the world before going to sea for a mere five weeks. But you know what? I didn't care. I'd made it. One hundred and eighty-five years after Samuel Allsopp's IPA first made its historic journey from Burton-on-Trent to India I had – approximately – recreated the journey. I gazed out at India, drinking it in, and thought, 'Bring it on.'

CHAPTER THIRTY-SEVEN

BURTON TAKES ON THE WORLD

Of doctors and medicines we have in plenty more than
enough ... what you may, for the love of God, send is
some large quantity of beer.

The dispatch from the colony in New South Wales, sent in
1854, was clear and emphatic. A couple of decades previously, the colonies in Australia were open prisons that made
Bencoolen and St Helena look like holiday camps. And then
someone discovered gold. In the 1850s, 400,000 Britons emi-
grated willingly.

India Pale Ale had gained its success – indeed its very
name – because it turned out to be the perfect antidote to
harsh, unforgiving conditions in which good beer couldn't be
brewed. As the nineteenth century progressed and the British
Empire took over the world, India became just one of many
places fitting this description.

By the 1850s, Bass and Allsopp were household names
both at home and around the world. In Burton, Bass built a
second brewery as large as the first. Eleven years later, a third
was added. Allsopp's New Brewery, built in 1858, was a
quarter of a mile long and devoted exclusively to the production of India Pale Ale. Any brewer wanting a piece of the
action could only partake if they had access to the wonderful
waters of Burton, and brewers from London and elsewhere
flocked to the town. In 1874 there were twenty-eight brewers
operating in Burton, producing 2.6 million barrels annually,
and Bass was the biggest brewery in the world.

In 1880, the anonymous author of *A Glass of Pale Ale and a Visit to Burton* spoke of the 'self-complacent French garçon' who, on encountering an Englishman, offers 'Biftik, Rosbif, Pell ell' and claimed that 'wherever Englishmen penetrate, they do carry with them their love of the Beef and Beer of Old England: for the former they secure the best substitute the land in which they are sojourning may afford; for the latter there is no substitute, and they never fail to obtain the genuine article in all its original excellence from home.' Boasting of the sun never setting on the Queen's Empire, he informs us that 'Bass's Pale Ale is found in the remotest corner of these dominions, and the natty scarlet triangle that constitutes the trade mark is ever hailed with welcome.'

With such success came new problems, and Michael Thomas Bass encountered a particularly ironic headache, given the dodgy tactics his father had employed in his attempts to enter the Baltic market over half a century earlier. Where Michael Bass had brewed beer to be passed off as Benjamin Wilson's, now it was Michael Thomas Bass whose beer was being widely imitated. In 1876, the 'natty scarlet triangle' became the first trademark ever registered in the UK. The beer made famous by the world's first multinational corporation, fittingly, became the world's first global brand, as universally recognizable as Coca-Cola or McDonald's today.

Exports to the rest of the world blossomed. By the early 1870s shipments to Australia were rivalling those to India. Henry Morton Stanley, in the diary he kept while journeying deep into the heart of Africa to find Dr Livingstone, recorded a pleasant surprise in his entry for 7th August 1876 (in *The Exploration Diaries*, published from the original manuscripts):

> Soon after camping, Kacheche came with supplies. 5 gal-
> lons of Rum. 4 sacks of rice, 2 sacks of potatoes. 1 bag of
> tobacco. 3 large loads of fish and 1 load of sundry small

things for myself such as tea, sugar, bread, butter, fish, jam, fruit in tin, English shag and cigarette paper, and three bottles of India Pale-Ale. The men gave three hearty cheers at the sight.[80] The skeletonized men began to revive, and this afternoon there is not a soul but is joyful. The long war against famine is over.

In the 1871–2 season Bass exported 131,000 barrels of beer, a sixth of Britain's entire ale exports. The firm was responsible for 73 per cent of British beer exports to the USA, and was also sending beer to the Azores, Madeira, the Canaries, Ascension, St Helena, Mauritius, Madagascar, Zanzibar, China and the Falklands. In each territory Bass competed with Allsopp and other brewers. In each case, it dominated.

In September 1883, *The Times* reported that 'the general way . . . in which beer is now exported is in bottles; and this has opened up a large and increasing business in bottling'. When St Pancras Station was built in London in the 1860s at the terminus of the Midland Railway, the station undercroft was specially designed to hold thousands of hogsheads of Burton ale. According to the *Royal Album of Arts and Industries of Great Britain*, published in 1887 to celebrate Victoria's golden jubilee, Bass alone had a storage space there for 8,000 butts of beer, as well as other stores in London and a depot at Poplar for the export and continental trade.

Of the 131,000 barrels exported by Bass in 1871–2, more than half of it was bottled. Bottling was a particular skill all of its own, ensuring that beer that was not yet fully 'ripe' was able to condition to perfection and not go off or explode in the bottle. James Herbert writes that 'it is most essential that the Ales should be perfectly clear and brilliant previous to bottling, so as to have the least possible sediment deposited in the bottles at the time of drawing the cork'. Just as hogsheads

---

80. Even though Stanley was clearly intent on sharing the IPA with nobody.

of IPA were not cask-conditioned, neither were the bottles seeded with extra yeast for a slow, secondary fermentation, as some beer fans believe. By 1878 there were no fewer than seventeen bottling companies in London, many clustered around St Pancras. One of them, Read Brothers, published a lavish booklet for the Sydney Exhibition in 1879, which explained why bottlers deserved as much credit as brewers for the quality of the beer:

> Beer reserved for export bottling is brewed from the choicest materials. It is indeed an altogether superior quality, and is charged accordingly.

> Messrs Bass & Co. do not themselves bottle their own Beer. They content themselves – very much to their own advantage – by brewing it only, and then selling it to professional bottlers, who thenceforth assume all responsibility of its management and outturn.

> This responsibility is a most serious one, for unless the ale is properly bottled at the right age, the consequences will probably be disastrous.

> Thus, if bottled too soon it turns thick and bursts the bottles, whereas if not bottled until it has passed its prime it will remain perfectly flat and wholly destitute of any of the refreshing pungency and flavour which characterizes ale in fine condition.

The popularity of bottling was in fact partly responsible for the first serious cracks that began to appear in Burton's monopoly of the global pale-ale trade. Scotland's brewers, particularly Edinburgh's, had been brewing pale ale since the 1820s, having found a 'magic circle' of wells under Edinburgh that possessed similar characteristics to Burton water. Alloa, home of Younger's, was similarly blessed, and Alfred Barnard, author of *Noted Breweries of Great Britain and Ireland*, christened it 'the Burton of the north'. When Barnard visited Younger's

Edinburgh site in the late 1880s he noted that 'their principal manufacture is India Pale Ale, which is well known and appreciated in all parts of Britain as well as foreign countries'. Originally developed for Scots working in the West Indies, Scottish IPA soon made its way to Africa, Asia, Australia, Europe and America, and was referred to in places as 'Scotch Burgundy'. Tennent's – which a century later would be famous for the bikini-clad 'lager lovelies' on the sides of its tins, and notorious thirty years after that for catering to the needs of park-bench alcoholics – brewed an ale that was particularly suited to shipping to hot climates: 'The peculiar excellence of the ales of Messrs Tennent, like those of Burton, is their remarkable keeping quality, and their retention of that delicate flavour of the hops, so often lost by the pale ale brewer, notwithstanding his utmost efforts to secure it.'

Barnard was also amazed by James Aitken's brewery in Falkirk, claiming that its success in the export trade was due 'not only to the quality of the beer, but to the cleanly, perfect, and careful nature of their bottling'. As bottling became the norm, the Scottish brewers grew to account for a quarter of all British beer exports.

This was the first chink in the armour of Burton's supremacy. It would crumble with astonishing rapidity.

CHAPTER THIRTY-EIGHT

INDIA'S NUMBER ONE BEER FAN

Outside the port gates, my world exploded. It was as if senses I'd not used for weeks were roughly shaken awake. The dusty roads were lined with busy-looking people, fetching and carrying, buying and selling. Freight trucks were painted and decorated in bright colours, like carnival floats, the constant bleating of horns their accompanying music. Green hills rose and fell dramatically as we twisted around the coastline.

It took two hours to get from the port into central Mumbai. The cut-and-pasted skyline I'd seen from the ship turned out not to be the city centre at all, but a mere suburb. As dusk fell, we crawled down a seemingly endless road lined with shacks built literally on top of one another. Shock at the extent of the poverty mingled with admiration at the skill of people building huts out of junk that were so solid that another dwelling could be built on top, with ladders up to them. And then a minute later we were in the clean, leafy Colaba district.

Originally a couple of islands, this was the first territory to be gifted to the East India Company by the Portuguese. The spaces between the islands were filled in and land reclaimed. After the opening of the Suez Canal, this is where the servants of the Raj alighted in India for the first time. Now, Colaba looked like a particularly well-preserved Victorian-era English town centre, only far more luxuriously verdant, and it's a magnet for travellers from around the globe, made famous by Gregory David Roberts's implausibly thrilling but allegedly true novel *Shantaram*.

After checking into my hotel, I hit the streets to sort out some money. I was in the middle of a huge collision between east and west, shops that were familiar from any city I've ever visited half-obscured by coconut vendors, tiny stalls selling bottled water, matches, cigarettes and snacks, random rails of clothes and boutiques of tourist tat. Every single vendor called to me as I walked past. It was impossible simply to walk down the street, you had to interact with it at every step.

I wasn't quite ready for this. As a long-time London-dweller, I knew the best policy was to keep my head down and pretend none of these people existed. But it became apparent that in India, this adult version of the child's I-can't-see-you-so-you-can't-see-me game doesn't get you very far. I moved on to the second stage – pretending to be speaking to someone on my mobile phone, the private bubble that's the only way to defeat the chuggers on London's pavements. But even this didn't work here. People approached me every few minutes trying to sell giant, three-foot-long orange balloons. I resisted the urge to ask, 'What the hell are they *for?* What would I do with it?' and walked on. This didn't deter them – they followed me, urging me to abandon my call because their balloons were more important than anything I might be talking about, and then had the panache to make out it was me who was being rude and unreasonable.

The first two cashpoints I found revealed a slight problem: none of my cards were working. As I walked up the main drag of the Colaba Causeway, past shop windows displaying Hugo Boss suits and Louis Vuitton bags, I started to worry.

Even the simple act of walking along the pavement could be interpreted as a rude snub. I like walking, and was particularly enjoying doing so hours after arriving in India for the first time in my life, after months of not being able to walk very far at all.

'Do you want a taxi?'

'No, thanks.'

'Yes, you do! Of course you do!'

'I'm happy walking, thanks!'

'What is wrong with my taxi? Where are you going?'

By the time I succeeded in getting some cash, the bars and shops were starting to close. It was almost midnight but, newly affluent, I had a craving to satisfy. I would contest that I love a late-night curry even more than the average English beer drinker. Added to this, I had endured five weeks of the food on the *Caribbean*, and had not eaten properly since disembarking nine hours ago. I found myself walking down a rubbish-strewn alley, in which stood a busy restaurant. One amazing 'lamb' curry – the first tasty food I'd had in two months – and a couple of large Kingfishers later, I was about £4.50 worse off. By local standards I'd been royally ripped off, but on London terms it was an outrageous bargain. I felt serenely happy.

As I went back to my hotel, whole families were bedding down for the night on the pavement. What struck me was the orderly way they did it: the neatly dressed parents carefully putting down bed rolls against concrete walls where their market stalls had stood until an hour ago, tucking in their children before turning in themselves, no differently than if they were in a semi in Croydon. I got back to my room, and felt unable to complain that my minibar hadn't been restocked as promised. Colaba was proving a challenge to how my brain worked. I was a fish out of water.

I spent the next morning holed up in an Internet cafe, trying to sort out my onward itinerary. I'd had no firm plans when I set off, save the fact that I wanted to open my beer in Kolkata (Calcutta). And there was no way I was flying there, with or without a heavy beer keg. I felt the thrill of freedom that, now I was in the country, after months of confinement in close spaces, I could wander wherever I wanted, albeit with more luggage than anyone could carry. There was a delegation from the British Beer & Pub Association in Delhi for a trade show. I'd agreed to join them at a press reception to talk about my journey, but that reception had happened while the *Caribbean* languished in the Gulf with a broken engine. I decided to head there anyway, if only because they might have some decent beer. And from there, we'd go on to Kolkata, for mine and Kevin's appointment with destiny.

At one point the plan had been to spend Christmas in India with Liz, but now circumstances at home had prevented her from coming and that took away some of the excitement. After the isolation of the ship, I was numbed by Mumbai's filth and glamour, the noise, the pace, the density of people, and was certain I would be loving and hating India in equal measure over the next couple of weeks. Delhi and Kolkata were likely to be more demanding. I wished I could relax into it, and maybe I would. But my thoughts were turning to home, to dark rainy streets, welcoming taverns and foamy pints of ale. I hadn't seen Liz – or tasted a decent beer for that matter (ice-cold, refreshing but tasteless iced beer in Brazil notwithstanding) – for months.

But I felt sure the afternoon would make up for it: I had an appointment with a man who is probably India's biggest beer fan.

Ashish Jasuja loves beer so much he took a job with Anheuser-Busch to get closer to the industry. I was due to meet him after his weekly German lesson. He was studying German because he hoped to go to the Munich Oktoberfest the following year, and was saving up for it. He loves beer so much that – and this is where it gets a bit worrying – he had found my details while browsing the website of the British Guild of Beer Writers, something he freely admitted to doing regularly.

While I was weeping tears of bored frustration as the *Caribbean* idled off the coast of Oman, my one-bar-of-signal BlackBerry buzzed with an email from him. He'd been following my journey via my sporadic blog posts from various Spanish and Brazilian ports, and felt an immediate kinship:

I too am on a quest to find the meaning of beer in my life! Your journey to India sounds super . . . I'm a big fan of the IPA and I've wanted to do something around it in India unfortunately no brands are available here. And that to me is a matter of national shame. Because here's this style which is a rage all over (how authentic the recreations are is plausible as you point out) the world and it's not available in the country that was the very reason for the style's existence!

After reading this, there was nothing I wanted to do in Mumbai more than have Ashish take me round its watering holes.

Ashish and his friend Pratyush from German class collected me from the hotel. They were both in their mid- to late twenties, Ashish fizzing like a bottle of pop, goateed and grinning constantly; Pratyush a little more quiet and thoughtful, possibly wondering what he had got himself into.

They took me to the kind of restaurant that manages to avoid the tourist guidebooks but not the patronage of discerning locals. I have a copy of their menu in front of me as I write and I suppose I should include its name, but I'm not sure Ash would thank me for doing so. The portents weren't good as we parked the car next to a crow feeding off a dead rat, but inside was the finest Indian meal I'd ever had at that point. We ordered drinks and Ash proclaimed, 'You are in India so you will want to drink Kingfisher.' He chose Budweiser (of course), and specified a warm one. I'd seen this in Kenya too – there's a real belief in some hot countries that cold beer upsets the stomach.

Over amazing tandoori fish we exchanged views on beer and drinking culture, and it turned out that Ash's were identical to mine. He'd gained all his knowledge on beer from the Internet, and while he was excited about my IPA and loved exploring Belgian beers on rare occasions when he could, the main thing he loved about beer was its essence of unpretentious sociability, something no other drink quite has.

The beery reality for affluent young professionals like Ash is currently frustrating, however. Though more relaxed than they were, India still has very tight import controls, as well as an additional level of bureaucracy in moving beer from state to state (my days as a smuggler of contraband beer were not yet over – something that would almost spell disaster in a few days' time).

Kingfisher, owned by United Breweries (UB), dominates the market with a share of nearly 40 per cent. United is owned by Dr Vijay Mallya, a billionaire entrepreneur and Member of Parliament, who is often described as India's answer to Richard Branson, especially since he founded Kingfisher Airlines in 2005. In beer he's sheltered to some extent by the complexities of red tape, but India is rapidly becoming a prize too big for his global rivals to ignore. With strong population and average income growth, and the average age of that population falling, the beer market is seeing sustained growth of around 9 per cent a year. SABMiller has bought breweries in the south, and Heineken has taken a 37.5 per cent stake in United itself. Anheuser-Busch, Carlsberg and InBev are establishing joint ventures or buying breweries outright, but SABMiller and United still control 80 per cent of the market. Having established themselves, the global brewers are just starting to launch brands like Bud, Foster's and Löwenbräu. Curiously Cobra – the twenty-year-old beer synonymous with India in Britain – has only entered the Indian market in the last couple of years.

But it's all lager – at least for now. India's moneyed elite has expensive tastes, and Ash said that in a few weeks' time, India's first microbrewery was due to open in Kingfisher's hometown, Bangalore, the centre of the booming IT industry. In one sense things were unrecognizable from IPA's heyday. In another, beer was once again all about the leading global brands and multinational corporations. But Ash seemed certain my barrel of India Pale Ale would have an interested audience.

After a sensational lunch, we rolled back out on to the streets of Colaba (the rat had gone), and approached a stall selling 'paan'. This is an everyday delicacy across many parts of Asia. You take a thick, green, shiny betel leaf and coat it with paste. Add slices of areca nut, a little lime and some seeds and spices, then you fold the whole lot up into a parcel and pop it in your mouth. The Mughal emperors picked up this habit from their subjects, and Company merchants also became addicted to its grainy, astringent bite. It was said to preserve the teeth, strengthen the stomach, comfort the brain and cure tainted breath. It took me about twenty minutes to chew my way through it, and when I'd finished my mouth had no idea it had just eaten several pungent, spicy dishes.

We spent the afternoon and evening trawling through Colaba's better class of pubs and bars. We were unable to pay for our drinks all day – Ashish didn't just sell beer to these guys, he was greeted by them like a long-lost friend.

Most bars were run by Parsis, the Zoroastrians descended from Persian refugees a thousand years ago. 'When the British left, the Parsis had paler complexions than anyone else,' said Ash. 'It just seemed to make sense that they would take over in bars, which were seen as being so Western.' While this may or may not be true (Freddie Mercury – real name Farrokh Bulsara – was Parsi, but had no practical problem in keeping his Indian ethnicity secret), there was also the fact that of all India's religious/ethnic groups, the Parsis had no taboo around alcohol. Wherever you look, there are wrinkles and quirks in India's complex demographics.

Between the bars we wandered along unbelievably leafy streets. Colaba on a sunny Sunday afternoon was tranquil and pleasant, the most noise coming from the games of cricket that sprang up on every flat surface, including the main roads, with balls being played in the brief gaps between traffic.

Arguably the centre of our day and evening was Leopold Cafe, another Parsi-run restaurant and bar that has become a Bombay institution.[81] The cafe on the ground floor offers a menu running from Indian food to burgers, pasta, fish and chips and chop suey. It's a mecca for travellers, every table bearing a well-thumbed copy of *Shantaram*, which was both strange and predictable given that much of the book centres around this bar. Upstairs was the dirty chrome of a grungy Sheffield nightclub with English Premiership football on the big screen. Naturally, we stayed here for some time. The boys enjoyed Bud and Foster's but I spotted something wonderful called London Pilsner, a 500ml bottle with a sort of fake Union Jack on it, establishing a seemingly effective but utterly fictitious link between London and lager brewing. It went down at least as well as the alternatives would have.

Dusk was falling outside and I was reaching the happy emotional state I attain whenever I'm drinking beer and making firm friends with people I've never met before in a part of the world I would never have visited if it had not been for the impact beer has had on my life. It's similar to the eternal 'you're my besht mate' caricature of drunken behaviour, but hits me earlier in the curve of inebriation, and feels far more profound. I thought about how I'd got here, about how I felt more familiar with India's history than its present, from James Lancaster and the *Red Dragon*, through the distinctly mixed legacy of the British in India, to how things were today. I felt like I were at the end of a long

---

81. Throughout this book I refer to the modern-day city as Mumbai because officially that's what it's called. But every time I said 'Mumbai' that afternoon, Ash or Pratyush would correct me to 'Bombay', and that's how they referred to it.

thread full of greed, death, cruelty, racism, wonder and fascination. There was something I'd been wanting to say since I began my historical research almost a year before, and these two seemed like the right people to say it to.

'Ashish. Pratyush.'

'Yes?'

'On behalf of the English people, I'd just like to apologize for what we did to your country. It was fucking inexcusable. I just want to tell you that throughout history, as well as the thugs and villains and racists, there were loads of us who fell in love with India and had nothing but respect for the culture and people here. I love this place. I want to stay here for months. I hope you can forgive us.'

'Pete, it was a long time ago. It's no problem, man. Most Indians alive today weren't born in 1947.'

'I'm not talking about that, I'm talking about before, I mean, for hundreds of years, we were responsible for millions of deaths . . .'

'Yeah, but seriously. It wasn't you, was it? That's what things were like back then. It's different now. Don't worry about it. Fancy another beer?'

'Ashish.'

'Yes?'

'I'd like to try some arak.'

'No.'

'Do you know where I could get some?'

'Yes, but I'm not going to tell you, man.'

'Please.'

'Why on earth would you want to drink arak? We are drinking good beer and there are much better spirits here.'

'I've just read so much about it, in the history of India. It was so important in the history of the British here, and the need to bring in IPA. Now I'm here I feel like I ought to try some, just to complete the story.'

'It could make you go blind!'

'I'm not talking about the cheap stuff, the stuff on the streets. Come on, let's try one of the quality brands.'

'The quality brands are the ones that could make you go blind! The cheap stuff will probably just kill you.'

'Oh, go on.'

'No.'

We finished our day together at the Khyber restaurant, one of Mumbai's finest. It surpassed even lunch at the secret place. I was in no condition to take notes by this stage, but I remember wishing we had Indian restaurants this good in London. Their website says it's 'an intriguing and classic place [that] reinforces your idea of elegance and authenticity. Adorned with a nostalgic décor, a careful melange of the classic and the modern, it leaves you mystified', and from what I can remember, that sounds about right.

It had been a fantastic day. As I took a cab back to the hotel, I reflected that India was stretching me to extremes of love and hate. After five weeks of solitary confinement I was struggling to cope with the noise and the pace and the weight of people. And I was finding it hard to cope with how obviously privileged I was compared with most of the people here – but not all of them. That week, new research had been published showing that Mumbai had leapfrogged New York to become the second-most expensive real-estate market in the world after London. I'm not saying that's a good thing. I wasn't sure what I thought about it. I felt as if I were only half there, a feeling I was sure would fade only slowly, like the sea tan on my legs.

'You want to go to nightclub? To see girls?' called my taxi driver.

'No. No, I'm exhausted. Thanks.'

'Yeah? These are very special girls.' He nodded to himself, like an old friend deciding he knew just the tonic to cheer me up. 'Yes. That's it. I take you to girls.'

'Please. Just the hotel.'

I was going to need all the sleep I could get if I wanted to keep up.

*

There was no room free in my Mumbai hotel after the week-end, so faced with the prospect of hauling my 80 kilos of luggage around the place I decided to go straight to Delhi. I wanted to travel by train so that I could see India, then realized that most of my journey would be in darkness. Ah well, it was still more of an experience than the plane, much cheaper and far less hassle with so much luggage.

The unlikely highlight of the journey occurred after a couple of hours, when the train began to slow. After miles of featureless darkness there were suddenly lines of white hotels crowned by neon signs, roads busy with traffic and every space between cars crammed with pedestrians. Tents lined the sides of the track, bonfires crowded by silhouettes, and then we were pulling into a station with Nescafé booths dotting the platform. The name of this bustling metropolis slid past the window: Surat. Here I was, alone in India, in the place where William Hawkins became the first-ever Eng-lishman to set foot in the country. It made me think again of what we'd done to the country since then. I knew from my conversation with Ashish that the antics of the Company and the Raj were fresher in my mind than in those of most living Indians, but I still felt as though I needed to apologize to everyone. Surat, though. I had no idea the place still existed, but the mangrove swamp had become a busy, lively city in the intervening four centuries. I was suddenly over-come with sweet melancholy, and got a bit tearful.

Delighted, I lay back in my bunk after dinner, serenaded by a sitar muzak version of Europe's 'The Final Count-down'. I wasn't sure whether it were meant to help lull us to sleep or not, but between the soundtrack and the violently rocking train, the Indian man sharing my cabin snoring like

Remus, and the constant tutting of the Frenchman also sharing my cabin, I didn't sleep much.

Thanks to my guidebook I was ready for the explosion of activity when I stepped off the train in Delhi just after 7 a.m., dishevelled but unmistakably Western. Within thirty seconds there were two porters carrying my heavy wheelie bag and the bag containing Kevin on their heads. I pointed out that both could be wheeled along by the handles, but they had their principles, so 30 kilos each pressing on the tops of their skulls it was. A third man, busy and smartly dressed, had kindly taken it upon himself to sort me out with transport to my hotel, but first he had to take me to an office to check that my reservation was OK.

Again, I'd read about this – it's a common scam to take sleep-deprived, disoriented travellers to 'the office', pretend to phone the hotel, discover there's no record of your reservation, and instead book you into a different, vastly more expensive hotel with which the office has a deal.

It probably had a higher success rate before the arrival of mobile-phone networks in India. As I sat waiting for my new friend to phone my hotel, I took out my mobile and my printed-off reservation confirmation, complete with phone number, and smiled pleasantly. Sure enough, my hotel reservation was fine. By the time I'd reached my hotel, I'd only paid the porters ten times the officially recommended rate, and been driven around the streets for twenty minutes to get to a hotel that was a few hundred yards away. I thought that a good result.

My room in a narrow, noisy street in Old Delhi proved a great incentive to getting out and exploring the city as soon as I'd dropped off my bags. Delhi is the city so good they might have only named it once, but they built it eight times. What we currently call Old Delhi was built by the Mughal emperors, and served as the capital of the Empire until the British crushed the Mutiny in 1857 and removed Bahadur

Shah Zafar II, the last Mughal emperor. When the British moved their capital of India here from Calcutta in 1911, New Delhi was designed by Edward Lutyens, and completed in 1931.

Connaught Place is where Old and New Delhi collide, a starburst explosion in the middle of the city street map, and like all visitors, I was drawn to this point first. As soon as I got there, loads of people were very keen to talk to me. Some of them were as young as ten; others were old men. Some were smartly dressed in suits and ties; others were filthy. Some spoke faultless English; others knew only a few broken phrases. Some were clever; others stupid. Some corpulent; others emaciated. Between them they represented an almost complete cross-section of Indian males. But they all wanted one thing: they were all desperate for me to go to Agra.

Some hid at shadowed corners, mumbling softly at me as I passed, like drug dealers or spies. Others took on the guise of officials, marching up and saying, 'Ah, yes, this way, please' and stepping off towards their 'brother's travel agency'. Others still fell into step beside me, friendly, immediately re-assuring me they wanted no more than a chance to practise their English, and plaintively called 'Just give me a chance!' at my retreating back when I rumbled them and walked away.

Agra, the ancient city where William Hawkins got drunk with an emperor four centuries ago, is home to the Taj Mahal, and is four hours' drive from Delhi. Together with Jodhpur, where you can see the stunning sixteenth-century Mehrangarh Fort, the three cities form 'The Golden Triangle'. It's a famous tourist route, recommended by Lonely Planet, and if I'd had more time, if I'd been here with Liz, I'm sure we would have done it. But I'd only just arrived in Delhi and there was a lot to see in the city itself. I was a little hurt that the entire population seemed to want me to leave again so soon.

Half a mile north of Connaught Place the roads crumble and their edges disappear into mounds of refuse and puddles, shored up by shop hoardings piled higgledy-piggledy atop each other, faded and dusty, advertising textiles and pure veg thalis under grey dust tans thrown up by never-ending autorickshaws, cars and lorries, bursting buses and weaving mopeds.

Half a mile south, the streets open out into broad, tree-lined avenues punctuated by pleasantly manicured round-abouts. After the four- and five-star hotels you're into government territory, where ministers flaunt their power through walled and guarded compounds, each with a sign boasting who it belongs to, each capable of housing an entire district of Old Delhi.

I explored both, soaking up the vibrancy of the Old, the elegance of the New. Crossing the streets in New Delhi was capable of ageing you ten years inside ten minutes, if you lived that long. Having survived my unwilling real-life par-ticipation in the eighties video game Frogger, I decided to go for a little variety, and took my life in my hands on wheels instead – three wheels, if anyone's counting. Autorickshaws are the flytraps of the motorized transport kingdom. They look nice, luring you in, before killing you violently. Death comes in the guise of another video game, the best never yet invented. You start off occupying an autorickshaw-shaped space in the middle of four lanes of bumper-to-bumper traffic moving at high speed. There's another auto-rickshaw-shaped space ten yards ahead of you, but absolutely no clear road whatsoever between your current space and the next one. The goal is to bend spacetime sufficiently to jump from one space to the other. If you do this several times over the course of a few miles, and you're still in one piece at the end of it, you've won. It costs about 200 rupees a go. This is of course an absurdly inflated price, but some of it goes to offsetting the costs of the holes you gouge in the thin upholstery of your seat as the angry insect whine of the engine approaches ramming speed.

I was on my way to meet Vikram Achanta, a friend of Ashish who was keen to hear about my journey in return for showing me a selection of Delhi's drinking spots. Vikram runs a design agency that does a lot of work with beer brands, so like Ash he was extremely interested in my quest and in talking about beer generally. We met at the Gymkhana Club, an outpost from the days of the Raj.

The institution of 'the club' was a focal point of Anglo-Indian life, the hub of society even in small country stations. In the last days of the Raj, civilians and army officers would meet at clubs to drink pegs of whisky and soda. Allowing membership to Indians was so controversial it 'almost split the empire' according to one old boy who was in favour of allowing well-bred Indians to join, 'considering not every Englishman who came out to India came out of the top drawer'.

Not coming out of the top drawer myself, I felt privileged now to be the English guest of an Indian member of one of the finest clubs in Delhi. Outside, the car park was full of the coolly retro but allegedly very uncomfortable white Ambassador cars that are standard issue for Delhi's politicians and diplomats. Inside we crossed a wide dance floor where the ghosts of women in ball gowns and officers in bright-red tunics were almost visible, and entered a long bar full of rotund Sikhs and old men with handlebar moustaches, all drinking whisky and soda.

Vikram seemed a little nervous at first, and when we talked about my day with Ashish I realized why. Vikram lowered his voice, looked me in the eye, and said, 'Ashish tells me you each drank fifteen litres of beer that night.'

I didn't want to betray my new friend and expose him as an arch-bullshitter, but my incredulous laughter was out before I could stop it. 'We had a few. But fifteen litres each would have killed us! Divide it by four and I think you're probably getting closer to the truth.' Confident now that he wasn't going to end the evening in a gutter, Vikram relaxed.

After this we went to one of the coolest bars in Delhi, on the ground floor of a smart, expensive hotel. It turned out to be an American-themed diner with Wurlitzer jukeboxes and 1950s pop memorabilia crowding the walls. It was great, but I felt like I'd stepped from one era of Western colonialism directly to the next, passing nothing in between.

I needed an antidote, so the next day I plunged into the winding streets of Old Delhi. Cows with brightly painted horns pulled rickety carts, or grazed on ten-foot-high piles of garbage in the streets. Rickshaw wallahs pulled in front of me, blocking my path, demanding I get in, forbidding me to walk. When I reversed and went round them they would keep pace with me for a hundred yards or so, yelling. My various maps soon lost their usefulness. There were unmarked forks in the road, unrecorded roundabouts and random streets, and there were no street names visible anywhere. Soon I was hopelessly lost.

But it didn't matter: every street was an open-air market. I wandered through stalls selling spices, fruit, leather goods, pans, watches ... It was cramped, loud and bewildering, and vibrant and engaging and simply human in a way no Western mall could ever be, even if it had the slightest desire to be so.

Eventually I stumbled into Chandni Chowk, the main thoroughfare leading to Old Delhi's main attraction, the Red Fort. I passed a man receiving a shave, then another having his ears cleaned, then one having his hair cut, then another having his armpits shaved. I imagined a bunch of scruffy, bleary people at one end of the street; lines of immaculately groomed executives at the other.

Finally, I made it inside the Red Fort. The stillness made me feel like I'd escaped into an immaculate cocoon.

This was where Company officials came to negotiate for the firman, their permit to trade freely in the Mughal Empire. Where huge, glamorous processions of painted elephants and hundreds of people carrying golden trays full of treasure had set off to celebrate royal weddings. And where the British army had slaughtered anyone with a brown face in the aftermath of the Mutiny. It was a palace of gardens and open walls. Once decked in beautiful fabrics, it had been stripped of its riches long ago, and yet was still magnificent. It made perfect sense that the Mughal emperors were often revered as poets. No sense at all that the British used these buildings as army barracks. It must have been hard for them to remember sometimes which side was the civilized benefactor, and which the heathen barbarian.

Delhi was every bit as exhausting as I'd expected. If you can deal with the filth, the smog, the spitting, the scammers and aggressive salesmen, if you can screen out the abject poverty at every turn, if you can turn your back on a toddler with a dirty face and huge eyes who sees your white face and totters towards you with an outstretched hand when he is too young even to know why he is doing so – then you can enjoy the city the same way you might enjoy a funfair ride. It's thrilling, unpredictable, a little dangerous, and it will make you want to throw up if you do it for long enough. Grow a scab over your sensitive nature. Lose a tender part of yourself. Forget your twee middle-class sensibilities. Become callous. It's not a one-sided relationship: stay pink and raw and Delhi will eat you whole. They're hard here. Meet them on their own terms, call a scam when you see it, reward kindness when it crops up, take it as it comes and keep your wits about you, and then – and only then – you can have a good time. But it's certainly not a place to relax, and relaxation was what I needed.

In a couple of days, I'd be opening my keg, and ending my quest.

CHAPTER THIRTY-NINE

THE SUDDEN DECLINE OF INDIA PALE ALE

In the middle of the nineteenth century, you could always rely on Charles Stuart Calverley for a witty verse to reflect the issues of the day. In 1862, he wrote a poem called 'Beer':

> O Beer: O Hodgson, Guinness, Allsopp, Bass!
> Names that should be on every infant's tongue!
> Shall days and months and years and centuries pass,
> And still your merits be unrecked, unsung?

Guinness is the only name there that most drinkers would recognize today, the only one that escaped Calverley's fear of remaining unsung – and it's the only one that was not an India Pale Ale. When he penned his ditty, IPA was conquering the world. But it took little more than twenty years for India Pale Ale to slip from global dominance into obscurity.

The change had been brewing for some time. In India, heavy drinking simply didn't fit with the refined climate the Anglo-Indians wished to create towards the end of the nineteenth century. In 1882 'F.E.W.' speculated that 'the severe forms of liver complaint, so common a quarter of a century ago, were probably due to the immense quantities of ale then consumed in India' and that the 'engagements of girls without the consent of their parents, and the elopements of wives with other women's husbands' was surely down to 'indigestion, begotten of ale and buffalo humps'.[82] Mr Stoequeler in

---

82. This insightful analysis of the causes of marital infidelity is of course still relevant today: how much longer must we put up with women (notice,

Bombay claimed that those who were still in thrall to the 'brutifying power' of drink were 'looked upon with mingled pity and contempt by all other classes of their fellow citizens'. The zeal to convert the whole country to Christianity, while officially disapproved of by the Raj, ran unchecked. As the nineteenth century progressed, bawdy theatres disappeared, thanks, according to a local journal, to 'the march of morality and the progress of fastidiousness'. When one army regiment staged a play to raise money for an orphanage that cared for the children of their fallen comrades, the money was refused because it had been gained in 'so unchristian manner', which could only 'hurt the feelings and principles of the orphans'. One chaplain refused to visit soldiers in the Calcutta Hospital suffering from alcohol-related ailments, because 'the very fact that they were ill was evidence of divine displeasure at their conduct and it was not for him to endanger his salvation by consorting with these lost souls'.[83]

India had always been a stage on which the English could play out their fantasies, obsessions, desires and neuroses on a grander scale than in the home country. When England was eating and drinking to excess, the Anglo-Indians turned gluttony into a national sport and many gorged themselves to death. Now, as sober Christianity ruled and the temperance movement reached its zenith at home, India became a Christian-fundamentalist theocracy as hardline as anything we've seen in Asia since.[84]

A small drink before lunch was still just about tolerated in

---

it's always women who cause it) gorging themselves on ale and buffalo meat then briefly considering popping a couple of Rennies before deciding instead to steal any man who isn't nailed down?

83. Which is a bit like Jesus encountering the lepers and shrieking, 'Ugh, I'm not going near them! I might catch something!' It's great to see that the more fundamentally and literally people believe in scripture, the less they seem to actually understand it.

84. Albeit a tad more *polite* than some.

some cities, but out in the mofussil drinking before sunset became frowned upon. In the local club, where responsible drinkers had been jeered as milksops a few decades before, anyone now showing evidence of being half-cut was swiftly removed.

Few mourned the decline of interest in beer. IPA may have been vital to the modern beer industry. For a long time it may even have been an important aspect of everyday life in India. But as far as the Honourable Company was concerned, it had never been central to their commercial interests. For one thing, the Company existed to create profit by trade overseas – either by shipping out bullion and currency and bringing home goods, or by triangular trade on the high seas, where they could use their ships to take goods produced in one place, trade them in a second place for goods produced there – and so on, increasing the value every time.

And while beer may have been a pleasant intoxicant and a vital part of the diet, it was bulky and difficult to carry. And in India, there emerged a more powerful, profitable intoxicant that took up far less precious hold space, and provided the perfect link in the coveted triangular trade among Britain, India and China.

Opium was used freely in Indian society. Fanny Parkes was offered it frequently when she visited the 'zenanas' (women's quarters) in the palaces of Bengal and Oude, where ladies took it as a preventative against common colds, and children were given it to keep them quiet. The Company saw a useful source of profit, and began investing heavily in poppy farming and opium production.

What they grew in India, they sold in China. When China banned opium imports, the Company ignored them. By the 1820s opium accounted for a seventh of the Company's total revenues, and was described as 'probably the largest commerce of the time in any single commodity'. When the

Chinese government insisted again on a ban in a desperate attempt to raise its population from druggy stupor, English ships shelled their cities until they changed their minds. At its very apex of power, the finances of the British Empire were utterly dependent on the Company's activities as an international smuggler of illegal drugs. As early as the 1840s, when beer was still experiencing burgeoning popularity in India, the bold, large-font beer ads for Hodgson, Bass and Allsopp had been displaced from the cover of the *Calcutta Gazette* by pages of formal, restrained notices advertising cases of opium for export. It would be nice to think that the opium trade died with the Company after the Mutiny, and that Queen Victoria's government would not countenance something so clearly immoral in return for nothing other than hard cash. But trading to China continued until 1907, with government-approved manufacture in India finally ending in 1911.

And then there was the Company's other export, the one it had less reason to be ashamed of. The ships that delivered opium to China stocked up on tea, which had long been a source of far greater profit to the East India Company than any of its administrative dealings in India. Manual labourers back in Britain had developed a preference for tea over beer as early as 1760, and by the 1830s Company tea imports were so vast that the duty on them accounted for 10 per cent of the Exchequer's revenue. In 1834 the Company looked into growing tea in India rather than having to buy it from China. The first few attempts were not successful, but by the 1860s retired army officers and civil servants began investing heavily in plantations. Tea stalls were set up in factories, mills and mines, and workers were treated to time off for tea breaks. From the highest servants of the Raj to the homeless on the streets of Calcutta, tea was available to all.

Even among those who still drank alcohol, fashions were changing. Brandy and soda was increasingly common from the 1840s. In 1869 the opening of the Suez Canal slashed journey times from Europe to just a few weeks, and the Victorian fashion for French cuisine was easily transferred to the subcontinent. Claret made a modest revival, drunk in moderation from the finest crystal glasses. Beer, gradually, became seen as the drink of the poor, and only the troops still enjoyed it freely. When French vineyards were devastated by phylloxera, and brandy supplies dried up and claret became scarce, the introduction of mass-marketed blended Scotch whiskies created the weak whisky and soda that became the symbolic drink of the Raj. In the 1860s tonic water was invented, a mixture of carbonated water and quinine, which helped safeguard against malaria.[85] This tasted far more pleasant when mixed with gin, and so the Anglo-Indians created the G&T. Following that, the gimlet – gin and lime juice – became the very thing to enjoy on the veranda at sunset. In 1883 'F.E.W.' lamented the passing of the old times, even with their liver damage and ale and buffalo-hump-crazed husband-stealers: 'That the new style of hospitality, which consists chiefly of lawn tennis in a sweltering climate, with whisky and soda water, or tea and cake, for refreshment, is all that can be desired is a question. Some persons profess to like that sort of thing, but it is repugnant to the old school of Anglo-Indians.'

The one practical advantage IPA had enjoyed was the favourable rates for shipping, but when protectionist policies made India a market for English textiles rather than vice versa, freight charges were no longer the bargain they had once been. With advances in refrigeration and brewing

---

85. As Professor Charles Bamforth of University of California, Davis, points out, the massive popularity of quinine demonstrates that bitterness was where the Anglo-Indian palate was centred – further proof that, while IPA may originally have been brewed to survive the journey, the aggressively hoppy flavour was a big part of its appeal.

science came calls for India to brew its own beer. In 1860, *The Times* in London argued:

> Plumpuddings have been made at Jerusalem, Christmas turkeys were cooked in the Crimea, and very good beef-steaks can be had everywhere except in Japan. Admitting that a supply of beer must precede a British establishment, just as the growth of mulberry trees must precede the produce of silk ... There are places in India as healthy and agreeable as Keswick or Eastbourne, if we would but take advantage of them, and the success of a brewery would not be a bad test of the salubrity of a station. Wherever sound beer could be brewed British soldiers could comfortably live, and a moral of deep import might be drawn from a fair commercial experiment.

It soon came to pass. In 1879, the Collector of Sea Customs in Calcutta reported in the introduction to the annual trade figures that imports of beer, ale and porter, 'which have always been considered the staple beverage of British subjects in India', had shown a 'remarkable decline', due to the 'great improvement and success in brewing malt liquors in the hills of Northern India'. By 1890 there were twenty-five Indian breweries. While the main cities were still too far away to reach economically, the messes and canteens up-country could now be supplied domestically. This was confirmed by a steady growth in the importation of hops. By the end of the century, domestic breweries were turning out 150,000 barrels of porter and ale a year, half of which were bought in bulk by the army, the rest by the civilian population.

But even as India was figuring out how to brew its own ale to supply a diminished market, IPA's final nemesis was gaining ground in all its golden glory.

The relationship between lager and IPA goes back to the 1830s. With Burton beers in the ascendant, legendary brewers Anton Dreher of Vienna and Gabriel Sedlmayr of Munich visited England on a mission to discover the secrets of their success. Brewers have always been sociable people happy to compare notes and show off their establishments to each other. Bass even presented Sedlmayr with a saccharometer so he could measure the fermentable sugars in his wort. But this openness didn't preclude a bit of industrial espionage. Legend has it that the wily Teutons carried hollowed-out walking sticks in which they secreted tubes of beer snaffled from Burton's fermenting vessels, and thermometers secretly to measure temperatures. They wrote home boasting 'we stole as much as we could', and 'It always surprises me that we can get away with these thefts without being beaten up.' Back in Austria, Dreher attempted to brew a pale ale, but it didn't sell well. He then married pale-ale malt with lager yeast (lager was as dark as any other beer until this point) and created a lighter, more refreshing brew known as 'Vienna Red'. A few years later, a renegade Munich brewer turned up in Pilsen and created a new sparkling beer that just happened to use pale malt, and Pilsner lager was born. Coming of age at the same time as refrigeration, it spread around the world with astonishing speed.

Beck's was one of several German lager brewers exporting modest amounts to India by the 1870s, and as ice machines reached the stations of the interior, its popularity bloomed. The whole reason for IPA's success had been the demand for a beer that could be drunk chilled, that was alcoholic but lighter in taste and effect than the heavier beers typical at the time. Just as India was finally sobering up, here was a beer that was even lighter, even crisper, and significantly lower in alcoholic strength.

The big Burton brewers ignored lager. In 1882, as German and American lager brewers opened for business across the planet, the *Brewers' Journal* complained that while 'bottled Bass has been found in every country where Englishmen have yet put foot', brewers like Allsopp, Barclay Perkins and Guinness, as well as Bass, were simply standing back and allowing the global beer market to be taken from under their noses. Critics in the sultry colonies had a new standard against which to judge pale ale, and began to find the British brew had 'too much alcohol, too much sediment, too much hops and too little gas' compared with its European cousin. But Burton's new town fathers had only just completed their new 'Leviathan breweries'. They would have had to redouble their investment to brew lager, and saw no immediate reason for doing so – they had a booming market for pale ale on their doorstep, and exports to India and the rest of the world were diminishing rapidly as a proportion of their business.[86]

Domestically they were proved correct – lager wouldn't destroy their business for almost a century. They were brewing weaker, fresher pale ales for the domestic market, beers that, according to the *Brewers' Almanack* in 1895, had an 'extreme freshness of palate with a degree of brilliancy and sparkle [the drinkers'] fathers never dreamt of'. But from an international perspective, this was an astonishing lack of business sense.

Encouraged by high import duties, new domestic breweries flourished in areas where brewing had been inconceivable a generation previously. By 1900, exports formed no more than 6 per cent of Bass's output. Sales in India were declining 20 per cent a year, and Pilsner lager was the runaway success, with Beck's being by far the most famous brand, now double the size of Bass. A full-page ad in the *Asylum Press Almanac* from Madras in 1895 proclaims the benefits of 'Pilsener lager from the Kaiser Brewery of Beck and Co', their beer 'the lightest purest and most wholesome in the market' as demonstrated by the medals it had won at exhibitions in Phila-

---

86. Allsopp's did build a big, new lager brewery in 1900, right in the middle of their financial meltdown, and advertised lager in the press in the early 1900s. It didn't sell much.

delphia in 1876 and – crucially – in Calcutta in 1884. IPA had been beaten on its own turf at what it claimed to do best.

McEwan's and Younger's of Scotland were outselling Bass. Allsopp's had seemingly disappeared altogether from the list of brands selling more than 10,000 gallons a year, and that list itself was shrinking as total beer sales declined. As well as the general move away from beer, the Boer War saw troops transferred from India to South Africa, and that vital market grew smaller.

In 1911, a year when Britain was in the grip of prohibition fever, *The Times* ran a feature on 'What to drink in India', claiming, 'the popularity of beer has greatly diminished, except among the rank and file of the Army, and "India Pale Ale" is no longer the favourite stimulant for men out snipe shooting.'

The sudden disappearance of the Indian market made little impact on the balance sheets of Burton's brewers. The endless barrels were still piled high in the yards and the trains were still running. Complacency had set in, and it was to prove fatal.

In 1900, Burton-on-Trent was brewing 3.5 million barrels of beer – about 10 per cent of all beer in the UK. This was astonishing for a time when brewing was still a very localized affair, with hundreds of brewers crowding every town and city in the country. At this point, the whole world looked to this small town for its perspective on beer. A century later, few would even be aware that Burton had ever held this position.

Just as in India, tastes changed and the prohibition movement grew powerful. The entire brewing industry contracted, so Burton, as its centre, was bound to suffer. But the fatal blow to the brewers' supremacy came as a result of their own success.

Burton led the field in establishing a scientific basis for brewing. The rigorous approach they pioneered in studying beer meant that, by the 1890s, brewers had discovered how to analyse precisely the mineral content of water, and replicate it. Water could now be 'Burtonized', given the same character as the well water of the Trent valley, wherever you were in the world. To this day ale brewers around the planet Burtonize their water, and Burton brewers still grumble that it's not the same. But by the close of the nineteenth century every brewer in Britain could brew Burton-style pale ale if they wished.

Brewers reacted to a declining market by financially tying the pubs that sold their beers. The complacent Burton brewers boarded this particular train late, and some suffered catastrophic losses. Allsopp's went into administration, and was finally swallowed by neighbour Ind Coope.

It was the ignominious end for the beer that inspired my journey – or so I thought. Sitting in the archives in Burton piecing the story together, I couldn't have guessed that there was one final chapter to be told in the Allsopp story – or that I would be a player in it.

Bass absorbed Worthington's, Salt's and others, was taken over itself, merged again, but still survived as Burton's iconic brewer, until it was bought by Belgian brewer Interbrew in 2000. Interbrew were told by the government they couldn't keep everything, and sold on the brewery and most of its brands to American giant Coors, but kept the Bass brand itself, moving control of it to its UK base in Luton. Back in Burton, Bass memorabilia was discounted for quick sale in the museum shop, which was no longer attached to the 'Bass Museum', but to the 'Coors Visitor Centre and museum of brewing'. Bass was airbrushed from Burton's history.[87] Coors

87. Just to confuse things further though, Bass is now being brewed in Burton again. Since Interbrew merged again, this time with South American brewer AmBev to become InBev, they have steadily withdrawn marketing support from their British ales. They don't support Bass with

now seem to be more sympathetic to ale than you might expect a Midwest American lager giant to be, but from their point of view, the name of the company, the plant, the heritage they had bought, was a name that now belonged to one of their fiercest competitors. What a bizarre situation. Bass, once the world's most famous brand not just in beer but in any product sector, is now a name that neither of its inheritors wants to admit knowing.

India Pale Ale's reign in the subcontinent ended with the nineteenth century. None of the breweries that supplied it survived the twentieth. Bass would go on to number among its fans Edward VII, Scott of the Antarctic and Buffalo Bill. Manet featured two bottles prominently in the foreground of his famous *A Bar at the Folies-Bergère*, and so far keen-eyed beerophiles claim to have spotted more than thirty bottles of Bass in works by Picasso. Even in decline, the UK's first registered trademark remained a global icon unmatched till the worldwide dominance of McDonald's and Coca-Cola.

Which makes it all the more agonizing that its new owners seem perfectly happy to let it rot.

---

advertising, and they no longer even brew it themselves – brewing has been contracted back out to Marston's in Burton, which is kind of poetic, but Bass is dwindling in the nation's consciousness, and the beer is a pale shadow – sorry – of its former self.

CHAPTER FORTY

RESCUED IN KOLKATA

The enormous, greasy blob sitting opposite me in his white pyjamas, legs splayed, leaned fractionally to one side and let rip. The sound of a ship's horn filled our compartment once again, ending in a smattering of wet pops as he really forced out the last bit, not wanting his monstrous fart to end, flirting dangerously with the possibility of following through. His wife, sitting next to him, took the full force of the blast. I marvelled at her. On the other side of the compartment I was close to retching. The velocity of the blast alone should have propelled her into the corridor, but she didn't even blink. Perhaps she didn't notice it any more. There had been three or four of these volleys an hour since we left Delhi seventeen long, sulphurous hours ago, and these two had obviously been together for years.

The blob barked something to his teenage son, who was sitting on the bunk beneath mine. The son obediently rose, crossed the cabin, picked up a pair of dirty socks from where they had lain since last night, when the blob took them off, and tossed them on our shared table just as dinner was being served. They were perhaps six inches from the blob's pudgy hand. His son handed them to his father, and returned to his seat.

The blob was sitting next to the window, and the morning sun was clearly bothering him. He barked at his son once again, and the young man duly rose, crossed the compartment again, and closed the curtains. My view of the Bengal countryside disappeared.

Including subdivisions, there are five or six different classes on Indian trains. This was the one at the very top: a 1AC sleeper compartment, air-conditioned, shared by only four people. It was so expensive that the ticket officer had looked at me in disbelief when I asked for the fare, warned me of its expense, and shrugged as if to say 'There's one born every minute' as he relieved me of the equivalent of thirty-two quid – half the price of a standard-class ticket for the two-hour journey from London to Sheffield back home. The train was now running ninety minutes late, meaning I got to spend eighteen and a half hours in close quarters with this rich Indian man and his cowed family. None of them spoke, apart from when the fat man barked a command. They had nothing to read, nothing to occupy their minds or hands, nothing to do at all except fart and breathe. Ten minutes after dinner, the blob had ordered his son to turn out the cabin lights and quickly began snoring like a wounded buffalo. And it was then – much earlier than I'd been expecting – that I began to feel nostalgic for my long evenings aboard the *Caribbean*.

By the morning I was sure Kevin had curdled. My English reserves of politeness were finally exhausted, burned away by blobby methane. I pointedly opened the curtains again. I've been on intimate terms with bullies in the past and know how they work – let the blob quarrel with me if he had a problem. He said nothing.

It was impossible to reconcile the images of famine and desperation we often associate with Bengal and nearby Bangladesh with the scenery rolling past the window. Streams threaded through lush green paddies and palm-lined fields of wheat. Plump goats were tethered to every tree stump. People were bent working the paddies, or gathered in groups, laughing, near the bars and shops that punctuated the red dirt roads snaking across the flats, under a big, eyeball-popping sky dotted with cotton-wool balls of cloud. I supposed the problem was that it wouldn't take very much for this paradise to flood with salty water from the tidal rivers flowing into the Bay of Bengal. When that happened, everything I could see would disappear.

The ludicrously pretty lakeside houses started to link to each other with proper roads and cluster together more densely. Soon there were factories and forests of tall chimneys, whole sides of buildings painted bright yellow with ads for soap powder and underpants, and the city began to thread around us. We slowed as the tracks became more congested and we jostled with other trains for priority over the points. Passengers who had paid fares fifty times smaller than mine spilled out of open carriage doorways, clinging to whatever they could, all looking forward into the cooling wind.

Even experienced travellers to India had raised their eyebrows when I told them I was going to Kolkata. In *The Great Railway Bazaar* Paul Theroux, fazed by so little on his epic inter-continental rail journey, seems to lose his nerve inside Howrah station, which he finds 'high and smoky from the fires of the people who occupy it; the ceiling is black, the floor is wet and filthy, and it is dark – the long shafts of sun streaming from the topmost windows lose their light in dust on the way down.' He reacts with disbelief when an Indian man he's just met tells him earnestly, 'You should have seen it *before* they cleaned it up.'

Howrah must have been cleaned again in the intervening thirty-five years. Yes, it was dirty and crowded, but no more so than Victoria Station in London. Outside I was mobbed by taxi touts. The queue for official taxis stretched halfway back to Delhi, and I relented. My two porters haggled a fare to my hotel of 250 rupees, a rip-off if you were going to be fussy about it, but a bargain to get me and my 75 kilos of baggage out of the mêlée. The porters – who had only been carrying one bag each – then asked me for 500 rupees. There had been a sign inside the station clearly stating that one trip for one porter was 15 rupees. I suggested this to them and they laughed, but not as hard as I had laughed at 500. We agreed on 150 each – a mere ten times the going rate. I was, I insisted to myself, getting better at handling India.

I was delighted to see that the groovy, retro Ambassador cars used by MPs in Delhi served here as cabs. They weren't very comfortable, but that wasn't the point: they were a wonderful way to travel and this one made me feel very grand. I perched high in a leather seat and watched the city unscroll.

The historical accounts I'd been reading for months collided with the evidence of my eyes and I saw the city not as a first impression on a Monday morning in December 2007, but as a point on a continuum stretching back 250 years. Here, for the first time, I could really understand the colonial mentality. Those Englishmen who had arrived here determined not to lose touch with home had built a resolutely English city. Tall tenement buildings completely unsuited to the climate had been stained a grimy grey by the pollution, just like the coal-etched sandstone of the Victorian town centres I'd known as a child in the north of England. Kolkata was Manchester with palm trees.

As I neared the end of my journey, my traveller's resolve was weakening. I'd booked myself a deluxe room in the Park Hotel, one of Kolkata's finest. I deserved porters, politeness, clean sheets, the choice of three decent restaurants and one of the city's most fashionable bars. My big, comfortable room had a minibar, fresh fruit and a turndown service. Even the endless buzz and beep of traffic on the nearby Chowringhee Road was a gentle lull compared to the neurotic activity outside my window in Old Delhi. And, most importantly, the room contained the first bath I'd laid eyes upon since the strange little one in the apartment on Tenerife, two-and-a-half months ago.

An hour later, I was lying on cool white sheets, clean and

glowing in a fluffy bathrobe, when my mobile rang. It was Janet Witheridge from the British Beer & Pub Association. And we had problems.

When I stepped off *Europa* back in Brazil, I still had no idea what I was going to do with my beer if I ever succeeded in getting it to India. I'd made a few enquiries with the Foreign Office in India but heard nothing back, and had simply run out of time before I set off. By the time I arrived in Brazil, fretting over how to get Kevin into the country, worrying about what I would do at the end of the journey was an unaffordable luxury. I had visions of me sitting in a hotel room on my own, wearing a party hat and some streamers, slowly getting pissed on strong, warm beer, tears streaming down my face.

And then, while I was frantically emailing, I received a message from Janet. She explained that she would be in Delhi for a trade show and invited me along, and I cheekily asked her if she might be able to arrange anything for me in Kolkata. Not only did she say yes, but she also extended her stay in India, and agreed to come on to Kolkata after the trade show to organize a media event for me.

Our plan had been that we would host the opening and tasting of Kevin the Keg of Calcutta IPA at the Oberoi, the only hotel in Kolkata that was grander than the one I was in. We'd had another keg of the same batch of Calcutta IPA flown in from Burton, so we could compare side-by-side the effects of the long sea journey with a beer that hadn't been through the same trauma. This second cask had successfully cleared customs and had relevant documents stating that it was imported legally and could be opened legitimately. Kevin didn't. And the Oberoi was refusing to allow him to be opened on their premises without the required documentation.

'They'd like to know – how did you get your beer into the country anyway, without the documentation?' said Janet.

'Well, I bribed the customs officials,' I replied.

'You bribed them to let the beer into the country?'

I was suddenly mindful that, while I was acting independently, Janet was here as a representative of an august British trading association.

'No, I bribed them to let *me* into the country, and I had the right documentation for me. After that, they didn't care about the beer. Go figure. What about the other keg? The one that flew in?'

'Well,' replied Janet, 'we could open that one. But it's stuck in Delhi and we can't get it here till Friday.'[88]

'And I fly home Tuesday evening.'

Invitations to the beer tasting had been sent out to the Calcutta press, India's food and drink magazines, attendees of the recent trade show, and British diplomatic staff stationed in Calcutta. After twelve weeks, 18,000 miles and one exploding beer keg, having finally got my beer here, it looked as though I wasn't going to be able to open it.

'We could always have a party in my hotel room and not tell anyone,' I suggested. 'That's what I'd have been doing anyway, without your help.'

'Leave it with me,' replied Janet, 'I'll see what I can do.'

I had no worry or stress left in me. I couldn't get wound up about this. I went for a slow, lingering lunch in one of the hotel restaurants, and read a Stephen King novel.

An hour later, Janet phoned back.

'Change of location,' she said. 'The British Deputy High Commission here has agreed to save the day. They've got a function suite, but the reason we didn't go there at first was because it's closed for refurbishment. But it's just about finished, and they've agreed to open it up a week early for us. They'll lay on a buffet, and they'll allow the beer to be

---

88. To the best of my knowledge, this second barrel is still in transit, somewhere in India.

opened on their premises. We need to go and meet them later. Simon Wilson, the Deputy British High Commissioner to India, will introduce you, so he'd like to meet you this evening. They'll re-contact all the people we've invited and tell them about the change of location, so we're sorted.'

The British Beer & Pub Association and the British Government were coming to my rescue because I'd smuggled twenty litres of beer into one of the most bureaucratic, alcohol-ambivalent countries in the world. Janet Witheridge and her husband, Robin, had extended their stay in India for a week because of me. The British Deputy High Commission were employing catering staff for an evening because of me. Someone was paying their wages and for the food they were about to serve. Someone was paying for Janet to be there. And that someone wasn't me. My knees buckled. I was ashamed of myself. 'Janet . . . how can I ever thank you enough? That's just . . . thank you.'

I hung up, stared into nothingness for several minutes as shudders ran through my body, then looked down at Kevin the Keg. 'I hope you're grateful,' I said to him. He didn't reply, but he looked proud. He was a benign entity, I thought, unlike his dead brother. But inside, hidden from view, he was brewing up one final humiliation for me.

I repacked Kevin and lugged him out to the lift. After an altercation in which I had to convince the helpful hotel staff that I was neither checking out nor doing a runner with my very heavy luggage, Kevin and I rode in the back of an Ambassador to the Oberoi, to pick up Janet and Robin, and then on to the British Deputy High Commission.

It was an unassuming building down a narrow side street off the main drag of Chowringee Road, though I suppose it would have been less than diplomatic if it had occupied one of Kolkata's grander buildings, and diplomacy was why it was here. After two separate security checks, we were shown into a long, low-ceilinged room with a kitchen and bar at one end, rows of seats in the middle and low leather sofas at the other end. The cool, subdued lighting made the marble floor glow softly, and a gentle hint of fresh paint filled the air. We met Kevin McCole, our host for the event, and talked through the arrangements for the following evening. I deposited Kevin (the keg, not the diplomat) carefully in the fridge behind the bar. 'He's got twenty-four hours to cool and settle in there,' I said to Robin as we stripped out the shelves from the fridge and slid the container gently in. 'We'll take him out a couple of hours before we're due to open him. That should be fine.'

With everything now ready, I turned to Kevin (the diplomat, not the keg) and said in a low voice. 'I wonder if you can help me with one last thing. I really owe Janet and Robin for all their help on this. We're going out to dinner tonight, and I'm going to insist on paying. I want to take them to the best Indian restaurant in Kolkata. No expense spared. I want to make it the meal of a lifetime.'

Kevin smiled. 'Then you have to take them to Peter Cat. It's not the most modern or stylish restaurant, but it's been here for years. It's a Kolkata institution. If you were only going to visit one restaurant in town, it would have to be that one.'

I remembered that Peter Cat had been described in similar terms by my Rough Guide. 'That'll be the one then. Thank you.'

We arrived at the restaurant half an hour later. Uniformed waiters showed us to a table under heavy red hanging curtains and threadbare carpets.

'Right,' I said as we sat down. 'This one is on me. No arguments. This is the best Indian restaurant in town and I want you both to fill your boots. No expense spared, this is the least I can do.'

And it was. This was the first restaurant I'd been to India that stocked a range of different beers. We tried them all. We ordered the most famous and luxuriant dishes they had, and ate until we could eat no more. And when I finally asked for the bill, it came to 1,219 rupees. Later, back home, this showed up on my credit-card statement as £15.21. It's the thought that counts.

CHAPTER FORTY-ONE

INDIA DECIDES FOR HERSELF

A Mrs Lushington, newly arrived in India towards the end of the nineteenth century, asked an elderly lady what she had seen of the country and its people since arriving years before. The lady replied, 'Oh, nothing, thank goodness. I know nothing at all about them, nor do I wish to. Really I think the less one knows of them, the better.'

Since the bloody 1857 Mutiny, the Anglo-Indians had lived a life completely isolated from their adopted country, but Indians had steadily been gaining rights and positions of influence within their own land. Thomas Macaulay had promoted an English educational system for Indians as early as the 1830s, hoping to produce a class of people who were 'Indian in blood and colour, but English in taste, in opinions, in morals, and in intellect', and Indian clerks, lawyers, doctors and engineers became common. The trouble with this was, being educated, they then started making bothersome demands about rights. The English fell back on racism to defend their position. The ironically named journal, *Friend of India*, was horrified at the thought of natives being in any position where they could have an impact on the whites. The editor asked his readers, 'Would you like to live in a country where at any moment your wife could be liable to be sentenced on a false charge, the Magistrate being a copper-coloured Pagan?' Indians, even the educated ones, were degenerate, simply incapable of self-rule. In the early nineteenth century, it had been suggested that the steamy climate and vegetarian diet in Bengal made the natives lazy and feeble. This charge was now renewed and strengthened – the dhal-munchers were weak and effeminate, no match for beery, beefy Britons.

But following the Mutiny and John Company's demise, even the English began to ask exactly why they were in India. Naked greed and profit was no longer acceptable as the right answer, so the English began to talk about how the poor Indians needed our help in being taught how to rule themselves, seemingly forgetting the decent job the Mughal Empire had been doing in looking after its people before the English came along and destroyed it. The fine, upstanding, superior Westerners would benevolently hang around until the heathens had been taught how to enjoy the benefits of civilization.

One of the results of the anglification of the natives was their adoption of English tastes. Educated Indians began to enjoy wine, beer and whisky. When Bhudev Mukhopadhyay attended the Hindu College in Calcutta, he found that 'in open defiance of Hindu social convention . . . to be reckoned a civilized person one had to eat beef and consume alcohol'.

But drinking had ceased to be the major pastime among Europeans by the early twentieth century. One old Anglo-Indian remembered that even though this was a land where 'sociability was gauged in very large measure by drinking habits', it was now a social crime to drink too much, 'or to be seen to drink too much before your servants'. Anyone showing signs of intoxication in the club would be hustled out by his friends. Clubs employed ex-army men who 'knew how to cope with that sort of thing'.

In 1911 *The Times* noted primly, 'the most welcome drink in India is the cup of scalding hot tea on awakening'. You never drank alcohol after sunset, and if you really had to partake the done thing was to order a long, weak whisky and soda. Lager had replaced pale ale for those who fancied a beer, but few did.

Some hard drinking still took place in the army, where drinking games abounded at the mess dinner. But this was away from prim society's gaze, and soldiers were expected to be able to hold their drink and not let it interfere with their appointment with the parade ground the next morning. Kincaid paints a desultory picture of the off-duty soldier's drinking experience: they would 'stroll without enthusiasm into Mr Pinto's Billiard Salon and order a beer, a warm pale tasteless beer, to drink at a froth-bedewed marble-topped table in a corner beside a declining palm ... to drink in lonely gloom ... Another beer; for there was little else to do.' And even this was a treat, because they 'seldom had enough money for beer'.

Things had seemingly changed from the era when the beer was brewed and packaged with the utmost care. In 1937 *The Times* reported on the small amount of beer that was still being imported from Europe with considerably less romance than it had sixty years previously, telling us that 'when it arrives in containers it can be aerated by means of an ordinary bicycle pump before it is poured out'. Maybe this helped explain why 'over 270,000 gallons of British beer are now being produced in the Empire oversea', and why this amount was now dwarfed by lager.

Others remembered beer slightly more fondly – it was cheap, good and strong. But the troops knew that 'when they came out of the wet canteen they didn't have to be offensive, they didn't have to be uproarious, they didn't have to be helpless, they just had to stagger and someone on duty outside the canteen would put them in the guard room for being drunk'.

After the social changes that swept Britain between the wars, the self-conscious Victorian Britishness of the Anglo-Indians began to look out of date. Visitors from Britain felt they were stepping back in time. Despite the fact that curry was becoming popular in Britain, for example, it was never

seen on any respectable Raj dinner table. The last generation of English people who remember what it was like to
rule India, now well into their dotage and fast disappearing,
reminisce about a stilted, formal faux-Victorian society where
stuffiness and convention prevailed. It was a mood that would
create a hangover long after the English left, and not just
through those who stayed on in the clubs, unable to accept
that things had finally changed.

India finally gained independence in 1947. Perhaps
inspired by the disastrous partition of India and Pakistan
along religious lines, and the movement of populations, mass
murder and starvation this entailed, many observers predicted
that with her myriad religious, social and ethnic diversities,
India would fragment into several nation states. Others
predicted revolution, bloodshed and political instability. But
India remains the only post-colonial country to have made
the transition to democracy pretty seamlessly. Gandhi and
Nehru, the architects of modern India, were both products of
English educational establishments. India's parliament and
legal system are modelled on the English one. In the end, the
English did contribute something of lasting value to Indian
society. Neighbouring China may be more powerful, but it
doesn't have a population of native English speakers like
India does, which means the latter is racing ahead in IT and
in the global call-centre industry.

This sense of a tradition of Anglified Indianness, combined
with swingeing trade barriers that were hastily erected to help
build up domestic industries, meant many of India's tastes
and attitudes remained frozen in the colonial fashions that
had held sway in 1947. The drinks market in particular was
almost in suspended animation for fifty years. Whisky remains
incredibly popular, and lager is still the beer of choice, though
in this respect India today is no different from the rest of
the world. But the brands that dominate the rest of the
planet are hardly known here – Kingfisher rules, and the likes

of Foster's, Budweiser and Carlsberg are only starting to establish themselves after the relaxation of import barriers in the 1990s. Some of those first Indian breweries founded in the Himalayas in the nineteenth century are still active today, but not one of them brews India Pale Ale, a style increasingly popular in most beer-drinking nations. In an echo of the prohibitive trade tariffs that killed the Baltic trade two centuries ago, India has obliterated any trace of the beer that bears its name. Before embarking on my journey, I'd failed to find anyone in India who had even heard of it.

Maybe that's because it had never really belonged to the Indians anyway. Today there's an ambivalent attitude towards alcohol, which is forbidden to both Muslims and devout Hindus. While staying in Nagpur in the 1930s, Prakash Tandon had seen 'dhoti-clad vegetarian-looking small businessmen' shuffling to the railway station to indulge in secret vices such as drinking beer and eating meat, newly acquired tastes that would have horrified their wives at home. But the people who mainly drank the beer – who actually no longer drank it anyway – had gone home.

Today there's a new generation of Indians with a different attitude, looking to the West for inspiration with little of the guilt felt by their grandparents. As in any developing country, beer is a symbol of the West, and is now being actively sought out by young Indians with money to spend. The beer market is about to explode, but so far with no sign of the ale that conjures up impressions of India around the world.

This was the country into which I had just smuggled Kevin the Keg. I was nearing the end of a long journey, both physically and historically. It struck me, having learned the story of the first multinational corporation, that a lack of awareness about what happened here was allowing modern corporations to do it all again. India's greatest disaster was not flood or famine, but the idiotic circumstance whereby a private corporation – bound by its articles of association to think only about returns to its shareholders – was given tax-raising powers, resulting directly in the deaths of 10 million people. We're not quite that bad yet, but modern corporations are being given powers over the lives of populations that extend far beyond those of a simple merchant – which is all they actually are. While the amount and variety of goods going in and out of India on ships like the *Caribbean* has changed, the basic concept seems little different to how things were when IPA came out on the East Indiamen.

The people drinking beer – the symbol of the West – in Kolkata as well as Beijing, Moscow, Kiev and Jakarta are looking for big global brands. The red star of Heineken and the – well, the red – of Budweiser have replaced the red triangle of Bass. At least this time the indigenous populations can afford the beer – although only the most affluent can afford the global brands, while the rest make do with local brew. How much has changed since Bass dominated the globe? I'm not in a position to answer that authoritatively, but suspect that despite my nostalgia for the golden age of IPA, a correct, if too brief, answer would be 'not enough'.

Britain's attitude to the legacy of John Company looks like the actions of a very guilty conscience. How many of us really have an idea about its role in our history?

The Honourable East India Company was finally wound up in 1864. In its early years, it had built its own ships at its dockyards in Deptford and Blackwall. Starting with the men employed directly in the building of ships, if you then add the crewing and victualling requirements, the Company was one of London's biggest employers. The Lascars – hands hired in India to crew ships back home – made up a quarter of all crews by 1700. When they reached London they were abandoned, thrown on the streets to survive as best they could, establishing London's multicultural identity. With its sprawling network of financiers, overseas agents, insurance men and speculators, the East India Company gave birth to London's financial sector as surely as it did the docks. Every way you look at it, modern London was built to the Company's specifications.

Who would even know that today? On the site of the East India Company's sprawling offices in Leadenhall Street now stands Richard Rogers' postmodern Lloyd's Building, and next to that – what else? – Starbucks. There's no blue plaque or statue, no memorial whatsoever to the East India Company offices that stood here, in one form or another, from the early years of Company exploration until the last structure was pulled down in 1862. There's no sign of, nor memorial to, the Company's vast warehouse complex, which once stretched from Fenchurch Street to Aldgate, save for one small corner building. That building is the only evidence in London that the Company ever existed, and – perhaps inevitably given our story – it's a pub.

The East India Arms on Fenchurch Street sits in the shadow of the Swiss Re building, or Gherkin, the newest addition to the skyline of the global financial centre the Company helped create. There's another Starbucks, right next door. On the red-brick wall of the pub, a plaque tells the history of the Company in a couple of hundred words, below a hanging pub sign depicting a crest with three tall ships in the middle.

The pub stocks three fine cask ales, but no IPA. Dried hops garland the bar and the walls are filled with old pictures and photographs of East Indiamen, Shepherd Neame beer logos and generic scenes of bygone London.

But the first thing you see as you walk in is the Company coat of arms on the far wall, and it's flanked by two big engraved mirrors: one branded Shepherd Neame (the brewery that owns the pub), the other Bass Ale. I've seen the Bass mirror in countless pubs before – it's a popular piece of memorabilia, ideal for creating that authentic traditional-pub atmosphere even in places that would never dream of actually serving Bass ale today. So it may just be coincidence that it's here. But as InBev continues to inflict a slow and humiliating death on the most famous of all Burton pale ales, that wall provides a quiet, unobserved signifier of the relationship between the first modern multinational corporation and the world's first global brand.

India Pale Ale provided the transition between strong, vatted ales, drunk in country houses by William Hickey's generation, and modern 'running' ales. In pioneering the use of pale malts, the Burton brewers possibly inspired the Pilsner lager brewers who now supply 90 per cent of the world's beer, while ale brewers the world over still 'Burtonize' their water as a matter of course. The Burton brewers pushed modern brewing science into the daylight. The reason we now refer to ales as 'bitter', even where they are fruitier and maltier, is testament to the character this beer once possessed, and its success in conquering the world's palate. And all because of the water in the wells of the Trent basin, and the fact that it was easier to ship a beer around the Cape on a five-month journey than it was to brew in the harsh climate of India.

The story is now mostly forgotten. Back in Burton, while this book was being written, the Coors Visitor Centre closed. The last link with Burton's glorious past has been severed. If things remain as they are, Beer Town will be buried for good.

But there is a grassroots campaign to resurrect what was once the Bass Museum, and recreate it as a national museum of brewing. Janet Dean is involved, the MP who saw me and Barry the Barrel off from the Brewery Tap, which at the time of writing stands dark and silent. There have been marches through the streets, petitions and overcrowded public meetings. Burton is still showing its stubborn spark.

And there's one more thing. Almost perversely, for all its modern facelessness, Burton-on-Trent remains Starbucks-free. The nearest branch of the global caffeine pusher is in Derby, twelve miles away.

Actually I got that wrong: there is a Burton Starbucks – Starbucks the newsagent, run by a man called Phillip Starbuck, in the tiny village of Rolleston-on-Dove, just round the corner from Rudgie's house. When Rudgie told young Mr Starbuck about this book, he replied, 'Course, my grandfather was a publican. Kept the Plough Inn on Horninglow Road, just opposite the old Salt's brewery.' So in a way, Burton had a Starbucks long before Seattle did, and it sold beer, not coffee.

I just can't help thinking that Beer Town might yet have a trick or two up its sleeve.

CHAPTER FORTY-TWO

CALCUTTA IPA

All told, I was in Kolkata for less than forty-eight hours. I never really got to see the city, apart from through the window of an Ambassador taxi. Tuesday 11 December – the day of the broaching of Kevin the Keg – dawned crisp, bright and warm as a lucky May Bank Holiday. It was three months to the day since I left Burton aboard *Remus* with dear, departed Barry, and with less than twenty-four hours before I boarded a plane home, I had a full day to do as I pleased before the reception in the evening. But I wanted to see Calcutta, not Kolkata. Instead of wandering the city, I decided to head for the library.

The district of Alipur still consists of the lush green gardens and grand white mansions of the colonial era. One of the finest is Belvedere House, originally built as a summer home for the Nawab of Bengal. In 1763, Mir Jafar gave it to Warren Hastings, and it was here, in the grounds, where Hastings fought an infamous duel against Philip French, his bitter rival within a fractious East India Company that was beginning to lose its grip on power. Belvedere House is now home to the National Library of India. I was here to dig into history – there couldn't have been a more perfect location.

It took me half an hour to confirm that they kept copies of the old *Calcutta Gazette*, and persuade them to let me have a look. I had six hours left to extract as much as I could. I picked up the first bound volume of newspapers from the 1780s, and set to work.

Worms had tunnelled through the pages, leaving crazed,

mazy patterns through notices about Company legislation and the imminent arrival of ships. Some were only held together by the ribbons wrapped around them. Each time I finished with a volume and gently closed it, the table had a light covering of crisped brown parchment, like desiccated, crumpled autumn leaves. In those pages I learned about what it was like to live here at the time of the nabobs, traced the emergence of beer from behind the shadow of Madeira, watched Hodgson grow to dominate the market, saw the tentative arrival of Allsopp and Bass, the spat between the brands before Bass' dominance, and finally the disappearance of beer as the opportunity for monstrous profits from opium captured the Anglo-English imagination. At one point, I finished transcribing the notice of an East Indiaman captain's auction and turned to the front page of the newspaper. A modest headline announced: 'We wish to update our readers on the Commotions in France'. I checked the date: 4 February 1790. I was reading about the French Revolution as breaking news, before it was even called the French Revolution.

I did as much as I could. I left the library in a daze, went back to my room, packed, and met Janet and Robin back at the Deputy High Commission.

The staff bustled around and fantastic smells drifted out from the kitchen. Seats had been set out for around fifty people, and I had a PowerPoint presentation ready to go on a laptop projector. The only preparation left was to open the beer.

Kevin had been standing here in this room, gently refrigerated, for just over twenty-four hours. The beer had been through a lot to get here, but I figured it should have had plenty of time to settle. Steve Wellington had supplied me with a jerrybuilt keg coupler, a clamp that fitted over the keg and led into a length of plastic tubing. It looked complicated, but wasn't. The device slid over the valve on the top of the keg, fitting snugly.

I lifted the keg carefully on to the bar.

'You might want to get a jug – it might come out pretty fast,' I said to Robin. He stood next to me, jug at the ready.

I pressed down the keg coupler.

The first India Pale Ale to reach Calcutta via its traditional route[89] for 140 years leapt out in a furious white foam. It spewed out of the end of the plastic pipe, which bucked and thrashed like a pissed-off snake. Beery suds soaked the first two neat rows of brand-new, upholstered chairs. Rich, copper-coloured ale spattered the newly laid marble floor tiles like slasher-movie blood, and Jackson-Pollocked walls whose cream paint was only just dry to the touch. Deputy High Commission staff stared at me in uncomprehending horror, before wordlessly disappearing to fetch buckets and mops as I grinned apologetically and wrestled to bring dead Barry's treacherous bastard of a brother under control. We filled jug after jug of foam, leaving them to stand and settle before our guests arrived. This fury would strip the beer of some of its flavour, releasing the volatile aroma compounds from the hops before we got to taste it, but there was nothing else we could do.

Simon Wilson, the Deputy British High Commissioner to India, took the destruction of his new hospitality suite quite well. He was very – sorry, but there's no better word – diplomatic about it. Well, to be fair, it wasn't as if he were going to have to repaint the walls himself, was it?

Our guests began to arrive. The tikka canapés had been prepared in a special masala that put even Colaba's secret restaurant to shame. It was Indian food, but more refined and delicate than any I'd tasted before, even as it lacked nothing in terms of its spicy punch.

Finally, Simon Wilson introduced me to the gathering. He impressed me – he'd done his homework, and gave a very

---

89. Give or take an eleven-hour flight to Brazil.

convincing impression that he'd had a detailed knowledge of the IPA story for years. He covered all the basics that I had ready on my PowerPoint slides, leaving me free to improvise around whatever themes I wished. ('Though I do think you should keep it brief,' he suggested.)

I didn't need notes – I didn't even need my slides really, though they had some nice pictures on, especially of me posing with Barry's corpse aboard *Europa*. But facing an Indian audience, having learned so much about both the structure and stability Britain had given India and the havoc we had wreaked here, about our casual abuse of my audience's ancestors and the deep, deep love many of my forerunners held for this country and culture, I could talk to them only about beer. I wanted them to have India Pale Ale – I wanted it to be *theirs*. I wanted them to be as excited by both the beer and the legend as I was, to tell their friends and to demand its return to modern India, to be savoured by Indians. I told them that this beer, India Pale Ale, was world famous, that India itself had a unique role in the history of beer, and that beer fans around the world revered the story. This beer had been created for their climate; it went astonishingly well with their food. It was the finest beer in the world. It was growing in popularity once again, and they deserved to enjoy it, to fall in love with it, more than anyone else. I received a polite round of applause, and no follow-up questions.

After I'd finished we moved over to the bar, where Simon and I posed for photos with Kevin, the decidedly non-photogenic beer keg. Finally, three months after tasting the Ratcliff Ale, I was – I hoped – about to taste a decent beer again.

I'm not discounting the possibility that being in Kolkata, and the sense of occasion after all this time and effort, affected my perceptions of the beer. I wanted it to be amazing. I wanted it to have changed, developed, matured. I wanted it

to have *ripened*. I tried to take this into account, to create a
buffer of scepticism with regard to what I was about to taste.
But it was no use: the beer was perfection.

It poured a rich, deep copper colour, slightly hazy from
the sheer weight of the hops. The nose was an absolute
delight: an initial sharp citrus tang, followed by a deeper
tropical salad of mango and papaya. And when I tasted it,
my tongue exploded with rich, ripe fruit, seasoned with a hint
of pepper. That bitter, hoppy spike had receded, the malt
reasserting itself now against the hop attack. As well as the
rich summer fruit, there was a delicate tracery of caramel,
not thick and obvious, but more the golden, gloopy kind you
get in Cadbury's Caramel bars, light and not too cloying.
The elements of the beer ran into each other, harmonizing.
The finish was smooth and dry, clean and tingling. And by
God it was damned drinkable for its hefty 7 per cent alcohol.

OK, so I might have been a little bit biased. But please
take into consideration the fact that, up to this point, the
nicest beer I'd tasted in almost three months – by a considerable margin – was Brahma lager. My palate was starved and
desperate. But this was a wonderful beer. It had definitely
matured since we sampled the young ale in Burton all those
weeks ago. In the global family of IPAs, it combined the
weighty hop character of the American beers I loved with the
balance of the more restrained English brews, the best of both
worlds.

It made perfect sense in the sultry climate, and I could
fully believe that this was what IPA tasted like here 150 years
ago. But I could also understand why it would be replaced by
lager so quickly. A few bottles of this, and you'd be dozing
pleasantly under the banyan tree for the afternoon. When
this was no longer the done thing, lighter alternatives simply
swept it away.

What I didn't know as we were tasting it was that we were
going to be able to do a comparison with the beer that hadn't

been on the sea journey after all. While I was getting drunk with Ashish in Mumbai, another keg of Calcutta IPA had been taken to a beer festival at London's legendary White Horse pub, and my beer-writing colleague Melissa Cole was there to taste it. She described the beer as having a spicy nose, little discernible maltiness and a 'medicinal spike' of hop, followed by an 'enormously long, dry hop finish'. She liked it, but in her write-up I sensed the same pause we'd had at our tasting back in Burton – it was going to turn into something even more wonderful, and hadn't yet done so. Unlike the beer that was now in my glass.[90]

The journey had matured and mellowed the beer. The legend was true after all.

The reaction of my audience was extraordinary, uplifting, and often hilarious. First, one short man with a neat moustache stormed up to me. He seemed less than pleased.

'What is this?' he demanded, waving his empty glass.

'Well, it's India Pale Ale, a British beer that—'

'This is not beer! What do you call this? Is it some kind of trick? This is wine! Why are you pretending this is beer?'

I realized then that the most characterful beer anyone in this country had ever tasted was Kingfisher lager. I tried to explain, but the small man stormed off in disgust, probably looking for hidden *Gotcha!* cameras.

He left me in the middle of a scrum of men who were very keen to give me their business cards. A dozen very similar rapid-fire conversations left me feeling confused and exhilarated.

'So when are you starting to import this beer?'

'How much will it cost?'

'Where can we place an order?'

I ran out of my own business cards, and ran into trouble.

'Um . . . I'm not importing the beer.'

---

90. And all over the walls, floor, ceiling and chairs.

'Well, where can we get it?'

'You can't. I'm sorry.'

'But you have brought this beer here! When are you bringing the rest?'

'I'm sorry. This is the only barrel.'

'So when are you bringing more?'

'I'm not.'

'Huh? So why did you bring this one?'

'I don't know! To show that I could. To prove that it could be done. To reintroduce it to India.'

'So when are you reintroducing this beer to India?'

'Well, I just did. That was it. I'm sorry, I'm just a writer. I just did this as a project. If I'd known . . .'

Eventually they drifted off. There was just me. And then there was the angry short man with the neat moustache again, the man who didn't believe this could be beer, the man who had all but accused me of perpetrating a practical joke on him before storming off.

'Can I have some more?' he asked.

A journalist approached, and in halting English asked for a picture of me standing next to Kevin the Keg. I obliged, and then he asked me a few questions.

'What is the keg made of?'

'Aluminium,' I smiled. 'We considered using a wooden keg, which would of course have been more traditional, but it just turned out to be too heavy.'

'What does the little bobble on the top do?'

'Well, that lets the beer out. It's pressurized inside the keg you see, and—'

'Why is the plastic rim around the top of the keg painted blue?'

'I don't know.'

'*You don't know?*'

'No, sorry, I'm not really an expert on kegs. Look, would

you like to know anything about the beer inside the keg? Would you like to try it?'

'No, I have everything I need. Thank you.'

And that was that. There was nothing left to do now other than grab a couple of hours sleep, get up again in the middle of the night, drive through Kolkata with a choking, burning sensation in the back of my throat, see the streets empty – something you only ever witness at 3 a.m. – and get the benefit of sixteen years' worth of scrimped-and-saved air miles on a business-class flight home, a luxury I felt I deserved. After taking three months to get to India, it would take me a mere, indecent eleven hours to get back home, to Christmas and to Liz, who would be waiting for me at Heathrow.

Everything had worked out. In the strictest sense, my quest failed when Barry blew in Tenerife – maybe even when I boarded a plane to get to Vigo because I couldn't go back on previous commitments. But I had carried twenty litres of beer across several international borders, and made it in one piece. I'd brought IPA home to India, for the first time in at least sixty years – and taken it on its original sea route – near enough – for the first time in at least a hundred and forty. My beer had travelled by sea, and that journey had changed it. All I'd had to do was put an awful lot of people to an awful lot of inconvenience, damage my marriage, my body and my mind, break several international laws, turn my friend into a beer smuggler, pay a few hundred dollars in bribes to corrupt customs officials and enlist the help of the Deputy British High Commissioner to India, and it had all turned out fine. All that remained was to finish the beer that had caused all this. It really was dangerously drinkable, and when the tandoori canapés came round it went beautifully, cutting through the heat and harmonizing with the spices so perfectly it was as if the beer had been designed specially to go with the cuisine, and perhaps it had. We stood in the British High

Commission, Englishmen (and women) in Kolkata, drinking
pale ale two centuries after William Hickey partied every day
like it was 1799, and slowly, we drained Kevin the Keg.

I'd like to think Hickey would have been proud of us,
as we addressed ourselves valiantly to the task in hand and
did not spare a single jug of Kevin's contents. Reader,
we did justice to him.

EPILOGUE

UP NAIROBI WEST

It's Monday afternoon, late August, three weeks before I'll cruise out of Burton aboard *Remus*. But I don't know that yet. With the confirmed legs of the voyage less than a month away, there are still big chunks I've not yet managed to arrange. I'm strung-out, wired, anxious, taking each day as it comes, just trying to get through all the work I've taken on to finance my imminent three months away.

Under any reasonably imaginable circumstances, an all-expenses paid, business-class week in Kenya should be one of the highlights of my year. The Serena is arguably Nairobi's finest hotel, and Tusker, East Africa's best-selling beer, is a brand I love and a beer that's potent with great memories.

But breakfast by the pool is spent with my head in a report. I don't see anything during my brief periods in the bar apart from my laptop screen. In the cracks between sessions where we're defining the future direction for Tusker, I'm trying to finish an overdue report for another client back in the UK. I'm 8,000 miles from home, and feel even further away from anything to do with my impending sea voyage to India. But in the unlikeliest of places, I'm about to discover – and then play my own cameo role in – a most unexpected footnote to the history of India Pale Ale.

August is the start of the rainy season in Nairobi. 'It is our winter now,' they keep telling us as if, one or two degrees south of the equator, this makes much difference. I've left behind the wettest, dullest, greyest summer on record in London, so I don't have much sympathy.

But no matter what the supposed season, there's weather, and then there's African weather. They do it bigger here. Thunderstorms come in director's cut widescreen Dolby 5.0 HD, complete with deleted scenes and extra commentary. Rain doesn't fall to the ground – that's far too passive. Here they have ACTION RAIN that throws itself at the earth, attacking the dust, attempting to sluice the whole city down into its own drains.

Mid-afternoon, the weather is only threatening, but we know it's more a promise than a threat. A yellow-grey, sick-looking sky squats on the city like the fat, bullied kid at school the day he realizes that, with his bulk acquiring a layer of muscle, he can now turn the tables on his tormentors.

We slide open the door of our 'matatu' (minibus), inhale the now familiar infusion of wood smoke, rubber, leaded petrol and a sweet hint of sewage, and step down on to dirty streets, striding over brown pools in the cracked concrete.

We're nearing the end of our tour of different classes of Kenyan bar. This would be even more fun than it sounds if we were drinking more Kenyan beer along the way, but the people we're with divide bars into six different segments, and we need to see one of each, and we have work to do afterwards.

We start off at the top of the pile with Segment One represented by Carnivore, an endless barbecue restaurant and bar that people drive miles to get to before wandering around its warren of bars and curving corridors clutching expensive bottles of premium beer or Smirnoff Ice. We follow this with a visit to a heppi, a stylish bar full of young Kenyans who come to drink slightly less expensive beer, watch football, play pool and listen to Snoop Dogg. From there we travel down subtle but noticeable distinctions between the segments, through the community bars that feel like local English boozers even though they couldn't look more different with their butcher's stalls near the entrance, where a man in a blood-spattered white coat slices ribs from a goat carcass, weighs the meat on an old-fashioned pan scale and sells it to you by the kilo.

Now we're walking into Bob's Rib Cage, a Segment Five bar. The Tusker Malt-branded ashtrays and tablecloths we saw in Three and Four have disappeared along with the corner-mounted TVs. The bar area sits behind a metal cage, with beers passed through a small gap at counter-height, like an English bank. The main bar area is dominated by a pool table with a paper sign reading WINNER STAYS propped against the overhead light. A few broken, mismatched chairs line the walls. Another faded, peeling POLITE NOTICE near the door reads NO HAWKERS OR IDLE SITTING. And behind the caged bar, behind the bored-looking woman serving drinks through the bars, stands a ghost.

'We don't really sell Tusker in Segment Five,' the local sales rep is telling me, 'in here it tends to be cheaper brands, like White Cap and Allsopp's.'

An electric shiver runs through me. 'Sorry? What brands?'

The rep repeats them.

'Allsopp's? They sell Allsopp's beer here?'

'Yes. It is one of our budget brands.'

East African Breweries Limited (EABL), formerly Kenya Breweries Ltd, has a monopoly over beer production in Kenya. Diageo, the world's biggest drinks company, bought a significant stake in EABL a few years ago, and is now helping EABL with its marketing, and that's why I'm here. Tusker is their (and therefore Kenya's) biggest brand. T-shirts bearing the brand's iconic and curiously stylish logo are the biggest sellers to tourists in Nairobi airport's duty free. It's more than just a beer: it's a symbol of the country, a source of national pride. When the ads come on the TV in a pub, it's not unknown for everyone to stand up and sing along with the patriotic jingle, arms slammed across chests in respectful salute.

But EABL has a whole range of other beers. Tusker Malt is a quality brew, superior to the main brand in brewing terms, on a par with good European lagers. But most of the market is below Tusker. Brands such as White Cap, Pilsner and Citizen grow progressively cheaper, using less malted barley and more brewing adjuncts, each with its special place down the hierarchy, all apart from Tusker Malt in the same scratched, reused brown half-litre bottles.

I've been here before, working on Tusker, about seven years ago, and I'm familiar with all these brands. But Allsopp's? That wasn't here last time. Is this some strange karmic joke?

'EABL reintroduced Allsopp's six years ago,' the rep is telling me. 'It sells for about sixty shillings[44p], compared to a hundred shillings[73p] for Tusker in a heppi. It is a medium-strength beer, five and a half per cent.'

Later, back in the UK, I'll learn that Allsopp's began brewing lager in Burton as early as 1897, in a doomed attempt to revive the fortunes of the then struggling brewery. It didn't work out, and the expensive, wasted investment in new plant accelerated the downward spiral. In the 1920s, production was transferred to Scotland's Alloa brewery. Lager was popular much earlier north of the border, and Allsopp's lager limped on. Long after Ind Coope had decided that Allsopp's served no further corporate purpose and dropped it from the brewery name, they still felt it had value as a consumer brand. As late as the 1960s, Allsopp's lager was still being sold, proudly bearing the Royal Appointment coat of arms, which implies that the Queen enjoyed opening a couple of cans to soothe a throat parched by asking 'And what do you do?' a hundred times a day.

In 1948, Ind Coope acquired an interest in Taylor's brewery in Nairobi. They launched Allsopp's White Cap Lager and the brewery was soon trading as Allsopp (East Africa) Ltd, Nairobi. In 1959 it merged with East African Breweries, which soon dropped the Allsopp's name from everything, including White Cap Lager. By the time the brewery decided to subdivide its volume a little further just after the turn of the millennium, Allsopp's was just another name in the back of the brand wardrobe. Few people knew where it had come from. Probably no one was aware of its story.

This is confirmed when I ask to look at a bottle. The sales rep says something to the barmaid, and she takes one down and passes it through the bars.

It's the same brown 500ml bottle as all the other brands, but decorated in an attractive gold metallic label with a regal blue shield. The blurb tells me it's 'brewed from extra roasted Equatorial malting barley, imported hops and the purest Aberdare water' and has '80 years of brewing excellence', which is wrong wherever you decide to date the history of the brand from – its inception, the decision to brew lager under the Allsopp name, its arrival in Africa, or its recent resurrection.

Later, when I check the EABL website, I find the following definition of what the brand is all about: 'Allsopps is the only beer that reassures that you have made a smart choice, because only Allsopps combines a distinctive taste and flavor while giving you the best value for your money.'

Translated, Allsopp's is the cheap lager for people who want to pretend they're not drinking a cheap lager. The perfect brand for segment Five or Six.

But we need to move on before we have time to sample one. Across the road and down the street, as the rain begins to spatter the muddy, oily pavements, we find Segment Seven on the six-segment scale, a place where any self-respecting global drinks company would rather not be seen, but where there is an important but depressing job to do.

We enter a market – tiny alleyways, three feet wide, breezeblock shelters on either side housing stalls selling food and clothes. Down the far end, against a high concrete wall, the final alley is full of benches and low Formica tables covered in yellow sheeting bearing the Tusker logo. But people don't drink Tusker here. They don't even drink Allsopp's here. Red and yellow bunting loops across our heads promoting a relatively new beer, held towards the camera in a traditional old English dimpled pint mug. Following the curious global rule of marketing whereby the more downmarket your brand, the posher the name you give it, we're here to sample Senator. The trouble is, there's none left. Everyone has sold out.

And then we spot a queue forming outside one outlet. The rumour spreads up the alley like a flood: a keg of Senator has just been delivered to this one establishment.

Our minders jump the queue and return with beers for us to try. The dimpled mug is made from plastic that gives the beer a strange purple hue. There's no aroma to it, and when I sip it there's no bitterness at all. Hops have been nowhere near this beer. It tastes sweet, the unimpeded, unaccompanied tang of 6.5 per cent alcohol reminding me of the synthetic taste of Cresta soda. A dirty aftertaste builds steadily after a few sips.

The guys tell us that a pint retails for around 25 shillings (18p), a quarter of the price of Tusker, for a beer that's far stronger. I'm silently appalled that any responsible drinks company could do this, until one of the marketing people makes me realize that, however perverse it sounds, they are performing a valuable service.

'The people who drink here in the market have very little money. Most of the time they do not buy beer at all, they make it illegally at home, using whatever they can find. These drinks are very bad – they can't control the alcohol level or the impurities, and there are many cases of people going blind or even dying after drinking this stuff. No one can stop people from doing this, we can only give them a reason not to want to do so. The government gives us a tax break to produce Senator, that's why it is so cheap. I understand that you may not like the beer, or the fact that it is so strong and so cheap, but it is far better that these people are drinking Senator than the alternatives. And once they are drinking our products, once they are buying beer rather than making this stuff at home, as their position improves we can trade them up from Senator to other beers.' Senator, in a way, is the IPA to Kenya's own arak.

Our last visit is to Nakumatt, Nairobi's biggest supermarket. Marabou storks hunch in the trees like a gang of winged Hell's Angels against the leaden sky. Barclays are trying to persuade everyone who enters the supermarket to apply for a credit card, working the crowd under banners proclaiming 'The most rewarding credit cards from your favourite store!' Tim, an American colleague who works across Africa, shakes his head. 'People here are all broke anyway. It won't make any difference to them if they go broke with credit cards.'

Like India, once you get to see Kenya in more detail than you do from a tourist minibus, it's impossible to see it as part of 'the third world' any more. You can use the term 'developing countries', but that feels like a euphemism, and is still too simplistic. These are places that are developing fitfully, growing in a lopsided, deformed way. An incredible spirit of optimism driven by a disproportionately young, energetic population with access to web cafes and mobile phones coexists with a rural tribalism that makes do without electricity and where Aids runs out of control. Barclays' attempts to sell credit cards hundreds of yards away from where people queue up for a beer that costs 18p a pint, which is one small but vital step away from home brew. And inside the supermarket, back down on the trivial level where I spend most of my time, Sierra Amber and Sierra Blonde – premium, all-malt beers from Kenya's first boutique, ultra-premium micro-brewery – sit in branded fridges next to EABL's beers, including Allsopp's.

I buy a couple of bottles of the last Allsopp's beer in the world and take them back to my room. One of them is stolen by the man who comes in to clean my room, along with the other beers I bought. But I get to taste the other. The promised 'distinctive taste' is absent from the thin, watery pale liquid. No hops, no barley, no aftertaste. Nothing.

The next day we go into our strategy session. We talk about every aspect of Tusker, from the product itself to the places it's served, and one of the conclusions we reach is the EABL has more different brands than it actually needs. You've obviously got to have Tusker. And we've learned that, at the bottom of the scale, Senator performs an important function. There's a lot of space between the beer that rich tourists are happy to take back home, and the beer that's drunk in Segment Seven on a six-segment scale. But with White Cap, Pilsner, Citizen and Allsopps all playing in that space, it's become very crowded. There's not enough distinction between any of them. With all of them belonging to one company, it becomes obvious there are too many. And it becomes obvious which among them has the weakest relationship with drinkers, and is therefore the easiest to make disappear.

And that's how, on the eve of a journey that seeks to be a fitting epitaph to a forgotten beer legend, I discover it alive and well one day, and help kill it the next.

*

Despite the guilt I feel at being one of the people who finally wipe Allsopp's beer from the face of the planet, I think it's for the best. That tasteless lager full of cornstarch and sugar is not what Samuel Allsopp envisioned when he turned his eye from Russia to India almost two centuries ago, and played his crucial role in creating the most wonderful, beguiling beer style the world has ever seen.

If the empty bottle of Allsopp's 'quality' lager now sitting in front of me now could talk, we'd be acting out hackneyed scenes from the movies. It could be a loving couple, or two buddies, or a heroic soldier and his officer who have just realized they don't hate each other after all, but it's always the same. One of them is lying in a hospital bed on a drip, or on a battlefield some distance away from limbs that were attached until moments ago. The other is gazing fiercely down with tear-filled eyes, declaiming undying love and a determination never to let go.

The stricken one smiles back, serene, reconciled with their fate, and says something like, 'Don't let the children/ my buddies/my fans see me like this. Remember me the way I was. Let me go.'

That thing in Nairobi was not Allsopp's. Let the marabou storks have that shadow, that empty shade. Allsopp's was the original Burton India Pale Ale, a beer that changed the world; that continues to give pleasure to millions of drinkers who enjoy flavourful, characterful beers through its hundreds of indirect offspring. Let Allsopp's stand in the memory as the IPA that caused whoops of joy when it was unloaded at Calcutta's wharves, and sighs of contentment when it was supped in the drawing rooms and public houses of the sweat-sodden Raj. Let it remain forever a precious cargo aboard glorious tall ships, ships that still draw gasps and tears of delight as they gallop over glitter-strewn sapphire waves.

'WINE OF MALT': THE RISE AND FALL OF INDIA PALE ALE IN THE UK

IPA became the template from which modern British beer was created. Its history in the UK is not directly a part of the story of this book, but for beer fans who wish to know a bit more about the history of this incredible ale, and the remarkable little town where it was brewed, here's a full version of the story (parts of which are referred to briefly in chapters thirty-nine and forty-one) that completes the link between the end of the historical chapters of this book and the beginning of my adventures. Think of this as a DVD deleted scene if you like.

It was a dark and stormy night. Of course it was.

Somewhere off the coast of Liverpool, sometime in 1827, a Calcutta-bound ship was getting into difficulty at the very start of her voyage. As the storm worsened it became clear she wasn't going to make it, and the cry went up to abandon ship. The next morning, wreckage and cargo were scattered up and down miles of Merseyside shoreline. The underwriters of the voyage had lost on this one, and had to pay out. But by the same deal, anything salvageable from the wreck now belonged to them, and amid the debris lay a sizeable number of intact hogsheads of beer. They auctioned these in the city, and made a great number of Scousers very happy indeed. No one in England had ever tasted bright, hoppy beer like this before, and word spread quickly. Soon, drinkers across the north of England were demanding that Burton brewers start selling their India Pale Ales a little closer to home.

Burton pale ales revolutionized English tastes to such an extent that they continued to shape our beer culture late into the twentieth century. And all thanks to this happy accident, this silver lining in the dark storm clouds over the Irish Sea.

So it's a shame really that, in fact, it never happened.

The well-known story (in beer circles) of the Liverpool shipwreck appears, with no substantiation, specific names, dates or references, in William Molyneux's *Burton-on-Trent: Its History, its Waters and its Breweries*, written in 1869. Oh, come on, 1869, it must be true! Well, perhaps the shipwreck did happen, but ships were wrecked off English shores all the time, and their contents were routinely auctioned by their insurers. Coastal pubs still use facsimiles of auction notices as part of their nautically themed decoration. And maybe this ship was carrying India Pale Ale. But the event did not introduce the beer to England in such dramatic fashion.[91]

Bass and Allsopp were already selling their beers in London and Liverpool by 1827, mostly for export, but not all. Within a few decades, this beer had changed the face of British social life at home as well as in the colonies. Its incredible success demands dramatic anecdotes. And if the truth is not quite as poetic, it's no less astonishing once you've nailed it down.

The real story of IPA in Britain begins in the early 1830s, and it's not Bass or Allsopp who kicks it off, but that greedy Londoner again. While John Bell was crowing in Bengal about the disappearance of Hodgson's ale, ads began appearing in English newspapers that revealed the brewer's new strategy. Hodgson's was universally famous in India, and a steady trickle of people were returning from the subcontinent. Some were ill, others just homesick. But most of them were substantially richer than before they left, and they'd acquired

---

91. Apart from anything else, the beer would not have conditioned yet, and would have been unfit to drink.

the taste for large quantities of Hodgson's Pale Ale. The first ad for 'Hodgson and Co.'s Bottled Pale Ale' appears in *The Times* in 1833, informing 'the Nobility, Gentry and others (especially Families from India)' that they may now be supplied with this celebrated beer. Two years later, in what seems to be the first public use of the term, Hodgson and Co's 'East India Pale Ale' was advertised in the *Liverpool Mercury*.

This was a shrewd move on Frederick Hodgson's part, but it was too little, too late. The pale-ale initiative had moved decisively to Burton, and there was nothing to stop the brewers there simply following suit. Bass ran boastful copy in newspapers declaring that their East India Pale Ale was 'more perfectly fermented, and approaches nearly the character of a dry wine'. And they couldn't resist resist a dig at their competitor, displaying shipment figures that showed Bass outselling Hodgson three-to-one in India.

Michael Thomas Bass and his partners Samuel Ratcliff and John Gretton realized that better communications between Burton and the rest of the country were key to their success, and when they heard of the proposed Derby to Birmingham railway they supported the scheme in any way they could. The line opened in 1839,[92] and was soon followed by another from Burton to Leicester. The whole domestic beer market was now easily available to Burton's brewers, and Bass was

92. If you don't have time to enter Burton via canal boat, the Derby to Birmingham railway is still the best way of getting there. It's humbling to sit on the train and marvel at the sheer volumes of beer that came down these very tracks. There are differences of course. I haven't done too much research on this, but I imagine they didn't have to unload all the beer off a little local stopper train when it reached Birmingham New Street, struggle with it up a long flight of stairs, past a really shit pub on the upper concourse, down another long flight of stairs and on to a strangely narrow and gloomy platform, then fight to squeeze it on to a hideously over-crowded Pendolino for the rest of the journey to London.

soon supplying customers in Kent, Cornwall and the north of Scotland, although a quarter of their entire output was still bound for London and Liverpool for export. By 1845, pale ale accounted for three quarters of their output.

Other Burton brewers joined the rush: Thomas Salt's was soon in a respectable third place behind Bass and Allsopp. Worthington's, which had made a quiet success out of the Baltic trade following a daring gamble by the first William Worthington and had been one of the few survivors of the Baltic crash, began shipping IPA in the late 1820s or early 1830s.

By 1849 Bass was brewing 80,000 barrels a year – an almost fivefold increase in fifteen years. Michael Thomas Bass bought a massive country pile, and in 1848 was elected Member of Parliament for Derby. The Burton brewers were on their way to becoming some of the most powerful industrialists of the Victorian age.

Circumstances began to conspire to make the rise of Burton pale ale seem preordained. The tax on glass was repealed, which meant that beer could be sold in bottles and drunk from glassware. Porter has many qualities, but looking clear and sparkling when you hold a glass of it up to the light is not one of them. Glassware became the fashion on any self-respecting table, and pale ale did it justice.

Apart from fashion, paler beer in vessels you could see through also meant that adulteration could be spotted much more easily. Porter was a beer that 'almost invited adulteration' according to brewing historian Ian Hornsey. The publication of *A Treatise on Adulterations of Food, and Culinary Poisons Exhibiting the Fraudulent Sophistications of Bread, Beer, Wine, Spiritous Liquors, Tea, Coffee, Cream, Confectionery, Vinegar, Mustard, Pepper, Cheese, Olive Oil, Pickles, and Other Articles Employed in Domestic Economy* in 1820 made adulteration techniques common knowledge to anyone who could stay awake past the book's title, describing how, due to the high price of malt and hops, brewers and publicans would add wood shavings to create bitterness, and 'vitriol' (iron sulphate), alum and salt to create a decent head. It was much harder to get away with this kind of thing in India Pale Ale – though the whole of Burton was shortly to be rocked by similar accusations of an even more sinister nature.

So railways and glassware created the conditions that allowed the expansion of IPA at home. But it fell to two seismic events to provide the impetus for growth, the first of which, in a roundabout way, related back to India.

By 1850 the British Empire stretched around the globe, but wasn't of much interest to the average Briton. For those who were even aware of British colonies abroad, they saw these foreign lands as heavy military and administrative responsibilities rather than wellsprings of treasure and glory. The Queen's husband decided to change that.

Victoria and Albert never visited India, but the Queen was fascinated by the country. Albert took this enthusiasm a stage further, and together with members of the Royal Society for the Encouragement of Arts, Manufactures and Commerce, organized the Great Exhibition of the Works of Industry of All Nations in 1851. A specially designed glasshouse, 1,848 feet long and 454 feet wide, was erected in Hyde Park and was nicknamed the Crystal Palace.[93] From May to October that year it hosted the most spectacular sights the country had ever seen, combining the atmosphere of a funfair with educational displays of art, science, natural history and industry from across the Empire. Six million people – a third of the entire population of Great Britain – visited the Crystal Palace and left with the sense that they were at the heart of the most prosperous, industrious and

---

93. In 1854 the Crystal Palace was moved to Sydenham Hill in south London. Even though it burned to the ground in 1936, that area is still known as Crystal Palace today.

gifted civilization the world had ever seen. It made the Millennium Dome look like a clueless, contrived white elephant with no real purpose.

It was a long, hot summer. Inside the glasshouse, in their stiff, formal clothes, the visitors developed a raging thirst. According to the definitive history of the brewery, Bass, Ratcliff & Gretton just happened to have signed agreements to supply the beer. Twenty years after the event, the *North of England Farmer*, tells how 'Jaded exhibitors and famished visitors from all the countries of Europe, America, and the furthermost ends of the earth slaked their parched lips and husky throats with pale and bitter ales.'

Which is another great story about how IPA conquered Britain. Perplexingly, once again, it's not true.

The Great Exhibition was far more controversial than you might think. While Karl Marx attacked it as a symbol of commodity fetishism, conservatives feared the sheer mass of visitors might mutate into a revolutionary mob. Alcohol, they felt, could only increase the likelihood of something kicking off, and they campaigned successfully for a booze ban inside Hyde Park. Some wily entrepreneurs were even prosecuted for selling beer through the railings. The only ale served inside Crystal Palace was Rawlings' ginger ale.

And yet, the Great Exhibition did do something for Bass' and Allsopp's fortunes. It lit a fire of interest in all things to do with the Empire, and with British industry and commerce. As India's beer, IPA acquired a halo of fashionability, and when the Crystal Palace was relocated and played host to other events with a lower quotient of poor people, beer was served. A craze for exhibitions swept the country, and the brewers took full advantage. Bass and Salt's exhibited their 'pale Burton, Australian and strong ales' at the Manchester Exhibition of 1862, and at the Paris Exhibition in 1867 the Burton brewery won a silver medal for its IPA.

Pale ale, having started off as the beer brewed in country

houses and demanded by the gentry on their visits to town, now became the most fashionable drink of the Victorian era, enjoyed in high society and lionized by nattily dressed young swells out on the town. Burton India Pale Ale was 'a bright sparkling bitter, the colour of sherry and the condition of champagne'. It was 'the high-fashion beer of the railway age'. The *Lady's Newspaper*, reporting on a performance of Boots, 'a favourite old farce' at the Swan theatre, described how Mr Robson, in the title role, quipped about India Pale Ale, 'This here ale went to Inghia, got frightened, grew pale, and came home again' – an explanation the paper felt was 'not strictly correct, [but] has at least the merit of originality'.

And then, in 1851, the chattering classes were rocked by a damning accusation. M. Payen, a French chemist, claimed that Burton's brewers used strychnine in their beer to get that bitter tang. Ignoring the fact that, to the best of my knowledge, there has *never* been a book or article in the whole field of business publishing with a title along the lines of 'Poisoning your customer base as a route to bumper profit!', it was the only way Payen could figure they could get their beers to taste the way they did. Large quantities of strychnine had allegedly been manufactured in Paris, bound for a secret destination. It was later 'discovered' that this poison was intended for Burton, 'in order to fabricate bitter beer'. The *Medical Times and Gazette* published these allegations in 1852, causing outrage in Burton. The editor later justified his decision to publish, arguing:

> As the statement referred to is one of deep importance . . . we would not give circulation did it not appear to have been made on perfect information . . . the fashionable longing for bitterness has surpassed the bitterness of hops, and the manufacturers have apparently been driven to their wits' end to satisfy the dyspeptic cravings of the British stomach.

The name of this editor? Well, that would be J. Stevenson Bushnan, MD . . . the same J. Stevenson Bushnan who later wrote *Burton and its Bitter Beer*, love letter to Samuel Allsopp, and source of everything we know about Campbell Marjoribanks, Job Goodhead and Allsopp's creation of Burton India Pale Ale.

Following publication of the allegations, Allsopp and Bass put down their metaphorical handbags and threw open their doors, challenging all comers to analyse their beers. Michael Thomas Bass roared off a letter to *The Times*, claiming he knew nothing about the strychnine that had apparently been manufactured in Paris and shipped to England, but argued, 'Why, Sir, India would long ago have been depopulated of its European inhabitants had there been anything pernicious in pale ale . . . We, and our eminent and respected competitors, only hope to maintain that favour by contending with each other in producing a beverage as palatable and as wholesome as it is possible to obtain from malt, hops, and the purest water.'

Visitors to the breweries over the ensuing months included a professor from the Royal College of Chemistry, a representative of the *Lancet* and Baron Justus Liebig, a German chemist who made major contributions to agricultural and biological chemistry, worked on the organization of organic chemistry, devised the modern laboratory-oriented teaching method, and is therefore regarded as one of the greatest chemistry teachers of all time. He's also known as the 'father of the fertilizer industry' for his discovery of nitrogen as an essential plant nutrient, and his formulation of the Law of the Minimum, which described the effect of individual nutrients on crops. And he invented Oxo cubes.[94] In other words, these

94. Do you ever feel that you're, I dunno . . . wasting your life? That perhaps your achievements don't come up to scratch? I first read about

were people who knew their stuff. They completely vindicated the brewers, and did so rather handily in the form of national press headlines. Liebig focused on Bass' pale ale, proclaiming: 'I convinced myself that the qualities of this excellent beverage depended mainly upon the care used in the selection of MALT and HOPS and upon the ingenuity exhibited in conducting the process of mashing and fermenting.'

So, not poisonous chemicals then.

In May 1852, professors Graham and Hoffman arrived at the 'comforting conclusion' that the allegations were utterly unfounded. They claimed the amount of strychnine required to achieve the levels of bitterness in Burton beer would have been twice the fatal dose, and pointed out that to sufficiently poison all the beer brewed in Burton in this way would require sixteen and a half times more strychnine than was manufactured in the world in an entire year.

That same month, no less a journal than the *Lancet*, the bible of the medical profession, proclaimed:

> From the pure and wholesome nature of the ingredients employed, the moderate proportion of alcohol present, and the very considerable quantity of aromatic anodyne bitter derived from hops contained in these Beers, they tend to preserve the tone and vigour of the stomach, and conduce to the restoration of the health of that organ when in a state of weakness or debility. They resemble, indeed, from their lightness, a Wine of Malt rather than an ordinary fermented infusion; and it is very satisfactory to find that a beverage of such general consumption is entirely free from any kind of impurity.

What had started off as a potentially ruinous scandal became a long-running free advertising campaign for the qualities of Burton pale ales.

Oxo Boy Liebig a month or two before my fortieth birthday. Thanks, Justus. Thanks for making me feel *soooooo* good about myself.

All of which left J. Stevenson Bushnan MD feeling . . . well . . . a bit uncomfortable. Having instigated what he referred to as 'the great pale ale controversy', he had to acknowledge his error, and visited Burton to pour oil on troubled waters. He wrote his 1853 book as an act of atonement, which might explain why Samuel Allsopp is described as 'a man of high courage, and with a spirit as stanch as ever warmed the breast of a true English gentleman', a man with 'the head to conceive . . . the hand to execute . . . having entered upon an undertaking he never failed to carry it out', a man who 'saw no difficulties which time, perseverance, resolution, consistency, and steady, unswerving honour could not overcome'. Clearly, we therefore have to read the whole story of Allsopp's invention of IPA, which I've faithfully repeated here, with one eyebrow raised sceptically.[95]

Having proven that IPA wasn't bad for you, the brewers went further, declaring that their beers were positively beneficial for health. Bass called in the eminent Dr Prout, who recommended their beer to 'weakly persons on account of its dryness, its tonic properties, and because it is not liable to turn in the stomach, as most other malt liquors are'. Allsopp responded by roping in Bass' old fan Liebig to recommend their ale 'in accordance with the opinion of the most eminent English physicians, as a very agreeable and efficient tonic, and as a general beverage both for the invalid and the robust'. According to George Robert Rowe MD, IPA was 'a boon to mankind'.

The Great Exhibition, the strychnine scandal, the fashionability and health benefits, plus the effect of people returning from India after a four- or five-year tour of duty with a thirst for IPA, meant there was no stopping Burton's domination of Britain and, ultimately, the beer-drinking world. By 1854,

---

95. Something I find hard to do – whenever I try, I look like a drunken Patrick Moore.

Bass and Allsopp were household names. Bass' 80,000 barrels in 1849 seemed impressive, but was still no match for the London Porter giants. In 1855 Bass was brewing 145,000 barrels – five years later, 341,000. In 1853 the firm built a second brewery, as large as the original, to cope with demand. Only eleven years later, a third brewery was added.

At fifty acres Allsopp's New Brewery was the largest single brewery in the world, an industrial marvel of the Victorian age. In 1858, in an article entitled 'A Leviathan Brewery', *The Times* described 'a brewery which when completed will cover nearly four acres of land, and present one facade of more than a quarter of a mile in length . . . intended for the exclusive production of East India Pale Ale, for which beverage the demand at both at home and foreign has of late so largely increased that all existing means of supply have altogether failed.'

Charles Stewart Calverley, always fond of a beery verse, wrote:

> He that would shine, and petrify his tutor
> Should drink draught Allsopp in its native pewter

Any brewer who wanted to take advantage of the booming pale-ale market could only do so courtesy of the wonderful waters of Burton. From the 1840s onwards London brewers such as Ind Coope, Truman, Charrington and Mann Crossman & Paulin opened shop in Beer Town. Boddingtons of Manchester, Everards of Leicester and various others soon followed.

Curiously, Hodgson's never took the train north. There are very few records of the brewery that created the first IPA. Frederick Hodgson eventually conceded defeat in Bengal, although Hodgson's ale is mentioned in the *Bengal Price Current* as late as 1862. But it seems that following his rout by Allsopp and Bass, Hodgson lost interest in the brewery. He recruited external partners to the firm and entered national politics.

By the 1840s, while 'Hodgson's beer' was still 'celebrated', it was brewed by 'Abbott's Bow Brewery', and specialized in private orders for wealthy families, particularly those that had returned from India. By 1888, when India Pale Ale was the world's most celebrated beer, 'A.H.' was writing to *Notes & Queries* to ask if anyone knew what had happened to Hodgson's IPA. The responses reveal that Frederick Hodgson died in 1854, and the brewery simply became known as Abbott & Son: 'But the special reputation of the beer had then passed away'. The brewery was sold to Smith, Garrett & Co., and was one of London's smaller concerns, brewing unremarkable 'pale ales, porter and stout', no longer using Hodgson's name to sell them. It was bought again by Taylor Walker in 1927, and demolished in 1933.

Meanwhile Bass had become the biggest brewer in the world, and Burton the globe's brewing centre. In 1874 the town was home to twenty-eight brewers. None could touch Bass and Allsopp, who between them accounted for 62 per cent of the town's output of an incredible 2.6 million barrels. Bass was averaging 957,000 barrels a year, Allsopp's just scraping 900,000 – figures that far exceeded anything the big London brewers were capable of. By the close of the century, Allsopp's had four breweries in the town, covering 180 acres. Bass, meanwhile, extended over 750 acres, with fifteen miles of railway track on brewery land alone. Houses and shops in the main streets were no more than façades, concealing brewery land behind. Three thousand men were employed by Bass in Burton, as well as hundreds at agencies around the country. In terms of value to the economy and numbers of people directly or indirectly employed, brewing was the second-biggest industry in Britain, behind cotton,[96] and Burton was its beating heart.

---

96. The fact that you almost certainly didn't know this – I didn't until just now – is perhaps the most significant victory of the temperance lobby. I

In 1871, Albert Edward, Prince of Wales, contracted typhoid, the disease that had killed his father. For days the nation held its breath as the future monarch hovered at death's door. Then, one day, he stirred and asked to be brought a glass of Burton pale ale. Several Burton brewers have claimed it was their beer that was used to nurse the prince back to health, and in later years he made special visits to both Bass and Allsopp. But in 1901, when he became king, it was Worthington's to whom he gave the Royal Warrant to supply his beer.

In 1878 Burton was incorporated as a borough. On 1 January 1879, William H. Worthington, 'magistrate, brewer and civic leader', raised a toast as the first mayor. S. C. Allsopp MP responded on behalf of Parliament. Many of the aldermen present made up a who's who of famous nine-teenth-century brewers. They proceeded to bestow churches, parks and civic buildings, all paid for by beer money, most of which, unlike the breweries themselves, are still standing. The beer men literally built the town, and now they ran it.

Burton brewers were recognized as the world's leaders, and they innovated on all fronts. This was a scientific age, but the idea of laboratories anywhere near a brewery raised the spectre of adulteration. The popular view was that brewing was a craft, not a science. Horace Tabberer Brown at Wor-thington disagreed. So did Cornelius O'Sullivan at Bass, and Dr Henry Bottinger, a pupil of Liebig and manager at All-sopp's. Louis Pasteur had revolutionized the beer world with his studies of yeast, published in 1876 as *Etudes sur la bière*. Brown, a Burton native hired by Worthington in 1866 at the age of seventeen with one year at London's Royal College of

---

clearly remember studying Victorian industry at school. We learned all about cotton, coal, steel, steam and railways. Brewing – which at this stage was contributing over a third of the Exchequer's total revenue and employing 1.5 million people – wasn't mentioned once.

Chemistry under his belt, devoured the book, and remarked that its findings were 'a full confirmation of my own observations on the principal organisms of beer'. He asked for a laboratory to analyse beer and figure out how yeast worked and why beer sometimes spoiled, and was rebuffed. Eventually he was given a small room in the brewery with windows that were blacked out, so that customers looking around the brewery would not see scientific apparatus and start to worry that the beer was being 'doctored'.

But the new scientific approach spread. Burton's brewing scientists were fêted by the Royal Society, and brewers from across Europe came to learn at their feet. One man who studied for several months with Evershed's brewery (later to become part of Marston's) was a young Dane called Carl Jacobsen – Carl as in 'Carlsberg'. India Pale Ale brewers were training the men who would one day put them out of business.

With scientific advances, pale ales no longer needed to be stored to 'ripen' like IPA. These 'running beers' were not as strong in alcohol nor as highly hopped, and could be sold soon after brewing. The incredible demand for Burton pale ale meant that any commercially minded brewer who was able to ship his beer without ageing it first couldn't resist doing so. In 1884, Michael Arthur Bass noted that 'practically all our pale ale now except that brewed in January and February and March may be said to be running beer – and even a large proportion is bottled at a very early date after brewing.' In redefining simpler, lighter 'pale ale', Burton had invented modern beer.

The strong stuff was still being brewed for export. The *Pall Mall Gazette* visited Bass' ale stores at St Pancras in 1880, and a Mr Bailey, the London manager, showed them around nine acres of beer across three floors. Coming to the export bottling cellar under the train station, Bailey inserted a screw into the side of a huge cask: 'forthwith there sprang a pipe-like stream of the purest amber which sparkled and shone in the dingy light of the oil lamps. "Look at that! Isn't that clear? That is eighteen months old. Our better classes of ale have to be kept for a time before sending them out, but the cheaper kinds are sent out almost as soon as we get them. The best ales need a little age upon them."'

The new pale ale spread around the country – no successful brewer could afford not to brew Burton-style beers. The obituary of one Edmund Greene in the *Bury and Norwich Post* in April 1891 claims: 'He was one of the first country brewers to discover that beer need not be vile, black, turgid stuff, but brewed a bright, amber-coloured liquid of Burton-type, which he sold at a shilling per gallon and made a fortune.'

Greene brewed in Bury St Edmunds, still home to Greene King – whose beer is the best-selling cask ale in Britain today and calls itself an IPA.

Success led to some high-quality problems in Burton. As early as 1840, production at Mr John Abbott's hop plantations, 'so much esteemed for their preservation quality in the celebrated Hodgson's Pale India Ale', was falling short of demand. In 1847 *London Markets* contained the plea 'choicest Goldings for Pale India Ale are greatly in request'. While English hops were considered undoubtedly superior, the UK became a net importer of hops, buying almost 150,000 hundredweight from the United States in 1878, as well as significant amounts from Germany and Belgium. One consignment of American hops was found to have a disagreeable flavour reminiscent of 'black currant leaf'. By 1880, down in St Pancras, Mr Bailey was enthusing that 'the Americans . . . are greatly improving their cultivation of hops, and some very fine ones come from the north-eastern States'. Bass was sourcing a quarter of its hops from Oregon as late as 1939, a clue perhaps that the wonderfully aromatic hops of the Pacific North West have a longer, more authentic heritage in IPA than anyone imagined.

Most IPAs sold in Britain today bear scant resemblance to the ales that went to India beyond being wet and mildly intoxicating. But without the development of beer for India, beer in Britain simply would not have looked and tasted the same. In the second half of the nineteenth century, with a rapidly expanding, thirsty population, a central location that – finally – had excellent transport links, and the unique Burton water making these the brightest, sparkling beers society had yet seen, it must have seemed like nothing could possibly go wrong. But we've all seen enough movies and read enough stories to know that that's precisely when something does.

The domestic climate was changing, just as India's had. After 1860 the temperance movement began a concerted anti-drink campaign in the national press. Britain was drinking itself to death, it was claimed, and the fat cat brewers sat in parliament, happy to let it do so, blocking any political reform to counter the binge-drinking epidemic. As the leading brewer of Beer Town, Bass, Ratcliff & Gretton felt compelled to take the fight to the temperance campaigners on behalf of more than a million people whose livelihoods depended on brewing.

The temperance movement never achieved its ultimate aim of outright prohibition. But for the brewing industry, the victory was hollow. Thanks to a growing range of leisure alternatives, the growth of a lower middle class that needed clear heads for clerical work, and the fact that temperance pressure simply made drinking unfashionable (always far more dangerous than mere legislation) beer consumption peaked in 1876, and began a long, slow decline that continues, with the odd blip, to this day.[97]

---

97. History is always cyclical. When the power of the temperance movement was at its peak, and its voice was loudest, the problem it was complaining about was actually in decline. Today, as media hysteria about

But before then, IPA was already being slowly strangled by legislation. Beer was traditionally taxed on the basis of the amount of malt used, and IPA used a lot of malt. Each time the country went to war (in other words, constantly) the tax on malt increased to pay for it. But at the same time, the duty on wine was decreased. This led William Ford, secretary of the Maltsters Association, to complain in 1862 that these measures had brought wine and beer almost to the same price:

> It has had a serious effect upon the consumption of ale termed 'India Pale', an article in great and increasing estimation with middle and higher classes of society . . . Thus has the government forced the sparkling ale (that beverage which was wont to be the pride, not only of the middle, but even the higher orders of society) from their tables to make room for the production of foreign countries.[98]

Brewers rejoiced when the tax on malt was reformed in 1864, but joy was short-lived. In 1880, Gladstone replaced the scattergun approach to beer tax with a single tax based on the original gravity of the beer – the measure of potential fermentation in the brew. Stronger beers were taxed more, weaker beers less.

The effect wasn't immediate: when the new system was first introduced the calculation worked out roughly the same as it always had. But under the new system, when taxes increased, as they inevitably did, or when business faltered, as it was about to, cutting the strength of beer and shipping it

---

'Britain's binge-drinking epidemic' reaches the point where you really, really want to slap the media around its collective face, government statistics monitoring the problem show a very clear downward trend in binge-drinking behaviour.

98. Anyone who has ever been to a British government or diplomatic reception and been offered French wine, Belgian or German lager but no choice of British beer will understand Ford's point.

more quickly meant you paid less tax. In the last twenty years of the nineteenth century, tax on beer accounted for a third of the Exchequer's entire revenue, and when Britain went to war against the Boers, tax was increased still further. The average strength of beer steadily declined. While India Pale Ale remained on some bottles in small print, from the early 1880s brewers like Bass simply referred to their beer as 'pale ale', which eventually acquired a reputation for weakness. Ultimately, IPA would refer to beers as low as 3.4 per cent – half of what they once were, shadows of their former selves, just another of those arcane acronyms on the bar. Having given birth to 'bitter beer', in the first half of the twentieth century, IPA became a subset of it, an interchangeable term applied to 'best bitter'.

Weaker beers that could be shipped quicker spelled the death of India Pale Ale, but Burton's brewers were happy to adapt. What killed the brewers themselves was another story entirely.

The 1872 Licensing Act increased the power of magistrates to grant, transfer and remove licences. This, plus the fall in the demand for beer, saw the number of licensed premises in England and Wales fall from 104,792 in 1886 to 88,445 in 1914, despite the population increasing by 45 per cent over the same period.

The brewers reacted by 'tying' the pubs they supplied, offering loans to landlords who needed to improve their premises to attract custom, in return for exclusive supply contracts. Or they simply bought pubs outright.

In 1886, Guinness became the first brewer to go public. Many other brewers followed, using the cash injection to build up their tied pub estate. Allsopp's floated in 1887, Bass the following year, Worthington the year after that.

With capital tight and shareholders demanding returns in a declining market, the argument for aged, stock ales became untenable. Weaker, running beers became universal.

When the national race to tie houses had begun, Burton's pale-ale brewers had seen little need to join in. Their beers were so popular surely they'd always be able to sell them in a free market? But as well as falling demand and the fact that a free market no longer existed, the investment in scientific rigour that Burton brewers had championed returned to haunt them, in the form of the discovery of 'Burtonization'.

Allsopp's suffered the most. In 1888 the chairman noted that the brewery was having trouble selling its beer because of the tied-house system, and leapt into the market with the proceeds of the stock-market flotation. They were reckless, impulsive, and far too late. Pub prices were doubling, even trebling, and the best ones had all been snapped up. The famous trailblazer of Burton IPA and the only serious con-tender to Bass for so much of the nineteenth century limped on from crisis to crisis, entering receivership in 1910. For the next two years Bass and Allsopp talked about a merger, but John Gretton of Bass couldn't agree with his board on the value of the offer. Allsopp's eventually merged with Ind Coope in 1934. The two breweries stood next to each other, and the dividing wall was simply knocked down to create Ind Coope and Allsopp Limited, leaving Bass to rue their hesitancy.

Bass didn't make the same mistake with Worthington's. Always far smaller than Bass and Allsopp, by 1900, Wor-thington's bottled ales nevertheless had a superior reputation, and were starting to cause so much concern for Bass that the giant brewer issued a warning to its bottlers – take any work from Worthington, and lose the Bass contract. It was nasty, mean business, but falling demand for beer was cited as justification. Antagonism and personal animosity existed between the two companies at every level of business, but circumstances forced them together. In 1926 the two brewer-ies merged.

The *Financial Times* reported on the curious arrangement that ensued: 'As the materials from which the famous Bass and Worthington pale ales are brewed are blended in an entirely different manner in each case, this giving a distinctive character to each pale ale, it has been decided that the two beers will be brewed as heretofore and thus the public will continue to have their choice.'

The name on the beer didn't matter. Access to the pubs was all any brewer cared about.

In 1906, Thomas Salt went into voluntary liquidation, but limped on. A year after the Worthington deal Salt's too was absorbed by Bass,[99] purely on the basis of acquiring their pubs and eliminating competition. The number of brewers in Burton fell from thirty-one in 1888 to seventeen in 1911.

The writing was on the wall for Beer Town, but the killer blow somehow failed to land. Bass continued to acquire breweries as they fell. Years later, the Burton-on-Trent Civic Society, formed to keep alive the memory of the Beer Capital of the World, seized upon the train layout that was still the main attraction in the Coors Visitors Centre when I began this book. The model depicted Burton in 1921, when the decline was already gathering a terrible momentum. 'But', the Society wrote, 'it is also close to being a model of the town in 1901 and as it still was in 1961.' Sixty years of growth in the nineteenth century was followed by sixty years of stasis in the twentieth. In 1935, the *Daily Express* ran a feature on this 'clean, curious town in open country thirty miles north of Birmingham'. Beer was still Burton's lifeblood. Six thousand people were still employed by the breweries, and the smell of hops filled the air. But close up, Burton was dying. 'Their industry is decayed and yet prosperous. All along the High Street, which used to be lined with busy breweries, are now derelict breweries: only one in that street is still working.'

---

99. My Calcutta IPA was a product of these mergers: Bass recipe, Worthington yeasts, Salt's water.

Burton was still proud, resistant. In April 1958, *The Times* was drawn to visit the town, and found it unbowed: 'Burton today still wears the grimy mantle of its Victorian prosperity, and both its buildings and its people tell the story of a town so dedicated to commerce that it has had little time or will to cultivate lighter pursuits. In the words of a prominent citizen: "Ours is a town of solid worth but few graces."'

IPA, the beer that had built Burton, had all but disappeared. In 1948, a book published by Whitbread claimed the term was 'now nearly obsolete'. Worthington's IPA, the last remaining beer that bore any resemblance to the original style, was officially rechristened as 'White Shield', the nickname by which it had been known since the shield and dagger trademark was developed in 1863. There was no longer any merit in referencing the style.

When the end finally came for Burton, it came suddenly and with brutal force. In the 1950s and 1960s, Canadian entrepreneur Eddie Taylor built a national brewing empire to get hold of a network of tied pubs through which he could sell his brand, Carling Black Label lager. Within thirty years, mainstream Britain would abandon pale ales such as Bass in favour of imitation Pilsner lagers. Half a century after the loss of Empire, a new generation of Britons finally put aside a measure of their haughty belief that British is best, and began to take on habits that reflected the rest of the beer drinking world.

Taylor's antics forced other brewers to form larger groups that would be safer from his grasp. Allsopp had been dropped from the corporate name of Ind Coope in 1959, the same year the brewery launched 'SKOL international lager'. In 1963, Ind Coope merged with Tetley, Walker and Ansell's, and a year later the new corporation was christened Allied Breweries. They launched 'Allsopp's Lager', which they brewed by appointment to the Queen. But this was not their biggest brand: that honour belonged to a beer that was notorious in the golden age of heavily TV-advertised keg bitters.

Double Diamond was first launched in 1899 by Ind Coope, but the trademark of two interlocking diamonds had been used by the brewer on their pale ales since 1856. In 1948, the advertising line 'Double Diamond works wonders' was introduced as part of a drive to help the beer compete against the two leading pale ales at that time: Bass Blue and Worthington Green. It was launched on draught as a keg beer in 1964, and five years later advertising agency Young & Rubicam launched the 'We're only here for the beer' campaign, burning the 'works wonders' jingle on to the cerebral cortex of an entire generation of drinkers.

Bass was struggling under the onslaught. Many of the smaller companies it had sold beer to were snapped up by the big new brewery combines. Sales of Bass beer had slipped behind those of Worthington for the first time, and Worthington E was launched to fight Double Diamond. It wasn't enough. In 1961, Bass became a subsidiary of Birmingham brewer Mitchells & Butlers. The new company, Bass, Mitchells & Butlers Ltd, would eventually merge with Eddie Taylor's Charrington, creating Bass Charrington, the UK's largest brewer.

Recognizing that their two main competitors were Burton-based, and that Burton was still recognized as the home of great pale ale, Allied went further in bigging up their new draught beer. Company literature proudly claimed that Ind Coope was synonymous with Burton-on-Trent, because this is where Double Diamond was brewed. Double Diamond, one of the mass-produced keg beers so reviled by the men who went on to form the Campaign for Real Ale, was touted as being the same beer as the first IPA produced by Samuel Allsopp. It's not true – Double Diamond was clearly being brewed by Ind Coope years before the merger with Allsopp's – nevertheless, a promotional booklet from the period boasts that 'Double Diamond Pale Ale, found in bottle in most bars in Britain and on draught on many, is a direct descendant of the first Burton IPA'. Across Burton, IPA's heritage was still being used to flog beer, but what was in the glass now bore scant resemblance to what had left Britain on the East Indiamen a century before. Allsopp's Lager disappeared quietly as stronger brands drove the market.[100]

At the same time as brewers were merging and launching new keg ales and lagers, Britain underwent a revolution in transport and communications that rendered the notion of a 'brewing town' obsolete. Motorways linked up the country with an unprecedented level of efficiency. At the same time, rising costs and industrial disputes on the railways made them increasingly impractical. The character of Burton was instantly transformed. The miles of track that criss-crossed the town's streets between breweries and the main line disappeared. As Bob Ricketts, a former Bass employee, remembers: 'Almost overnight the brewers gave the town back to its people, leaving vast, unwanted areas in the centre.' In 1892 there had been forty-two working breweries in Burton. By 1960 there were five.

Burton still looked like a Victorian town devoted to brewing, but the 'background noise of coopers hammering, steam hissing from the trains and the urgent clang of the crossing bells, whilst the aroma of brewing and malting floated over all' was gone. The magnificent buildings were crumbling, derelict. After avoiding the truth for decades, there was only one course of action. Nunneley's brewery was demolished in 1963 (it's now a shopping centre, derelict at the time of writing). The Bass middle yard was demolished in 1966 (now a drive-through KFC and a car park). Robinson's brewery and Worthington's both went in 1968 (both now shopping malls), the Bass old brewery in 1969 (another car park), and the Bass middle brewery in 1973 (offices), the same year as the Worthington maltings (the public library, where

100. Double Diamond still exists somewhere, now owned by Carlsberg.

I'm sitting as I write this). William Worthington's old town house, still recognizable by the shield and dagger logo above the door, is now occupied by a firm of solicitors.

In 1984, the Victorian Society shut the metaphorical stable door eleven years after the tortuously analogous horse had bolted, and published *Brewery Buildings in Burton-on-Trent*, a pamphlet critical of the extensive demolition. It's fair to say that it had no one quaking in their boots. Even the Burton-on-Trent Civic Society noted that the report expressed 'the point of view of an industrial archaeologist which may not be entirely shared by those who live in Burton'.

To be fair, it needed to happen. The old buildings were expensive and difficult to maintain, and there was simply no need for them. Brewing continued in the town, but the new, state-of-the-art lager breweries took up far less space. The problem was, the town planners made a complete and utter balls-up of a sadly necessary task. Like the US invasion of Iraq, there seems to have been no idea of what to do once they had gone in and smashed everything up. And to make matters worse, this happened in the late sixties and early seventies, when architects were hitting every building they could with a massive Ugly Stick. There was no attempt to retain any of Burton's unique character. In the space of a decade, Beer Town mutated into one of the blandest, most anonymous urban spaces in the UK.

While Marston's ploughed its quiet furrow on the outskirts of the town, surviving as it had always done, the Bass red triangle remained visible everywhere. But Bass was a much changed business now. The Carling Beer Company would have been a more accurate name for the brewing arm, which had itself become overshadowed by the corporation's other interests. Burton was only one of Bass' breweries, and brewing itself now only accounted for a third of the business – as well as Pontin's holiday camps, Bass owned more than 3 per cent of the global hotel market, including the Holiday

Inn, Crowne-Plaza and InterContinental chains. In 1999, Mike Jennings, a senior brewery manager, burned his career bridges by telling the *Burton Mail* that few Bass directors even understood brewing.

In late 2000, fresh from its acquisition of Whitbread, Belgian brewer Interbrew bought Bass' brewing interests. The Department of Trade and Industry stepped in, worried about the concentration of brewing capacity in so few hands, and insisted the Belgian corporation sell on large chunks of what it had acquired. They didn't have a problem with those chunks being bought by an American corporation that was almost as big as Interbrew, and so Coors moved into Burton. Interbrew sold them all the Bass breweries and major Bass brands such as Carling, Grolsch and Worthington, but kept Bass the beer for itself, transferring it to its new UK headquarters, the former Whitbread offices in Luton. Burton locals tried to stop Coors taking down the red triangles from all the breweries, raising arguments about local character and then, when that failed, insisting they were nesting sites for rare birds. It was all to no avail. The last direct link between Burton and its illustrious past was broken.

Acknowledgements

With each book I write, I seem to call upon more people to do more for me. For my next trick, I'd like to write a book that doesn't put anybody out, doesn't upset anyone, doesn't require anyone to do anything except lean back and enjoy a beer and a chat. I'd love to think that I might one day succeed.

This is the story of a voyage that's no longer possible according to the people who know best. Urs Steiner at Station Weggis made it possible.

Getting on the ships was only part of it though. I lived at the mercy not only of the winds and the seas, like James Lancaster, but also of customs officials, bureaucrats, pirates, scammers, touts and my own incompetence and misfortune. It's still a very big world out there, and I travelled through it – and through the history of India and IPA – far more comfortably, far happier, and far more successfully than I had any right, thanks to Vikram Achanta, Pamela Brown, Pratyush Chalasani, Melissa Cole, Dennis Cox, William Dalrymple, Mark Dorber, Klaas Gaastra, Chris Gittner (who comes from a family of punsters and thought of the name for this book), Robert Humphreys, Ashish Jasuja, Rupert Ponsonby, Roger Protz, Dave Ryder, Cilene Saorin, Graham Smith, Viking Afloat and WERNER.

Special thanks must go to Jeff Pickthall, who saved the whole thing when it would otherwise have fallen apart, and who is now an international beer smuggler as a result.

At the end of the journey, it had a proper finale thanks

entirely to Janet and Robin Witheridge of the British Beer & Pub Association, who went far beyond the call of duty for someone they hadn't even met when they set off for India, aided very kindly by Simon Wilson and the Deputy British High Commission in Kolkata.

Back home, thanks to Janet Sherry for navigating me from the events described in chapter thirty-four to the real end of the journey.

The reason for going on the voyage was to bring a legend back to life. If I managed to succeed in this object, then Steve Wellington and Paul Rudge must be regarded as co-authors of this book. Their passion and commitment to make this project work equalled my own. They were involved because they work for Coors. But they went to the lengths they did to help me because they are great people, unrivalled in their passion for beer, and by the end, great friends. Paul Hegarty, Jo White, Ian Ward and Lisa Needham at Coors also gave invaluable help, and I was privileged to be given free rein in the archives at the Visitor Centre before it was mothballed – thanks to Roger Sellick, Peter Orgill and all the archivists who helped me there. I don't like everything that Coors do, but as an organization they fully supported Rudgie and Steve in supporting me, and probably spent as much money as I did myself in helping to make it happen. I'm sure they did this in the hope that it will create some favourable publicity for them, and I hope it does – they deserve it. They didn't have to help as much as they did, and as a corporation they made this whole enterprise possible.

Thanks to my agent, Jim Gill, for instantly saying 'Yes – it's a no-brainer' as soon as he heard the idea, and Pan Macmillan for doing the same when he took it to them. Thanks particularly to Jon Butler who had the daunting task of wrestling the manuscript down from a completely unworkable length, and to Dusty Miller for her enduring enthusiasm and support beyond the call of duty.

Three weeks before I started the engine on *Remus*, Michael Jackson (aka the 'Beer Hunter' not, as he liked to point out, 'The Gloved One') died. I came relatively recently to the world of beer writing, and I can't claim to have known him well, much as I would like to. I was present at the same dinners and drinks receptions as he was for several years, but he was always surrounded by a dense cluster of acolytes and fans, and though I always told myself I just didn't want to be a sycophant, the truth is I was too nervous to approach him. I think we had maybe three proper conversations in total, but when we had one of them he inscribed a copy of the latest edition of his *Guide to the Beers of Belgium* with a dedication that means a lot to me. Most of us who write about beer would not be doing so – and many of the beers we love wouldn't be around – if it hadn't been for his passion and his ability to communicate it to others. I set off for Burton days after his funeral, and in the time before I left a couple of people who were with him shortly before he died told me that he'd heard of what I was trying to do, and supported my doing it. That knowledge helped 'toughen me up' at times when all I wanted to do was book a flight home. I'd like to dedicate this book to Michael's memory.

And that would be the sole dedication, emblazoned across the fly pages at the front, were it not for my wife. On hearing about my stupid idea, my beery mates said, 'Christ, I'd never get away with that.' Liz's friends backed this up by telling her, 'I wouldn't let him do that.' The fact that Liz not only 'let' me do it, but stayed married to me, and supported me and encouraged me and lifted me up when I fell down, might imply that my wife is a soft touch, who allows her husband to walk all over her. Anyone who knows Liz knows that this could not be further from the truth, and if I've done her justice in this narrative, you'll know that too. I don't know how I won her love, but my greatest fear is that, if the Buddhists are right, in about forty years time I'm coming back as a slug, whereas she'll be a dolphin. Apart from the obvious grim reality of life as a permanently homeless snail[101] this would definitely rule out a next-life reconciliation. I'd be willing to have a go at overcoming the physical incompatibility, but the salt water would do for me in an instant.

Cheers.

Pete Brown
London
2008

---

101. Why don't you ever see hermit slugs, the way you do crabs? Are slugs really more stupid than crabs? *Homeless* crabs? Crabs walk sideways for Christ's sake! Oh boy, stupider than a crab: I am definitely coming back as a slug. No doubt about it.

BIBLIOGRAPHY

Primary Sources

Scrapbooks and corporate literature. Bass Brewery Archive and Allsopp's Brewery Archive: Coor's Visitor Centre, Burton-on-Trent.

Correspondence between Madras, Bombay and Calcutta with the Honourable East India Company. East India Company Archive: British Library, London.

Bell, John – *A Comparative View of the External Commerce of Bengal 1824–35 to 1836–37.* Baptist Mission Press: Calcutta.

Collector of Sea Customs, Calcutta – *Annual Statement of the Trade and Navigation of the Bengal Presidency 1878–79.* Custom House: Calcutta, 1879.

Government of India – *Annual Statement of the Trade and Navigation of British India.* Government of India: 1880.

Macpherson, D. J.: Introduction to the *Annual Accounts of the Sea-Borne Trade and Navigation of the Bengal Presidency 1899–1900.* Custom House: Calcutta, 1900.

Parker, Harrington – *The Critic Criticised. Remarks on the Case Epsilon v Dr Carpenter, FRS, Relating to the Use of Allsopp's Pale Ale in Indigestion.* Petter, Duff & Co: London, 1853.

Phipps, John – *A Guide to the Commerce of Bengal.* Calcutta, 1823.

Prinsep, G. A. – *Remarks on the External Commerce and Exchanges of Bengal.* Kingsbury, Parbury and Allen: London, 1823.

Wilkinson, E., *The Commercial Annual, or A Tabular Statement of the External Commerce of Bengal during the years 1846–47 and 1847–48.* W. Ridsdale, Military Orphan Press: Calcutta, 1848.

Wilson, Horace Hayman, *A Review of the External Commerce of Bengal from 1813–14 to 1827–28*. Baptist Mission Press: Calcutta, 1830.

Secondary Sources – Books

India, the East India Company

Allen, Charles – *Plain Tales from the British Empire*. Abacus: London, 2008.

Asylum Press Almanac – *Directory and Compendium of Intelligence for 1895*. Lawrence Asylum Road: Madras, 1894.

Atkinson, George Franklin – *Curry and Rice on Forty Plates*. London, 1859.

Beames, John – *Memoirs of a Bengal Civilian*. Eland: London, 1984.

Bernier, Francis – *Travels in the Mogul Empire*. William Pickering: London, 1826.

Brown, Hilton (ed.) – *The Sahibs: The Life and Ways of the British in India*. William Hodge: London, 1948.

Burton. David – *The Raj at Table*. Faber: London, 1993.

Clemons, Mrs Major – *The Manners and Customs of Society in India*. London, 1841.

Collingham, Lizzie – *Curry: A Tale of Cooks and Conquerors*. Vintage: London, 2006.

Cordiner, James – *A Voyage to India*. A. Brown & Co: London, 1820.

Dalrymple, William – *White Mughals*. Harper Perennial: London, 2002.

——— *The Last Mughal*. Bloomsbury: London, 2006.

D'Oyly, Charles – *The European in India*. London, 1813.

Evans, Robley D. – *A Sailor's Log: Recollections of Forty Years of Naval Life*. Appleton and Company, 1901.

Hickey, William, Quennell, Peter (ed.) – *Memoirs of William Hickey*. Hutchinson: London, 1960.

Hunter, Sir William Wilson – *A History of British India*. Indian Reprints, 1972.

Keay, John – *The Honourable Company*. HarperCollins: London, 1993.

Kenny-Herbert, Colonel Arthur Robert – *Wyvern's Indian Cookery Book*. Higginbotham & Co: Madras, 1904.

Kincaid, Dennis – *British Social Life in India 1608 to 1937*. Routledge: London, 1938.

Luce, Edward – *In Spite of the Gods: The Strange Rise of Modern India*. Little, Brown, 2006.

Milton, Giles – *Nathaniel's Nutmeg: How One Man's Courage Changed the Course of History*. Hodder & Stoughton: London, 1999.

Parkes, Fanny – *Begums, Thugs and White Mughals*. Eland: London, 2005.

Riddell, Dr R. – *Indian Domestic Economy and Receipt Book*. Madras, 1850.

Robins, Nick – *The Corporation that Changed the World: How the East India Company Shaped the Modern Multinational*. Pluto Press: London, 2006.

Thackeray, William Makepeace – *The Tremendous Adventures of Major Gahagan*. Scholarly Publishing Office, University of Michigan Library, 2006.

Theroux, Paul – *The Great Railway Bazaar*. Penguin: London, 1977.

Yule, Sir Henry, and Burnell, A. C. – *Hobson-Jobson: A Glossary of Colloquial Anglo-Indian Words and Phrases*. John Murray: London, 1886.

Burton-on-Trent: History

Burton Civic Society – *Burton upon Trent: The Years of Change 1962–1987*. Burton Civic Society, 1987.

Greenslade, M. W., and Jenkins, J. G. (eds) – *The Victoria County History of Staffordshire*. Oxford University Press, 1967.

Owen, C. C. – *The Development of Industry in Burton upon Trent*. Phillimore, 1978.

Underhill, Charles Hayward – *History of Burton upon Trent*. Tresises: Burton upon Trent, 1941.

India Pale Ale, Breweries and Brewing

Anon, *Notes and Queries*. 7th Series, vol.1, 1888.

———— *Collection of English Ballads from the Beginning of the Present Century when They were First Engraved and Published Singly with Music*. 1790.

———— *A Glass of Pale Ale and a Visit to Burton*. Wyman & Sons: London, 1880.

———— *One Hundred Years of Brewing*. H. S. Rich & Co: Chicago, 1903.

Barnard, E. A. B. – *Noted Breweries of Great Britain and Ireland*. Causton: London, 1889.

Bickerdyke, John – *The Curiosities of Ale and Beer*. Spring Books: London, 1886.

Bushnan, J. Stevenson, MD – *Burton and its Bitter Beer*. William S. Orr & Co.: London, 1853.

Cornell, Martyn – *Beer: The Story of the Pint*. Hodder Headline: London, 2003.

———— *Amber, Gold and Black: The Story of Britain's Great Beers*. Zythography Press (e-book), 2008.

Defoe, Daniel – *Tour of the Whole Island*. G. Strahan: London, 1724–7/1948.

Donnachie, Ian – *The Brewing Industry in Scotland*. John Donald: Edinburgh, 1979.

Faulkner, Nicholas – *Allied Breweries: A Long Life*. Allied Breweries Ltd, 1988.

Foster, Terry – *Pale Ale: History, Brewing, Techniques, Recipes*. Brewers Publications, Boulder: Colorado, 1999.

Gourvish, T. R., and Wilson, R.G. – *The British Brewing Industry 1830–1980*. Cambridge University Press, 1994.

Hawkins, K. H. – *A History of Bass Charrington*. Oxford University Press: Oxford, 1978.

Herbert, James – *The Art of Brewing India Pale Ale and Export Ale*. London, 1865.

Hornsey, Ian S. – *A History of Brewing*. RSC: Cambridge, 2003.

Marchant, W. T. – *In Praise of Ale*. Redway: London, 1888.

Matthias, Peter – *The Brewing Industry in England 1700–1830*. Cambridge University Press, 1959.

Molyneux, William – *Burton-on-Trent: Its History, its Waters and its Breweries*. Trubner, 1869.

Neame, Alan – *The Exploration Diaries of H. M. Stanley*. Vanguard Press Inc.: New York, 1961.

Owen, C. C. – *The Greatest Brewery in the World: A History of Bass, Ratcliff & Gretton*. Derbyshire Record Society: Chesterfield, 1992.

Protz, Roger – *The Ale Trail*. Eric Dobby: Orpington, 1995.

Protz, Roger, and La Pensee, Clive – *Homebrew Classics: India Pale Ale*. CAMRA: St Albans, 2001.

Staffordshire County Council – *Pale Ale and Bitter Beer*. Staffordshire County Council Education Dept, 1977.

Tizard, W. L. – *The Theory and Practice of Brewing*. Gilbert & Rivington, 1843.

Tulloh and Co – *Circular on the Beer Trade of India*. Calcutta, 1829.

Ships and the Sea

Brookesmith, Frank – *I Remember the Tall Ships*. Seafarer Books: Rendlesham, 1991.

Chatterton, E. Keble – *The Old East Indiamen*. Rich & Cowan Ltd: London, 1914.

Cotton, E. – *East Indiamen*. Batchworth Press: London, 1949.

Keevil, J. J. – *Medicine and the Navy*. Churchill Livingstone, 1961.

Lloyd, Christopher – *The Nation and the Navy*. Cresset Press: London, 1954.

McCamish, Thornton – *Supercargo: A Journey Among the Ports*. Lonely Planet: Melbourne, 2002.

Melville, Herman – *Moby-Dick*. Penguin Classics revised edition: London, 2003.

Miller, Russell – *The East Indiamen*. Time Life: Virginia, 1980.

Nixon, Larry – *Vagabond Voyaging: The Story of Freighter Travel*. Little, Brown: Boston, 1939.

Northcote-Parkinson, C. – *Trade in the Eastern Seas*. Cambridge University Press: Cambridge, 1937.

Pack, James – *Nelson's Blood: The Story of Naval Rum*. Kenneth Mason: Hampshire, 1982.

Sargent, A. J. – *Seaways of the Empire*. Black: London, 1918.

Secondary Sources – Periodicals and Papers

17th–18th Century Burney Collection newspapers. Digital Archive, British Library: London.

Bamforth, Charles – 'The Art of Ale'. *Brewers' Guardian*. July 2004.

Calcutta Gazette. Archive, National Library of India: Kolkata.

Periodicals Archive. British Library: London.

Protz, Roger – 'Pale and Interesting'. www.beer-pages.com.

The Times. Digital Archive 1785–1985. British Library: London.

Thomlinson, Thom – 'India Pale Ale'. www.brewingtechniques.com.

Thomlinson, Thom, Meeting Report: British Guild of Beer Writers India Pale Ale Conference, 21 May 1994. www.brewingtechniques.com.

Thompson, Adrian, Burton upon Trent: 'The Development of a Brewery Town', unpublished thesis for BA Hons degree in Architecture. Liverpool University, 1980.

WEBSITE DISCOUNT OFFER

Purchase any of Pete Brown's beer trilogy from www.panmacmillan.com for just £4.99 each.

£1 postage and packaging costs to UK addresses; £2 for overseas.

Hops and Glory   Man Walks into a Pub   Three Sheets to the Wind

---

To buy the books with this special discount

1 visit our website, www.panmacmillan.com

2 click on the titles you wish to buy

3 add to your shopping basket

4 use the discount code **BEER** when you check out
